Praise for

International Libel and Privacy Handbook
Second Edition

A Global Reference for Journalists, Publishers, Webmasters, and Lawyers

Edited by Charles J. Glasser Jr.

"A clear understanding of the laws of this country and the rest of the world is essential if the news media and book publishers are to act as public watchdogs. Charles Glasser's book is a wonderful resource—both clearly written and concise."

CHRISTOPHER FINAN
President, American Booksellers Foundation for Free Expression

"With a section devoted to overarching issues of global interest, including special issues affecting book publishers, the *International Libel and Privacy Handbook* is an invaluable resource for editors and in-house counsel and belongs on the reference shelf of every publishing house."

JUDITH PLATT
Director, Freedom to Read, Association of American Publishers

Praise for the First Edition

"For many years, attorneys have awaited publication of a single volume summarizing libel and privacy law throughout the world. At long last, we can now compare on a nation-by-nation basis how countries in the Americas, Asia, and Europe deal with libel and privacy issues and how that treatment differs from that in the United States. **This book offers a sophisticated and reader-friendly response to the core questions that any practitioner frequently must consider.**"

FLOYD ABRAMS

"Charles Glasser's impressive book could not have come at a better time. We've entered the post–*Gutnick v. Dow Jones* era, where the protection of geographical borders is history and where the online media face exposure to liability in every corner of the globe. **This welcome volume offers practical guidance about the legal environment in many jurisdictions**

abroad. Mr. Glasser, a former journalist and now the media law counsel for Bloomberg worldwide, is ideally suited to the challenge this eminently useful work meets."

Richard N. Winfield
International Senior Lawyers Project
Clifford Chance US LLP

"For thirty-five years, the Reporters Committee has helped journalists navigate American laws regarding their rights to publish. **But in the Internet age, we increasingly are required to know media laws around the world. Charles Glasser's *International Libel and Privacy Handbook* is an indispensable addition to our law library.**"

Lucy Dalglish
Executive Director, Reporters Committee for Freedom of the Press

"Bloomberg's *International Libel and Privacy Handbook* is a highly readable guide to the legal standards that affect media reporting and publishing in a selection of countries in the Americas, Europe, and Asia. Today's journalists inevitably speak to the entire world no matter where they may be based. Prudence dictates that they recognize the differing legal rules and norms they will encounter beyond their own borders. **Charles Glasser has assembled a blue-ribbon panel of legal experts who provide essential information in a series of accessible outlines that make quick checks of specific issues easy. Additional essays on special topics such as book publishing, Internet and copyright issues, and enforcement of foreign judgments will be particularly useful for media attorneys.** But anyone who speaks or writes for a living—or who advises those who do—will benefit from consulting this handbook."

Jane E. Kirtley
Silha Professor of Media Ethics and Law
Director, Silha Center for the Study of Media Ethics and Law
School of Journalism and Mass Communication
University of Minnesota

INTERNATIONAL LIBEL & PRIVACY HANDBOOK

INTERNATIONAL LIBEL & PRIVACY HANDBOOK

A Global Reference for Journalists, Publishers, Webmasters, and Lawyers

SECOND EDITION

Edited by Charles J. Glasser Jr.
Global Media Counsel, BLOOMBERG NEWS®

Foreword by Matthew Winkler
Editor in Chief, BLOOMBERG NEWS

Viva Books
New Delhi | Mumbai | Chennai | Kolkata
Bangalore | Hyderabad | Kochi | Guwahati

First Indian Edition 2010

VIVA BOOKS PRIVATE LIMITED

- 4737/23 Ansari Road, Daryaganj, New Delhi 110 002
  E-mail: vivadelhi@vivagroupindia.net, Tel. 42242200
- 76, Service Industries, Shirvane, Sector 1, Nerul, Navi Mumbai 400 706
  E-mail: vivamumbai@vivagroupindia.net, Tel. 27721273, 27721274
- Jamals Fazal Chambers, 26 Greams Road, Chennai 600 006
  E-mail: vivachennai@vivagroupindia.net, Tel. 28290304, 28294241
- B-103, Jindal Towers, 21/1A/3 Darga Road, Kolkata 700 017
  E-mail: vivakolkata@vivagroupindia.net, Tel. 22836381, 22816713
- 7, Sovereign Park Apartments, 56-58, K. R. Road, Basavanagudi, Bangalore 560 004
  E-mail: vivabangalore@vivagroupindia.net, Tel. 26607409, 26607410
- 101-102 Mughal Marc Aptt., 3-4-637 to 641, Narayanguda, Hyderabad 500 029
  E-mail: vivahyderabad@vivagroupindia.net, Tel. 27564481, 27564482
- First Floor, Beevi Towers, SRM Road, Kaloor, Kochi 682 018, Kerala
  E-mail: vivakochi@vivagroupindia.net, Tel: 0484-2403055, 2403056
- 232, GNB Road, Beside UCO Bank, Silpukhuri, Guwahati 781 003
  E-mail: vivaguwahati@vivagroupindia.net, Tel: 0361-2666386

www.vivagroupindia.com

Published by arrangement with

Bloomberg Press
731 Lexington Avenue
New York, NY 10022

ISBN: 978-81-309-1125-0

Published by Vinod Vasishtha for Viva Books Private Limited, 4737/23, Ansari Road, Daryaganj, New Delhi - 110 002. Printed and bound by Raj Press, R-3, Inderpuri, New Delhi - 110 012.

CONTENTS

Appendixes

FOREWORD

I'll never forget the day in 1982 when a London-based colleague realized as we were opening our mail that he was reading something destined to become a front-page scoop. Inside a manila envelope with no return address was a half-inch-thick document prepared by one of the four largest clearing banks in the UK. The text was riveting. A country-by-country breakdown of each South American nation's nonperforming indebtedness to the British bank leapt off each page. Almost every major American and European bank was having difficulty reducing bad debts to Latin American countries. The UK bank's shareholders and competitors would be eager to learn the extent of the bank's bad loans derived from South America. Here at last was the answer.

As the document was sent anonymously, we had to determine its authenticity. Within thirty minutes, my colleague confirmed that someone unknown to us, or to the bank, had obtained something prepared by bank employees and that we were the recipients. He told his editors that we had an exclusive. When he called bank officials for comment, they inadvertently revealed the authenticity of the document by asserting that we couldn't publish something that was "stolen."

Publishing our discovery suddenly became a race against legal jeopardy: Before the bank could get a restraining order from a London judge, we needed to get the story outside of the country, where UK law wouldn't apply. Seconds before we received a hand-delivered writ forbidding us from publishing our story about the document, my colleague pressed the "send" button on his video display terminal, delivering it to New York and ensuring that our newspaper could publish the piece in the United States the next day. British newspapers and magazines, prevented from publishing anything derived from the original document, printed dozens of stories citing our scoop.

Since that episode more than twenty years ago, the challenges of reporting amid diverging and idiosyncratic press laws worldwide are more intimidating than ever.

That's why every serious journalist, publisher, lawyer, and webmaster should embrace the *International Libel and Privacy Handbook,* edited by Charles J. Glasser Jr., the media counsel to Bloomberg News. The most important issues in media law are explained in this global reference manual consisting of specific entries from forty-one experts in more than twenty-four countries. At Bloomberg, no one has safeguarded the process of editorial integrity better than Charles Glasser. So we are delighted that his experience can now be shared with the widest possible audience of professionals committed to getting the facts legally, without fear or favor.

—MATTHEW WINKLER
Editor in Chief
BLOOMBERG NEWS®

ACKNOWLEDGMENTS

IN THIS SECOND EDITION, as was the case with the first, many people deserve a public "thank you" for the help they have given me, as professionals and as friends. Many in the legal and academic worlds were kind enough to nurture my passion for media law, and deserve my thanks: Sandra Baron, executive director of the Media Law Resource Center, who gave me my first legal job and taught me how to really read cases; Professors Burt Neuborne and Diane Zimmerman of New York University School of Law, who were so generous with their knowledge and experience; Judge Harry T. Edwards of the U.S. Court of Appeals for the District of Columbia, who taught me to trust myself to argue persuasively; Judge Robert D. Sack of the U.S. Court of Appeals for the Second Circuit, who in writing *Sack on Defamation* inspired me to try to contribute to the literature of media law; and Jon Piper and Michael Kaplan of Preti Flaherty Beliveau Pachios & Haley in Portland, Maine, who gave me the first opportunities to prove myself as a lawyer on the briefs and in the courtroom. The attorneys at Willkie Farr & Gallagher are due thanks not only for their contributions to this book, but for my relying on them day in and day out for so much hard work and commonsense advice. I cannot overstate the quality and quantity of learning I received working under the late Rick Klein. In particular, Willkie's Tom Golden deserves credit for remaining the best sounding board, reality check, and consultant that an in-house lawyer could have. An acknowledgment is also in order to the memory of Cam Devore, who served in several capacities for the then-named Libel Defense Resource Center while I was working there as a law student. He was not just a leading light in protecting the press, but was a warm and generous man who encouraged my career path.

Matthew Winkler, editor in chief of Bloomberg News, is central to why I believe I have the best job in the best news organization in the world. When there is the slightest question about a story, Matt's default query is always "what is the right thing to do?" Matt puts clarity, fairness, and accuracy ahead of legal defenses, making my job all that much easier. He has given me the moral and intellectual breathing room to be a lawyer, ombudsman, journalist, researcher, psychologist, advocate, and ethics coach to a great newsroom, and I am deeply in his debt. Likewise, many wonderful people at Bloomberg News are owed thanks. Our Executive Editors are a superstar roster of great journalists who put responsible reporting and good writing ahead of other interests, which makes my job so much easier. Reto Gregori, our chief of staff, deserves thanks for always cutting through the static and helping me resolve problems, as does the late Fred Wiegold, a craftsman of an editor whose gentle manner was exceeded only by his deep-rooted commitment to plain decency and fairness.

On a personal level, I owe some friends and family my thanks: Cyndi Johnson, who has had to put up with so many dinners interrupted by urgent phone calls from reporters in trouble; Sean and Barbara Brogan, Chris Otazo, Karen Pearse, Stephanie Phillips, the entire Pascotto family, and Jean Marie Bonthous, friends in the deepest sense of the word; and most of all Prem Rawat, known to millions as Maharaji, who taught me that life's greatest gift is a joy to be found inside each of us.

PREFACE

Understanding Media Law in the Global Context

THERE IS NO single body of "international law" that explains the risks a reporter, editor, or webmaster faces. There is no such unified theory of law in securities litigation or in environmental or health care law, so why should there be one in publishing?

Spend five minutes at the United Nations or any international congress—where arguing about the shape of a meeting table can go on for a day—and it will come as no surprise that media law around the world is a crazy patchwork quilt of laws, with each square reflecting a nation's cultural biases, political history, and economic structure. Most of us in the mass media—and especially in newsrooms—believe that free speech isn't merely an economic or political activity, but is one rooted in basic and transnational human rights. The desire to express oneself is a part of who we are. Indeed, many jurisdictions recognize this by making free expression a constitutionally protected right.

In the United States, those of us who practice journalism or media law often echo the language of Supreme Court Justice William O. Douglas, who referred to the "preferred position" of the First Amendment in order to "bring fulfillment to the public's right to know."[1]

Americans tend to believe that it is the *First* Amendment, because the right to speak freely is the right from which all other freedoms flow. One can't make informed decisions about the virtues of legalizing marijuana, the right or wrong of abortion, the illegal activities of Wall Street CEOs, or the wanton sex lives of movie stars without the right to speak openly. Free speech is part of—and maybe even responsible for—the American culture.

For better or worse, "everyone has a right to his opinion" is a concept Americans learn at an early age. As thick-skinned as we are, we also learn on the playground that "sticks and stones may break my bones, but names will never hurt me." In short, it takes a lot in America to say something so hurtful, in such a context, and with such loudness that the law will punish it.

But punishment does occur, even in the home of free speech. Libel cases, even those in which the press is victorious, are long, expensive, and often emotionally painful experiences. Susan Antilla, now an award-winning columnist for Bloomberg News, was sued by businessman Robert Howard over a 1994 story Antilla wrote when she was a reporter for the *New York Times.*[2] Howard was the chairman of two publicly traded companies whose stock price had been fluctuating enough to draw Antilla's attention. After extensive investigation and research, Antilla determined that the market might have been reacting to rumors that Howard may have had a dual identity, the "other" identity being Howard Finklestein, a convicted felon.

Antilla, after interviewing more than thirty people during the course of a month, wrote an article that didn't adopt as "fact" that Howard had a dual identity. Instead, it simply reported that the rumor was being passed around Wall Street and that it may have had an impact on the companies' share prices. The article also contained Robert Howard's unequivocal denial.

In 1997, three years after the publication, Howard brought a libel and privacy suit, not against the *Times,* but against Antilla. Although the eventual outcome—at the appellate level—vindicated Antilla's reporting on First Amendment grounds, the trial was a grueling and abusive experience for Antilla.

Antilla tried to be fair and clear in her story, which she knew was reported thoroughly, but the experience of being sued scared her and shook her confidence, and it took a long time for her to recover from it.

"From the very beginning, the plaintiff did everything to grind me down. He wanted revenge," says Antilla. Even before Howard filed his suit, a burly private investigator showed up at her house and questioned her about her sources and the way she reported the story.

Things didn't improve. The trial process, including two days of depositions and six days of trial, made her feel "picked apart." "They had looked at everything I had ever written, even going back to where I grew up," says Antilla. "They questioned my competence and training as a reporter. In the end you feel so naked and like there's nothing that's safe to write. . . .you lose your confidence. It's the worst thing I've ever gone through."

Afraid that the jury might sympathize with Antilla, Howard's lawyer began his arguments by saying, "Sometimes good people can do bad things." The jury believed him.

Even though Antilla and her reporting were eventually vindicated on appeal, the experience took its toll not just on Antilla's confidence, but on the way she felt back in the newsroom. "After the trial, I went back to writing and having tremendous complications working with an editor again because I was quadruple reporting everything," she says. "The way journalists look at you after being sued is never the same. Even though fifteen people approved the story, the shame really hung around my neck. You don't end up being a hero: everyone runs for the hills and you have a sense of it being your fault. My lawyers were great, very supportive, but you're the one holding the bag. I still get defensive about it."

The financial consequences of being sued for libel can be more devastating than the emotional toll. Newspapers have been put out of business by the cost of libel litigation and the subsequent monetary judgments.

In the late 1990s, Barricade Books, a division of Lyle Stuart, published *Running Scared,* a book about Steven Wynn, one of the best-known and most highly regarded casino operators in the world. The book and its advertisements alleged that Wynn had improper connections to the Genovese crime family, and ostensibly based some of that writing on reports from England's Scotland Yard, generated when Wynn applied for a casino license in London.

Long and arduous litigation followed. In 1997, a jury found those allegations false and defamatory, and awarded Wynn $3.2 million. That judgment was litigated throughout Nevada's legal system. The Nevada Supreme Court eventually overturned the judgment and ordered a new trial. Wynn declined to prosecute his case further, saying through his lawyers that he felt vindicated. By that time, the damage had been done, and not just to Wynn's reputation. The libel suit forced Lyle Stuart into bankruptcy.

There may be good reason to argue that the damage to Lyle Stuart was self-inflicted. The case raised questions of whether a UK police report qualified to be protected under Nevada law or if UK law regarding police reports could, or should, be applied in Nevada. It seems that this international aspect was never fully examined.

Even discounting these episodes as aberrant, there is no doubt that being sued for libel is something to avoid. When questions of international law appear, it raises the stakes even higher.

The threat of libel litigation is now exacerbated by the reach of the Internet. Today, bloggers are breaking news that is chased down by mainstream media. They are now credentialed at national political conventions and even at the White House. Acting as self-appointed mass-media watchdogs, bloggers have claimed credit in ending the careers of a famous television news commentator and various news executives.

More news media are distributing their content across borders. Bloomberg, the news provider for whom I am fortunate to work, is American-owned, but its success is built on global reach. In more than 100 newsrooms around the globe, headlines and stories are flashed on desktops at the speed of light. There is no telling where the next story will come from or what it will say. A reporter in Milan is working on a story about a deal involving an Italian bank, a Spanish executive, and a Japanese bond issuer. A New York-based reporter is moving a story about a Russian oil company headed by a British resident and his battles in a U.S. bankruptcy court with French investors. These stories will be read in Hong Kong, London, Kansas City, and places the reporter may not even be able to locate on a map.

Given that libel suits are often ruinous, if not emotionally grueling, given that words are sent instantly around the world and archived forever, are there guidelines that reporters and editors should use? What is needed is a global approach requiring that reporters and editors review their practices and philosophy toward global newsgathering, and that they develop an understanding for the basic moral engine that drives each nation's media laws.

American editors and their lawyers generally review news stories from a solely U.S. perspective, publish stories conforming to a level of risk under U.S. law, and hope that either the facts are good enough to win a libel suit, or, in the alternative, that either their publisher has no assets to attach in a foreign country or that an adverse judgment won't be enforced in the United States.

In essence, the U.S. model is based on the press-friendly moral engine that drives American media law. As a democracy, constitutionally derived rights (like the right to speak freely) transcend other rights rooted in common law or statute. As mentioned previously, the right to publish is embedded in the First Amendment of the U.S. Constitution and is considered paramount. The "personal" rights of privacy, to enjoy a good reputation, to be free from defamation or other assault on personal identity, aren't constitutionally protected in the U.S. Thus, under U.S. law, the press's rights trump these "personal" rights.

I once attended a libel law conference where I sat next to the general counsel of a large media conglomerate. The panel was discussing a libel case in Europe where the press had enormous burdens to meet in court.

"Haven't they ever heard of the First Amendment?" asked this American lawyer.

The answer is that they may have heard of it, but don't give it any weight. In many nations, there is no constitutional right to press freedom, but the constitution does recognize the personal rights (also called "dignitary rights" in some jurisdictions). In many of these nations, there simply is no "First Amendment" that trumps other rights. Yet other nations' press law represents a balance of the two: a constitutional right of a free press is on an equal footing with personal rights. In balancing the two, courts weigh the rights of the press against the responsibilities to avoid harming dignitary interests.

The danger of taking a strictly American approach is highlighted by the British case of *Berezovsky v. Michaels and Others (Forbes)*.[3] From an American perspective, everything seemed right about this hard-hitting story. In December 1996, a *Forbes* magazine story about Boris Berezovsky retold stories about the Russian media, oil, and finance oligarch's rise to riches.[4] Introduced with a headline that read "Power, Politics, and Murder. Boris Berezovsky can teach the guys in Sicily a thing or two," the story was the result of months of reporting by a team of some of the most experienced journalists in the world. They spoke to dozens of first-hand witnesses who alleged that they knew that Berezovsky left behind "a trail of corpses, uncollectible debts and competitors terrified for their lives."

The article called Berezovsky a "powerful gangland boss," and basing their reporting on police reports, corporate documents, and interviews, the reporters strongly suggested that Berezovsky was behind the murder of Vladislav Listyev, a popular television host and top official at Russian Public Television.

In the United States, such reporting would be protected by a plethora of privileges, and *Forbes*'s editors didn't expect that a libel case would be brought, let alone brought in the United Kingdom. Berezovsky filed a libel claim in Britain, where few privileges protect the press and sued-upon stories are assumed by the court to be false. Since Russian prosecutors never charged Berezovsky for Listyev's murder, how could a magazine on the other side of the world conduct a criminal investigation to convict Berezovsky of murder?

Forbes fought the case the best way it knew how: challenge the location of the suit in London. The House of Lords disagreed with their American cousins and allowed the case to continue, because Berezovsky convinced the court that even though the story was published by an American newsroom, and was about a Russian citizen, enough Britons had read the article (published simultaneously on *Forbes*'s website) to damage Berezovsky's reputation in England.[5]

The case dragged on, and millions of dollars later, *Forbes* was finally forced to relent, reading a statement in open court that apologized to Berezovsky and issuing a detailed retraction.[6]

Following the American model may place reporters and news organizations at risk in other ways. For example, American reporters are often shocked to learn that the UK (and most of Europe) often places considerable restriction on the ability to quote arguments and documents from court cases.

Where American law presupposes the right of access to court proceedings, the United Kingdom and many other nations use "publication bans" to restrict the ability of the press to publish many parts of court proceedings. Following the theory that juries might be unfairly persuaded by "evidence" they read in the newspapers but do not examine in court, these jurisdictions set out strict limits as to what can and cannot be published.

This problem was underscored in 2005 when a publication ban was issued in a trial about corruption in Canada's Liberal Party. The court banned publication of testimony on the Internet. American webmasters, especially those with nothing to lose and no assets at risk in Canada, began to publish articles about the trial. Canadian news organizations then linked their Web sites to the U.S.-based Web sites. Although some of those Canadian news organizations later removed the links for fear of contempt of court prosecution, the court did not try to punish the U.S. webmasters.[7]

Although the American webmasters may have struck a blow for Canadians' right to know, the problem remains and looms large for bona fide news organizations, especially those who do business or maintain offices in Canada. Although the webmasters might have been too small for the courts to go after, it is by no means certain that large, well-established news organizations will not come within the courts' crosshairs.

The global model suggests that the right guidelines might satisfy some of the international constants. In other words, if the highest standards of accuracy, clarity, and fairness are met, then a story should be suitable for publication anywhere. Distilling those universal constants to a few principles, global publishers should consider the following:

Put Accuracy Ahead of Style and Speed. Unlike U.S. law, the laws of many nations assume that a sued-upon story is false, and places the burden of proof on the publisher. This means that every fact should withstand close scrutiny prior to publication and should be subject to exacting proof with notes, interviews, documents, and other primary source material prior to publication. It is also worth noting that some nations, like France, do not allow reporters to prove the truth of their stories with information gathered in the course of a lawsuit. If the reporter did not have it to rely upon while writing the story, then the reporter may not rely upon it at trial. There's a world of difference between a story that you *know* is correct and one you can *prove* is correct.

Publishers should also be aware that "the rush to publish" is a nearly fatal accusation in many nations. In those countries without a First Amendment analogue, courts give less weight to the "public's need to know" than to a person's dignitary right, especially in light of an error committed because the reporter did not have time—or take the time—to adequately research a story and seek comment. Many of these same nations do not recognize competitive pressures and deadlines as reasons that justify an allegedly damaging and inaccurate story.

Make Fairness an Obvious and Primary Element of All News Stories. Failure to provide a meaningful opportunity to comment is often the most damaging element of a libel claim in Europe. In an English case, George Galloway, a politician known for pro-Arab views and opposition to the Iraq War, won a libel judgment of almost $300,000, plus attorney's fees, against the *Daily Telegraph* after the paper published an article the court found fundamentally unfair.[8]

The paper's reporter, who was in Iraq after the 2003 invasion, claimed to have found a set of documents showing that Galloway had been receiving illicit payments from Saddam Hussein and had meetings with Iraqi intelligence officers. The reporter telephoned Galloway on the evening of April 21, and in that conversation, Galloway denied the allegations and told the reporter he had never seen the documents in question.

The next morning, the *Telegraph* published a five-page spread with the headline "SADDAM'S LITTLE HELPER" and a story that began: "George Galloway, the Labour backbencher, received money from Saddam Hussein's regime, taking a slice of oil earnings worth at least £375,000 a year, according to Iraqi intelligence documents found by the Daily Telegraph in Baghdad."

Under English law, the seriousness of the allegations has to be met with an equal zeal to allow a meaningful opportunity to respond. This was the failure that may have most damaged the *Telegraph*'s case. Reviewing the facts of the case, Justice Eady pointed out that the *Telegraph* admitted it did not have the documents examined for authenticity prior to publication, and did not read the documents to Galloway when asking him for comment.

The reporter did not tell Galloway that the story would be published the next morning, nor that it would be featured in a five-page spread. The reporter refused to tell Galloway where and how the damning documents were obtained. Instead of presenting Galloway with the specific allegations that he would surely have to answer later, the reporter merely told Galloway that the documents had "come to light." Given that Galloway was accused of nearly treasonous acts that would surely damage his career, the court found that Galloway was not given a reasonable and meaningful attempt to comment.[9]

The *Telegraph* appealed the decision and sought a defense of qualified privilege based on the premise that the documents were of public interest. The Court of Appeal, however, deemed that the allegations made by the *Telegraph* were so unfair as to abuse the privilege, and upheld the lower court ruling.[10]

The lesson from this case is: *the more serious the allegation, the more detailed and fair must be the reporting.* The reporter must make a concerted effort to contact the subject. One phone call may not be enough, and asking people to comment on documents they have never seen is even more troublesome. Consider follow-up e-mails, faxes, and, if necessary, hand-delivered letters setting out the details of what a subject is going to be accused of, and asking for comments.

The real tragedy of the Galloway case, however, is that it turned out the *Telegraph* did have a legitimate story about Galloway. Although the truth of the documents that the *Telegraph* based its stories on was not an issue considered in the case, the papers did, in fact, turn out to be authentic.

In July 2007 Parliament published a report conducted by Sir Philip Mawer, which included two forensic expert's conclusions that the documents were genuine and that it could be assumed that they reported the truth. It is unconfirmed, however, whether Galloway benefited personally from the donations; the authenticity of the papers confirmed only that Galloway received funds from Saddam Hussein's regime for the British political campaign against sanctions on Iraq, the Miriam Appeal.[11]

If the reporter had been more careful and thorough in his attempt to reach Galloway and in presenting the details in a less accusatory manner, Galloway would have had a weaker case against the *Telegraph*.

More often than not, doing less simply looks unfair. In nations without a rich tradition of a First Amendment, facts that look like a "cheap shot" usually work against the press. The journalist should aim for neutral reporting. Adopting questionable facts as true and then commenting on them without clearly acknowledging whether or not they are known to be true and without giving the subject a fair chance to respond can lead to trouble.

Serve the Public Interest. In many nations, especially those without a constitutional counterweight to dignitary rights, even truth is not an absolute defense to libel claims. These courts require that such intrusions serve the public interest. American law is on the whole very generous to the media in determining what is and isn't in the public interest. Guided by the First Amendment's "marketplace of ideas" theory, American law generally defers to that marketplace.[12] Editors, after all, know what interests the public, and they try to provide that kind of story. If the story isn't of interest to the public, then readership and circulation decline. This free market approach assumes that the public interest is indicated by what the public consumes.

But in most of the world, courts don't grant such deference to journalists, and what is of interest "*to*" the public is not the same thing as what is "*in*" their interest. For example, Italian courts ask whether journalists are "fulfilling their mission to inform the public about news it needs to protect itself."

Bloomberg's editor in chief, Matt Winkler, says that a fundamental element in all news stories is "what's at stake." In his handbook, *The Bloomberg Way,* Winkler explains that "people need a sense of what's at stake in order to know why they ought to care about an event."

When reporting a story, the "what's at stake" underscores the public interest by asking and answering the same questions: Is there an effect on public health? Is there a risk of harm to a nation's economic or physical security? Is there a chance that an act of wrongdoing might go unpunished and repeated? Are society's more vulnerable members likely to become victims?

Reporters and editors should be encouraged to find the angle in each story where society can be said to benefit from publication of information that it can use to protect itself. The merely prurient and prying—although popular—may not meet the court's standards of public interest.

Cultural Sensitivity Counts. Phrases that may be innocuous in one culture are often offensive—and even libelous—in others. For example, in the United States, to say that someone was "fired" is not by itself defamatory. Yet the same statement in France or Japan will almost always raise eyebrows and get the libel lawyers' sabers rattling. Why the difference? The answer is cultural.

In the United States, people are used to the notion of an unfair dismissal. People can be fired in many states for no reason at all, or for reasons that people think are unfair. In isolation, it doesn't imply that the former employee did something wrong. By contrast, French unions and employment law make it next to impossible to "fire" a person without a strong showing that the employee violated some duty. Thus, a person who was "fired" must have done something wrong, or at best have been incompetent.

Similarly, in Japan, where people are expected to work for one company their entire adult lives, being fired is a shameful event. This is why Asian and European publishers often use the phrase "made redundant" to describe persons who are laid off for economic savings reasons.

Assuming the public interest, one can report that an executive was fired, but the publisher of that statement had better be prepared to prove it with direct quotes or documentary evidence.

Cultural differences are reflected in the varying definitions of defamatory meaning. What is offensive or worthy of ridicule in one place might make no difference in another. To be called "gay" in San Francisco would not raise contempt, hatred, or scorn, while using the same term in Hong Kong may cause an uproar.

It's not just rude or imperialistic to assume that your nation's moral values are the appropriate yardstick; it may be considered intrusive or libelous.

Similarly, iconographic figures or political doctrines may be so ingrained in the culture that the laws specifically proscribe attacks upon them. Statements that question the integrity and political wisdom of Chairman Mao will almost certainly set alarms ringing in China, and endorsement of an independent Taiwan are expressly criminalized.

In the United States, some might characterize Singapore's Lee Kuan Yew as a plutocrat. Yet in that nation, he is genuinely revered by most of the populace as a founding father and strong, benevolent leader. Reporters and editors should at the very least be aware of these potential pitfalls.

Translation in reporting from various languages also raises problems. In reviewing a story about warring Mexican shareholders in a takeover bid, I noticed the original draft had one side accusing the other of actions that were "illegal." Although I'm not a Mexican securities lawyer, it seemed far-fetched to say that offering a certain price for stock was a criminal act, so I asked the reporter to check back and see if the sources meant against the law (*contrario a la ley*) or instead merely not legally binding (*sin precedente vinculante*). It turned out to be the latter, not the former, and we accurately described ordinary business litigation, rather than accusing someone of committing a crime.

Don't Confuse the Right to Publish with What's Right to Publish. Common sense and good taste will almost never steer you wrong. Reporters' competitive nature leads them to use facts that are "exclusive" without asking if any of those facts move the story forward. But should they?

A reporter's job is not to gratuitously inflict damage. Nor is it to be "hard-hitting." It is to "seek truth and report it." In order to do that, the truth has to be contextualized, and presented in a fair manner. The fact that some detail may be true is not always by itself an ethical justification for publishing it. The more sensitive the fact, the closer reporters and editors must look at whether the public truly needs to know that fact. Asking whether the fact is gratuitous or if it answers a question the public needs answered is a good start. These are not often easy or pleasant choices, yet asking these questions helps guide us to a more ethical outcome that also serves the public interest.

In the early days of the Enron collapse and scandal, Bloomberg News obtained through entirely legal and ethical means a copy of a suicide note left by an executive who had taken his own life. The note was addressed to his wife, and did not discuss Enron. Should we publish the contents of the note?

We had to ask ourselves the same questions outlined above. Sure, it was interesting, even sensational, made more so by the fact that we had it exclusively. But did it move the story forward? Did it answer a question that the public needed to know, or was it voyeurism?

After a close look and a lot of discussion, we realized that the larger public debate was whether the executive had actually committed suicide or was instead killed by people afraid he would disclose damaging information. Publishing the note helped answer that question. But our inquiry could not end there. Did the note disclose personal details about the surviving family? Would disclosing those details move the story forward, or merely subject the family to intrusive examination? Fortunately, the note did not contain that kind of detail.

We believed that our decision to publish the suicide note helped answer the debate about the executive's death. But this kind of inquiry is exhaustive and soul-searching.

In conclusion, we do well to avoid terse justifications for publishing sensitive material. "He deserves it" or "that's his tough luck" are not substitutes for thoughtful analysis. Putting ourselves in the position of the subject, and asking ourselves if we are really being fair—how we would like it if the roles were reversed—goes a long way to answering these questions.

There's often no single "right" answer, but we have an ethical obligation, as well as a legal one, to ask the right questions.

—Charles J. Glasser Jr.
August 2008

Chapter Notes

1. *Branzburg v. Hayes,* 408 U. S. 665, 721 (1972).

2. *Howard v. Antilla,* 294 F.3d 244 (1st Cir. 2002).

3. *Berezovsky v. Michaels and Others,* http://www.parliament.the-stationery-office.co.uk/pa/ld199900/ldjudgmt/jd000511/bere-1.htm.

4. http://www.forbes.com/forbes/1996/1230/5815090a_print.html.

5. Since the Berezovsky case, British courts have become less of the libel tourist's destination. See Laura Handman and Robert Balin, "It's a Small World After All: Emerging Protections for the U.S. Media Sued in England," available online at http://www.dwt.com/related_links/adv_bulletins/CMITFall1998USMedia.htm.

6. http://www.carter-ruck.com/Newsletters/200306-Berezovsky.html.

7. The problems of publication bans are explored at http://www.dcexaminer.com/articles/2005/04/20/opinion/op-ed/10oped19adamson.txt.

8. *Galloway v. Telegraph Group Limited* [2004] EWHC 2786 (QB); Case No. HO03X02026 (appeal pending).

9. It is worth noting that the *Galloway* court took a dim view of the publisher's argument that time constraints justified the meager opportunity to respond, and

when pressed, the publisher admitted that it was not so much the public's need to know that drove the rush to publish, as it was a sense of competitive pressure for fear of losing a big scoop. The court found that this hurt rather than helped the *Telegraph*.

10. http://www.carter-ruck.com/articles/George%20Galloway%20v%20Telegraph%20Group.html.

11. Standards and Privileges Committee, 6th Report, Session 2006-07, House of Commons, 16 July 2007. http://www.publications.parliament.uk/pa/cm200607/cmselect/cmstnprv/909/90902.htm.

12. See, e.g., *Huggins v. Moore*, 94 N.Y.2d 296, 303 (1999). ("Absent clear abuse, the courts will not second-guess editorial decisions as to what constitutes matters of genuine public concern.")

ABOUT THE EDITOR

Charles J. Glasser Jr. is global media counsel to Bloomberg News. Prior to joining Bloomberg, he represented a wide range of broadcasters, magazines, and newspaper publishers. A former daily newspaper and wire service journalist, he has litigated many of the issues covered in this book. Glasser collects vintage sports cars, is an accomplished classical guitarist, and resides in the New York metropolitan area.

ABOUT THE CONTRIBUTORS

Nellie Alexandrova of Denton Wilde Sapte has been practicing for fifteen years as a Russian-qualified lawyer, much of that time in international legal practice. She has extensive experience in corporate and commercial matters with an international element (including acquisitions and joint ventures) and cross-border financial and securities matters (including project and trade finance, and financial markets). She also has substantial intellectual property experience and has advised a variety of clients on transactions involving licensing, copyright, trademarks, software imports, service agreements, and customs duties. Alexandrova is a graduate of Moscow State University, where she holds a degree in law (with distinction) and a doctorate degree in international law. She has also completed a special program at Cambridge University. She regularly speaks at various high-profile forums and contributes to Western and Russian business publications such as *Eastern European Forum Newsletter* and BNA's *Eastern Europe Reporter.* Alexandrova is a member of the Moscow City Bar and sits on the editorial board of *Kollegia,* the first Russian professional journal for practicing lawyers.

Almudena Arpón de Mendívil is head of the telecommunications and audiovisual department at Gómez-Acebo & Pombo (Spain). She has extensive experience advising corporations with business in the communications area, which includes telecommunications, media, and IT. Arpón de Mendívil is a council member of the IBA Legal Practice Division, immediate past co-chair of the IBA Committee on Communications (Cm), and chair of the Regulatory Commission of the Spanish Association of Corporate Communications Users. She is also a member of the Telecommunications and IT Commission of the ICC and of the European Space Law Center. She has been designated by the Spanish Regulator as independent arbitrator at the Spanish Arbitration Court for telecommunications conflicts.

She has published widely and is a correspondent for several specialized international publications. She is author of *International Joint Ventures in Spain* (Butterworths, 1992 and 1997). In Spain, she directed *Comments to the General Telecommunications Law* (Aranzadi, 1999), is co-author of *Legal Regime of Acquisitions of Companies* (Aranzadi, 2001 and 2004), of *Regulation and Competition in Telecommunications* (Dykinson, S. L. 2003), and of *Electronic Communications and Competition* (Bosch, 2004). Her department's leadership in the telecommunications and media sectors has been recognized most recently by, among others, the rankings *Chambers & Partners* (2004), *European Legal 500* (2004), *PLC Which Lawyer?, Practical Law Company* (2004/2005), and *Euromoney's Best of the Best Telecom Media and IT* (2004).

Rolf Auf der Maur is a partner at VISCHER, one of the leading Swiss law firms with offices in the main commercial centers of Zurich and Basel. He is head of the IP/IT practice group. He studied at Zurich University and University of California, Los Angeles, and published his thesis in the area of copyright law. Before beginning his career as a lawyer in 1991, he was an entrepreneur in the IT and media sector and a journalist. As early as 1994, he began advising clients on Internet-related legal matters. The global communication network and the converging industries (IT, media, and telecommunications) remain his core interests and practice areas.

Auf der Maur advises leading international and Swiss corporations in the media, telecommunications, and IT sectors in litigious and nonlitigious matters as well as in regulatory affairs. Auf der Maur is vice president of the executive board of the Simsa Swiss Interactive Media and Software Association (the Swiss Internet industry organization) and a member of the board of the International Association of Entertainment Lawyers. He also serves as a vice chair of the Technology Law Committee of the International Bar Association. He speaks and publishes regularly on IT and media-related legal issues and takes part actively in the further development of the Swiss regulatory environment for the converging industries.

Barbosa, Müssnich & Aragão is one of the top ten business law firms in Brazil with important practices in almost all areas of business law, including the intellectual property area. The practice of law at Barbosa, Müssnich & Aragão is characterized by rigorous legal analysis, coupled with creative solutions that maximize clients' business opportunities. In relation to intellectual property, Barbosa, Müssnich & Aragão provides services in matters involving trademarks, copyrights, and entertainment law, which covers, among other areas: cinema, television, music, theater, literature, print and electronic media, art exhibition, and advertising. The firm works with specialized lawyers in this area, such as Laura Fragomeni, coordinator and professor at the IP Post Graduation Course of Getulio Vargas Foundation, with an LLM degree from Harvard Law School, an MBA in law and economics from the Getulio Vargas Foundation, and an LLB from the Catholic University of Rio de Janeiro; and Paula Mena Barreto Pinheiro, teaching assistant at the IP Post Graduation Course of Getulio Vargas Foundation, with a postgraduate degree in intellectual property law and an LLB from the Catholic University of Rio de Janeiro.

Peter Bartlett is chairman of Minter Ellison, the largest law firm in Australia in terms of number of lawyers, and ranked the largest legal group in the Asia Pacific (according to *Asian Legal Business*). He is national head of the Minter Ellison Media and Communication Group. Bartlett has more than twenty years' experience in media and telecommunications and a comprehensive knowledge of media-related issues, including defamation, prepublication advice, contempt, suppression orders, legislative restrictions on publications and advertising codes, together with e-commerce (content) and privacy issues.

Minter Ellison has acted for *The Age* newspaper since 1863 and Bartlett is its chief legal adviser. He has worked on behalf of an extensive range of media-related clients, including Fairfax in Victoria, *Business Review Weekly*, SBS Television, Simon & Schuster Australia, and Pan Macmillan Australia. He has also acted for Qantas airlines on various matters, including the recent high-profile deep vein thrombosis litigation. Bartlett is also chair of the Media Committee and coordinator of the Intellectual Property, Communications and Technology Section of the International Bar Association.

The highly respected "Asia Pacific Legal 500 2003/2004" ranked Bartlett as a "leading individual" lawyer in media and named Minter Ellison as a "leading technology, media and telecommunications firm."

Marco Consonni is a partner of Dewey & LeBoeuf, based in the Milan office. He has for many years been active in the IT, telecommunications, and media sectors, advising major Italian and foreign companies in their corporate and commercial activities and litigation, including company reorganization and associated human resources matters. His clients include major telephone and Internet companies, advertising and media agencies, publishers, software houses, and technological services companies. Before joining Dewey & LeBoeuf, Consonni practiced in the Milan office of the English law firm Frere Cholmeley Bishoff and at Andersen Legal. With Davide Contini, in 1998 he founded the Milan office of Galgano, where he was responsible for the commercial and TMT areas. Consonni is qualified to practice in Italy and is a member of the Bar Association of Milan.

Edward J. Davis is a partner in the New York office of Davis Wright Tremaine LLP. He specializes in representing media organizations, especially in matters of libel, privacy, press access, reporter's privilege, copyright, and trademark. His clients include leading magazines, newspapers, book publishers, television and electronic news organizations, entertainment companies, and nonprofit institutions, as well as authors and artists (or their estates). He has represented coalitions of publishers, authors, museums, and advocacy groups in landmark cases to protect freedom of expression. He provides prepublication and prebroadcast advice for clients and often represents them in business litigation as well as cases where First Amendment freedoms may be at stake. Davis has served as vice-chair of the American Bar Association's Committee on Media Law and Defamation Torts, chair of the Committee on Copyright and Literary Property of the Association of the Bar of the City of New York, and a member of the latter Association's committees on the Judiciary, Communications and Media Law, Civil Rights, and Drugs and the Law. He graduated magna cum laude from Harvard Law School and Harvard College and received master's degrees in economics and in Chinese studies from the London School of Economics and the School of Oriental and African Studies of the University of London, where he studied as a Marshall Scholar.

Iacopo Destri obtained his JD with maximum marks from the University of Pisa. After an initial period with a law firm based in Chicago, he joined Baker & McKenzie. In October 2007, he became member of the Milan office of Dewey & LeBoeuf. His specific areas of practice are IT, IP, and Litigation. In particular he represents media and technology companies in a full range of issues advising in trademark, copyright, technology, privacy and data protection, defamation, advertising, and commercial matters, both contentious and transactional. He has been lecturer in the master programs organized by the University of Venice Ca' Foscari and the Bocconi University of Milan. He has also been invited as a guest speaker at several professional conferences. He is qualified to practice in Italy and is a member of the Bar Association of Milan.

Evaristo de Moraes law firm has a long tradition in Brazil. Founded in 1894 by Antonio Evaristo de Moraes, the firm presently is run by Antonio Eduardo de Moraes and Renato de Moraes (grandsons of the deceased Evaristo) who, with the support of experienced lawyers, continue the tradition initiated by their ancestors.

Steven De Schrijver, a partner at Van Bael & Bellis, an international law firm with over sixty lawyers based in Brussels (www.vanbaelbellis.com), has concentrated his practice on corporate transactions and information technology. De Schrijver advises Belgian and foreign companies, banks, and investment funds on mergers and acquisitions, joint ventures, corporate restructuring, financing of acquisitions, private equity, and venture capital. His work in the area of corporate transactions has involved him in several national and cross-border transactions in the telecom, IT, biotech, petrochemical, and cement sectors. In addition, De Schrijver has handled numerous complex commercial agreements and projects dealing with new technologies (e-commerce, software licensing, website development and hosting, privacy law, technology transfers, digital signatures, and IT outsourcing). For instance, he has coordinated several pan-European data protection compliance programs. De Schrijver received his JD (magna cum laude) from the University of Antwerp (Belgium) in 1992 and received an LLM from the University of Virginia School of Law in 1993.

H. R. Dipendra is an advocate and solicitor with an active practice in Kuala Lumpur, Malaysia. He graduated with an LLB (Hons) from the University of London in 1997, Certificate in Legal Practice in 1998, and an LLM from the London School of Economics and Political Science in 1999. He has been in active practice since 2000. Since 2007, H. R. Dipendra has been the deputy chair of the National Young Lawyers Committee of the Malaysian Bar Council. He is also the head of the Freedom of Expression and Media Defense Working Group of the Malaysian Bar Council's Human Rights Committee for the year 2008–2009. He is also part of the South East Asia Media Defense working group, a coalition of lawyers, academics, and like-minded organizations, all sharing a common and determined belief in protecting the freedom of expression and media defense. He is currently a partner in the law firm Tengku Hishamudin Ram Dipendra, where his primary focus is litigation.

Rick Glofcheski teaches law at the University of Hong Kong. He obtained his BA and LLB in Canada and his LLM at Cambridge University, England. He practiced law in Canada, mainly in civil litigation, for four years. He joined the University of Hong Kong in 1989. His primary areas of teaching and research are tort law and labor and employment law. He has also taught criminal law, contract law, the legal system, and medical law. He is past Head of the Department of Law (1996–99). Glofcheski is General Editor of the *Hong Kong Law Journal* and the author of *Tort Law in Hong Kong* (Hong Kong: Sweet and Maxwell Asia, 2nd ed., 2007). In 2004, he was appointed

University Teaching Fellow in recognition of his outstanding teaching and his contribution to the advancement of teaching in the university.

Thomas H. Golden and **Stephen B. Vogel** are attorneys in the litigation department of Willkie Farr & Gallagher LLP, which serves as primary outside counsel to Bloomberg News. Golden received his bachelor's degree cum laude in 1988 from the College of the Holy Cross and his law degree magna cum laude in 1991 from New York University School of Law, where he was awarded membership in the Order of the Coif. Vogel received his bachelor's degree cum laude in 1998 from Dartmouth College and his law degree in 2003 from Columbia University. Willkie Farr & Gallagher LLP is an international law firm of over 600 attorneys with offices in New York, Washington, DC, Paris, London, Milan, Rome, Frankfurt, and Brussels. The firm is headquartered in New York City.

Jan Hegemann is a partner in the Munich office of Hogan & Hartson Raue LLP, and is a member of the Intellectual Property, Litigation, Corporate, Securities and Finance Groups. His practice focuses on intellectual property, information technology, press and media, the arts, and entertainment. His clients include numerous publishing companies, theaters, universities, and several internationally known artists and authors. Hegemann represents major newspaper publishers and advises politicians and artists with regard to press and media law. In addition, he provides advice for German literature publishers and represents several information technology companies, with a particular emphasis on intellectual property protection and software rights.

Prior to joining Hogan & Hartson Raue, Hegemann was a partner in the Berlin office of a leading German law firm. He studied law and philosophy at the Universities of Bonn and Munich and passed his First State Exam. He served as a judicial clerk in Berlin and Tokyo and passed the Second State Exam. In 1995, he received his doctorate, magna cum laude, from Humboldt University in Berlin. Since 1996, Hegemann has been an associate lecturer for culture and media law at the Academy of Music "Hanns Eisler" in Berlin and obtained the title of professor in 2002.

Fluent in English and German, Hegemann is an active member of the German Association for Intellectual Property and Copyrights (GRUR) and the German-Japanese Law Association.

Kim & Chang, founded in 1972, is the largest and the most specialized law firm in Korea. It is a full-service law firm based in Seoul with approximately four hundred professionals including lawyers, tax lawyers and accountants, and patent and trademark attorneys.

The expertise and multicultural background of Kim & Chang's professionals make the firm the recognized leader in providing specialized legal services for cross-border transactions and uniquely qualified to address the legal needs of international companies doing business in Korea. The firm is active in practically all areas of commercial practice. Its practice groups include securities, capital markets and banking, mergers and acquisitions, privatization, foreign investment, bankruptcy/corporate restructuring, human resources, antitrust and fair trade, international trade, product liability, real property/construction, environment, telecommunications, health care, intellectual property, litigation and arbitration, tax, and maritime law. Kim & Chang handles legal matters in English, German, French, Japanese, Chinese, and Swedish as well as Korean. Whether career attorneys, former judges, prosecutors, or regulators, Kim & Chang's professionals are committed to the firm's philosophy of providing clients with custom-tailored legal services of the highest quality. Kim & Chang's professionals and staff are taught to meet the needs of clients by finding creative solutions to help them succeed in Korea. It is due to this underlying philosophy that the firm has established its present status and reputation around the world within thirty years.

Kochhar & Company is one of the leading and largest corporate/commercial law firms in India with full-service offices in Bangalore, Chennai (Madras), Mumbai (Bombay), and New Delhi with resident partners in each of these offices.

Kochhar & Co. offers a wide range of legal services in the areas of corporate and commercial law and specializes in representing foreign corporations in connection with their business interests in India. The firm represents some of the largest multinational corporations from North America, Europe, and Japan (including many Fortune 500 companies). Kochhar's major practice areas include antitrust, unfair trade practices, arbitration, banking and finance, bankruptcy and reorganization, commercial contracts, corporate and securities laws, e-commerce transactions, environmental law, foreign investment, information technology, infrastructure projects, insurance, intellectual property, international trade and customs, joint ventures and technical collaborations, labor law, litigation, media and entertainment, mergers and acquisitions, privatization and disinvestment, real estate, regulatory approvals, shipping, taxation (international and local), and telecommunications.

Janmejay Rai is a senior associate with the New Delhi office.

Amber Melville-Brown is an English solicitor specializing in media law advice as a consultant at niche London media law firm David Price

Solicitors & Advocates from where she runs her own media law practice. Her expertise is in defamation, privacy, and media litigation and media and crisis management. Prior to becoming a consultant, she was a partner at London media specialist law firm Schillings, where her client base included claimants seeking advice in defamation, privacy, and other media litigation matters. Before that she was head of defamation practice at London-based Finers Stephens Innocent, acting mainly for major U.S. media defendants, including CNN, the *New York Times,* and *Time* magazine.

Melville-Brown provides crisis and media management advice and assistance to both claimants and defendants in relation to various media issues. Her clients include celebrities, television presenters, entertainers, and other individuals and national and international corporations including those involved in health care, diamond mining, and construction. She advises UK and U.S. photographic agencies on privacy issues in connection with publications in the UK.

Melville-Brown is the media columnist for the biggest-circulation news magazine for lawyers in Europe, the *Law Gazette,* in which she writes a regular legal update column in addition to features and reviews. She also writes and contributes on legal issues to national newspapers, including the *Times* and the *Independent.* In 2005, she was asked to write, present, and coproduce a training program for lawyers for Legal Network Television on "Knowing the Media," with an audience of lawyers nationwide including at least half of the top 100 legal firms and in-house practitioners in the UK Melville-Brown is also the external examiner for media for the College of Law, the largest postgraduate law school in Europe.

Slade R. Metcalf, a partner in the New York office of Hogan & Hartson LLP since March 2002 focuses his practice on media law and litigation for various media and entertainment companies. He counsels newspapers, television stations, syndicated television programs, magazines, and book publishers on prepublication and prebroadcast issues. He also represents media companies, reporters, authors, and photographers in litigations regarding issues of libel, invasion of privacy, copyright, and trademark. His practice is nationwide, with many of his cases outside the state of New York.

Metcalf is a member of the Forum on Communications Law of the American Bar Association, a member and past chair of the Committee on Media Law of the New York State Bar Association, and a member of the Association of the Bar of the City of New York.

Prior to joining Hogan & Hartson, Metcalf was a partner at Squadron Ellenoff Plesent & Sheinfeld (which merged with Hogan & Hartson in 2002) from 1981 to 2002, and prior to that an associate at the Squadron firm from 1977 to 1981. Metcalf was an associate at Townley Updike Carter & Rodgers from 1973 to 1977. He is a former chairman of the Legal Affairs Committee of the Magazine Publishers of America, and has participated in numerous bar association committees regarding media, communications, art, copyright, and literary property. He has lectured extensively on media law at forums including conferences of the Media Law Resource Center, Practicing Law Institute, the Magazine Publishers of America, and the American Society of Magazine Editors.

Metcalf is the author of a legal treatise entitled *Rights and Liabilities of Publishers, Broadcasters and Reporters,* which is updated annually and has been a leading media law resource book since 1981. He is also the founder of the Media Law Update, a quarterly Hogan & Hartson publication. He received his JD from New York University School of Law in 1973 and his AB from Princeton University in 1968. He is admitted to the New York Bar as well as to several federal courts.

Dominique Mondoloni, a practicing avocat admitted to the Paris Bar, is a partner in the Litigation Department of Willkie Farr & Gallagher LLP, and a member of the Paris Bar Council. He has significant experience as a civil and commercial litigator. He has handled, notably for U.S. and European clients, matters involving French civil, commercial, and criminal law. He has developed an extensive experience in corporate-related disputes. He has acted for plaintiffs in a number of libel cases and regularly assists a U.S.-based media firm in relation to French press law issues. He has authored a number of articles on issues involving French private international law, civil law, and bankruptcy law.

Mori Hamada & Matsumoto is a full-service international law firm based in Tokyo, with offices in Beijing and Shanghai. The firm has more than two hundred attorneys and a support staff of more than two hundred and fifty, including legal assistants, translators, and secretaries. It is one of the largest full-service firms based in Japan and is particularly well known for its work in the areas of mergers and acquisitions, finance, litigation, insolvency, and intellectual property. The firm was formed through the merger on December 1, 2002, of Mori Sogo and Hamada & Matsumoto, two well-established Tokyo-based firms. On July 1, 2005, the firm merged with Max Law Offices, a Tokyo-based firm with highly regarded expertise in the areas of copyrights, trademarks, and patents, as well as information technology, the Internet, media, and entertainment law. The firm's senior lawyers include a number of highly respected practitioners and leaders in the Japanese and international legal community, including the current president of the Daini-Tokyo Bar Association, the former president of the Japan Federation of Bar Associations, the former president of the Tokyo Bar Association, the former secretary-general of the Inter-Pacific Bar Association, and a prominent professor of law at the University of Tokyo. In addition, a former senior partner of the firm now sits on the Japanese Supreme Court. The firm has lawyers with primary legal qualification in Japan, the United States, the People's Republic of China, and the Philippines.

Anna Otkina is based in the Moscow offices of the international law firm Denton Wilde Sapte, where she has been advising foreign investors on international corporate and financial projects. She graduated from MGIMO Ministry of Foreign Affairs of the Russian Federation with distinction. She also holds an LLM in International Trade Law from the University of Georgia School of Law, USA, and a Master of International and Comparative Law/European Studies from Vrije Universiteit Brussels, Belgium.

Otkina regularly advises on corporate as well as regulatory issues involved in transfer and registration of rights to issued share capital in international transactions, telecommunications, as well as aviation law matters.

Monica Pa is an associate in the New York office of Davis Wright Tremaine LLP. She represents U.S. and foreign broadcasters, magazines, newspapers, and artists in the areas of libel, privacy, copyright, trademark, and other aspects of First Amendment, publishing, media, and entertainment law. Pa is a member of the Committee on Entertainment Law of the Association of the Bar of the City of New York, and a member of the steering committee for the New York State Bar, Entertainment and Sports Law Section. She was previously a law clerk for the Honorable Rosemary S. Pooler, United States Court of Appeals for the Second Circuit. She graduated magna cum laude from New York University Law School, where she received the Walter Derenberg Prize for Copyright Law.

Brian MacLeod Rogers of Toronto, Canada, practices media law and litigation, with an emphasis on libel, privacy, copyright, freedom of expression, and Internet-related issues. He represents writers, newspapers, magazines, book publishers, producers, broadcasters, and electronic media and has an extensive practice of prepublication/broadcast review. He has conducted hundreds of freedom of expression and libel cases and has appeared before all levels of courts, including the Supreme Court of Canada. He is currently acting as counsel for a coalition of fifty-one international, U.S., and Canadian media-related organizations intervening in the Ontario Court of Appeal in *Bangoura v. Washington Post* on the issue of jurisdiction and

Internet publication. He was founding president of Advocates In Defence of Expression in the Media (Ad IDEM, the Canadian media lawyers association) and the first Canadian member of the Defense Counsel Section, Media Law Resource Center, for which he co-authors annual surveys on Canadian libel and privacy laws. Rogers has authored and edited articles and books on media law, constitutional law, and civil litigation and co-founded the media law course at Ryerson University's School of Journalism. He has been peer-rated as "AV" by Martindale-Hubbell and "most frequently recommended" by Lexpert. He was graduated from Queen's University (Hons. BA.) and University of Toronto (LLB) and was admitted to the Ontario Bar in 1979. He is located in the offices of Stockwoods, Barristers, a litigation boutique firm in Toronto.

Mark Stephens has been described by the *Law Society Gazette* as "the patron solicitor of previously lost causes." It is this reputation for creativity with law that leads international publishers and broadcasters to his door. He has created a niche in international comparative media law and regulation. His practice takes him to Africa, the Commonwealth, Europe, and the United States. Stephens was appointed by the foreign secretary to the Foreign and Commonwealth Office free-expression advisory panel and is chair of the management board of the postgraduate Program in Comparative Media Law and Social Policy at Wolfson College, Oxford University. He is regularly asked to litigate privacy, free speech, and public interest issues before domestic and international courts (including the European Court of Human Rights and the Privy Council) and has given expert evidence before courts in three jurisdictions. In 2005, Stephens was asked to draft a new EU- and NATO-compliant freedom-of-information law for Romania. He is a trustee of *Index on Censorship* and sits on the editorial boards of *Communications Lawyer, Copyright World,* and *EIPR.* He has litigated points arising from libel tourists visiting London and founding claims merely on the basis of Internet publication. As founding chair of the Internet Watch Foundation, Stephens has lectured for the Foreign and Commonwealth Office and the Department of Trade and Industry on Internet content control and regulation and has run courses and tutorials on media law and policy for the Commonwealth Parliamentary Association and World Bank Institute. He is also a regular commentator on legal matters in both print and electronic media.

Tay Peng Cheng is a partner in Wong Partnership. He has extensive experience in litigation and arbitration, encompassing corporate and commercial disputes, construction and civil engineering matters, insolvency, receivership and judicial management, and libel. Tay has acted for a division of a

U.S.-based publishing house in a defamation suit commenced in Singapore pertaining to the publication of allegedly defamatory words in an online real-time electronic publication.

Wong Partnership, a full-service law firm, is one of the largest firms in Singapore with over 120 fee earners. In addition to its very highly regarded Litigation & Dispute Resolution Practice, Capital Markets, and Corporate departments, the firm offers specialized practices in China, India, Competition, and Intellectual Property. The firm has a Shanghai representative office, through which it has advised on a number of cross-border corporate and M&A transactions and represented parties in arbitrations held in China and Singapore. Wong Partnership also has a joint law venture in Singapore with Clifford Chance, LLP, known as Clifford Chance Wong.

Sinfah Tunsarawuth is an attorney in Thailand and is currently the Regional Coordinator for the Open Society Foundation, specializing in networking and interaction among media lawyers in Southeast Asia. Previously in private practice for various firms including Kanung & Partners, Tunsarawuth was also instrumental in creating the Thai Media Policy & Advocacy Center (Thai MPAC) at Chulalongkorn University in Bangkok, which includes media law advocacy as a main component of its activities. A former journalist for Reuters, Dow Jones, and *The Straits Times,* Tunsarawuth was admitted to practice in Thailand in 2002.

Jens P. van den Brink, an associate at Kennedy Van der Laan attorneys in Amsterdam, specializes in intellectual property and media law. Apart from the more classical intellectual property rights, his practice concentrates on unlawful publications, media law, the law pertaining to counterfeit, as well as the gaming industry. Van den Brink acts for several major players in the Dutch media industry, including both conventional (newspapers, broadcasters, publishers) and new media (Internet, mobile telephony). He regularly publishes on these subjects. Van den Brink studied French at the University of Nice, France, and international and Dutch commercial law (specializing in intellectual property law) at the University of Amsterdam and Columbia University in New York. He also obtained a Master of Laws (LLM) at King's College London, United Kingdom.

Vincent Wang is a legal consultant in the Shanghai office of Davis Wright Tremaine LLP. He represents and counsels clients on a wide range of activities in China, including media and Internet issues, intellectual property, telecommunications, foreign direct investment, corporate structure, commercial transactions, customs, land use, engineering, and dispute resolution. He received his BS and LLB degrees from Shanghai Jiao Tong

University, where he chaired the Legal Forum. He is fluent in Mandarin, English, and the Shanghai dialect and has published articles in English and Chinese concerning legal issues on the Internet, e-commerce, intellectual property, employment, and contract law in China.

Doreen Weisenhaus is director of the Media Law Project and an assistant professor teaching media law and ethics at the Journalism and Media Studies Centre at the University of Hong Kong. She is author of *Hong Kong Media Law: A Guide for Journalists and Media Professionals* (Hong Kong University Press 2007) and founder of http://hongkongmedialaw.net. Formerly, Weisenhaus was an assistant district attorney in Brooklyn, NY; city editor of *The New York Times,* law and political editor of *The New York Times Magazine,* and editor in chief of the U.S.-based *National Law Journal.* She holds a JD from Northwestern University's School of Law and a BS from the Medill School of Journalism, also at Northwestern. Her research areas also include media law developments in the People's Republic of China and elsewhere in Asia, media ownership trends, journalism history, and newsroom practices.

International Libel and Privacy Handbook

INTRODUCTION

How to Use This Book

In preparing this book, we submitted a list of the most commonly troublesome libel issues to lawyers around the world with expertise in media and privacy law. The questions are not exhaustive, and of course, no book or outline is a substitute for careful editing and legal review.

The best way for journalists and other publishers to avoid legal problems is to understand those problems *before* setting pen to paper. For that reason, the material presented here is designed for use by journalists to help *avoid* libel suits; it is not oriented toward tactics and defenses in litigation *after* a suit is filed. If you are not a lawyer experienced in the language of media law, I strongly recommend that before consulting the nation-specific chapters in this book, you read this section to familiarize yourself with the concepts explained. They are:

1. What is the locally accepted definition of libel?
2. Is libel-by-implication recognized, or, in the alternative, must the complained-of words alone defame the plaintiff?
3. May corporations sue for libel?
4. Is product disparagement recognized, and if so, how does that differ from libel?
5. Must an individual be clearly identified (by name or photograph) to sue for libel? Can a group of persons sue for libel, even though not named?
6. What is the fault standard(s) applied to libel?
   a. Does the fault standard depend on the fame or notoriety of the plaintiff?
   b. Is there a heightened fault standard or privilege for reporting on matters of public concern or public interest?
7. Is financial news about publicly traded companies, or companies involved with a government contract, considered a matter of public interest or otherwise privileged?

8. Is there a recognized protection for opinion or "fair comment" on matters of public concern?
9. Are there any requirements upon a plaintiff, such as demand for retraction or right of reply, and if so, what impact do they have?
10. Is there a privilege for quoting or reporting on papers filed in court, government-issued documents, or quasi-governmental proceedings?
11. Is there a privilege for republishing statements made earlier by other, bona fide, reliable publications or wire services?
12. Are there any restrictions regarding reporting on ongoing criminal investigations, criminal prosecutions, regulatory investigations, civil litigation, or other judicial proceedings?
13. Are prior restraints or other prepublication injunctions available on the basis of libel or privacy, and if so, what are the standards for obtaining such relief?
14. Is a right of privacy recognized (either civilly or criminally)?
    a. What is the definition of "private fact"?
    b. Is there a public interest or newsworthiness exception?
    c. Is the right of privacy based in common law, statute, or constitution?
15. May reporters tape-record their own telephone conversations for note-taking purposes (not rebroadcast) without the consent of the other party?
16. If permissible to record such tapes, may they be broadcast without permission?
17. Is there a recognized evidentiary privilege preventing the disclosure of confidential sources relied upon by reporters?
18. In the event that legal papers are served upon the newsroom (such as a civil complaint), are there any particular warnings about accepting service of which we should be aware?
19. Has your jurisdiction applied established media law to Internet publishers?
20. If established media law has been applied to Internet publishers, are there any ways in which Internet publishers (including chat room operators) have to meet different standards?
21. Are there any cases where the courts enforced a judgment in libel from another jurisdiction against a publisher in your jurisdiction?

The Key Questions Explained

1. What is the locally accepted definition of libel?

In the broadest terms, a libel claim usually requires that a publisher:

1. makes a statement to a third party;
2. that is false; and
3. defamatory, meaning that it exposes a subject's reputation to harm.

This third element—"defamatory meaning"—is central to most libel issues. If a statement is false but not defamatory, in most nations there is no libel. For example, if a statement that a cabinet minister drives a blue car turns out to be false, and his car is in fact green, it would take an unreasonable stretch to attribute reputational harm to the error: no one would think less of him for driving a blue car instead of a green one.

In many countries, to be considered defamatory, a statement must expose the subject to "hate, ridicule, contempt, or scorn" or to "lower the subject's reputation in the eyes of right-thinking members of society." Generally, defamatory words are those that would damage reputation, and would reasonably cause people to stop associating or doing business with the subject. Typically, these are statements of criminal or ethical wrongdoing, professional incompetence, lack of integrity, impending financial insolvency, loathsome disease, or immorality.

Each jurisdiction has different limits regarding what is and isn't considered defamatory, and these standards are reflective of the societal norms of that culture. Of course, some statements would put the subject's reputation into disrepute globally: an accusation of thievery or violent crime is universally condemned. However, less obvious issues require looking at the society in which the subject would complain. For example, in cosmopolitan cities such as New York and San Francisco, being called homosexual is not considered defamatory, because the society does not assume that it is something of which one should be ashamed. By contrast, in rural Georgia, being called "gay" is actionable, because that society considers homosexuality as a moral wrong.

Some jurisdictions allow a libel claim to be brought on seemingly innocent statements that would injure reputation if the reader happens to be aware of certain undisclosed facts. The law calls this *libel per quod.* For example, consider the statement: "Mr. Smith was seen kissing a blonde-haired woman in a restaurant last night." This in and of itself shouldn't expose his reputation to harm—unless the reader knew that Mr. Smith was in fact married to a dark-haired woman!

One common mistake journalists and publishers make here is to confuse "falsity" with "defamatory meaning." In most jurisdictions, even if a statement exposes a person to reputational damage, if it is true, it may not be the basis of a libel suit. But conflating truth with defamatory meaning leads to problems. With the exception of the United States, if sued upon, the publisher or journalist carries the burden of proving the truth of the statement in court, which is not as easy as it sounds. The proof must be hard, documented, and reliable enough to stand up in court. (See the discussion of fault standards in Question 6 below.) The safest, most responsible approach for any journalist or publisher is, as a first rule, to determine whether the statement at issue is capable of defamatory meaning: will it harm the subject's reputation? If so, the next step is to determine how much solid, incontrovertible proof you can offer that the statement is indeed true.

There are certain circumstances when the statement is considered "privileged." This is when the subject matter is considered by law to be so important to society that a publisher is relieved of the duty to determine the truth of defamatory allegations. These "privileged" circumstances are usually found in situations where *the fact that the statement was made* is in itself newsworthy. For example, allegations made in court pleadings, police reports, government agencies' reports, or legislative debates are important because society needs to be informed about what transpires in courts and government. Thus, many nations treat these circumstances as "privileged," and provided they are accurately and fairly reported, the press may republish these statements without liability. (See the discussion of privilege in Question 10 below.)

In many nations, truth is not always an absolute defense, and if the statement at issue exposes the subject to reputational injury, it need not be false to be actionable: In these nations, a true statement that exposes a person to reputational damage may still be sued upon if the court finds that the statement does not serve the public interest. Mere curiosity or gossip may not satisfy the court that the public "needed to know" the damaging facts, despite their truth, or that telling these facts was an example of fulfilling a journalist's mission. (See the discussion of fault standards in Question 6 below.)

2. Is libel-by-implication recognized, or, in the alternative, must the complained-of words alone defame the plaintiff?

Some statements are defamatory "on their face," meaning that, by themselves, they may defame the subject, for example, "X is a murderer." By contrast, libel-by-implication can occur either by arranging innocent facts in a way that suggests wrongdoing, or by leaving out information that the reader ought to know to have a less damaging view of the subject.

In the first instance, a common occurrence in libel analysis is the juxtaposition of a series of facts: "A is a child-care specialist. The government is investigating child-care specialists for evidence of child abuse." Put together, a reader could reasonably infer that "A" might be under investigation for child abuse. *This is true even though there is no specific statement that "A" is under investigation.* Courts often allow a hypothetical reader to make reasonable inferences, even though such implications were not necessarily the intent of the writer. Avoiding this problem requires clarity and precision of language.

Similarly, leaving out facts that clarify a story can also create the impression that someone has committed wrongdoing or is subject to other defamatory meaning. For example, to say that "University Professor X failed to report to the school that he made extra money tutoring students at his home" implies that he had a duty to report his extra income, and may have committed a wrongful act. But something is omitted here: is the professor actually *obligated* to make this disclosure? If the story omitted that fact, the reasonable reader might assume that the professor violated some trust or even a legal obligation. Did he really *fail* to do something he should have?

It is also worth noting that in many jurisdictions, raising hypothetical questions may be a form of libel-by-implication. To ask: "Is X wanted by government investigators?" raises the question that he *might* be a wanted criminal.

3. May corporations sue for libel?

The question of whether a company has the right to sue for libel comes up frequently in the areas of consumer reporting, financial news, and product reviews. Some jurisdictions severely limit the ability of companies to sue for libel, and other jurisdictions do not allow companies (as corporate entities) a right of privacy. Individual executives, of course, may still bring libel claims subject to the laws of the applicable jurisdiction.

The question also comes up when a story or publication targets an individual who may be closely associated with a particular company.

4. Is product disparagement recognized, and if so, how does that differ from libel?

Product disparagement (sometimes called "trade libel") issues arise when a product or brand of goods is held in disrepute. This occurs often in product reviews, consumer reporting, and comparative advertising. Some jurisdictions apply the same substantive standards as a libel claim, while others allow these kinds of claims to apply only when competitors make statements that might be construed as unfair competition or deceptive trade practices.

5. Must an individual be clearly identified (by name or photograph) to sue for libel? Can a group of persons sue for libel, even though not named?

Also referred to as the "of and concerning" doctrine in libel, jurisdictions have differing degrees of specificity with which the subject of a story is described. Usually, the law does not require that a subject be named: if he or she is reasonably identifiable from the details provided, that will suffice for a libel claim. Other jurisdictions, such as France, however, adopt a "libel par ricochet" doctrine, through which not only the subject, but people with whom the subject is normally associated by the public, may also have a libel claim.

6. What is the fault standard(s) applied to libel?

Misapprehension of the "fault standard" is probably responsible for more sloppy journalism—and libel suits—than any other doctrine in law. Moreover, the plain fact of the matter is that reporters, writers, and editors do sometimes get their facts wrong.

Too many publishers overlook the fact that the fault standard is essentially a legal excuse for making a mistake: "the right to get it wrong." In many nations, courts and legislators have realized that the public would be shortchanged if the press were strictly liable for every mistake. This is because the press would be forced to "self-censor" and cut off the flow of information, lest it face a bankrupting libel claim for any mistake. The fault standard seeks to strike a balance between the public's need for important news and the right that citizens have to be free from libelous statements. Without some leeway for good faith error, the chilling effect of libel suits would prevent most publishers from taking the financial risk of publishing important news, especially about the powerful and well-funded. Publishers must recognize that in most jurisdictions, the complained-of story is assumed to be false as a starting point for most courts.

Fault standards generous to the press have in some cases been relied upon by unscrupulous journalists who see it as a license to print whatever they want without due care for whether the material they publish is accurate. On the other hand, thoughtful publishers and journalists see the fault standards as a guidepost of due care, a minimum standard of professional responsibility and behavior.

a. Does the fault standard depend on the fame or notoriety of the plaintiff?

In some nations, courts differentiate libel plaintiffs in varying degrees as "public" or "private" figures, and may apply a more stringent set of hurdles for a "public figure" to overcome as a plaintiff in a libel suit. This is not, as some journalists think, rooted in a theory that public figures are "asking for it." Instead, the law in nations applying a "public figure" test assumes that public figures have the ability to command attention and can easily dispel false stories by issuing a press release or holding a press conference to challenge stories. Their fame or notoriety will help ensure that their side of a story is heard. In these cases, public figure plaintiffs will have to show more than mere falsity or defamatory meaning: they usually have to show that the reporter breached all standards of ethical or professional duty in making the mistake.

In some jurisdictions, such as the United States, the plaintiff will have to prove that the reporter knew his or her story was incorrect or entertained serious doubt about its falsity but chose to publish anyway. This is often referred to as *actual malice.* By contrast, in nations with heightened fault standards, private figures, or persons involved in a matter not deemed of public importance, do not have to meet such a difficult task. They often need only prove negligence on the part of the journalist. *That comes down to a court asking in sometimes detailed terms if the reporter did that which a reasonable reporter should have done.* In journalism, this commonly includes:

- Extensive fact-checking and note-taking;
- Exhaustive documentary research and personal interviews;
- Clear and precise writing without a malicious tone;
- Providing an opportunity to fairly and fully respond; and
- Asking whether the story is so important to the public interest that it cannot wait for further research or fact-checking.

It is important to recognize that in most jurisdictions, the fact the reporter simply *believed* in good faith that the material was accurate is not enough to satisfy the test.

b. Is there a heightened fault standard or privilege for reporting on matters of public concern or public interest?

In jurisdictions where the story is assumed to be in error, or where there is in fact a defamatory inaccuracy, some courts allow this error to go unpunished if it is made in "good faith" *and* the matter is one of public concern. The definition of "public concern" is informed by each jurisdiction's approach to excusing error. In other words, in nations such as the United States where adherence to the First Amendment is seen as a primary goal, and protection for the press is at its greatest, courts will generally allow editors—not lawyers—to determine what is and isn't in the public interest. Some U.S. courts have gone as far as to say that if an editor chose to publish the story, it must be, by definition, a matter of interest to the public.

By contrast, courts in most other jurisdictions take a very close look at the question of "public concern" and ask actively whether the story at issue was something that served the public welfare, not the public's idle curiosity or appetite for gossip.

7. Is financial news about publicly traded companies, or companies involved with a government contract, considered a matter of public interest or otherwise privileged?

In some jurisdictions, the courts recognize that the press is the "watchdog" of the activities of publicly traded companies. Thus, reports on their activities may be "privileged" to one extent or another, heightening the legal protections. When companies or their products are the subject of reporting, one important risk publishers should take into account is the varying degree of damages that companies may be able to claim are the result of an inaccurate and defamatory story. Companies can in some cases claim that lost sales, lost value of assets, failed transactions, and even a drop in stock price are recoverable.

Although not generally recognized in the United States, some nations recognize a cause of action for "negligent publication," which some academics describe as a "libel claim without the libel." In essence, these are claims where the false statement does not necessarily expose the subject to reputational damages, but is somehow relied upon by readers to the subject's detriment. For example, if a news story inaccurately describes a company losing a big contract, and based on that story the company has trouble borrowing money, the company may claim that the higher cost of financing is attributable to the erroneous story. Similarly, under this theory claims have been brought on the publications of faulty recipes that made people sick, product reviews that "encouraged" people to buy defective products, or instructions for mechanical engineering procedures that resulted in personal injury.

8. Is there a recognized protection for opinion or "fair comment" on matters of public concern?

Most jurisdictions allow some leeway for the expression of opinion on matters of public concern, subject to varying restrictions. Intellectually, the defense is based on the following syllogism: if libel claims require a false fact and opinions are not capable of being proven true or false then opinions are not subject to libel claims.

On a more practical level, opinions can be the subject of a libel claim if they are not "pure" opinion (e.g., "I don't like Mercedes-Benz automobiles") but are instead opinions that imply undisclosed fact (e.g., "I don't think Mercedes-Benz automobiles are safe"). The second example implies to the reader that there is something *factually provable* about the Mercedes that serves as a basis for the opinion. In many jurisdictions, unless the writer disclosed to the reader *why* she thinks the Mercedes is unsafe, a libel claim might arise. Note that those facts have to be accurate, of course. Despite this framework, a surprisingly high number of editors and commentators are subjected to libel claims because of the false comfort to be had from couching otherwise defamatory statements in the language of opinion, such as "I think" or "it is believed that . . . ."

Many jurisdictions also place restrictions on the "tone" of the opinion. In the United States, the more vitriolic, or at least hyperbolic the language, the closer to "pure" opinion the article will be found, on the theory that "heated rhetoric" is patently obvious as a writer's opinion, rather than stating actual facts. Thus, American defendants have been able to call subjects "nazis," "pigs," "butchers," and in one case, "a chicken butt." Many nations are not as generous with wild language, and may hold publishers liable for the use of "uncivil" or "ridiculing" language.

9. Are there any requirements upon a plaintiff, such as demand for retraction or right of reply, and if so, what impact do they have?

The "right of reply" is grounded in two different theories, each of which should be understood by publishers. Some jurisdictions, particularly those that have a generous press-friendly body of law, are driven by the belief that "more speech is better," in other words, that the public interest is best served by having opposing sides of a story brought into the open. These jurisdictions usually reward publishers who publish replies from story subjects by limiting the amount of damages that may be awarded at trial. Other pro-press jurisdictions even deny libel plaintiffs the right to sue at all if they do not make specific written demands for retraction within certain time periods.

By contrast, some jurisdictions approach the right of reply from a "press responsibility" theory, namely, that because publishers control access to the press, fairness requires that people who take issue with stories have a right to be heard. These jurisdictions place a serious requirement on publishers who do receive such demands from libel plaintiffs, and publishers who fail to publish responses in a specified manner may be subjected to civil fine.

10. Is there a privilege for quoting or reporting on:

a. Papers filed in court?

Variants on the "fair and true report" privilege essentially allow reporters to reproduce potentially defamatory statements made in court without independently verifying those facts. This is because courts often accept that the reporting is about what transpires in civil or criminal proceedings, and accordingly, the public has a need to be informed about the administration of justice. That said, great care should be taken when reproducing the allegations made in court. First, because court cases (whether civil or criminal) usually involve some degree of wrongdoing, the odds are high that a potentially defamatory statement will arise.

Second, very few jurisdictions allow the press absolute, unfettered ability to publish defamatory statements plucked from courtrooms or court papers. This second caveat is the heart of the "fair and true" doctrine: the report must be fair to the subject of the allegations, and true, meaning it must accurately describe the legal argument or court document at issue. Although by no means exhaustive, reporters should consider the following guidelines:

"Fair" generally means:

- Reporting not just the damaging facts or allegations, but including the counterarguments or defenses raised by the subject;
- Making clear the distinction between unproven allegations and an actual finding of fact;
- Providing an opportunity to respond.

"True" generally means:

- Accurately describing the legal argument or allegation made;
- Refraining from adding conjecture about innocence and guilt;
- Quoting from the documents or statements when possible, instead of paraphrasing.

b. Government-issued documents?

Jurisdictions have differing views on what kind of government papers may or may not be subject to the fair and true report privilege. In most areas, public statements, reports, fact-finding papers, and statements made by government agencies are privileged to one degree or another, as are usually legislative or parliamentary debates.

Not all jurisdictions allow defamatory allegations contained in documents or statements made by a government agency to be quoted without some limitations. Jurisdictions also vary widely in defining what a "government document" is: for example, in some places police reports are privileged, in others they are not. As a general rule, an "official" statement will be one that is:

(i) made by a government employee authorized to speak on behalf of the agency; and (ii) made in a situation or occasion expressly convened for the purpose of disseminating information to the public at large, such as press conferences, press releases, public meetings, or e-mailed statements to the press.

c. Quasi-governmental proceedings, such as those issued by professional associations (for example, disciplinary proceedings)?

As described above, jurisdictions have varying definitions of what is and isn't a government agency for purposes of applying a privilege to reporting defamatory allegations contained in their documents. Many jurisdictions apply this privilege to the statements, reports, findings, and hearings of "quasi"-government agencies. These may be loosely defined as bodies that have been given a degree of authority to make decisions on behalf of the public, or of bodies that have the authority to discipline specific industries on behalf of the public interest, such as medical or bar associations, or self-regulating bodies such as those that oversee stock brokers and traders.

11. Is there a privilege for republishing statements made earlier by other, bona fide, reliable publications or wire services?

As a basic rule, those who repeat a libel are as responsible as those who first published it. Nonetheless, some jurisdictions allow publishers to rely on the reporting of bona fide, reputable news agencies in certain circumstances, particularly in jurisdictions that require a plaintiff to show more than mere negligence to recover libel damages. The application of this privilege varies, but courts generally require that the "republisher" did not alter the language of the original report, did not excise any exculpatory information from the original report, and did not have specific knowledge or reason to believe that the original report was wrong.

Publishers find themselves in a quandary when the fact of the original report is *in itself* newsworthy. There are often instances when the fact that a major publication or broadcaster publishes a groundbreaking and important story has an effect on the marketplace or the political dialogue. Courts that recognize this privilege often require that those republishing allegations made by other publishers should try to craft their story in a manner that does not adopt those allegations as a fact, but rather sets forth the controversy in an even-handed manner.

12. Are there any restrictions regarding:

a. Reporting on ongoing criminal investigations?

Few areas are as fraught with landmines as reporting ongoing criminal investigations. Aside from the libel issues (see Questions 10a. and b. above), non-U.S. courts generally take a dim view of publishers perceived as "interfering" with law enforcement or regulatory activities. This is because of the argument that the publication may be inadvertently "tipping off" suspected individuals and allowing them to escape detection or to destroy evidence.

b. Reporting on ongoing criminal prosecutions?

Several nations place restrictions on reporting ongoing investigations because the law is concerned with publications that might taint the public's perception of a case from which a jury pool might be selected. In these cases, reporters and publishers who reveal details about criminal proceedings may be charged with Contempt of Court, and be subject to fines or imprisonment.

Restrictions on the reporting of criminal proceedings include, variously, "blackout" periods of publishing between the time of arrest and verdict, names and identifying information about suspects and witnesses, details about the crime, and speculation about guilt or innocence. Contempt of Court in many of these nations is a "strict liability" crime, meaning that there is no justification defense available: if the forbidden material is published, the reporter or publisher faces charges.

c. Reporting on ongoing regulatory investigations?

Reporters may face the same difficulties reporting on regulatory investigations as they might in criminal cases.

d. Reporting on ongoing civil litigation or other judicial proceedings?

Although civil cases are usually subject to fewer restrictions, reporters should be advised that courts may declare certain types of material "off limits" depending on what kind of civil case is being litigated. For example, the publication of proprietary trade information, personal private data, identities of minors, material in family court such as paternity issues, and other sensitive material may be proscribed.

13. Are prior restraints or other prepublication injunctions available on the basis of libel or privacy, and if so, what are the standards for obtaining such relief?

"Prior restraints" are judicial actions whereby the court forbids a publisher from disclosing or reporting certain information before it is published. The United States is one of the few jurisdictions that bans "prior restraints" under its Constitution.

Prior restraints are generally granted when the subject of the story has a reasonable basis for believing that the material is about to be published, and can convince the court ahead of time that the story is false and damaging. Publishers or webmasters served with notice of a hearing for a prior restraint should consult local counsel immediately, and should never ignore such a notice.

Even if the publisher believes that the story is accurate under the local law, failure to obey the prior restraint without attending the hearing may subject the publisher to criminal charges. The bad news is that attending such a hearing may delay publication, or even ruin the exclusivity of the story. The good news is that in most nations that allow prior restraints, the person requesting relief will have to put up a bond and bear the publisher's legal costs if the restraint is not granted.

14. Is a right of privacy recognized (either civilly or criminally)?

The right of privacy should be understood as separate and distinct from defamation. Where defamation addresses the reputation of entities impacted by false speech, "privacy" addresses not damage to reputation (what others think of the subject) but instead the damage to the subject's *feelings*. The truth or falsity of the statement at issue is rarely germane to privacy claims.

At its core, privacy claims center on the offensiveness of having material published about a person that (the plaintiff claims) has no business being disclosed to the public at large. Although corporations can bring claims based on the disclosure of private data or trade secrets, they usually do not have standing to bring "invasion of privacy" claims because these claims are designed to repair "hurt feelings" or "emotional damage," both injuries that corporations (as opposed to human individuals) do not have the ability to suffer.

a. What is the definition of "private fact"?

In those nations that recognize a right of privacy, the central question is whether the sued-upon story discloses a fact that is generally personal and private, and the disclosure of which is highly offensive. Defining a "private" fact is not an easy task for plaintiffs. The fact at issue may not be known, but if it is *knowable* to the public (for example, through easily accessed public records), it may not be considered "private."

Even if the fact at issue is secret, mere secrecy is not enough to make a claim. Courts will examine the nature of the fact itself, and its inherent "offensiveness." Courts will generally find "privacy" to have been violated when a fact discloses something of an *intimate* nature. Medical information, information about sexual preferences or behavior, information about children, marital matters, and the like are more likely to be actionable. Publishers should also be aware of restrictions in the European Union and elsewhere about disclosure of data that is considered private under Data Protection Laws.

b. Is there a public interest or newsworthiness exception?

Some jurisdictions that recognize a right of privacy still protect publishers if the fact at issue is "rationally related" to a public controversy. This usually becomes a very fact-specific examination. Broadly speaking, media superstars such as notoriously misbehaving pop singers are often deemed to have almost no right to privacy at all, while other celebrities, although famous, may be allowed to pursue claims of privacy *when the private fact at issue is not rationally related to the reason he or she is famous.* Superstar fashion model Naomi Campbell was allowed to pursue privacy claims in the United Kingdom when a tabloid showed photographs of her leaving a drug rehabilitation clinic. Campbell argued that the disclosure of her medical condition was private and not in the public interest. The UK courts and the European Court of Human Rights agreed.

c. Is the right of privacy based in common law, statute, or constitution?

Several jurisdictions also have statutes addressing a form of privacy claim called "misappropriation of likeness." This claim is similar to a false endorsement, trademark, or unfair competition claim, wherein people—usually celebrities—who have a value in their image claim that it is being misused for the purpose of profit. Some celebrities have tried to use this claim as an end run around substantive defamation laws, arguing that because newspapers or broadcasters are in the business of making a profit, their image shouldn't be used in newspaper stories without their consent. Courts have almost universally rejected this approach, and apply a "newsworthiness" exemption to this claim as well. This protection has also been extended to unauthorized biographies, movies, posters, and even artwork. It should be noted that there have been several cases where the claim was allowed to proceed because the story underlying the unconsented use of the photo was erroneous, or, in the words of one judge, "so infected with substantial falsity" that the judge said it would be illogical to allow a newsworthiness defense to a story that was clearly not news.

15. May reporters tape-record their own telephone conversations for note-taking purposes (not rebroadcast) without the consent of the other party?

Many jurisdictions forbid the recording of telephone conversations without the consent of all parties to the phone call (also called "two-party" consent). In these places, the mere act of making the recording itself may be a crime, and it does not matter whether the tape is disclosed to a third party or not. In some of these jurisdictions, such an improperly made tape might not be admissible as evidence in a libel trial in the event that the recording is needed for the reporter to prove that something in particular was said.

16. If it is permissible to record such tapes, may they be broadcast without permission?

Even in areas where it is permissible for reporters to tape-record their telephone interviews without the other person's consent, that is not a guarantee that such tapes may be broadcast without consent. The act of making the tape is separate from disclosing the tape (or its contents), which might be a violation under statutory privacy laws, or broadcasting regulations.

17. Is there a recognized evidentiary privilege preventing the disclosure of confidential sources relied upon by reporters?

Using confidential sources is something that reporters should never take lightly. A "shield law" or "reporters' privilege" is a doctrine that protects reporters from having to disclose their confidential sources. This comes up in a variety of ways:

1. when parties are in litigation and seek to obtain reporters' notes or outtakes to prove their case (usually through a subpoena);
2. when law enforcement agencies want to investigate or prosecute someone who may have been interviewed by the reporter (also demanded through a subpoena); and
3. when the reporter or publisher is sued for libel in a story that uses confidential sources (usually demanded in discovery or disclosure).

Nations that do have shield laws are usually protective to the press in the first instance when civil litigants seek to use a reporter's notes, especially when those notes might reveal the identity of a confidential source. The second instance, however, is not as clear-cut, and generally, law enforcement agencies have been successful in convincing courts that reporters should disclose their confidential sources. Judges in these matters are generally required to balance the harms at issue. On the media's side, forcing disclosure makes the press an official "arm" of law enforcement, and erodes the press's independence. Press freedom advocates add that this has a "chilling effect" on sources who want to tell the press important information but are afraid of being targeted for retribution. On the other hand, law enforcement agencies have been able in some cases to convince courts that reporters have no higher standing or more rights than "ordinary" citizens, and, like "ordinary" citizens, must come forward and testify as to facts they have that the government might need to protect the public.

Shield laws may not apply to the third situation, when the press is sued and the plaintiff seeks the identity of the confidential source. Because plaintiffs in most cases have a right to attack the credibility of reporters or sources, the press is often barred from relying on confidential sources to defend a libel claim unless it is willing to disclose the identity of the source. This puts the press in a difficult position, because sources who are promised confidentiality by the press have been allowed to sue the press for breach of contract when their identity is disclosed without consent. Moreover, some European jurisdictions make it a criminal act for reporters to disclose the identity of confidential sources.

18. In the event that legal papers are served upon the newsroom (such as a civil complaint), are there any particular warnings about accepting service of which we should be aware?
Each nation has its own set of procedural laws regarding the manner in which legal papers such as subpoenas and complaints (and sometimes demands for retraction) must be delivered. Failure to respond properly to such papers might result in a default judgment against the publisher or reporter, and local counsel should be consulted immediately in all cases.

19. Has your jurisdiction applied established media law to Internet publishers?
It should not be assumed that all established media law and case decisions will be applied the same way. For example, the archival aspect of the Internet has established different rules for statutes of limitations, whereby claims can "expire" if not acted upon within a certain date of the publication. Where stories published on paper might not be sued upon after a set period (say three years after the first publication in any medium), many courts outside the United States have said that on the Internet, each day that the offending Web page is available brings a new publication, and the claim renews. Thus, Internet publishers might face "infinite" exposure for their stories.

20. If established media law has been applied to Internet publishers, are there any ways in which Internet publishers (including chat room operators) have to meet different standards?
Federal communications law in the United States provides a "safe harbor" for most operators of ISPs, chat rooms, and electronic bulletin boards, protecting them from liability for the defamatory statements made by others without the operator's prior knowledge. However, many non-U.S. jurisdictions apply a strict liability rule, making the operators of websites

and the like responsible for defamatory statements, whether they are aware of the falsity of the statements or not.

Website operators outsides the United States have also been held accountable for the unknowing use of their websites for the improper posting of copyrighted material and materials that violate the European Data Privacy Act.

21. Are there any cases in which the courts enforced a judgment in libel from another jurisdiction against a publisher in your jurisdiction?
A judgment in one nation against a publisher or reporter might not be enforceable in others. The enforcement of judgments is determined by a patchwork of statutes, treaties, and common law. Although judgments issued outside of the United States rooted in non-U.S. libel law might not be enforceable in the United States, the same is not necessarily so for entities who have employees or assets elsewhere. For example, judgments in a European country may be enforced fairly easily against entities with assets in another European nation.

PART **ONE**

Americas

Brazil

Canada

United States

CHAPTER 1

Brazil

LAURA FRAGOMENI, PAULA MENA BARRETO,
Barbosa, Müssnich & Aragão

AND EDUARDO DE MORAES
Evaristo de Moraes

Barbosa, Müssnich & Aragão
Av. Almirante Barroso, n0 52, 32 Floor
Rio de Janeiro/RJ/Brazil 20031-000
Phone: (55 21) 3825-6001
Fax: (55 21) 3824-6069
www.bmalaw.com.br
lfo@bmalaw.com.br
pmb@bmalaw.com.br

Evaristo de Moraes
Rua México, n0 90 sala 402
Rio de Janeiro/RJ/Brazil 20031-141
Phone: (55 21) 2240-6128
Fax: (55 21) 2240-6128
evaristomoraes@uol.com.br
edumoraeseva@uol.com.br

Introduction to the Brazilian Legal System

The Brazilian legal system is derived from traditional civil law theories and is guided by the Brazilian Federal Constitution, which was drafted in 1988. The "new" system has significantly streamlined a Brazilian system that was infamous for having an excessive number of laws.

The current judicial system has two branches, a federal branch and a state branch. There are two levels of federal courts in Brazil. Federal districts, composed of states and municipalities, each have their own court, called the Federal District Court. The second level of the federal branch is the Supreme Court of Justice, the highest federal court in the country. The state system is composed of states and municipalities within each state. Each state has its own uniquely organized judicial system, and each state's courts, judges, and jurisdiction are determined by a state constitution. State legal powers are limited by the federal constitution, but are otherwise unhindered. Municipalities have constitutional equivalents, called organic law, but no court system, and must obey all federal constitutional laws.

Brazilian Civil Code and Media Law

Persons producing content subject to Brazilian law are advised to familiarize themselves briefly with the structural framework of Brazil's legal system and its approach to media law. Article 5 of the Constitution of Brazil (CB, in force since 1988) places a high value on freedom of the press;[1] however, the CB also provides citizens with the inviolability of privacy and private life. Therefore, the various constitutional guaranties must be weighed against each other in any given case. In addition, certain restrictions on press freedom have been established via legislative means.

The Brazilian Civil Code (BCC), which was passed in 2002, introduced changes in the area of personality rights, including the right to private life. The BCC provides that the private life of natural persons is inviolable and that the courts, on application by an interested party, may adopt such measures as may be necessary to prevent any act contrary to the inviolability of private life or to cause such acts to cease.

1. What is the locally accepted definition of libel?

The CB guarantees both freedom of the press and the right to privacy. Provision is made for the freedom of artistic and scientific expression and communication that is free from censorship or restriction. On the other hand, the CB also states that "honor, dignity, image, and the right to privacy are all inviolable rights," breach of which gives rise to an entitlement to damages. Libel is both a criminal offense and a civil wrong in Brazil.

Chapter 3 (Capítulo III) of the Press Law[2] sets out the offenses arising from abuse of the right to freedom of thought and information using communication/information media. The term media, in this context, covers newspapers and periodical publications, radio transmission, and other news services.

Media crimes are divided into two classes: on the one hand, public order offenses or the divulging of state secrets, and on the other, defamation ("crimes against reputation"). Depending on the conduct of the agent, libel (in a broad definition) can take, according to Brazilian law, three different forms: calumny (*calúnia*), defamation (*difamação*), and injury to dignity or decorum (*injúria*). These three crimes are defined as follows:

Calumny: To falsely accuse someone of committing a criminal act (punishable by six months' to three years' imprisonment plus a fine ranging from one to twenty minimum salaries).[3]

In the offenses of calumny (Art. 20) and defamation (Art. 21), the publisher alleges a provable fact. In the former (calumny), the publisher must have knowledge of the falsity prior to publication. It is important to note, however, that in certain circumstances the defendant accused of the crime of calumny or defamation may rely on the defense of truth. This defense is generally available in calumny (Art. 20) but only in limited circumstances in defamation (Art. 21), and not at all for injury to dignity (Art. 22). The defense of truth, where applicable, is an absolute defense, whereby the defendant avoids conviction.

Examples of calumny include the following: The unproven allegation that a judge, in the city of Canoinhas, had committed the offense of threatening behavior (which constitutes a crime) against the owners of a publishing company, saying that if the editor in chief did not stop writing about the mayor of the city, he would be severely punished, with payment of fines and, additionally, imprisonment. The publisher published such threats. The truth of the allegedly calumnious statement was not proved and, for this reason, the owners of the company were convicted.[4] In a city in the State of São Paulo, a public agent was accused of manipulating the results of a public contest and making false representations. The court decided that such a statement would constitute a crime of calumny.[5]

The following statements were found not to constitute calumny: A news report was published of a charge of manslaughter filed against a medical practitioner. Because the charges had in fact been brought, the court found the statement justified by truth and held there was no crime of calumny.[6] A journalist authored an article in which he referred to the plaintiff as a drug dealer, for being criminally convicted and currently on conditional release. However, the court decided that libel was not present, once the defendant had established his fact-finding on the *animus narrandi* ("willing to tell").[7]

Defamation: To allege that someone has performed a disreputable act (punishable by three to eighteen months' imprisonment plus a fine of between two and ten minimum salaries).[8]

In the lower-level offense of defamation, the act that the victim is stated to have performed is not a criminal act, but is nonetheless conduct that is detrimental to the victim's reputation (*disreputable*). An individual's reputation is the person's "standing in society." The law seeks to uphold and protect the esteem in which a person is held by society—called his *objective dignity.*

Examples of defamation include: Blaming the mayor of a municipality for improper accounting procedures at City Hall, saying he had "never been transparent" in his accounting and that the "public authorities were reluctant to publish the accounts" because of fear of reprisals.[9] In another case, an article referred to the mayor of a certain city as "mentally disordered." The court understood this conduct as defamatory, and no public interest was present in the context of this statement. For this reason, the statement was not supported by the principle of freedom of speech in the Brazilian Constitution.[10]

The following statements were found not to constitute defamation: A newspaper reported the filing of administrative proceedings against an educational institution. The court held that the aim of the report was to inform the community of an issue of public interest. The journalist's intention was not to defame the legal entity referred to or its partners.[11] In another case, a journalist published a satire *animus jocandi* ("willing to make fun") that alleged provable facts. Because they were true, the way they were published was considered a legal form of expression by the journalist.[12]

Injury: To offend someone's dignity or decorum (punishable by one to twelve months' imprisonment or a fine of between one and ten minimum salaries).[13] The offense of injury (Art. 22) involves making statements that simply offend the subjects' "decorum and dignity." Decorum (in Portuguese *dignidade*) refers to a person's moral attributes, whereas dignity (in Portuguese *decoro*)[14] refers to the individual's physical and intellectual attributes. The mere use, to describe a person, of words that express a negative concept or image and which offend "subjective" honor (the victim's self-image, as opposed to that person's image in society) constitutes grounds for prosecution for this offense.

Examples of injury include: An article describing one of the candidates standing for presidency of a municipal legislative assembly (City Hall) as a "hypocrite," "false moralist," and "a man of limited cultural resources" was held to show a clear intention of offending the individual's dignity and decorum rather than making a criticism based on public interest.[15] In another instance, a newspaper published an article stating that the mayor of a city in the State of Rio de Janeiro was a "scoundrel" and his behavior was harmful to the poor population. The court understood that the use of the word "scoundrel" constituted a violation of the subjective honor of the mayor and the newspaper was convicted.[16]

The following examples found that injurious publications had not been committed: A politician was called "selfish" and a "political opportunist" by his political opponent. The court decided that such conduct did not characterize injury because it constitutes (legitimate) criticism.[17] The case of a person named to a public function and who was called "incompetent" and "unable to exercise such function" was adjudicated not injurious because the court held that the expressions were used not to offend the individual but in order to instigate the public opinion against the politician's appointment.[18]

2. Is libel-by-implication recognized, or, in the alternative, must the complained-of words alone defame the plaintiff?

Most expressions need to be interpreted in the context in which they are written in order to determine whether or not one of the three crimes referred to above (calumny, defamation, or injury) has been committed. Expressions that in isolation are not offensive may be held by the judge to be so following examination of the circumstances and manner in which they were used.

3. May corporations sue for libel?

Although there is a divergence in both the precedent and authorities on this question, the dominant position in the Brazilian Superior Court of Justice (Superior Tribunal de Justiça—STJ) is that crimes against honor (which include calumny, defamation, and injury) can only be committed against natural persons. Therefore, corporations could not sue third parties based on libel for criminal purposes. However, legal persons can bring a civil action for damages if they believe they have been defamed.

4. Is product disparagement recognized, and if so, how does that differ from libel?

The mere allegation that a product is unequal (inferior or superior) to another does not constitute a crime against reputation. Neither the Brazilian legislature nor the courts therefore consider the affirmation made in the media that a given brand is better than its competitor to be a criminal offense (crime against reputation).

Denigration of a competitor's product, in the guise of promoting a given trademark, could constitute the crime of defamation and could amount to contravention of other provisions relating to crimes against industrial property (Law no. 9.279/96, Industrial Property Law—IPL). In this sense, and according to Article 195 of IPL, the publication of false information or false statements about a competitor in order to obtain any advantage is considered to be a crime.[19]

5. Must an individual be clearly identified (by name or photograph) to sue for libel? Can a group of persons sue for libel, even though not named?

In order to bring an action, the plaintiff must be identified (by any means, such as name or photograph) or at least identifiable (as in the case where reference to a position or function allows the individual to be identified). The same rule applies to a group of persons that can be identified by reason of the function they exercise, even if they have not been referred to by name and their image has not been published.

6. What is the fault standard(s) applied to libel?

a. Does the fault standard depend on the fame or notoriety of the plaintiff?

The fame or notoriety of the plaintiff is not relevant to the question of whether defamation has occurred, although the dominant position among the authorities is that public personalities generally enjoy less protection with respect to their private lives.

b. Is there a heightened fault standard or privilege for reporting on matters of public concern or public interest?

The general rule in Brazilian law is that there are no aggravating or attenuating factors in crimes against honor in connection with reporting on matters of public concern, although the circumstances mentioned in the paragraph below should be observed. Nonetheless, courts will allow a limited "public interest" defense in civil cases.

With respect to the public interest in reporting criminal matters, and specifically in connection with the crime of calumny, the CC provides for truth as a defense. However, by statute, truth is not a defense when calumny is committed against the president of the Republic, the head of a foreign state, the president of the Senate, the president of the Chamber of Deputies, or the ministers of the Supreme Federal Court (Supremo Tribunal Federal—STF). However, it is important to mention that the CC was passed when Brazil was under a dictatorship, and the same can be stated with regard to the LP. For this reason, both laws are strict in relation to this matter, but their application is doubtful. Nowadays, in cases of publication considered to be calumnious against any of the public persons mentioned above, the public interest may be invoked (and used as a defense) in order to justify such publication.

In cases of defamation, proof of truth of the statement will be admitted as a defense if the subject is a public servant and the offense is related to the exercise of the office held.

Under civil law, the public interest may prevail over the principle of inviolability of a person's honor, private life, and privacy, if the facts reported are true. Thus, even if the plaintiff's honor has been affected by the report, if the facts reported are true and there is a relevant public interest in the report, the plaintiff has no right of redress. The same principle applies in conflicts between the right to inform and the right to preservation of an individual's image or an individual's right to private life, provided, here again, that the facts reported are true.

In contrast, in cases where there is no relevant public interest in the facts, they should not be reported, regardless of their truth. It should be borne in mind that a crime may be committed even when the aim of the reporting is based upon the exercise of the right to serve the public interest, but such right is exercised with malice—a clear intent to damage the reputation of a subject.

7. Is financial news about publicly traded companies, or companies involved with a government contract, considered a matter of public interest or otherwise privileged?

The CB provides that the public administration must comply with the principles of legality, impersonality, morality, efficiency, and publicity, among others. Likewise, Law 8666, which governs government contracting, provides for the publicity of acts and contracts entered into with the public administration. Accordingly, all contracts entered into with the government are public, unless they contain a confidentiality clause. In relation to the financial news of publicly traded companies, they are required by law to publish their financial information periodically, in the form of quarterly reports and annual reports. Therefore, all information published in this manner can be relied upon by a journalist to show relevant public interest.

8. Is there a recognized protection for opinion or "fair comment" on matters of public concern?

The LP sets out in two provisions (Art. 21, Paragraph 2 and Art. 27, Section VII), that criticism made on the grounds of public interest does not constitute an abuse of the exercise of freedom of thought and information.

In addition to the grounds of public interest, the specific legislation further excludes *inter alia* from the roll of crimes committed via abuse of the exercise of the freedom of expression and information the following (save where there is manifest intention to prejudice the third party):

1. adverse literary, artistic, scientific, or sporting criticism or commentary (Art. 27, Subsection I);
2. the reproduction of reports, expert opinions, decisions, or other acts performed by the relevant organs of the legislature, save where such information is confidential (Art. 27, Subsection II);
3. the reproduction of written or oral debate/argument in court, as well as the reporting of court orders and decisions and such other orders or communications as may be made by the judiciary (Art. 27, Subsection IV);
4. the reporting of statements or allegations made during court hearings by the parties to the proceedings or their representatives (Art. 27, Subsection V).

Thus, critical commentary, irritating though it may be, provided it falls within the limits referred to, does not in itself amount to media crime.

9. Are there any requirements upon a plaintiff, such as demand for retraction or right of reply, and if so, what impact do they have?

Yes. The LP provides for a right of reply, in the following terms: any natural or legal person which is accused in, or offended by, a report published in a newspaper or periodical, or in a broadcast, or about whom an untrue or incorrect fact is published through the information media, has the right of reply or rectification. The reply or rectification must be submitted in writing within a period of sixty days from the date of the publication or transmission.

Under the Brazilian CC, the right of reply consists of:

1. publication of the response or rectification of the offended party, in the same newspaper or periodical, with the same characteristics as the original report;
2. transmission of the written reply or rectification of the offended party, by the same broadcaster and on the same program and at the same time as the original report; or
3. transmission of the reply or rectification of the offended party, by the news agency, to all media to which the original report was transmitted.

The broadcaster, newspaper, or news agency must comply with the demand for reply or rectification within twenty-four hours. If the twenty-four hour time limit is not met, the offended party may bring a judicial proceeding to enforce the right of reply. It should be noted that publication or transmission of a reply or rectification does not affect the offended party's right to seek redress through criminal and civil actions. Under the Brazilian CC, if the accused retracts the calumnious or defamatory statement in an appropriate manner at any time prior to judgment, the accused is exempted from criminal liability.

10. Is there a privilege for quoting or reporting on:

a. Papers filed in court?

Yes. The LP authorizes, in whole or in part, the reproduction of news, reports, or transcriptions of oral or written debate before judges or courts, and the publication of orders and judgments and all other communications and orders by judicial authorities. The privilege is absolute: even if the reproduction or report contains calumny, defamation, or injury to dignity and decorum, it will not constitute an abuse of the freedom of information if it is accurate and is not disclosed in a manner that shows bad faith.

b. Government-issued documents?

Yes. The LP authorizes reproduction in whole or in part of reports, opinions, decisions, or acts performed by agencies or departments of the Legislative Houses, unless they contain reserved or secret material; and reports and comments on bills and acts of the legislative branch of government, and related debates and criticism.

c. Quasi-governmental proceedings?

Yes, although the extension of immunity to quasi-governmental proceedings is a closer question, depending on the specific legislation governing the various professional associations at issue. Because the publication of administrative acts of this nature has the potential to violate the members' right to privacy, the legality of such publication will depend on the public interest in the published information and, of course, on the truth of the information reported. In the case of attorneys, for example, who are members of the Order of Attorneys of Brazil, disciplinary proceedings are secret and only the parties, their attorneys, and the directors and other officers of the OAB are allowed to be present. In any event, the question of whether the proceedings of a given professional association are public can only be answered on a case-by-case analysis.

11. Is there a privilege for republishing statements made earlier by other, bona fide, reliable publications or wire services?

Yes. The Brazilian legislature provides for the imposition of a penalty for calumny only for circumstances in which the defendant publishes or transmits allegations of criminal conduct that the individual knew to be false (i.e., the reporting of an allegation that amounts to calumny, and which the reporter knows to be false) (Art. 20, Paragraph 1).

In relation to the crime of defamation, the courts have consistently held that the reporting of facts previously published in other newspapers, when the intention is merely to divulge the information and there is no bad faith or wish to prejudice a third party, is not a crime. It is important to state that if, in the opinion of the judge, the person who retransmitted or republished the offending item acted in good faith, that individual should be acquitted.

12. Are there any restrictions regarding reporting on:

a. Ongoing criminal investigations?

Generally, there are no restrictions in this regard, and Brazilian law recognizes the freedom of expression and information in relation to reporting ongoing criminal investigations. Liability may attach only in cases where there is malice—an "unmistakable intent"—on the part of the reporter to defame the person who is the subject of the report. A newspaper report that a certain individual is being investigated for involvement in a criminal organization, for example, is not a crime against reputation or an abuse of the exercise of freedom of information, provided the report is not malicious or in bad faith.

b. Ongoing criminal prosecutions?

As has been set out above, Brazilian law expressly states that the whole, partial, or summarized reproduction, publication, or outline of a written or oral argument before courts or tribunals, and the reporting of court orders and sentences and any other measures taken by the judiciary, shall not be deemed an abuse of the freedom of expression and information (Art. 27, Subsection IV). The same applies to "articulation, citations (references/quotations) or allegations made in court by the parties or their representatives" (Subsection V).

Brazilian law also recognizes a "presumption of rehabilitation." The law prohibits the reporting of an individual's completed prison sentence, unless there are public interest grounds for the publication.

c. Ongoing regulatory investigations?

No.

d. Ongoing civil litigation, or other judicial proceedings?

No; however, in some legal proceedings, either criminal or civil, e.g., those relating to child-care issues or where sensitive issues of state security are involved, the court may order that the proceedings be heard in private (on camera). Any breach of such order, for example by reporting on any aspect of the case, is a serious criminal offense.

13. Are prior restraints or other prepublication injunctions available on the basis of libel or privacy, and if so, what are the standards for obtaining such relief?

No. There is no provision for preemptive censorship of information, even with a view to protecting privacy. There are no means within the criminal law with which to prohibit the publication of news/journalistic material. Specific legislation provides for seizure of printed material that contains war propaganda, discriminatory material relating to race or social class, incitement to subversion of the social and political order, or offense to public decency or values.[20]

14. Is a right of privacy recognized (either civilly or criminally)?
As mentioned in the introduction to this chapter, the right of privacy is recognized in the CB (Art. 5, Subsection X), the BCC (Art. 21), and the CC (crimes against the inviolability of correspondence and secrets).

a. What is the definition of "private fact"?
There is no definition of private fact in the law of privacy. It can be said that "the right to private life can be defined as the right to live one's own life in isolation, without being subjected to publicity that one neither asked for nor wanted."[21] Privacy interests often outweigh priority over the right to inform, which may prevail only if the necessary public interest in disclosure exists.

b. Is there a public interest or newsworthiness exception?
As mentioned above, the constitutional protection of privacy may give way in the face of public interest. However, such cases are exceptional and must usually be authorized by a court order. A typical example would be access to confidential banking information (which falls within the sphere of privacy), when authorized by a court to serve an overriding public interest.

c. Is the right of privacy based in common law, statute, or constitution?
As mentioned above, the right of privacy is provided for in the CB (Art. 5, Subsection X). The BCC, which came into effect in January 2003, deals expressly with personality rights, including the right of privacy (Art. 21).

15. May reporters tape-record their own telephone conversations for note-taking purposes (not rebroadcast) without the consent of the other party?
Although the courts and the scholars are not unanimous on this point, the dominant opinion is that it is legal to record one's own telephone conversation without the consent of the other party. The Court of Justice of São Paulo, for example, decided that recording a conversation on an answering machine is not illegal, even though the recording was made by only one of the participants in the conversation. The court found that "what the Constitution forbids is the interference of third parties in the dialog, without the consent of the speaker or the listener: that which is referred interception, resulting in clandestine recording. But it is permissible for one of the parties to make a recording of an ordinary conversation between people who accept each other as speaker and listener, in the free expression of their thoughts, just as it would be possible to record the content of direct conversations, carried on without the use of the telephone."

16. If permissible to record such tapes, may they be broadcast without permission?

No. Because publication or broadcasting of telephone conversations represents, in principle, a violation of the privacy or private life of another, the other party's consent is required. Disclosure of the contents may result in a civil action.

If the conversation contains confidential information, disclosure of such information can constitute the crime of breach of confidentiality provided for under the CC, unless there is just cause for disclosure.

17. Is there a recognized evidentiary privilege preventing the disclosure of confidential sources relied upon by reporters?

Yes. The CB guarantees reporters confidentiality of the source of information, whenever necessary to the exercise of a profession (Art. 5, Item XIV). Article 7 of the LP also provides for confidentiality of the source or origin of information received from or collected by journalists.

In addition, journalists who disclose such information may themselves be subjected to civil liability under the LP, which treats such dissemination as a violation of professional confidentiality. It is also a crime under the CC.

18. In the event that legal papers are served upon the newsroom (such as a civil complaint), are there any particular warnings about accepting service of which we should be aware?

Criminal liability is successive. In other words, primary liability for a media crime lies with the author of the published or transmitted material, and, should the author not be identifiable, the material shall be deemed to have been reprinted by the editor of the section in which it was published or by the director or by the editor in chief or the manager.

A criminal summons must be served personally on the person named in it. The Court Official (Process Server) cannot, in criminal proceedings, effect service by leaving the document at the company office (e.g., with a secretary). In the case of civil litigation, however, depending on the nature of the claim, service may be effected on any company employee, so that for example the Court Official can in theory effect service by leaving the documents with the receptionist. It is therefore advisable to provide training to certain "key" employees (e.g., receptionists, door staff) so that they are aware that any formal legal document of this nature must be immediately forwarded to the responsible manager/editor or other such designated person.

All other staff should be instructed to refer the Court Official to the identified "key" staff, so that if, for example, the Court Official attempts to effect service on the trainee, the employee knows that the correct procedure is to direct the official to reception, where the citation will be appropriately dealt with. Given that court deadlines in Brazil are frequently very tight, all official legal documents should be referred to the company's attorneys at the earliest possible moment, if necessary by means of fax or electronic communication, and the legal advisers should be alerted immediately by telephone or personally that an official court document has been received.

19. Has your jurisdiction applied established media law to Internet publishers?

Brazilian law is not clear on this issue. Because the LP dates from 1967, it does not contemplate Internet publishing. However, the trend among the scholarly authorities and the courts is to accept application of the LP to publication on websites. The Superior Court of Justice (STJ), in a case concerning publication on a website of a letter containing accusations against an elected representative, admitted a criminal complaint against the author of the document, based on the provisions of the LP. In another case, a São Paulo court found that the commission of crimes against honor on websites dedicated to journalistic activities in general should be subject to the LP.

20. If established media law has been applied to Internet publishers, are there any ways in which Internet publishers (including chat room operators) have to meet different standards?

Depending on the structure and content of the website, it can be very difficult for publishers to have complete control over all the published content, since part of the content is created by third parties without the express authorization of the publisher, as in the case of chat rooms and bulletin boards.

For this reason, some specialists in the field believe that the LP should not apply where end users supply content, such as chat rooms and blogs. Even if the website has mechanisms to filter out undesired messages, it would be impossible to review and, if necessary, block information that is automatically inserted or updated.

However, in cases where the website has journalistic content, the application of the LP would be appropriate. In certain cases, the Internet service provider could also be held jointly liable for defamatory postings. However, the ISP would not have any liability if its only function was to publish content inserted by third parties who are identifiable and therefore liable for the publication of the information.

21. Are there any cases where the courts enforced a judgment in libel from another jurisdiction against a publisher in your jurisdiction?
It should be borne in mind that, as we have stated above, libel in Brazil takes the form of three crimes (calumny, defamation, and injury). Jurisdiction lies with the court where the offending matter was printed, or the location of the studio of the radio transmission service and/or head office of a news agency. If in a jurisdiction where defamation (libel or slander) is a tort, the court makes a civil law order; such order may be enforced in Brazil by means of an application to the Brazilian Superior Court.

Chapter Notes

1. Federal Law 5250 of 1967, known as the "Law of the Press" (LP).
2. *Id.*
3. Art. 20 (LP).
4. TJSC, ap. n. 97.005781/4, 1998.
5. TACRIM SP, p. 723.743/1, 1993.
6. TACRIM SP, ap. n. 348.899.
7. TJRJ, p. n. 2002.051.00404, 2003.
8. Art. 21 (LP).
9. TJRJ, 1999.
10. TJRJ, 1999.050.05049, 2001.
11. TACRIM SP, ap. n. 775847/9, 1993.
12. TACRIM SP, p. n. 348.879/2, 1984.
13. Art. 22 (LP).
14. Please note that the terms are false cognates.
15. TACRIM SP, p. 838.797/7.
16. TJRJ, p. 2002.050.05.477, 2002.
17. TACRIM SP, p. 221443, 1980.
18. TACRIM SP, p. n. 401.059/1, 1985.
19. Furthermore, note that comparative advertising is acceptable, but the Code issued by the National Agency of Publicity Regulation (Conselho Nacional de Auto-Regulamentação Publicitária) must be observed. Some of its principles, in relation to comparative publicity, are (i) the clarification and defense of consumers, (ii) objectiveness in the comparison, and (iii) the possibility of proving such

comparison, among others. Please note that general statements, such as "the best," and subjective information, such as "the most beautiful," are not considered to be offensive to competitors, nor have to be proved.

20. Art. 61, Subsections I and II.

21. William Swindler, cited by Enéas CostaGarcia, in *Responsabilidade Civil dos Meios de Comunicação*. Juarez de Oliveira, ed. São Paulo, 2002.

CHAPTER 2

Canada

BRIAN MACLEOD ROGERS

Brian MacLeod Rogers
150 King Street West, Suite 2512
Toronto, Ontario Canada M5HIJ9
Phone: 416-593-2486
Fax: 416-593-8494
brian@bmrlaw.ca

Introduction to the Canadian Legal System

Every province in Canada uses a common law system except Quebec, which uses civil law. Quebec's civil law system is based on a Civil Code enacted in 1991. There are four basic levels to the Canadian common law court system: the first level is the provincial courts; the second level includes the provincial and territorial superior courts and the federal court, trial division; the third level is the provincial courts of appeal and the federal court of appeal; and the highest level is the Supreme Court of Canada.

Provincial courts are located in each province throughout Canada. The Provincial Court is the court of first resort for most criminal offenses, claims over smaller amounts of money (limit varies in the various provinces), family court issues, and other small offenses. There are also several provincial courts designated for specific types of crimes—domestic violence, for example. The most serious criminal offenses and many appeals from provincial courts are heard in the Provincial Superior Court. The superior court has jurisdiction over every legal matter in its province except those specifically reserved for provincial courts and handles most serious civil cases. Some provinces organize superior courts by subject—family law, property claims, and so on. Appeals from the superior courts are heard in the courts of appeal. This court generally sits in panels of three judges who will hear and adjudicate cases. Provincial Superior Courts have inherent jurisdiction over all matters except those specifically banned by statute. Conversely, the Federal Court of Canada

(FCC) only has jurisdiction over claims against the federal government and others specified in federal statutes.

The FCC is similar in hierarchy to a superior court, but with solely civil jurisdiction. The FCC is divided into a trial division and an appeal division; it shares jurisdiction with superior courts.

1. What is the locally accepted definition of libel?

Libel is defamation in written or other material form, including a broadcast (as confirmed by statute). A defamatory statement "tends to lower a person in the estimation of right-thinking members of society" and should be judged from the perspective of a "reasonably thoughtful and well-informed person who has a degree of common sense."

Examples of defamatory statements are: taxi driver and owner alleged to be "trafficking in licenses";[1] lawyer acting for a real estate developer said to have engaged in a "serious breach of faith" and to have been "practicing deception";[2] lawyer said to have improperly paid himself legal fees from funds belonging to a community organization;[3] politician said to be part of "the Jewish Mafia";[4] politician said to be racist;[5] engineer said to be lacking integrity and not competent to design certain facilities;[6] doctor on a government-appointed committee said to have been in a conflict of interest.[7]

2. Is libel-by-implication recognized, or, in the alternative, must the complained-of words alone defame the plaintiff?

Libel may arise by implication. This may occur by an inference drawn from the published words alone or by "legal innuendo," based on unpublished facts that would be known to some readers.

3. May corporations sue for libel?

Corporations may sue for libel but will generally only recover "nominal damages" unless they can prove economic injury.

4. Is product disparagement recognized, and if so, how does that differ from libel?

A separate tort for malicious falsehood exists and deals with disparagement of a product. It requires the plaintiff to prove that the defendant published a false statement about the product with malice, or the intention to cause injury, and that actual financial injury occurred as a consequence. Therefore, the plaintiff must prove falsity, malice, and actual injury flowing from the statement in question. A libel claim may be included where the disparagement reflects on the individuals or company producing, distributing, or selling the product.

5. Must an individual be clearly identified (by name or photograph) to sue for libel? Can a group of persons sue for libel, even though not named?

An individual must be identifiable, but need not be named or have his photograph published, in order to sue for libel. In these cases, the issue will be whether the published information serves to identify the plaintiff.

An unnamed group of persons cannot sue for libel as a group. However, insofar as individual members of the group are identifiable and have personally been defamed by what was published, each such individual has a cause of action in libel. This approach generally imposes a limit on the size of groups that may be involved, but no clear line has been drawn on what size is too large.

6. What is the fault standard(s) applied to libel?

a. Does the fault standard depend on the fame or notoriety of the plaintiff?

In general, libel is a strict liability tort and does not require the plaintiff to prove any degree of fault on the part of the defendants. The standard does not depend on the position, fame, or notoriety of the plaintiff. The plaintiff need only show that a defamatory statement that is identifiably about him or her has been published by the defendant, and falsity and malice are presumed. The defendant then must establish one or more defenses, and defenses of truth and consent are the only ones that cannot be defeated by a plaintiff who can show that the defendant acted with malice.

b. Is there a heightened fault standard or privilege for reporting on matters of public concern or public interest?

Apart from certain reporting privileges for newspapers and broadcasters protected by statute, the common law defense of qualified privilege may be available for media reporting on matters of public interest. This would require overruling earlier Supreme Court of Canada decisions, which held that any publication in the media amounted to "publication to the world" and put it beyond the scope of a privilege defense, but some trial and appeal decisions, as well as recent English cases, give some hope.

In *Hill v. Scientology*,[8] the Supreme Court of Canada explicitly rejected a *New York Times v. Sullivan* defense on the facts of that case. However, the more recent UK House of Lords decision in *Reynolds v. Times Newspapers*[9] acknowledges a common law defense of qualified privilege for media on the basis of public interest; it has not yet been specifically ruled on by any senior Canadian court. However, references to that decision in appeal decisions appear to treat it as a persuasive authority, and it may lead to a broader qualified privilege defense at common law along the lines proposed in that decision.

7. Is financial news about publicly traded companies, or companies involved with a government contract, considered a matter of public interest or otherwise privileged?

No statute or case law has established that financial news about public companies or companies with government contracts amounts to a matter of public interest or would be automatically protected by a defense of qualified privilege. If the publication was based on information contained in a report or other document released to the public by government or a related agency, a statutory qualified privilege would be available.

8. Is there a recognized protection for opinion or "fair comment" on matters of public concern?

Yes, the common law defense of fair comment protects statements of opinion on matters of public interest, provided the plaintiff cannot establish that they were published with malice. The dividing line between statements of fact and opinion can be difficult to draw, and the facts upon which the opinion is based must be contained in the article in question or be generally known, and must be proven true by the defendant. A recent case, *Leenan v. CBC,*[10] suggests that an objective test of fairness should be applied in light of all the facts available to the defendant at the time. Traditionally, the defense only required that the opinion be honestly held by the defendant. Almost all provincial statutes protect defendants when they publish the opinions of others that they do not share. The defense of fair comment will not fail simply because the defendants (or even the person who expressed the opinion) did not hold the opinion as long as "a person could honestly hold the opinion."[11] This overcomes a Supreme Court of Canada decision, *Chernesky v. Armadale Publishers Ltd.,*[12] which held that an honest belief in the opinion was essential for a newspaper defendant even for letters to the editor published by it.

9. Are there any requirements upon a plaintiff, such as demand for retraction or right of reply, and if so, what impact do they have?

The rules vary among provinces. For a libel published or broadcast by a publisher or broadcaster in Ontario, plaintiffs must serve written notice of libel specifying the matter complained of within six weeks of the alleged libel coming to their attention. This has recently been extended to cover online versions as well. A failure to give the required notice is an absolute bar to bringing an action. (There is also a three-month limitation period in Ontario.) Further, the notice triggers a period of time (three days in

Ontario) within which the defendant can publish a "full and fair retraction in as conspicuous a place and type as the alleged libel" in order to limit the plaintiff to recovering only actual damages (actual, provable losses directly attributable to the libel). Other provinces require written notice to be given at least seven days before the commencement of an action so that a retraction can be published before an action is started, and most provinces have a six-month limitation period. However, British Columbia has no notice requirement, and it, Alberta, and Manitoba have a two-year limitation period. In the event that a demand for retraction is received, publishers are advised to contact local counsel immediately.

10. Is there a privilege for quoting or reporting on:

a. Papers filed in court?

A common law qualified privilege is available for fair and accurate reports of documents and records in court files that are publicly available, as established by *Hill v. Scientology, supra.*

b. Government-issued documents?

As long as the documents were issued by the government for the public, a statutory qualified privilege is available for any fair and accurate report of all or part of such a document, or a synopsis of it. This defense is established by provincial defamation legislation and varies to some extent among jurisdictions. Arguably, there would also be a common law qualified privilege for fair and accurate reports of such publicly available information, issued for the public's benefit.

c. Quasi-governmental proceedings?

There is a qualified privilege available for fair and accurate reports of public proceedings of administrative tribunals. In Ontario, disciplinary proceedings for legal and health professionals are governed by legislation, and fair and accurate reports of their proceedings are protected by statutory qualified privilege as they are in other provinces. Such a privilege also applies to other nonstatutory bodies that govern their members, such as "an association formed in Canada for the purpose of promoting or safeguarding the interests of any trade, business, industry or profession, or persons carrying on or engaged in them" (or "any game, sport or pastime open to the public") where its constitution provides such disciplinary powers. Fair and accurate reports of their disciplinary decisions (or findings) are protected by statutory qualified privilege.

In all cases, the statutory privilege can be lost if the defendant refuses to publish a "reasonable statement of explanation or contradiction" on behalf of the plaintiff. This may be considered a modified right of reply but can often be provided by inviting a response from the person affected for the initial publication or publishing one in a follow-up article.

11. Is there a privilege for republishing statements made earlier by other, bona fide, reliable publications or wire services?

There is no such privilege. Each republisher is liable for whatever is published and must prove at least one of the available defenses.

12. Are there any restrictions regarding reporting on:

a. Ongoing criminal investigations?

Apart from the general law of libel, there is no restriction on reporting on ongoing criminal investigations. Insofar as an article reports on an investigation, without imputing guilt, it can be defended as true merely by proving the fact of the police investigation. However, if serious criminal charges already exist against those being investigated, attention should be paid to (b) below.

b. Ongoing criminal prosecutions?

The traditional common law of contempt of court continues to apply in Canada. A publication that causes a serious risk of prejudice to the fair trial of an action can lead to a contempt citation against the publisher and all those involved. This is a criminal proceeding. Over the past ten to fifteen years, strict enforcement of law of contempt has waned, and a more considered approach is taken as to whether the publication actually poses a serious risk of prejudice. Previously, any publication of an accused's prior criminal record or bad character would be strictly prohibited after arrest. This is no longer the case, but enforcement varies from province to province; Alberta is the strictest, and Ontario, British Columbia, and Quebec are the most lenient. As a result, a precise test can no longer be given. A number of factors need to be considered, such as the time intervening before trial, the size of the community involved, the potential impact of the information, and the public interest being served by publishing it now. At all times, disclosing a confession or other admission by an accused is the most risky since it is highly prejudicial and yet may not be admissible at trial.

However, it has been deemed almost impossible to prejudice a judge sitting alone in a criminal case, and even in jury trials, publication well in advance of trial, depending on all of the circumstances, should not give rise to a real risk of prejudice. Change of venue, challenges for cause, and strict jury instructions can be used to minimize any such risk. In addition, a respected appeals judge in Alberta recently proposed a defense of public interest in contempt cases. Simply put, this is a gray area of the law, and it requires close judgment calls based on the facts at hand.

In addition to the law of contempt, the Criminal Code provides for various statutory publication bans, so that reports of bail hearings and preliminary inquiries are severely restricted, and bans on identifying sexual complainants and certain other witnesses can be obtained as a matter of course. There is also a discretionary right for the court to impose broader publication bans on identifying witnesses, but normally notice must be given to the media when such orders are being sought.

During jury trials, nothing can be reported about what occurs when the jury is not present since they are not sequestered. Such information can only be published when the jury retires to render its verdict. In general terms, such statutory publication bans are purportedly intended to protect the fair trial process, acting as a specific means of enforcing the more general law of contempt. Anonymity orders are based on the risk of possible harm to the person in question and the societal interest of encouraging victims and witnesses to come forward, especially in underreported crimes such as sexual assault.

c. Ongoing regulatory investigations?

No, other than the general law of libel.

d. Ongoing civil litigation, or other judicial proceedings?

The law of contempt may be applied where a civil jury trial is being conducted, and nothing should be published during a trial about what occurs in the jury's absence. In particular, publication of the damages being sought in a statement of claim can lead to a mistrial since jurors are not advised of these amounts. There can also be specific publication bans (including anonymity orders) in civil proceedings, but they are more unusual than in criminal cases. Otherwise, there are no restrictions on reporting on publicly conducted proceedings, and the defense of qualified privilege is available for fair and accurate reports of them.

13. Are prior restraints or other prepublication injunctions available on the basis of libel or privacy, and if so, what are the standards for obtaining such relief?

No prepublication injunctions have been awarded in the last fifteen years on the basis of allegations of libel alone. To succeed, the plaintiff would first have to meet the usual requirements for an interlocutory injunction in these circumstances; in essence, that there is a serious (or arguable) issue to be tried and a real risk of irreparable harm. The plaintiff would also have to counter any defenses that might be raised by the defendants. Essentially, any bona fide defendant should be able to defeat a motion for such an injunction by asserting a willingness to defend on the basis of a legally permissible defense.

Certain provinces (British Columbia, Saskatchewan, Manitoba, Quebec, and Newfoundland) have privacy statutes that create statutory torts for invasion of privacy. With the exception of Quebec, these have been very seldom used against the media. Other provinces have not recognized such a tort, but as in England, the tort of breach of confidence has been used against the media to obtain prepublication injunctions with some success.

In these cases, the traditional test for injunctions (as set out above) is applied, and the plaintiff need only show that confidential information might be published, causing irreparable harm. The media have usually been successful in subsequently setting aside these preliminary injunctions, and the significant additional publicity garnered for the broadcast or publication in question has made plaintiff counsel more wary of using such tactics.

14. Is a right of privacy recognized (either civilly or criminally)?

Apart from provincial privacy legislation (British Columbia, Saskatchewan, Manitoba, Quebec, and Newfoundland), there is federal legislation that restricts the use by private organizations of third party information, the Personal Information Protection and Electronic Documents Act.[13] It now applies not only within the federal jurisdiction but also provincially, where a province does not have its own legislation. All privacy legislation has an exception for newsworthiness or for journalists, as set out below.

In Quebec, privacy rights are much more established and are even given specific protection in its provincial *Charter of Human Rights and Freedoms.* For example, publication of a photograph should not take place without the subject's permission unless he or she is simply part of some public event.[14] However, evidence must be given of damage. At common law, no tort of invasion of privacy has been recognized with the exception of commercial misappropriation of personality, which generally requires some unauthorized suggestion that a known personality endorses a particular product or company.

a. What is the definition of "private fact"?

There is no definition of "private fact" at present that has any broad application. Generally, the courts have focused on whether there was a reasonable expectation of privacy in the information involved.

Examples include: publishing the identity of a complainant in a criminal sexual assault case where her identity was protected by court-ordered publication ban;[15] broadcasting without consent a videotape of hair transplant surgery;[16] concealed videotaping by a landlord of a woman using a washroom;[17]

and in Quebec, publishing without consent a photograph of a young woman sitting in a doorway by a sidewalk on a public thoroughfare.[18]

b. Is there a public interest or newsworthiness exception?

Provincial privacy legislation recognizes a form of newsworthiness exemption where the matter published was of public interest, was fair comment on a matter of public interest, or would be protected by privilege under defamation law (with some variation among provinces). In Quebec, public interest is also cited as a defense, recognizing newsworthiness in articles about public issues and public figures. The federal Personal Information Protection and Electronic Documents Act[19] specifically exempts organizations collecting, using, and disclosing personal information for "journalistic, artistic or literary purposes."

c. Is the right of privacy based in common law, statute, or constitution?

Privacy rights are defined by provincial and federal statutes, discussed above.

15. May reporters tape-record their own telephone conversations for note-taking purposes (not rebroadcast) without the consent of the other party?

Yes.

16. If permissible to record such tapes, may they be broadcast without permission?

No. By Canadian Radio-television and Telecommunications Commission regulations, such interviews cannot be broadcast without consent.

17. Is there a recognized evidentiary privilege preventing the disclosure of confidential sources relied upon by reporters?

No. However, at a minimum there is judicial discretion to require such disclosure only in limited circumstances, essentially where the evidence is truly necessary because it is relevant and not available by other means and where the value of requiring the evidence outweighs the potential harm of disclosure. The Supreme Court of Canada refused to rule on this issue under the *Canadian Charter of Rights and Freedoms* in *Moysa v. Alberta Labour Relations Board*[20] on the facts of that case, but it also cast doubt on whether protection of confidential sources even amounted to an element of free expression protected by Section 2(b) of the *Charter.*

A recent case in Ontario ruled in favor of a "qualified" privilege, on a case-by-case basis, for protection of a journalist's confidential sources relying on the *Charter* and common law; it is under appeal.[21] Such an approach to journalists' sources was specifically cited in obiter by the Supreme Court of Canada in *R. v. McClure*.[22] In Ontario, the "newspaper rule" developed in England applies in libel cases to prevent disclosure of journalists' confidential sources at the discovery stage of litigation. This rule does not apply in British Columbia and a number of other provinces.

18. In the event that legal papers are served upon the newsroom (such as a civil complaint), are there any particular warnings about accepting service of which we should be aware?
No. However, the very short time periods for responding to libel notices (which need not follow any particular form) mean that a lawyer should be immediately advised if anyone on staff receives a document complaining of damage to reputation.

19. Has your jurisdiction applied established media law to Internet publishers?
In general, the existing common law of libel and privacy applies to all communications media, including the Internet in its various forms. However, thus far there have been few cases to reach trial involving Internet libel or privacy concerns.

The Ontario Court of Appeal has pointed to the "ubiquity, universality, and utility" of the Internet and its potential as "a medium of virtually limitless international defamation."[23] This breadth of potential dissemination has an impact on defenses such as common law qualified privilege, as well as on damages, unless website access has been limited to those to whom publication is properly directed.[24]

20. If established media law has been applied to Internet publishers, are there any ways in which Internet publishers (including chat room operators) have to meet different standards?
To date, neither the courts nor the legislatures have developed special standards or laws for Internet publishers in these areas. However, the defense of "innocent dissemination" may be available to bulletin board or chat room operators where they had no knowledge, nor ought to have had knowledge, of the alleged libel.[25] This is beneficial to these operators and ISPs generally where no attempt is made to monitor postings. However, once notice is received of an alleged libel, a decision will have to be made whether to remove the offending posting, and the operator can no longer rely on its "innocence." As a result, it is useful to publish on the website clear notice that the chat room is not being monitored but the operator will respond to complaints that are made in a prescribed fashion.

There also remains an issue as to whether a website or online publication qualifies for the special provisions for newspapers and broadcasters under provincial legislation (see above, Question 9). It has, however, been ruled that the online version of a magazine otherwise qualifying as a "newspaper" does not lose that benefit.[26] However, one appeal court has rejected a "single publication" rule with respect to Internet publication, and subsequent accessibility may extend limitation periods.[27] Differences in legislative definitions from province to province could well produce different results.

21. Are there any cases where the courts enforced a judgment in libel from another jurisdiction against a publisher in your jurisdiction?

The leading case on this issue is a British Columbia case: *Braintech Inc. v. Kostiuk.*[28] The court refused to enforce a default judgment obtained in Texas under its long-arm rules over bulletin board postings by a B.C. resident concerning a company with principal operations in British Columbia. As stated by the court:

> It would create a crippling effect on freedom of expression if, in every jurisdiction the world over in which access to the Internet could be achieved, a person who posts fair comment on a bulletin board could be hauled before the courts of each of those countries where access to the bulletin could be obtained.

In a recent case with profound implications for the application of Canadian jurisdiction against foreign publishers, the Court of Appeal for Ontario recently found that the *Washington Post* was not subject to Canadian process based upon the libel claims of former U.N. diplomat Cheickh Bangoura. In 1997, at the time of the alleged libel appearing in the *Washington Post,* only seven subscribers in Ontario received the paper physically, although its online edition was theoretically available to many Canadians. The plaintiff had not moved to Ontario until 2000. The court found that it was not reasonably foreseeable that the *Post* would have been sued in Ontario, and it was unfair to assume that a newspaper can be sued anywhere in the world by virtue of its publication on the Internet. "To hold otherwise would mean that a defendant could be sued almost anywhere in the world based upon where a plaintiff may decide to establish his or her residence long after publication of the defamation."[29] The court added that the Internet publication involved did not create a substantial connection between the *Post* and the forum. A contrary holding would result in "Ontario publishers and broadcasters being sued anywhere in the world with the prospect that the Ontario courts would be obligated to enforce foreign judgments filed against them."

Chapter Notes

1. *Ross v. Lamport* (1956), 2 D.L.R. (2d) 225 (S.C.C.).

2. *Sykes v. Fraser* (1973), 39 D.L.R. (3d) 321 (S.C.C.).

3. *Botiuk v. Toronto Free Press Publication Ltd.* (1995), 126 D.L.R. (4th) 609 (S.C.C.).

4. *Snyder v. Montreal Gazette Ltd.* (1982), 49 D.L.R. (4th) 17 (S.C.C.).

5. *Chernesky v. Armadale Publishers Ltd.* (1979), 90 D.L.R. (3d) 321 (S.C.C.).

6. *Hiltz and Seamone Co. v. Nova Scotia* (Attorney General), [1997] N.S.J. No. 530 (S.C.); [1999] N.S.J. No. 47, 172 D.L.R. (4th) 488 (N.S.C.A.).

7. *Leenan v. C.B.C.*, [2000] O.J. No. 1359; aff'd [2001] O.J. No. 2229 (C.A.); leave denied [2002] S.C.C.A. 432.

8. [1995] 2 S.C.R. 1130.

9. [1999] H.L.J. No. 45.

10. [2001] O.J. No. 2229; 54 O.R. (3d) 612 (C.A.) (leave to S.C.C. denied).

11. s. 24, Libel and Slander Act, R.S.O. 1990, c.L.12.

12. [1979] 1 S.C.R. 1067.

13. S.C. 2000, c. 5.

14. *Aubry v. Editions Vice-Versa Inc.*, [1998] 1 S.C.R. 591.

15. *J.M.F. v. Chappel and News Publishing Company Ltd.*, [1995] B.C.J. No. 1438 (B.C.S.C.), varied (1998), 158 D.L.R. (4th) 430 (B.C.C.A.), leave dismissed [1998] S.C.C.A. No. 154.

16. *Hollinsworth v. BCTV*, [1996] B.C.J. No. 2638 (B.C.S.C.); [1998] B.C.J. No. 2451 [1999] 6 W.W.R. 54 (B.C.C.A.).

17. *Malcolm v. Fleming*, [2000] B.C.J. No. 2400 (S.C.).

18. *Aubry v. Editions Vice Versa Inc.*, [1998] 1 S.C.R. 591.

19. S.C. 2000, c. 5, s. 4(2)(c).

20. [1989] 1 S.C.R. 1572.

21. *R. v. National Post*, [2004] O.J. No. 178 (S.C.).

22. [2001] 1 S.C.R. 445.

23. *Barrick Gold Corp. v. Lopehandia*, [2004] O.J. No. 2329 (C.A.); (undefended claim over Web postings).

24. *Christian Labour Association of Canada v. Retail Wholesale Union*, [2003] B.C.J. No. 3100 (S.C.) (union website available to public).

25. *Carter v. B.C. Federation of Foster Parents Assoc.*, [2004] B.C.J. No. 192 (S.C.), but on appeal, this defense was ruled to be not available where the operator was negligent in leaving the offending posting on the website long after receiving notice: [2005] B.C.J. No. 1720 (C.A.).

26. *Weiss v. Sawyer,* [2002] O.J. No. 3570, 61 O.R. (3d) 256 (C.A.).

27. *Carter v. B.C. Federation of Foster Parents Assoc.*, [2005] B.C.J. No. 1720 (C.A.).

28. [1999] B.C.J. No. 622, 171 D.L.R. (4th) 46 (C.A.); leave denied, [1999] S.C.C.A. No. 236.

29. Decision available at http://www.ontariocourts.on.ca/decisions/2005/september/C41379.htm; [2005] O.J. No. 3849 (C.A.).

CHAPTER 3

United States

THOMAS H. GOLDEN AND
STEPHEN B. VOGEL
Willkie Farr & Gallagher LLP

Willkie Farr & Gallagher LLP
787 Seventh Avenue
New York, NY 10019-6099 USA
Phone: 212-728-8000
Fax: 212-728-8111
www.willkie.com
tgolden@willkie.com
svogel@willkie.com

Introduction to the U.S. Legal System

The U.S. legal system is a common law system modeled after the British common law system. There are two distinct court systems in the U.S. judiciary: the state systems of each of the fifty states and the federal system. Each state has at least one Federal District Court, which, with the exceptions of bankruptcy, tax, and other specialized matters, is the federal court of first instance. Judges in the federal system serve life terms: state judges may serve life terms or be elected by the citizenry.

Each system is governed by its respective constitution, the federal constitution, and each individual state constitution; however, the federal constitution is considered the "supreme law of the land" and trumps any conflict between state and federal constitutions. The federal constitution reserves certain powers for the federal government and reserves the rest for the states.

The progression of a case is similar in both court systems. A jury composed of citizens often decides verdicts. Appeals courts and specialized courts do not have juries, but have panels of judges. The courts of first instance hear both civil and criminal cases.

The judge determines the issues of law at hand and the jury, or judge sitting without a jury, will determine findings of fact. The trial court is the only court in which new facts can be presented and considered in a given case. In the federal system, cases are appealed to a geographically determined appellate court organized by "circuits." Some states have intermediate appellate courts, while others have appeals heard directly by the State Supreme Court.

Appeals in the federal system are made thereafter to the Supreme Court of the United States, and the hearing of such cases is granted at the discretion of the Supreme Court. State supreme courts can recommend cases to the federal Supreme Court, too; however, since the federal Supreme Court has the ability to choose which cases it hears, most recommended cases are never accepted. The U.S. Supreme Court is composed of nine justices appointed for life by the president and approved by Congress.

1. What is the locally accepted definition of libel?

Although the definition varies significantly by state, a cause of action for libel often includes the following elements: (a) a statement of fact; (b) that is false; (c) and defamatory; (d) of and concerning the plaintiff; (e) that is published to a third party (in written or otherwise tangible form); (f) that is not absolutely or conditionally privileged; (g) that causes actual injury (unless obviated by the presence of presumed harm); (h) that is the result of fault by the defendant (usually); (i) that causes special (pecuniary) harm in addition to generalized reputational history (on occasion).[1]

Libel claims rise and fall on defamatory meaning. There are many definitions of "defamatory," and these are reflective of the cultural constraints embedded in the common law of the states. What is defamatory in Georgia may not be so in New York. The RESTATEMENT (SECOND) OF TORTS § 559 (1997) defines defamatory communications as those that tend "to harm the reputation of another so as to lower him in the esteem of the community or to deter third persons from association or dealing with him." Similarly, other treatises define a defamatory statement as that which "tends to injure 'reputation' in the popular sense, to diminish the esteem, respect, good-will, or confidence in which the plaintiff is held, or to excite adverse, derogatory or unpleasant feelings or opinions against him."[2]

In essence, to "defame" means to damage one's reputation, usually by the assertion (or implication) of something shameful or worthy of scorn. Defamatory meaning may vary from state to state, and is largely dependent on context.

Some examples of statements found to be defamatory are: playing a role in an alleged kidnapping and murder;[3] incompetence of a professional;[4] being a communist;[5] or being a "liar and a fraud."[6] The following are examples of nondefamatory statements: calling someone "a bum";[7] calling a college basketball player a disgrace;[8] or referring to someone as "short, ugly and stupid."[9]

2. Is libel-by-implication recognized, or, in the alternative, must the complained-of words alone defame the plaintiff?

Courts generally agree that libel by implication is allowed in the United States: "Falsity can be either express or implied. . . . A story that contains only truthful statements may nonetheless be false and defamatory as it relates to the plaintiff if it omits material facts. . . . It is not enough to get the details right if you fail to put them in the proper context."[10] Thus, courts generally consider the challenged statement in the context in which it was used and examine the totality of the circumstances.[11] Some states, however, are more demanding in the requirements that must be met in order to plead libel by implication.[12]

3. May corporations sue for libel?

Yes. Generally, a corporation has reputational interests and is protected against false and malicious statements affecting its credit or property, and against statements impugning corporate honesty, efficiency, or matters of business performance.[13] It is worth noting that in several states, corporations are deemed public figures, which are required to meet a higher standard in order for a libel claim to succeed.

4. Is product disparagement recognized, and if so, how does that differ from libel?

Most U.S. jurisdictions recognize "product disparagement," also known as "trade libel," as a cause of action. This tort is generally defined as a false communication that damages the reputation of a company's goods or services. The same requirements that govern defamation appear to govern claims for product disparagement, and the same First Amendment protections that apply to libel also apply to trade libel.[14]

This tort differs from traditional libel in that it is primarily a business tort designed to protect economic interests, and therefore requires a specific showing of special harm in the form of actual pecuniary damages (usually a demonstrable loss of sales, customers, or contracts).[15] Also, it is more likely that punitive or injunctive relief may be available in a product disparagement claim.[16]

5. Must an individual be clearly identified (by name or photograph) to sue for libel? Can a group of persons sue for libel, even though not named?

To be actionable, the defamatory statement must be "of and concerning" the plaintiff, and the hypothetical average reader would have to understand who is being referenced. It is incumbent on the plaintiff to demonstrate that in "some definite and direct sense, the plaintiff was the person against whom the defamatory statements were directed, and by whom the reputational damage was suffered."[17] It is not necessary that every recipient of the communication identify the plaintiff, so long as there are at least some who reasonably do.[18]

Most American law rejects "group libel." The Supreme Court has also held that it is constitutionally insufficient to equate statements defaming a government agency with statements defaming the head of the group merely on the presumption that to libel one is to libel the other.[19] This has been extended to protect criticism of other groups and businesses.[20] To the extent that actions by a member of a group are allowed, a plaintiff would need to show that the statement about a group is "of and concerning" the particular individual. Factors to be considered include: (1) the size of the group; (2) the degree of organization of the group (is the composition definite and its size fixed?); and (3) the prominence of the group and its individual members.[21]

6. What is the fault standard(s) applied to libel?

The U.S. Supreme Court, in *New York Times Co. v. Sullivan,* 376 U.S. 254 (1964), and *Gertz v. Robert Welch Inc.,* 418 U.S. 323 (1974), has established minimum constitutional fault levels that must be met before recovery is possible in an action for defamation. Individual states are free to adopt higher standards.

a. Does the fault standard depend on the fame or notoriety of the plaintiff?

Yes. A central distinction in libel law is the distinction between public and private figures.[22] A plaintiff who is a public figure must prove, by clear and convincing evidence, that the defendant made a defamatory statement with actual malice, which is defined as "knowledge that [the statement] was false or . . . reckless disregard of whether it was false or not."[23] By contrast, a plaintiff who is a private figure must merely prove the defendant's negligence,[24] though it is possible that the Supreme Court would allow for a strict liability standard where the plaintiff is a private figure and the defamatory statement does not concern a matter of public interest.[25]

The majority of states have adopted a negligence standard for private figure cases, though a number of states have adopted a standard that requires actual malice in cases involving private plaintiffs in matters of public concern.[26] The plaintiffs, as part of the *prima facie* case, carry the burden of proof in establishing the requisite fault standard. In short, the difference is that whereas "actual malice" requires "knowing falsity" or, at best, "purposeful avoidance of the truth," defendants adjudged by the negligence standard may face liability if they did not report the news in a manner which any "reasonable" reporter would have followed. The former is difficult to prove because it requires the subjective knowledge of the reporter be shown. The negligence standard is subjective, and expert witnesses (such as journalism professors or retired journalists) may give testimony as to the reportorial shortcomings of the defendant.

b. Is there a heightened fault standard or privilege for reporting on matters of public concern or public interest?

Yes. In matters of public concern, plaintiffs may not recover presumed or punitive damages absent actual malice, without regard to whether the plaintiff is a public or private figure.[27] American publishers generally enjoy great latitude as to what constitutes "public concern": "[a]bsent clear abuse, the courts will not second-guess editorial decisions as to what constitutes matters of genuine public concern."[28]

7. Is financial news about publicly traded companies, or companies involved with a government contract, considered a matter of public interest or otherwise privileged?

Many jurisdictions employ a case-by-case methodology to determine whether a company is a public or private figure, and assume that if it is a public figure, the matter is one of public concern. The Fifth Circuit identified two factors that were important in differentiating between public and private figures: (1) public figures are better able to counteract false statements because of their access to channels of effective communication; and (2) public figures "invite attention and comment" and, thus, assume the risk of greater scrutiny.[29] In order to apply these factors, there must be a case-by-case assessment of the extent to which they are implicated by the circumstances giving rise to the alleged defamation.[30] Some courts have applied the pre-*Gertz* test and attempted to determine whether the defamatory statement concerned a topic of public interest either "because of the nature of the business conducted or because the public has an especially strong interest in the investigation or disclosure of the commercial information at issue."[31]

To make this assessment, courts will often consider the notoriety of the corporation in the relevant geographical area, the nature of the corporation's business, and the frequency and intensity of media scrutiny that the company receives.[32]

8. Is there a recognized protection for opinion or "fair comment" on matters of public concern?

Yes; however, only "pure" opinion—that which does not imply a discernable fact—enjoys complete First Amendment protection. The Supreme

Court in *Milkovich v. Lorain Journal Co.*, 497 U.S. 1 (1990), refused to recognize a blanket First Amendment privilege for opinion. In that case, students were being interrogated under oath in a high school athletics scandal. When discrepancies among the students' stories were discovered, the local newspaper opined that they had changed their stories at the behest of the wrestling coach, and ran a headline that said: "Milkovich Teaches the Big Lie." Although the newspaper asserted that it was merely their opinion, Milkovich argued that this headline reasonably implied that he had encouraged the youngsters to commit perjury: a crime. The Court agreed, holding that defamation actions can be based on statements of opinion that imply undisclosed defamatory facts.

The dispositive inquiry is whether a reasonable reader would view the statement in question as conveying defamatory facts about the plaintiff and, if so, whether these statements can be proved false.[33] Defamation suits cannot be based upon "imaginative expression," "rhetorical hyperbole," or "loose, figurative, or hyperbolic language" that would signal to the reasonable reader that what is being said is opinion, and not an assertion of fact.[34]

9. Are there any requirements upon a plaintiff, such as demand for retraction or right of reply, and if so, what impact do they have?

Over half of the states have statutes covering retraction. A number of states require a plaintiff to demand a retraction in writing, and failure to do so often limits recovery to actual damages.[35] Florida, for example, requires the plaintiff to serve a retraction demand before a suit can be filed.[36] States that do not have a retraction requirement often allow a retraction to be used as evidence of lack of malice or for mitigation of damages.

10. Is there a privilege for quoting or reporting on:

a. Papers filed in court?

There is a well-recognized privilege to publish fair and accurate reports of certain judicial, legislative, and executive proceedings, commonly known as the "fair report" privilege. This privilege exists in common law, but has been codified in many jurisdictions. The latitude varies from state to state. In some jurisdictions, reporters may only be immune for the near-verbatim reporting of the court documents: in other states, almost any statement reasonably related to the court proceedings will be privileged.

The "fair report" privilege allows reporters to republish or report on documents filed in court without liability so long as the report itself is accurate and fair.[37] "The accuracy of the summary, not the truth or falsity of the information being summarized, is the 'benchmark of the privilege.'"[38]

There is often an exception, however, for defamatory statements made by the person who files defamatory statements in a pleading and then reports to others what he has said (or forms a collusive arrangement with the person who reports on the contents of the filing).[39] Also, some jurisdictions have held that a complaint is not a public document until there has been some official action in the proceeding.[40]

b. Government-issued documents?

Generally, yes.[41] The scope of this privilege varies by jurisdiction.[42]

c. Quasi-governmental proceedings?

Many jurisdictions include the "reports of bodies which are by law authorized to perform public duties (e.g., bar association disciplinary proceedings, findings of blue-ribbon panels)" in their definition of an official proceeding.[43]

11. Is there a privilege for republishing statements made earlier by other, bona fide, reliable publications or wire services?

Some jurisdictions recognize a "wire service" defense for republication of materials, provided that there was no substantial reason to question the accuracy of the material or the reputation of the original reporter.[44] Many other jurisdictions appear to provide a narrower defense where a local media organization republishes a release from a reputable news agency without substantial change and without actually knowing that the article is false.[45] Regardless of whether a particular jurisdiction recognizes this defense, the plaintiff must still prove the requisite level of fault.

12. Are there any restrictions regarding reporting on:

a. Ongoing criminal investigations?

In order to determine whether there is a right of access to records and proceedings, a court must determine whether: "the place and process have historically been open to the press and general public" and "public access plays a significant positive role in the functioning of the particular process in question."[46] There is a split of authority as to the right of the news media to gain access to pre-indictment access to search warrant affidavits. Some courts have held that there is no right of access,[47] while others have held that there is a right of access.[48] A third group has held that, while there is no First Amendment right of access, there is a "common law qualified right of access . . . committed to the sound discretion of the judicial officer who issued the warrant."[49] The judicial officer may deny access when sealing is essential to preserve higher values and is narrowly tailored to serve that interest.[50]

b. Ongoing criminal prosecutions?

Open trials are a fundamental feature of the American system of justice. The Supreme Court has held that open access is fundamental to both pretrial hearings[51] and trials and thus, there is a qualified First Amendment right of access to criminal proceedings.[52] It stated that a trial can be closed "only if specific findings are made demonstrating that, first, there is a substantial probability that the defendant's right to a fair trial will be prejudiced by publicity that closure would prevent and, second, reasonable alternatives to closure cannot adequately protect the defendant's fair trial rights."[53] Many states do restrict the distribution of certain information in special cases, such as juvenile matters, sex crimes, and other sensitive matters.

The Supreme Court has struck down a number of laws that prohibited press access to criminal proceedings and public records relevant to them. Specifically, the Court has held that: (1) there can be no tort liability for the publication of facts obtained from public records—more specifically, from judicial records which are maintained in connection with a public prosecution which themselves are open to public inspection;[54] and (2) a statute which absolutely bars access to rape trials where the victim is a minor is unconstitutional.[55]

c. Ongoing regulatory investigations?

There is no fundamental right of access to administrative proceedings. Many courts have analogized this situation to that of the right to attend civil proceedings and have employed the *Richmond Newspapers, Inc. v. Virginia,* 448 U.S. 555 (1980), "experience and logic" test.[56] In determining whether there is a right of access, a court must consider: whether there is a tradition of accessibility for the proceeding and whether the Supreme Court has traditionally considered whether public access plays a significant positive role in the functioning of the proceeding.[57]

d. Ongoing civil litigation, or other judicial proceedings?

Generally, there are few restrictions,[58] although the Supreme Court has never decided whether the public has a First Amendment right to attend civil proceedings. However, several federal appeals courts and state courts have held that civil cases are presumed to be public under the First Amendment,[59] and it has been generally accepted that there is a common law right of press access. In certain circumstances certain pleadings may be filed under seal. The Sixth Circuit has stated that "while District Courts have the discretion to issue protective orders, that discretion is limited by the careful dictates of Fed. R. Civ. P. 26" and "is circumscribed by a long-established legal tradition" that values public access to court proceedings. Rule 26(c) allows the sealing of court papers only "for good cause shown" to the court that the particular documents justify court-imposed secrecy.[60]

13. Are prior restraints or other prepublication injunctions available on the basis of libel or privacy, and if so, what are the standards for obtaining such relief?

Aside from restricting the ability to report on criminal cases, prior restraints are presumptively invalid. "In addition to the First Amendment's heavy presumption against prior restraints, courts have long held that equity will not enjoin a libel."[61] In its nearly two centuries of existence, the Supreme Court has never upheld a prior restraint on pure speech.[62] The First Circuit has stated: "as the Supreme Court made clear in *Nebraska Press Association,* a party seeking a prior restraint against the press must show not only that publication will result in damage to a near sacred right, but also that the prior restraint will be effective and that no less extreme measures are available."[63] It added that although the Supreme Court has "implied that such a restraint might be appropriate in a very narrow range of cases, when either national security or an individual's right to a fair trial is at stake. An individual's right to protect his privacy from damage by private parties, although meriting great protection, is simply not of the same magnitude."[64]

The Supreme Court has established a three-part test to determine whether a trial court can issue a prior restraint, which prohibits the media from reporting information that imperils a defendant's right to a fair trial. Courts must consider: (a) "the nature and extent of pretrial news coverage"; (b) "whether other measures would be likely to mitigate the effects of unrestrained pretrial publicity"; and (c) "how effectively a restraining order would operate to prevent the threatened danger."[65] These orders face a very high presumption of their invalidity; in fact, Justice White in his concurring opinion expressed "grave doubt" that any prior restraint in the area would "ever be justifiable."[66]

14. Is a right of privacy recognized (either civilly or criminally)?

Yes, a right of privacy is civilly recognized in certain jurisdictions in the United States.

a. What is the definition of "private fact"?

A "private fact" is a fact concerning a truly intimate or private matter such as one's private sexual affairs or the health of one's self or one's family, which is not already known to the public, and the disclosure of which is offensive to a reasonable person.[67]

b. Is there a public interest or newsworthiness exception?

Yes. Statements "of legitimate concern to the public" are not actionable. This privilege is broader than the one associated with defamation and, thus, a factually accurate statement is not tortious when newsworthy even though "offensive to ordinary sensibilities."[68] This privilege encompasses such matters as births, deaths, marriages, divorces, crimes, accidents, arrests, personal tragedies, and the activities of celebrities and other prominent individuals.[69]

c. Is the right of privacy based in common law, statute, or constitution?

The right of privacy is primarily based in common law, although the First, Fourth, Fifth, and Fourteenth Amendments to the Constitution have been read to protect a number of privacy rights. Also, there are a number of state and federal statutes that protect various privacy interests.

15. May reporters tape-record their own telephone conversations for note-taking purposes (not rebroadcast) without the consent of the other party?

The majority of states and the federal government allow reporters to record telephone conversations without the consent of all parties.[70] A number of states, however, have enacted criminal and/or civil penalties for the recording of telephone conversations without the consent of all parties (commonly called "two-party" states).[71] In general, state statutes apply to conversations that take place within a single state, while federal law applies to conversations between states. However, an individual state may attempt to enforce its laws and it is unclear whether the federal law, which allows one-party-consent recording of conversations, will preempt a conflicting state law.

16. If permissible to record such tapes, may they be broadcast without permission?

The FCC has adopted a rule that requires a reporter, before recording a telephone conversation, to inform the other party of her intentions to broadcast the conversation unless it is "obvious that it is in connection with a program in which the station customarily broadcasts telephone conversations"[72] (such as call-in shows or contests).

17. Is there a recognized evidentiary privilege preventing the disclosure of confidential sources relied upon by reporters?

Yes. The Supreme Court has recognized a limited qualified privilege wherein the asserted privilege should be judged on its facts by striking a balance between freedom of the press and the obligation of all citizens to give relevant testimony.[73] Many states have enacted shield laws, or constitutional amendments, which give journalists varying degrees of protection against the compelled production of confidential sources.[74]

18. In the event that legal papers are served upon the newsroom (such as a civil complaint), are there any particular warnings about accepting service of which we should be aware?

In the United States, the time within which a defendant is obligated to respond to legal papers typically begins to run on the date it is served with those papers. Consequently, news employees should bring such papers—including all enclosures, attachments, and the envelope in which they were contained—to their legal advisers immediately. They should also make note of the date and time at which such papers were received.

In addition, most U.S. jurisdictions provide that only limited categories of employees are authorized to accept service on behalf of their employer. Employees should not assume that they have such authority, and should not indicate that they are authorized to accept service unless they are certain that they have such authority.

19. Has your jurisdiction applied established media law to Internet publishers?

A number of cases have applied libel law to the Internet, and Congress has acted in this area, as discussed below.

20. If established media law has been applied to Internet publishers, are there any ways in which Internet publishers (including chat room operators) have to meet different standards?

The most significant substantive development related to libel law on the Internet is the "safe harbor" portion of the Communications Decency Act of 1996, which protects "provider[s] or user[s] of an interactive computer service" by providing that they shall not be treated as the "publisher or speaker of any information provided by another information content provider."[75]

Also, some courts have applied the single-publication rule (there may be only one cause of action by a plaintiff for any edition of a written publication) to libel cases involving Internet publications in the same manner as they do to traditional materials.[76] These courts found that failure to apply this rule would subject Web publishers to almost perpetual liability and would seriously inhibit the exchange of free ideas on the Internet. The Firth court also stated that the addition of other, unrelated information to the website containing the defamatory statement is not a republication.[77]

Finally, there are important issues relating to personal jurisdiction for Internet publications. Two federal appellate courts have considered whether a court has jurisdiction over defendants from outside the court's jurisdiction. In one, two Connecticut newspapers published articles criticizing the state of Connecticut for housing some of its prisoners in Virginia facilities. A warden of one Virginia facility sued the newspapers in federal district court in Virginia. The court found that there was no personal jurisdiction as the newspapers directed their activities to Connecticut readers, had no connection to readers in Virginia (even though the articles could be read online in Virginia), and did not intend or attempt to serve a Virginia audience.[78]

21. Are there any cases where the courts enforced a judgment in libel from another jurisdiction against a publisher in your jurisdiction?

Generally, the U.S. courts have not been receptive to libel judgments from jurisdictions outside of the country, as they often do not meet First Amendment requirements. For instance, courts have declined to enforce judgments from the United Kingdom.[79] A U.S. court would be more likely to enforce a judgment from a foreign jurisdiction that complied with the requirements of the U.S. Constitution.

Chapter Notes

1. Rodney A. Smolla, *Law of Defamation* § 1:34 (2d ed. 2004).

2. W. Page Keeton, *Prosser & Keeton on Torts* § 111 (5th ed. 1984); *Prosser & Keeton on the Law of Torts* § 111 at p. 773.

3. *Condit v. Dunne,* 317 F. Supp. 2d 344 (S.D.N.Y. 2004).

4. *Scripps Texas Newspapers v. Belalcazar,* 99 S.W.3d 829 (Tex. 2003).

5. *MacLeod v. Tribune Publ'g Co., Inc.,* 52 Cal 2nd 536 (Cal. 1959).

6. *Raymond U v. Duke University,* 91 N.C. App. 171 (N.C. 1988).

7. *Kilcoyne v. Plain Dealer Publ'g Co.,* 112 Ohio App. 3d 229 (Ohio 1996).

8. *Bauer v. Murphy,* 191 Wis. 2d 518 (Wis. 2002).

9. *Grillo v. John Alden Life Ins. Co.,* 939 F. Supp. 1685 (D. Minn. 1996).

10. See, e.g., *Mohr v. Grant* (Wash. Ct. App. 2003); *Turner v. KTRK TV, Inc.,* 38 S.W.3d 103 (Tex. 2000); *Memphis Publ'g Co. v. Nichols,* 569 S.W.2d 412 (Tenn. 1978).

11. See *Boule v. Hutton,* 138 F. Supp. 2d 491 (S.D.N.Y. 2001); *Smith v. Cuban Am. Nat'l Found.,* 731 So. 2d 702 (Fla. Dist. Ct. App. 1999).

12. See, e.g., CAL. CIV. CODE § 45a (West. 2004) (plaintiff must allege and prove special damages to recover for defamation not libelous on its face).

13. Smolla, *Law of Defamation* § 4:75.

14. See *Nat'l Life Ins. Co. v. Phillips Publ'g, Inc.*, 793 F. Supp. 627 (D. Md. 1992); *Suzuki Motor Corp. v. Consumers Union of U.S., Inc.*, 292 F.3d 1192 (9th Cir. 2002); but see *Procter & Gamble Co. v. Amway Corp.*, 242 F.3d 539 (5th Cir. 2001); *World Wrestling Fed'n Entm't, Inc. v. Bozell*, 142 F. Supp. 2d 514 (S.D.N.Y. 2001).

15. See Smolla, *Law of Defamation* § 11:45.

16. *Id.* §§ 11:46, 11:47.

17. See Smolla, *Law of Defamation* § 4:40.50 (citing, *inter alia, Serv. Parking Corp. v. Wash. Times Co.*, 92 F.2d 502 (D.C. Cir. 1937)); *Michigan United Conservation Clubs v. CBS News*, 485 F. Supp. 893 (W.D. Mich. 1980), *judgment aff'd*, 665 F.2d 110 (6th Cir. 1981); *Blatty v. N.Y. Times Co.*, 728 P. 2d 1177 (Cal. 1986).

18. Smolla, *Law of Defamation* § 4:44 (citing, *inter alia, Geisler v. Petrocelli*, 616 F.2d 636 (2d Cir. 1980); *Bindrim v. Mitchell*, 155 Cal. Rptr. 29 (Cal. App. 1979); Prosser & Keeton § 111).

19. *Rosenblatt v. Baer*, 383 U.S. 75 (1966).

20. See *QSP, Inc. v. Aetna Cas. & Sur. Co.*, 773 A.2d 906 (Conn. 2001); *Auvil v. CBS "60 Minutes,"* 800 F. Supp. 928 (E.D. Wash. 1992); *Isuzu Motors Ltd. v. Consumers Union of U.S., Inc.*, 12 F. Supp. 2d 1035 (C.D. Cal. 1998).

21. *Brady v. Ottaway Newspapers, Inc.*, 445 N.Y.S.2d 786 (2d Dep't. 1981).

22. In *Gertz*, 418 U.S. 323 (1974), the Supreme Court identified two classes of public figures. An individual may have such "pervasive fame or notoriety" so that he or she is a public figure for "all purposes and in all contexts," a general-purpose public figure (*Gertz*, 418 U.S. at 345). Or, more commonly, an individual "voluntarily injects himself into" a particular public controversy and thereby becomes a public figure with respect to the limited range of issues surrounding the controversy, a limited-purpose public figure. *Id.*

23. *New York Times Co.*, 376 U.S. at 280.

24. *Gertz*, 418 U.S. at 347.

25. *Dun & Bradstreet, Inc. v. Greenmoss Builders, Inc.*, 472 U.S. 749 (1985).

26. New York has adopted a "gross irresponsibility" standard, which compares the defendant's conduct to the "standards of information gathering and dissemination ordinarily followed by responsible parties." *Chapadeau v. Utica Observer-Dispatch, Inc.*, 379 N.Y.S.2d 61, 64–65 (1975).

27. See, e.g., *Dun & Bradstreet, Inc. v. Greenmoss Builders, Inc.*, 472 U.S. 749 (1985); *Levinsky's, Inc. v. Wal-Mart Stores, Inc.*, 999 F. Supp. 137 (D.Me. 1998).

28. *Huggins v. Moore,* 704 N.Y.S.2d 904, 908 (1999).

29. *Snead v. Redland Aggregates Ltd.,* 998 F.2d 1325 (5th Cir. 1993).

30. Smolla, *Law of Defamation* § 2:98.

31. *Jadwin v. Minneapolis Star & Tribune Co.,* 367 N.W.2d 476, 487–88 (Minn. 1985); see also *Martin Marietta Corp. v. Evening Star Newspaper Co.,* 417 F. Supp. 947 (D.D.C. 1976); *Dairy Stores, Inc. v. Sentinel Publ'g Co.,* 465 A.2d 953 (N.J. Super. Ct. Law Div. 1983).

32. *Snead,* 998 F.2d at 1329; see also *Reliance Ins. Co. v. Barron's,* 442 F. Supp. 1341, 1348 (S.D.N.Y. 1977) (company found to be public figure because it was a large, publicly traded company, had been the subject of great public interest, was in a heavily regulated industry, filed financial reports, and was in the process of offering its stock to the public); *Global Telemedia Int'l, Inc. v. Doe 1,* 132 F. Supp. 2d 1261 (C.D. Cal. 2001) (company is a matter of public interest because it has 18,000 public investors and is the topic of thousands of Internet postings); but see *Blue Ridge Bank v. Veribanc, Inc.,* 866 F.2d 681(4th Cir. 1989) (extensive government regulation not sufficient to make company a public figure).

33. See *Levin v. McPhee,* 119 F.3d 189 (2d Cir. 1997).

34. *Cochran v. NYP Holdings, Inc.,* 58 F. Supp. 2d 1113 (C.D. Cal. 1998).

35. See, e.g., Cal. Civ. Code § 48(a) (West 2004); Ga. Code Ann. § 51-5-11.

36. Fla. Stat. Ann. § 770.01-02 (2004).

37. See, e.g., Mich. Comp. Laws § 600.2911(3) (2004) (privilege for reporting on "matters of public record, a public and official proceeding, or of a governmental notice, announcement, written or recorded report or record generally available to the public, or act or action of a public body . . ."); N.Y. Civ. Rights Law § 74 (2004) ("a civil action cannot be maintained against any person, firm or corporation, for the publication of a fair and true report of any judicial proceeding, legislative proceeding or other official proceeding"); Cal. Civ. Code § 47(d) (West 2004) (applying to judicial, legislative, or other public official proceeding); *Langston v. Eagle Publ'g Co.,* 719 S.W.2d 612 (Tex. Ct. App. 1986) (applying Tex. Civ. Pract. & Rem. Code § 73.002).

38. *Myers v. The Telegraph,* 773 N.E.2d 192, 198 (Ill. App. Ct. 2002).

39. See Restatement (Second) of Torts § 611 cmt. c (1997); *Amway Corp. v. Procter & Gamble Co.,* 346 F.3d 180 (6th Cir. 2003).

40. See *Amway,* 346 F.3d at 186 (citing Restatement (Second) of Torts § 611 cmt. e (1997)); but see *First Lehigh Bank v. Cowen,* 700 A.2d 498 (Pa. Super. Ct. 1997).

41. See *Stewart v. Sun Sentinel Co.,* 695 So. 2d 360 (Fla. Dist. Ct. App., 1997) (qualified privilege to accurately report on the information received from

government officials, including broadcast of contents "of an official document"); MICH. COMP. LAWS § 600.2911(3) (2004); N.Y. CIV. RIGHTS LAW § 74 (2004); CAL. CIV. CODE § 47(d) (West 2004).

42. See, e.g., *Wilson v. Slatalla,* 970 F. Supp. 405 (E.D. Pa. 1997) (presentence reports and letters from an A.U.S.A. to a judge conditionally privileged); *Bowers v. Loveland Publ'g Co.,* 773 P.2d 595 (Colo. Ct. App. 1988) (report of police reports was a matter of public concern subject to constitutional protection); *White v. Fraternal Order of Police,* 909 F.2d 512 (D.C. Cir. 1990) (ad hoc investigatory police department committee with no adjudicatory powers was a governmental proceeding); *Edwards v. Paddock Publ'ns, Inc.,* 763 N.E.2d 328 (Ill. App. Ct. 2001) (privilege protects news accounts based upon the written and verbal statements of governmental agencies and officials made in their official capacities).

43. See, e.g., RESTATEMENT (SECOND) OF TORTS, § 611 cmt. d (1977) (the privilege . . . is also applicable to public proceedings and actions of other bodies or organizations that are by law authorized to perform public duties, such as a medical or bar association charged with authority to examine or license or discipline practitioners); *Harper v. Walters,* 822 F. Supp. 817 (D. D.C. 1993).

44. *Jewell v. NYP Holdings, Inc.,* 23 F. Supp. 2d 348, 371 (S.D.N.Y. 1998); see also *Karaduman v. Newsday, Inc.,* 435 N.Y.S.2d 556, 565–66 (1980).

45. *Brown v. Courier Herald Publ'g Co.,* 700 F. Supp. 534, 537–38 (S.D. Ga. 1988); see also *Nelson v. Associated Press, Inc.,* 667 F. Supp. 1468, 1478–80 (S.D. Fla. 1987); *Appleby v. Daily Hampshire Gazette,* 478 N.E.2d 721 (Mass. 1985); *Howe v. Detroit Free Press,* 555 N.W.2d 738 (Mich. Ct. App. 1996); but see *Friedman v. Israel Labour Party,* 957 F. Supp. 701 (E.D. Pa. 1997) (wire service defense not available in Pennsylvania).

46. *Press-Enterprise Co. v. Superior Court of California,* 464 U.S. 501, 505 (1984); *Press-Enterprise Co. v. Superior Court of California,* 478 U.S. 1 (1986).

47. *Times Mirror Co. v. United States,* 873 F.2d 1210 (9th Cir. 1989).

48. *In re Search Warrant for Secretarial Area, Outside Office of Gunn,* 855 F.2d 569 (8th Cir. 1988).

49. *Baltimore Sun Co. v. Goetz,* 886 F.2d 60 (4th Cir. 1989).

50. *Id.* at 65–66.

51. But there is no right of access to grand jury proceedings. See *Douglas Oil Co. v. Petrol Stops Northwest,* 441 U.S. 211, 219 (1979); but see *Butterworth v. Smith,* 494 U.S. 624 (1990) (state statute that banned witnesses from disclosing own grand jury testimony was unconstitutional).

52. *Press-Enterprise Co. v. Superior Court of California,* 478 U.S. 1 (1986).

53. *Id.*

54. *Cox Broad. Corp. v. Cohn,* 420 U.S. 469 (1975); see also *Smith v. Daily Mail Publ'g Co.,* 443 U.S. 97 (1979) (challenge to application of W.Va. law making it illegal to publish name of child prosecuted in a criminal proceeding).

55. *Globe Newspaper Co. v. Superior Court,* 457 U.S. 596 (1982).

56. See *North Jersey Media Group, Inc. v. Ashcroft,* 308 F.3d 198 (3d Cir. 2002) (immigration hearing); *Detroit Free Press v. Ashcroft,* 303 F.3d 681 (6th Cir. 2002) (same); *United States v. Miami Univ.,* 294 F.3d 797, 824 (6th Cir. 2002) (university's student disciplinary board proceedings); *First Amendment Coalition v. Judicial Inquiry & Review Bd.,* 784 F.2d 467 (3d Cir. 1986) (access to records of disciplinary measures against a judge); *Soc'y of Prof'l Journalists v. Sec'y of Labor,* 616 F. Supp. 569, 574 (D. Utah 1985) (administrative hearing), vacated as moot, 832 F.2d 1180 (10th Cir. 1987).

57. *Press-Enterprise Co. v. Superior Court of California,* 478 U.S. 1, 8 (1986).

58. See, e.g., *Tex. Civ. Prac. & Rem.* § 73.002 (2004) (allowing fair comment on judicial proceedings, other proceedings to administer the law, executive or legislative proceedings, proceedings of a public meeting, or comment on or criticism of an official act of a public official or other matter of public concern).

59. *Publicker Indus., Inc. v. Cohen,* 733 F.2d 1059 (3d Cir. 1984) (preliminary injunction hearing); *In re Cont'l Ill. Sec. Litig.,* 732 F.2d 1302 (7th Cir. 1984) (hearing on motion to dismiss); *In re Iowa Freedom of Info. Council,* 724 F.2d 658 (8th Cir. 1984) (contempt hearing); *Newman v. Graddick,* 696 F.2d 796 (11th Cir. 1983) (pre- and post-trial hearings); *NBC Subsidiary (KNBC-TV), Inc. v. Superior Court,* 980 P.2d 337, 353 (Cal. 1999) (presumptive right to access to civil trial unless court expressly finds: (i) an overriding interest supporting closure and/or sealing; (ii) a substantial probability that the interest will be prejudiced absent closure and/or sealing; (iii) the proposed closure and/or sealing is narrowly tailored; and (iv) there is no less restrictive means of achieving the overriding interest).

60. *Proctor & Gamble v. Bankers Trust Co.,* 78 F.3d 219 (6th Cir. 1996) (citations omitted).

61. *Metro. Opera Ass'n v. Local 100,* 239 F.3d 172, 177 (2d Cir. 2001).

62. *In re Providence Journal Co.,* 820 F.2d 1342 (1st Cir. 1986).

63. *Id.* at 1351.

64. *Id.* at 1350.

65. *Nebraska Press Ass'n v. Stuart,* 427 U.S. 539, 562 (1976).

66. *Id.* at 570.

67. See Smolla, *Law of Defamation* §§ 10:39, 10:42.

68. Restatement (Second) of Torts, § 652D (1977); see also Smolla, *Law of Defamation* §§ 10:49, 10:50.

69. See Smolla, *Law of Defamation* § 10:50.

70. See, e.g., 18 U.S.C. § 2511(2)(d) (West 2004).

71. See, e.g., Cal. Penal Code §§ 631, 632 (West 2004); Fla. State Ann. § 934.03 (West 2004); Mich. Comp. Laws § 750.539c (2004).

72. 47 C.F.R. § 73.1206 (2005).

73. *Branzburg v. Hayes,* 408 U.S. 665, 710–11 (1972).

74. See, e.g., N.Y. Civ. Rights Law § 79-h (2004) (providing unqualified protection for journalists' confidential sources and materials); Cal. Const. Art. 1 § 2(b) (reporters may not be held in contempt for refusing to disclose sources or unpublished information obtained during news gathering); Fla. State Ann. § 90.5015 (West 2004) ("professional journalists" cannot be compelled to be witnesses or disclose information that they have obtained while actively gathering news, but which may be overcome by a "clear and specific" showing that: (a) the information is "relevant and material," (b) the information cannot be obtained elsewhere, and (c) a compelling interest exists for requiring disclosure).

75. 47 U.S.C. § 230 (West 2004); see also *Batzel v. Smith,* 333 F.3d 1018 (9th Cir. 2003) (providers of interactive computer services not liable for publishing or distributing defamatory material written or prepared by others); *Doe v. GTE Corp.,* 347 F.3d 655 (7th Cir. 2003); *Zeran v. Am. Online, Inc.,* 129 F.3d 327 (4th Cir. 1997); *Ben Ezra, Weinstein, & Co. v. Am. Online, Inc.,* 206 F.3d 980 (10th Cir. 2000); *Green v. Am. Online, Inc.,* 318 F.3d 465 (3d Cir. 2003).

76. *Firth v. State,* 747 N.Y.S.2d 69 (2002); *Traditional Cat Ass'n v. Gilbreath,* 13 Cal. Rptr. 3d (Ct. App. 2004); *Van Buskirk v. N.Y. Times Co.,* No. 99 Civ. 4265 (MBM) 2000 WL 1206732 (S.D.N.Y. Aug. 24, 2000).

77. *Firth,* 98 N.Y.2d at 372.

78. *Young v. New Haven Advocate,* 315 F.3d 256 (4th Cir. 2002); see also *Revell v. Lidov,* 317 F.3d 467 (5th Cir. 2002) (plaintiff could not gain personal jurisdiction in Texas over a defendant located in Massachusetts posting to a Columbia University website); but see *Bochan v. La Fontaine,* 68 F. Supp. 2d 692 (E.D. Va. 1999) (Virginia court had personal jurisdiction over out-of-state defendant who posted his message through a Virginia-based ISP, but not over a different out-of-state defendant who posted through a California or New Mexico ISP (but the court had jurisdiction over this defendant because he regularly solicited business in Virginia)).

79. *Bachchan v. India Abroad Publ'ns, Inc.,* 585 N.Y.S.2d 661 (Sup. Ct. 1992) (declined to enforce because English courts do not adhere to First Amendment standards); *Matusevich v. Telnikoff,* 877 F. Supp. 1 (D.D.C. 1995) (same).

PART **TWO**

ASIA AND AUSTRALIA

Australia

China

Hong Kong

India

Japan

Korea

Malaysia

The Middle East

Singapore

Thailand

CHAPTER 4

Australia

PETER BARTLETT
Minter Ellison

Minter Ellison
Rialto Towers, 525 Collins Street
Melbourne, VIC 3000
Phone: +61 3 8608 2677
Fax: +61 3 9620 5185
www.minterellison.com
peter.bartlett@minterellison.com

Introduction to Australian Media Law

While the Internet has largely neutralized the tyranny of distance in the communications area, Australian courts have not followed many of the trends appearing in offshore jurisdictions. Australian Media Law is moving further away from other common law jurisdictions.

Since early 2006 Australia has had one uniform defamation law to replace the eight separate laws previously enforced across the Australian States and Territories. This is a recognition that the State and Territory borders are largely irrelevant to the media.

1. What is the locally accepted definition of libel?

The uniform defamation law does not include a definition of what is defamatory. By leaving the definition open, it gives the courts flexibility to decide cases according to community standards at any given time.

The classic definition is found in *Parmiter v. Coupland*:[1]

> Matter . . . calculated to injure the reputation of another, by exposing him to hatred, contempt and ridicule.

A more modern test is found in *Mirror Newspapers v. World Hosts*:[2]

> [A] statement about the plaintiff of a kind likely to lead the recipient as an ordinary person to think less of him.

In reality, material is defamatory if it lowers the reputation of someone in the eyes of others. Defamatory material can be expressed in any mode of communication capable of being comprehended by a reader or a listener. Libel is defamatory material in permanent form. The uniform defamation law removes the distinction between libel and slander. Television and radio broadcasts are deemed to be broadcast in permanent form.[3]

Australian law has a fairly broad interpretation of what statements subject a person to defamatory meaning. For example, statements that a restaurant owner was going bankrupt,[4] or that a minister in the Australian government was an adulterer,[5] or that a publisher acted dishonorably in negotiations to settle a former employee's compensation claim were held to be defamatory. The courts have also found that publications, while not accusing the subject of wrongdoing but nonetheless holding him or her up to ridicule, could be actionable. In one case, a professional football player brought a claim for libel after a newspaper published a photograph of him in the shower.[6] The court found that his reputation was tarnished because the photograph made him look "ridiculous" and the public may have believed that the athlete intentionally posed for the photograph.

In rare cases, criminal liability will attach to the unlawful publication of defamatory material in certain, limited circumstances. Even though the offense has been codified, its exact terms differ across the states and territories, and there are often a number of defenses available.

2. Is libel-by-implication recognized, or, in the alternative, must the complained-of words alone defame the plaintiff?

Defamation can arise either from the ordinary and natural meaning of the words published, or from the imputations the words carry. This may be determined by examining the context and tone of the statement at issue. It is worth noting that the intention of the publisher is irrelevant. The question is whether a defamatory meaning is capable of arising and then whether it in fact arises. The jury decides these questions.

3. May corporations sue for libel?

A corporation cannot sue for libel unless it is a private body and is either a not-for-profit organization or employs fewer than ten people and is unrelated to another corporation. This does not prevent an individual associated with a company from suing in cases in which the material defamatory of the company is also defamatory of the individual.

In a rather surprising decision, the High Court of Australia has recognized a class of defamation, described as business defamation:

> where published material conveys a defamatory imputation that would injure a plaintiff and the plaintiff's business, trade or profession.[7]

Companies need to look at other possible remedies such as under the Trade Practices Act 1974 (Cth) (misleading and deceptive conduct, although they will need to avoid the media defense), injurious falsehood or negligence.[8] The media defense does not apply to the publication of an advertisement, a promo for a future program, or statements made in the course of a media investigation for a story.

Government bodies cannot sue for defamation, as political discussion is seen as a crucial element of freedom of speech.

4. Is product disparagement recognized, and if so, how does that differ from libel?

Yes, although the cause of action is referred to in Australia as "injurious falsehood" where a false and malicious statement against a person's business, property, or goods causes provable economic loss.

An action for injurious falsehood is separate from an action for defamation, although both actions can be run in conjunction. The difference between the two is that an action for injurious falsehood protects a person's business, while an action for defamation protects a person's reputation. An injurious falsehood claim was recently dismissed in *Griffith & Anor v. ABC & Anor.*[9]

A publication need not be defamatory to ground an action in injurious falsehood. In other words, it need not subject the target to reputational damage, but need only be false and reasonably linked to damages suffered by the business. For example, an inaccurate story that says that "Company X has lost its key employees in the widget-making department" might be actionable if Company X could show that the statement is false, and that contracts to sell widgets were canceled by buyers because they believed that X could not produce the sought-after widgets.[10] An action may also lie under Section 52 of the Trade Practices Act 1974 (Cth), which prohibits conduct that is misleading and deceptive.

5. Must an individual be clearly identified (by name or photograph) to sue for libel? Can a group of persons sue for libel, even though not named?

A person needs to show that the material complained of identified him or her as the subject of the defamatory imputations contained in the article.[11]

The person does not need to be named in the material published, rather only be identifiable by other persons acquainted with him or her.[12] Basically, any connection that one can reasonably make between the material published and the person will identify the person.[13]

Group libel is possible in limited circumstances. Defamatory statements about a group of unnamed persons are actionable by one of those persons if the statement is shown to be referring to individual members of the group. The members of the group can only sue if they can show that the statement refers particularly to them.[14]

This is usually the case where the group is so small as to make members easily identifiable. You can potentially defame each member of a group because it is small enough to allow the defamatory meaning to apply to each member of that group.

6. What is the fault standard(s) applied to libel?

There are a number of defenses that provide protection from liability for otherwise defamatory statements in the uniform law. This is in addition to any other defense or exclusion of liability available at common law or under statute unless modified or repealed by the Uniform law. The main defenses in the Uniform law are:

Truth. It is a defense if the defendant proves that the defamatory imputations pleaded are substantially true. This is consistent with the common law.

The defense of contextual truth was upheld in *Fawcett v. John Fairfax Publications.*[15]

Fair comment and honest opinion. (See discussion in Question 8 below.)

Absolute privilege. This defense protects statements made in the course of parliamentary or judicial proceedings. Journalists and webmasters should note that this defense is not available for anyone but the participants in the proceedings (i.e., parliamentarians, lawyers who are taking part, the judges, and the witnesses giving evidence).

Qualified privilege. This is the defense relied upon by publishers producing reports of parliamentary proceedings and judicial proceedings. It is available to the media as long as the material published is in the public interest, is not founded on malice, and is fair and accurate.

The defense in the uniform law is similar to that previously in existence in the New South Wales (NSW) Defamation Act 1974.

Publishers are not required to be under a duty or to have an interest in publishing information on a particular subject. They must instead prove either that the recipient had an interest, or they had reasonable grounds to believe that the recipient had an interest, in having the information published and the defamatory matter was published to the recipient in the course of giving him that information.

The publisher's conduct in publishing must also be reasonable. The uniform law lists the circumstances the courts may take into account to decide whether the defendant's conduct in publishing was reasonable. Except for one new circumstance, which could assist the media, namely the nature of the business environment in which the defendant operates, they are the same as those previously existing under the NSW Act.

The requirement to prove reasonableness could be considered a major drawback to the media because what is "reasonable" has been interpreted narrowly by the NSW courts, making this defense very difficult to rely on for the media.[16] An example of the defense being upheld in a non-media case is *Jerry Lee Bennette v. Cohen.*[17]

The defense is defeated if the plaintiff proves the defendant acted with malice. Proof of malice is determined according to the common law.

The common law defense of political discussion has been preserved.

Innocent dissemination: This statutory defense essentially adopts the English common law defense by protecting subordinate publishers. Subordinate publishers will not be liable for defamatory publication on services they provide, unless they knew or ought reasonably to have known the material was defamatory or their lack of knowledge was not due to negligence on their behalf. The new defense extends the protection currently available to ISPs and Internet content hosts under the Broadcasting Services Act 1992 (Cth) to cover a range of providers of Internet and other electronic and communications services who will generally be considered subordinate distributors. This includes wholesalers and retailers of publications and broadcasters of a live program (where they have no effective control over the person who makes the defamatory statement).

Triviality: This defense is new to the common law states and is available if the defendant can prove that the circumstances of publication were such that the defendant was unlikely to sustain any harm.

a. Does the fault standard depend on the fame or notoriety of the plaintiff?

There is no differing fault standard in the case of the fame or notoriety of the plaintiff except where qualified privilege is claimed for publication of a matter of public interest or concern, or the publication concerns government and political matter. The fame or notoriety of the plaintiff may be relevant in calculating damages.

b. Is there a heightened fault standard or privilege for reporting on matters of public concern or public interest?

i. To succeed in a qualified privilege defense, other than a report of parliamentary or judicial proceedings, it is necessary to show that:
   - Recipients had an interest in receiving the information;
   - The matter was published to the recipient in the course of giving the recipient information on that subject; and
   - The conduct of the publisher in publishing the matter was reasonable and there was no malice.

ii. The "subject" must necessarily be of public interest. The defamation will occur as an unavoidable incidental to giving information on that subject. The defense of qualified privilege is extremely difficult for the media to establish. To prove reasonableness, a journalist researching a story must at least:
   - Contact, or attempt to contact, the persons or company referred to in any story to provide them with the opportunity to comment on the allegations made in the story;
   - Include their comments (if any) in the publication;
   - Take care to use reliable sources and verify each available source of information; and
   - Check the accuracy and authenticity of any material contained in the report.[18]

iii. There is a separate qualified privilege to respond to attacks published elsewhere.

iv. A publisher will have a qualified "public interest" defense to a defamation action where the material published discusses government or political matters and publication of the material was reasonable in the circumstances. These are subject to the limitations enumerated in section (ii) above.

Australia has not yet moved as far as the UK decisions in *Reynolds v. Times Newspapers*[19] and *Yousef Jameel v. Dow Jones & Co Inc.*[20]

The statutory qualified-privilege defense under the uniform defamation law will provide a broader basis than the common law for finding that a recipient had the necessary interest in receiving the defamatory information. However, courts have interpreted reasonableness under statute narrowly, making it more difficult than at common law for publishers to prove that publication was reasonable in the circumstances. The plaintiff will still defeat the defense, proving that publication was actuated by malice.

7. Is financial news about publicly traded companies, or companies involved with a government contract, considered a matter of public interest or otherwise privileged?

There would be a strong argument to suggest that "financial news about publicly traded companies, or companies involved with government contracts," is a matter of public interest and privileged, but it is still necessary to satisfy the test that:

- The recipients had an interest in receiving the information;
- The matter is published to the recipient in the course of giving to the recipient information on that subject; and
- The publisher's conduct in publishing the material was reasonable and not actuated by malice.

It is necessary to show that the publisher's conduct was reasonable.

8. Is there a recognized protection for opinion or "fair comment" on matters of public concern?

While the common law defense of comment remains, the Uniform law introduces a similar defense of honest opinion. At common law it is necessary to show that

- Each meaning where the defense is pleaded arises as comment (either opinion, a conclusion, or an inference);
- The opinion was honestly held;
- The comment relates to a matter of public interest; and
- The comment was based on facts stated in the report or adequately referred to, which are true or based on privileged material.[21]

The defense of comment was upheld in *Fawcett v. John Fairfax Publications.*[22]

Under the Uniform laws it is necessary to show that:

- The matter complained of was opinion rather than a statement of fact;
- The opinion related to a matter of public interest; and
- The opinion is based on proper material.

The High Court of Australia decided in *Channel Seven Adelaide Pty Ltd v. Manock*[23] that the comment defense is only available if the facts are set out in the publication, sufficiently indicated or are notorious. The High Court also suggested that for the defense to succeed, any comment must be "reasonable." This claim concerned a promo for a future current affairs program. In that case, Justice Kirby noted that the majority judgment "would seriously reduce the availability and utility of the fair comment defense to the media in Australia" and that this was "a step that has the potential to erode freedom of speech." The *Manock* decision was followed in *Hore–Lacy v. Cleary and Allen and Unwin*.[24]

9. Are there any requirements upon a plaintiff, such as demand for retraction or right of reply, and if so, what impact do they have?

There are no requirements in Australia upon a plaintiff to demand a retraction or a right of reply. An apology is relevant on the question of damages, but is not a defense.[25]

The uniform defamation laws contain a codified offer-of-amends procedure similar to that in the United Kingdom. Rejection of a publisher's reasonable offer of amends, made in accordance with the legislation, can provide a complete defense to a defamation claim. In considering the reasonableness of an offer, the court must consider any correction or apology published before trial and its prominence compared with the matter in question, and the time elapsed between publication of the matter in question and the apology. An unsuccessful party who unreasonably failed to make or accept an offer of amends can be ordered to pay indemnity costs. The offer can be made in respect of all or some of the defamatory statements made.

10. Is there a privilege for quoting or reporting on:

a. Papers filed in court?

Papers filed with the Court Registry in most states are not protected by privilege until they have been accepted into evidence by the judge. Affidavits that have not been read out in open court or taken as read by the judge are not protected.

The Uniform laws provide a privilege for a fair quoting or summary of any document filed or lodged with a court that is open to inspection by the public.

b. Government-issued documents?

Depending on the content of the documents, there may be an argument for qualified privilege, subject to a "fair and accurate" reporting or other requirement.

The Uniform laws generally provide a defense for publication of a fair copy or summary of a public or government document. The defense is defeated if the plaintiff proves that the material was not published honestly for the information of the public or for the advancement of education. The New South Wales Court of Appeal rejected an argument that remarks about a skydiver on a disability pension were a fair and accurate summary of a protected report.[26]

c. Quasi-governmental proceedings?

Again, depending on the circumstances, findings, or decisions of an association, a committee of an association, or the governing body of an association relating to a member or to a person subject to the association's control may in some circumstances be covered by a defense of qualified privilege.

The subject matter must be one in which the public has a genuine interest in the outcome of the proceedings, which generally embraces associations:

- for the advancement of learning;
- for the promotion or protection of the interests of a trade, business, profession, or industry; or
- for the promotion of a public spectator sport, pastime, or game and the promotion or protection of the interests of persons in connection with the sport, pastime, or game.

Any such report must be accurate and balanced and published in good faith for public information. It must be a précis of what happened in the proceedings. In some states and territories, such reports have specific statutory protection.

11. Is there a privilege for republishing statements made earlier by other, bona fide, reliable publications or wire services?

There is no privilege for republishing such material except where an innocent dissemination defense may apply (see discussion in Question 20, below). The publisher is deemed to have published that republished material and, if defamatory, is liable in damages.

12. Are there any restrictions regarding reporting on:

a. Ongoing criminal investigations?

Clearly it can be defamatory to report ongoing criminal investigations to the extent that the report suggests that the person or persons being investigated are guilty or even that there is sufficient evidence available to justify the continuing investigation.

There are statutory restrictions on areas such as identifying the victim of sexual assault, or minors. A publication that has a real and definite tendency to prejudice a pending trial could be held in Contempt of Court.[27]

b. Ongoing criminal prosecutions?

Certain restrictions are placed upon reporting of ongoing criminal prosecutions, such as:

- where the matter involves children;
- where it involves a sexual offense;

- where a court order suppressing publication is in place; or
- where a witness is in the witness protection program.

The publisher does not have a potential problem with Contempt of Court until charges are laid. It would be in Contempt of Court to publish material that would prejudice the fair trial of the matter. The publisher should be particularly careful where the matter is being heard by a jury, and avoid publishing facts not heard by the jury.

Generally, reporters may repeat any evidence given in open civil or criminal proceedings so long as it is a fair and accurate report of the matter and is not in Contempt of Court, such as by being the subject of a non-publication order.

c. Ongoing regulatory investigations?

There are various statutory restrictions on reporting some ongoing regulatory investigations and prosecutions, and journalists should consult local counsel prior to publishing such reports or investigatory material.

d. Ongoing civil litigation, or other judicial proceedings?

Certain restrictions are placed upon the reporting of civil litigation where:

- the matter is before the Family Court or the Children's Court;
- a court order suppressing publication is in place; or
- the civil litigation involves evidence of sexual offenses.

Unless the report is a fair and accurate account of the proceeding, the normal rules relating to defamation and contempt apply.

13. Are prior restraints or other prepublication injunctions available on the basis of libel or privacy, and if so, what are the standards for obtaining such relief?

It is generally considered that injunctions will rarely be granted in Australia to prevent the publication of defamatory material, as courts are reluctant to prevent freedom of speech on matters of public interest and there is always the right to sue for damages after publication if a person has been defamed.

An injunction could be granted if monetary damages are not an adequate remedy. That would be very rare. An injunction can be obtained to prevent the publication of confidential material, in some circumstances.

The Nine Network was able to publish some confidential documents that were accidentally disclosed by Corrections Victoria. Nine was prevented from publishing other documents such as patient profiles.[28]

14. Is a right of privacy recognized (either civilly or criminally)?
There is no general right of privacy in Australia, but the civil laws against breach of confidentiality and trespass, and the criminal laws against secretly recording private conversations, are important privacy protections.

In *Channel Seven Perth Pty Ltd v. 'S'*[29] the Western Australian Supreme Court, Court of Appeal prevented Channel Seven from broadcasting a hidden camera recording of a private conversation.

Australia has not followed the trend in the UK to extend confidentiality or the trend in Europe or New Zealand to extend privacy as a civil remedy. That said, the Australian Law Reform Commission and the New South Wales Law Reform Commission both favor a statutory tort of invasion of privacy. The privacy commissioner favors weakening the media exemption in the Privacy Act. In addition, the 2007 case of *Jane Doe v. ABC*[30] is presently on appeal to the Victorian Court of Appeal. In that case the plaintiff is seeking the recognition of a common law tort of invasion of privacy.

a. What is the definition of "private fact"?
To the extent that a privacy claim would be recognized, the Privacy Act 1988 (Cth) is concerned with the protection of personal information of individuals (being information from which a person's identity is reasonably ascertainable) that is handled by organizations, especially the protection of the collection and distribution of such information without that person's consent, i.e., how that information is disclosed. There are stricter limitations on the disclosure of health or sensitive information in the Privacy Act and also State- and Territory-based health records legislation.

b. Is there a public interest or newsworthiness exception?
The Privacy Act affords exemptions to journalists.[31] Acts engaged in by a media organization that are *in the course of journalism* are exempt. The easiest way to ensure this applies, when collecting information about an individual, is by making sure that it is used for the purposes of writing the story and not for some other sideline purpose, such as advertising. The privacy commissioner is looking at the possibility of weakening the exemption.

c. Is the right of privacy based in common law, statute, or constitution?
The Privacy Act is statutory in nature, and the causes of action sounding in breach of confidence are founded in common law.

15. May reporters tape-record their own telephone conversations for note-taking purposes (not rebroadcast) without the consent of the other party?

Tape-recording one's own telephone conversation by placing a tape recorder next to the telephone's speaker or mouthpiece is permitted. It is preferable to obtain the consent of the other party to the conversation, but this is not strictly required.

Putting in place special technology that intercepts a telephone conversation over the line, even internally in one's receiver, is illegal in Australia, unless all parties to the conversation are aware that tape-recording is taking place and consent to the conversation being recorded.

16. If permissible to record such tapes, may they be broadcast without permission?

Illegal tape recordings are inadmissible in court cases; thus, interviews that may be challenged in libel cases later should be made with an eye toward admissibility, and local counsel should be consulted during the preparation of such material.

Legislation in many states and territories means tape recordings obtained by recorders external to the phone cannot be broadcast without the permission of all parties to the conversation, subject to limited exceptions such as when used in legal proceedings, or where their use would be in the public interest.

17. Is there a recognized evidentiary privilege preventing the disclosure of confidential sources relied upon by reporters?

No. Currently, journalists have no legal right to withhold their source of confidential information, although journalists in Australia do maintain and uphold an ethical right not to reveal sources. Journalists who refuse to reveal the sources of confidential information before the court will be held in contempt. They can be penalized by fine or imprisonment or both. There is a current push for enactment of "shield laws" to protect journalists in such circumstances, but it is unclear whether this will occur. There is such a shield in New South Wales but it is reasonably ineffective in protecting reporters.[32] Judges would normally only order a journalist to disclose a source where the judge takes the view that it is essential for the fair determination of the case for the identity to be disclosed. That is rare. Following an article on Government cuts to war veterans' entitlements, two reporters were ordered to disclose their sources.[33]

18. In the event that legal papers are served upon the newsroom (such as a civil complaint), are there any particular warnings about accepting service of which we should be aware?

There are no particular warnings about accepting service of process in Australia, other than that the documents served should be forwarded to the publisher's lawyers as soon as possible to ensure the proper response is made to the service and that any action is defended appropriately. Any offer of amends under the Uniform law needs to be made within twenty-eight days of receipt of the complaint. Normally, documents would be served on the registered office of the publisher's company.

19. Has your jurisdiction applied established media law to Internet publishers?

Defamation law has been applied to Internet publishers. In *Dow Jones & Company Inc. v. Gutnick*[34] it was held that defamation on the Internet occurs in the jurisdiction where the material is downloaded (i.e., read or heard). Australia has not followed the UK, U.S., or Canadian cases in this area. As would be expected, the Internet-related case law is building. The State of New South Wales was found not to have published (consented, approved, adopted, or promoted) articles on a Yahoo-hosted site accessed via a school's computers.[35]

There is potential liability for content in published links.[36] The NSW Supreme Court declined to grant an injunction to restrain publication of a Web page as the order would be unenforceable against the publishers, in the United States. ". . . an injunction is not designed to superimpose the law of NSW relating to defamation on every other State, Territory and country of the world."[37]

Justice Betty King ordered that a thirteen-part television series based on real-life events, *Underbelly*, not be broadcast on television or on the Internet in the state of Victoria, as it might prejudice a forthcoming trial.[38] The decision of Justice King, insofar as it related to the Internet, is largely unenforceable. The decision illustrates how difficult the courts are finding it to grapple with the new issues thrown up by the Internet. The outer limits of the fair dealing exceptions in the context of "new media" were considered in *Telstra Corporation Pty Limited v. Premier Media Group Pty Ltd & Anor.*[39]

20. If established media law has been applied to Internet publishers, are there any ways in which Internet publishers (including chat room operators) have to meet different standards?

1. ***"Primary" Publishers***

   For primary publishers (i.e., online newspapers) there are no different standards for defamation. They are liable for defamatory material published on their site.

2. ***Internet Intermediaries (Web Hosts)***

The Broadcasting Services Act 1992 (Cth) provides a statutory defense to defamatory "Internet content" carried, hosted, or cached by Internet content hosts and Internet service providers where they are not aware of the nature of the material.

This defense extends to material held on a data storage device (i.e., server or hard drive), a posting to a newsgroup, and postings to a chat room, but does not protect defamatory ordinary e-mail messages, instantaneous chat services, or information transmitted in the form of a broadcasting service, i.e., streaming television or radio programs.

The uniform defamation laws contain a defense of "innocent dissemination," meaning most Internet intermediaries would not be liable for defamatory matter they republish so long as they are not the author of the material and do not exercise any editorial control over the content of the matter.

21. Are there any cases where the courts enforced a judgment in libel from another jurisdiction against a publisher in your jurisdiction?

We are not aware of any such cases. It is likely that Australia would enforce a judgment from a common law country. It would be unlikely to enforce an award from a country with more restrictive libel laws than Australia.

The Foreign Judgments Act 1991 (Cth) sets out the reciprocal arrangements for the enforcement of judgments.

Chapter Notes

1. *Parmiter v. Coupland* (1840) 6 M&W 105 at 108; 151 ER 340 at 342, per Parke B.

2. *Mirror Newspapers v. World Hosts* (1979) 141 CLR 632, at 638 per Mason and Jacobs JJ.

3. Broadcasting Services Act 1992 (Cth), Section 206.

4. *Id.*

5. *Morosi v. Mirror Newspapers* (1972) 2 NSWLR 749.

6. *Ettinghausen v. Australian Consolidated Press Ltd.* (1991) 1 NSWLR 443.

7. *John Fairfax Publications Pty Ltd v. Gacic* (2007) 235 ALR 402 at 422.

8. *Alan Bond v. Paul Barry, News Limited & Anor* [2007] FCA 1484; *TCN Channel Nine Pty. Ltd. v. Ilvariy Pty. Ltd.* [2008] NSWCA 9; *ACCC v. Seven Network Limited* [2007] FCA 1505.

9. *Griffith & Anor v. ABC & Anor* [2007] NSWSC 711.

10. *Palmer Bruyn & Parker Pty Ltd. v. Parsons* (2001) 208 CLR 388 at 404-16.

11. *Kasic v. Australian Broadcasting Corporation* [1964] VR 702, 707.

12. *Lloyd v. David Syme & Co. Ltd.* (1985) 3NSWLR 778.

13. *Andrews v. John Fairfax & Sons Ltd.* [1980] 2 NSWLR 225.

14. *Channel Seven Sydney Pty Ltd. v. Parras* (2002) Australia Torts Reports 81-675 at [30]

15. *Fawcett v. John Fairfax Publications* [2008] NSWSC 139.

16. *Echo Publications v. Tucker* [2007] NSWCA 73.

17. *Jerry Lee Bennette v. Cohen* [2007] NSWSC 739.

18. See *Lange v. Australian Broadcasting Corporation* (1997) 198 CLR 520.

19. *Reynolds v. Times Newspapers* [2001] 2 AC 127

20. *Dow Jones & Co Inc v. Jameel* [2005] EWCA Civ 75; (2005) 149 S.J.L.B. 181 Times, February 14, 2005.

21. *Herald and Weekly Times Ltd. v. Popovic* [2003] VSCA 161.

22. *Fawcett v. John Fairfax Publications* [2008] NSWSC 139.

23. *Channel Seven Adelaide Pty Ltd v. Manock* (2007) 241 ALR 468.

24. *Hore–Lacy v. Cleary and Allen and Unwin* [2007] VSCA 314.

25. *Carson v. John Fairfax* (1993) 178 CLR 44, at 66. The Australian Press Council (APC) provides a forum for complaints about and against the press based on a "Statement of Principles." In considering complaints, the APC will consider whether the publication has made amends "for publishing information that is found to be harmfully inaccurate by printing, promptly and with appropriate prominence, such retraction, correction, explanation or apology as will neutralise the damage so far as possible." The APC cannot impose sanctions or remedies.

26. *Macquarie Radio Network v. Dent*, [2007] NSWCA 261.

27. See, e.g., *Hinch v. Attorney General* (Vic) (No.2) 164 CLR 15 and

Attorney General (NSW) v. TCN Channel Nine Pty Ltd. (1990) 20 NSWLR 368.

28. *State of Victoria v. Nine Network*, [2007] VSC 431 514.

29. *Channel Seven Perth Pty Ltd. v. 'S'* [2007] WASCA 122.

30. *Jane Doe v. ABC.*

31. Privacy Act 1988 (Cth), Section 7B(4).

32. *Obeid v. John Fairfax Publications Pty Ltd.* [2006] NSWSC 1059.

33. *Harvey & McManus v. County Court of Victoria* [2006] VSC 293.

34. *Dow Jones & Company Inc. v. Gutnick* (2002) 210 CLR 575.

35. *Frawley v. State NSW* [2006] NSWSC 248.

36. *Cooper v. Universal Music* [2006] 156 FCR 380.

37. *Macquarie Bank Ltd v. Berg* [1999] Aust. Defamation Reports 53, 035.

38. *DPP v. Mr X*, Unreported, Supreme Court of Victoria, 12 February 2008.

39. *Telstra Corporation Pty Limited v. Premier Media Group Pty. Ltd. & Anor* [2007] FCA 568.

CHAPTER **5**

China

VINCENT WANG AND EDWARD J. DAVIS
WITH MONICA PA
Davis Wright Tremaine LLP

Davis Wright Tremaine LLP
Suite 640 East Tower
1376 Nanjing Xi Road, Shanghai 200040
Phone: 011-86-21-6279-8560
Fax: 011-86-21-6279-8547
www.dwt.com
vincentwang@dwt.com

Davis Wright Tremaine LLP
1633 Broadway
New York, NY 10019
Phone: 212-489-8230
Fax: 212-489-8340
www.dwt.com
eddavis@dwt.com

Introduction to the Chinese Legal System

The Chinese legal system is based on a civil code that has expanded dramatically in recent decades. New laws have been issued on specific topics as the government has perceived needs to arise. The laws often reflect the influence of other modern legal systems, as well as some aspects of traditional Chinese law and the primary role of the Communist Party, a role that is enshrined in the Constitution of the People's Republic of China. The government closely controls and regulates the media and owns many of the media outlets. (This chapter's appendix describes some ramifications of the government's involvement.) Although the private law of defamation and privacy may not be as extensively developed in China as in some other countries, the laws governing defamation and mass communication are evolving rapidly.

The legal rights of parties to defamation cases are governed by the Constitution, the Criminal Law, the General Principles of Civil Law, and "judicial interpretations" issued by the People's Supreme Court. The Supreme Court's judicial interpretations explain and clarify the application of broadly worded statutes to specific situations—often based on the facts of actual cases—to provide guidance for lower courts. They are viewed as definitive. In 1993 and 1998, the Supreme Court issued judicial interpretations that addressed questions regarding defamation. In addition, the Supreme Court has issued "replies" in response to questions presented by lower courts regarding particular defamation cases. Decisions made by lower courts in many cases have been reported, but, because China does not employ the common law system, the decisions in individual cases serve as references rather than binding precedents.

1. What is the locally accepted definition of libel?

Chinese law protects the right to reputation more broadly than U.S. law does. The Chinese Constitution provides that "[t]he personal dignity of citizens of the People's Republic of China is inviolable. Insult, libel, false accusation or false incrimination directed against citizens by any means is prohibited."[1] Legal action may be taken based on acts that most courts worldwide would recognize as defamation: denigrating the character of another by publishing false statements of fact. Going further, however, Chinese law punishes speech that is often not actionable in many Western nations: tarnishing the reputation of another with malice, or harming someone's reputation by way of insult.[2] Insulting statements may be found actionable even if they do not contain false statements of fact. Derogatory words such as "shameless," "bastard," "monster," "hooligan," "presumptuous," "rotten," and "human scum" have been cited as examples of actionable insults.[3]

Criminal proceedings may be brought for public insults and defamation based on the knowing publication of false statements, with penalties of up to three years in prison, surveillance, and loss of political rights.[4] The State prosecution department generally does not initiate criminal libel proceedings unless the victim presses for them, but prosecutions are not unknown. Leftist activists in the city of Zhengzhou were prosecuted for a commemorative essay about Mao Zedong that was posted on a website and distributed in leaflets in the city's business district on the anniversary of Mao's death. The essay criticized the increasing capitalism of Chinese society and criticized former Chinese leaders Deng Xiaoping and Jiang Zemin for allowing "capitalist-roaders" to get rich while China's workers suffered poverty, pollution, and poor health. The court sentenced both the writer and the distributor of the leaflets to three years' detention for defaming Jiang Zemin. (The court held that criminal charges for defaming Deng Xiaoping could not be maintained because he was no longer living.)[5] Where the interests of the State are not at stake, criminal prosecution is much less likely.[6]

As a general matter, the Supreme Court has directed judges to consider the following issues before a finding of defamation may be made:

1. whether the reputation of the plaintiff has been harmed;
2. whether the activities of the defendant were in violation of the law;

3. whether the illegal activities caused damage to the plaintiff's reputation; and
4. whether the defendant was at fault.[7]

2. Is libel-by-implication recognized, or, in the alternative, must the complained-of words alone defame the plaintiff?

Chinese courts have not readily recognized libel-by-implication. A good illustration of the difficulty for plaintiffs came in a case decided in 2000.[8] Two newspapers published a news story praising a young man for the life-saving support he provided for an elderly lady. The article stated that all the woman's children had died and that she was living in misery and distress before the young man began supporting her. In fact, the woman had two daughters who were alive. One of her daughters was living in another city and could not conveniently visit and take care of her mother on a regular basis. The other daughter was living in the same city as her mother, but she was living in poverty herself and could visit her mother only on national holidays and at times when her mother was ill. When the two daughters read the news story, they thought it implied that they were bad daughters who did not treat their own mother well, in addition to stating falsely that they had died. They sued the newspapers for defamation, but judgment was rendered in favor of the newspapers. Although the court agreed that part of the news story was untrue (the statement that the children had all died), it held that the plaintiffs failed to prove that their reputation was harmed in any way by the untrue statement. The court's decision emphasized that the article focused on the young man who was being praised and that readers would interpret it as intended to praise him rather than to criticize the woman's daughters. They were not even named and were in fact asserted to be dead.

It is possible, however, that courts may entertain claims based on libel by implication. One instance, unreported in the law journals, involved the author Yang Mo. An article reported that Yang had said in an interview that he met then U.S. President George H.W. Bush in 1989 when Bush visited China. Yang alleged that the article defamed him because, although it would be an honor to meet the U.S. president, in fact Yang had not met him, had not been interviewed for the article, and had never said he met President Bush. The article, therefore, made him look like a boastful liar. Yang won the lawsuit.[9] His victory indicates that courts may be open to claims of libel by implication if plaintiffs can provide evidence of extrinsic facts that will render words defamatory in the minds of certain readers, even though the statements look innocuous on their own.

3. May corporations sue for libel?

Yes. Publicly traded companies, limited liability companies, governmental agencies, nonprofit institutions, associations, and schools may all sue for libel. Suits are often filed over reports that a company's products are of inferior quality, unfairly high in price, or so poorly made that they compromise the quality of other products into which they are incorporated.

4. Is product disparagement recognized, and if so, how does that differ from libel?

Yes, product disparagement is recognized. The same fundamental legal principles apply to claims of product disparagement and defamation, but additional procedural options are available for product disparagement claims under administrative law.

Product disparagement claims are governed by the Anti-Unfair Competition Law (1993). A victim of product disparagement may file a complaint in court or submit a complaint to the relevant administrative agency, usually the State Administration of Industry and Commerce (SAIC), which polices commercial markets in China. The SAIC conducts an investigation and, if product disparagement is determined to have occurred, may impose fines. In addition to assessing fines to be paid to the government, the SAIC may also require payment of damages to the complainant, including costs incurred in investigating the unfair business practice. Either side may appeal the administrative determination to court.

Administrative complaints are ordinarily filed by business competitors. In the event that a media defendant—not a competitor—is alleged to have defamed a product, a civil action for damages would be appropriate. Such a suit would not significantly differ from a suit for defamation. In fact, the Supreme Court recognized, in its 1998 interpretation, that defamation law may be used to address losses suffered in manufacturing, distribution, and other business operations if criticisms or comments in the media regarding the quality of products or services are not "basically true."[10] The Supreme Court specified that such losses may be measured by the value of products returned or contracts canceled, or other pertinent evidence of losses or reduced profits.

A 2007 decision by a Beijing district court illustrates how Chinese libel law has been applied to product disparagement.[11] 360 Safe Network Technology Co., Ltd. (360 Safe) was held to have disparaged certain online search software created and distributed by the Baidu companies, which provide online information services in China. 360 Safe's "anti-badware" software identified the search software developed by Baidu as malicious software and deleted it from 360 Safe's customer's computers, but 360 Safe could not provide evidence sufficient to prove that Baidu's software was in fact malicious. Baidu demanded an apology and 2.55 million yuan ($363,403) as compensation. The court found that 360 Safe had damaged the reputation of Baidu and the reputation of its products by classifying them as harmful without sufficient factual and legal basis. 360 Safe was required to post a written apology approved by the court on its website, but the court imposed a judgment of only 100,000 yuan ($14,251), including costs.

5. Must an individual be clearly identified (by name or photograph) to sue for libel? Can a group of persons sue for libel, even though not named?

It is not necessary for an individual to be identified by name or photograph, and a group of persons can sue for libel although their names are not used in the allegedly defamatory material. Such questions arise regularly in China, perhaps because of the practice of expressing social and political criticism indirectly, through ostensibly fictional stories and historical allegories, to avoid the risk of censorship. Pursuant to the Supreme Court's judicial interpretations of 1993, the publication of insults, defamation, or private facts may be actionable even if the real name and identity of the person referred to are not provided, so long as readers can conclude that a specific identifiable person is being referred to and the reputation of that person is harmed by the reference.[12]

In a case in the 1990s, the defendant wrote a novel set at a time before the Chinese Revolution of 1949, which was published in a newspaper as a serial. The physical characteristics of a drug dealer, a brothel boss, and a hooligan in the novel matched those of three workplace colleagues with whom the author did not get along, but the author did not use their names and he changed their social backgrounds in the book. He did everything, however, to insult and denigrate the three characters in the novel. When his three colleagues read parts of the novel, they recognized their portrayals and asked the newspaper not to continue publishing the story, but the newspaper refused. They sued the author and the newspaper, and they won.[13] According to the judgment, although the three characters and the novel were made up, the descriptions of the three characters were so detailed that it was easy for people who knew the plaintiffs to recognize that the three characters were meant to represent them. They had been shown in a false and insulting light, and the author was therefore found liable for defamation. The newspaper was held liable, as well, although it did not know before it began to publish the installments that any characters would evoke real people, because it continued publishing the novel after being informed by the plaintiffs that the story contained defamatory depictions of them.

On the other hand, if a character is not based on a real person but just happens to be similar in some ways to that person, a defamation suit would not succeed. In another case of alleged libel in fiction, an author created a novel about malpractice in a hospital after gathering information from several hospitals.[14] All the names, including the names of the hospital and all the characters in the novel, were fictitious. After publication of the novel, the director of one of the hospitals the author had visited to gather information filed a lawsuit against the author for defamation, claiming that the character of the director of the fictitious hospital was meant to represent him. After reading the novel, the court held that it would be impossible for anyone, even someone who knew the plaintiff well, to think that he was the hospital director portrayed in the novel. According to the judgment, the descriptions of the hospital and the director were too general, and there were readily apparent differences between the real and fictional hospital and director.

In another case, not involving a work that was presented as fiction, an article reported erroneously that human flesh was used as a filling for buns in an unnamed restaurant.[15] Because the article did not refer to any identifiable person or restaurant, the report could not be actionable.

In a 2006 case, however, a group police department and a TV station in Anhui Province were held liable for defamation after the station broadcast a videotape provided by the police of a lineup during a rape investigation. Six male minors who were not involved in the incident appeared in the lineup.[16] Although their names were not used and their images appeared on screen for only two seconds, the two-second exposure was sufficient for people familiar with those six individuals to recognize them. The face of the actual suspect was shown later in the broadcast, but the court held that a false impression was nonetheless created with respect to all six others in the lineup because the broadcast did not make it clear that they were there only because they were similar in height and appearance to the suspect, rather than because one or more of them had some involvement with the case or with the police.

6. What is the fault standard(s) applied to libel?

a. Does the fault standard depend on the fame or notoriety of the plaintiff?

In China, the defendant's fault in a libel case is judged by an objective standard of negligence: whether the defendant has exercised the due care that would be exercised by someone in the same profession or by a person with comparable knowledge and experience acting in good faith.

Regardless of whether the defendant actually anticipated the consequences of publishing the statements or not (i.e., whether the defendant actually knew something was false and defamatory or knew it might be false and defamatory), the defendant is deemed to be capable of anticipating the consequences if others in the same profession or position would anticipate them and exercise greater care.

b. Is there a heightened fault standard or privilege for reporting on matters of public concern or public interest?

The fault standard does not depend on the fame or notoriety of the plaintiff, nor is there a heightened standard or privilege for reporting on matters of public concern or public interest. However, commentators have noted an unresolved tension between the constitutional protection for reputation, on the one hand, and the constitutional guarantees of freedom of speech, freedom of the press, and freedom to criticize any State organ or State official, on the other.[17]

A good example of the application of the negligence standard comes from a commentary on a case in 1988 provided by a judge of the Supreme Court of China in a treatise he authored.[18] A newspaper published an article about a fire in an apartment next door to the apartment of the vice secretary of the Politics and Law Commission of the county. (The Politics and Law Commission ensures that the Chinese Communist Party's policies are fully implemented in government law enforcement departments.) The article said that, at the time of the fire, the vice secretary kept his door closed and neither helped fight the fire nor allowed the firefighters to take water from his home. The vice secretary sued for defamation. In his complaint, he explained that he was doing carpentry work at the time of the fire and did not know there was a fire in the neighborhood. He closed his door to prevent the wind from blowing the sawdust everywhere in his home. The judge of the Supreme Court commented that, although the criticism in the article was not well founded, at the time the article was written it was impossible for the author and the newspaper to guess what the vice secretary was doing at home when there was a fire next door. Therefore, neither of them knew or should have known that the article would defame the vice secretary. As a result, the author and the newspaper were not at fault, and no liability for defamation could be found in the case.

In contrast, in the 2006 Anhui case involving the police lineup described above, the court found the television station liable for defamation even though the broadcast did not state that any of the plaintiffs had been suspected in the crime and even though the police who provided the videotape had failed to notify the station that the six boys requested that the video not be used.[19] The court held that the station was liable because it should have anticipated that the general public would not know how the lineup had been organized and therefore should have either blocked the minors' faces on the screen or clarified that they were in the lineup simply because they were similar in height and appearance to the rape suspect.

A similar example of a finding of journalistic fault came in the 1994 case of Song Jianping.[20] Police authorities informed a newspaper that they had detained Ms. Song and her husband for scalping tickets. The newspaper printed a front-page story about them without contacting Ms. Song. It turned out that Ms. Song was a telephone operator, not a ticket scalper, and was not married. A ticket scalper had used Ms. Song's name when the police detained her. The newspaper and the police were found negligent and held liable for defamation. The facts that led to the finding of negligence in the *Song* case were not fully explained, beyond the fact that the newspaper had not contacted Ms. Song.

In a string of cases in 2006 involving matters of clear public concern, the courts reached judgments for the plaintiffs without apparent reference to any heightened fault standard for such matters. Fang Shimin, a well-known Chinese critic of scientific and academic misconduct who has exposed many cases of inaccuracy, fraud, and plagiarism on his website and in other publications, was found liable in cases in Beijing, Xi'an, and Wuhan. In July 2006, a court in Wuhan held Fang liable for defaming a professor of surgery at Huazhong University, after Fang accused the professor of exaggerating his credentials. Fang was ordered to make a public apology and pay 30,000 yuan (US$3,750) in damages.[21] The Wuhan Intermediate Court affirmed the decision.[22] On November 21, 2006, the Beijing Intermediate Court ruled that Fang libeled Liu Zihua, a scholar who had claimed that he used an ancient philosophical theory to predict the existence of a planet in the late 1930s.[23] Fang called Liu's theory a fraud and reported that a famous astronomer had branded Liu "a big cheat." Liu had died in 1992, but his wife and son sued Fang for libel. The court held that although Fang could legitimately criticize Liu's theory, he committed defamation by repeating the statement calling Liu a big cheat, and the court ordered Fang to pay Liu's family 20,000 yuan (U.S. $2,500).[24] On November 22, 2006, Fang lost another libel case, for criticizing Xi'an Fanyi University in an article in *Beijing Sci-Tech Report.* The article alleged that a U.S. report stating that the university was one of China's ten most outstanding universities and that its president was one of the most respected university presidents was a "self-paid advertisement" and that the poor English of the report cast doubt on its credibility. Fang and the publisher of *Beijing Sci-Tech Report* were ordered to pay 150,000 yuan (U.S. $18,750) to the university.

In defamation cases where fault is in question, it should be possible to introduce evidence of standard journalistic practices. It has been reported that professional journalists have been added to judicial panels in some defamation cases in Hefei, Anhui Province, presumably to reflect the standards of the profession and help inform the judges as they determine what may constitute negligence.

7. Is financial news about publicly traded companies, or companies involved with government contracts, considered a matter of public interest or otherwise privileged?

Financial news is protected if it (1) is based upon true statements that do not constitute private facts or State secrets; (2) accurately reflects statements made by the publicly traded companies concerned; (3) is a republication of news reported by the Xinhua News Agency; (4) is based on official government documents that have not been amended or rescinded; or (5) qualifies as "fair comment" as elaborated below.

There have not been many court decisions to illuminate the boundaries between the confidential information of private businesses or government agencies and information that may be freely published because it is of legitimate interest to the public. Chinese enterprises fall into several categories along a spectrum from completely private to completely State-owned, and information concerning particular enterprises may be protected from disclosure as a trade secret or a State secret (both of which are protected, by separate laws). More information is becoming routinely available to the public, however, especially regarding publicly traded companies. An archive of information about all companies in China is kept by the SAIC, which maintains a publicly available database. The operations of private and State-owned enterprises and the prices they charge for their products and services are regularly reported on in the media, but the fear of lawsuits for defamation prompts most news organizations to ask all businesses involved in a news story to confirm the facts in a news report before publication. News organizations usually will not publish if a company denies the facts.

The legal definition of State secrets in China is broad enough to encompass information that would be considered of legitimate public concern elsewhere in the world. Publishers and broadcasters in China have historically been careful, therefore, especially in reporting on sensitive information about State-owned enterprises, even outside the military/security sphere. Economic data and social information can be State secrets. Information about private or State-owned enterprises that provide products or services for the military or related to State security is, of course, likely to be highly protected. For example, individuals have been prosecuted for disseminating

State secrets in cases in which employees have revealed the nature of a project on which a defense contractor is working.

Pursuant to the Law on Maintaining State Secrets (1988) and its related regulations and rules, the following matters are regarded as State secrets:

1. matters kept secret in decision-making in State affairs;
2. secret matters pertaining to the military forces and defense activities;
3. secret matters concerning diplomatic activities, foreign affairs, and matters on which the State has an obligation of confidentiality to another country;
4. secret matters pertaining to the economy and social development;
5. secret matters of scientific technology;
6. secret matters pertaining to State security activities and the investigation of crime; and
7. secret matters as determined by the governmental agencies dealing with State secrets. (Internal reviewers employed by newspapers may consult the agencies for such determinations prior to publication.)

The definition of "secret" matters is broad. Information may be "secret" if its release or dissemination would:

1. undermine the strength and defense capacity of the State;
2. affect the unity of the State, the unity between ethnic groups, and social stability;
3. damage the political and economic interests of the State in its external activities;
4. affect the security of State leaders or important officials of foreign countries;
5. hinder major State safety and security work;
6. reduce the reliability of, or render ineffective, measures for the maintenance of State secrets;
7. weaken the economic, scientific, or technological strength of the State; or
8. deprive State agencies of the safeguards necessary for the exercise of their lawful power.

Some documents containing State secrets are marked with a "secret" or "super-secret" chop (an official signature stamp), but others are not, and their status is subject to the determination of relevant government authorities. Journalists working in China develop a feeling for whether the State will object to disclosure in certain circumstances. The one foolproof clue that a document has been classified as containing State secrets is the mark of a chop with the characters "confidential" or "super-confidential" on it.

Disclosure of the confidential content of such documents is forbidden, and it is doubtful that the fact that another party has already disclosed such material may be relied upon in defense.

China has, however, enacted regulations on the freedom of information, the Provisions on the Disclosure of Government Information, scheduled to take effect on May 1, 2008. Under the regulations, government agencies are required to release information on a range of topics of public interest, and a mechanism for requesting disclosure of particular information is available. Each government department must compile information directories and respond to requests for information within thirty days. The regulations, nonetheless, require government officials to block the release of any information judged to be a State secret or confidential commercial information and any information that would harm State security, economic activity, public safety, or social stability, or infringe on an individual's privacy if it were released. The regulations provide that individuals who believe their interests have been harmed by the disclosure of confidential information may sue for compensation.[25] It is expected that government agencies will be allowed broad discretion not to release information.

8. Is there a recognized protection for opinion or "fair comment" on matters of public concern?

No specific provision of Chinese law protects opinion or "fair comment," but protection may be accorded at the discretion of judges.

In a treatise on media torts, a judge of the Supreme Court who is responsible for trials of civil cases has explained that, to be protected, an expression of opinion must be on a matter of public concern, and it must be fair.[26] Generally, the following subjects may be held to be of public concern, depending on the circumstances: (1) the policies and measures of the State and of local governments and legislative and judicial bodies (the Constitution enunciates a right to criticize the government, in Article 41); (2) the decisions and activities of enterprises, companies, institutions, and associations, to the extent that they relate to the public interest; (3) scholarly, literary, and artistic performances or works; (4) public figures and newsworthy events (there is no definition of public figures and newsworthy events, so the determination is subject to the discretion of the court); and (5) major events such as natural disasters, major accidents, or serious crimes that attract public attention and therefore merit analysis.

For an expression of opinion or comment to be deemed fair, the following requirements should be met: (1) the comment must be made in good faith, which means that the opinion is honestly held by the commentator, whose standing is impartial and fair; (2) the facts on which the opinion or comment are based must be true; and (3) in the case of opinion and commentary on literary, scholarly and artistic works, the expression should qualify as discussion or debate regarding literary, artistic, or scholarly value, and not be defamation in disguise.

The facts on which critical comments are based need not be literally true, only substantially accurate. In one case, three party officials were criticized for spending 117 yuan (US$16.67) of public money on a private feast, when it was actually a group of four officials who had spent 112 yuan (US$15.96) on the feast.[27] The court held that the inaccuracy was not significant enough to render the criticism actionable. In another case, officials in a municipality in Hunan Province sued a newspaper for reporting that they had spurned requests for help after a murder took place, sticking their heads out the window and saying that no one was in their office.[28] The windows were built in a way that would have prevented anyone from putting a head out, but the officials did not prevail, presumably because the gist of the claim was that they were actually in the office and did not respond to the requests for help, which apparently was true.

In addition to the two cases cited above, the *Beijing Evening News*, for instance, was sued by a soft drink factory that had been fined by the government for poor sanitary maintenance. The article said the factory was "full of flies," while the government report had referred to only "a few flies."[29] The suit failed, despite the exaggeration, but the court warned the newspaper about reckless use of words.

Most press entities in China are arms of the government. They are often shielded from liability for critical statements they publish, particularly if such statements reflect policy initiatives of the State.

9. Are there any requirements upon a plaintiff, such as demand for retraction or right of reply, and if so, what impact do they have?

No such requirements are imposed on a libel plaintiff under Chinese law. However, not properly responding to a demand for retraction may trigger liability under certain circumstances, particularly on the Internet if the defendant is the website owner and not the poster of the allegedly libelous material. (See Questions 19–20, below.)

10. Is there a privilege for quoting or reporting on:

a. Papers filed in court?

Yes. Pursuant to the Supreme Court's 1998 judicial interpretation on the trial of defamation cases, there is a privilege for reporting on official court documents and the public actions of government agencies so long as such reporting is "objective and accurate" and does not reveal State secrets.[30]

However, if a court decision is later reversed or the court paper quoted is subsequently corrected, the quoting or reporting party must report the reversal or correction in later editions. Otherwise, if the original report damages the reputation of the parties concerned, and the correct information goes unreported, the privilege will be lost.

A 1996 decision illustrates this principle. An official in the prosecutor's office of Guangxi Province issued a press release to a newspaper based upon documents prepared by the prosecutor regarding the arrest of two judges who were alleged to have committed the crime of official malpractice.[31] Afterward, however, the two judges were found not guilty and their acquittal was recorded by the court. The official and the newspaper did not update or correct the previous press release. The two judges sued the official and the newspaper, and won. The court reasoned that there was no wrong when the official and the newspaper first reported that the two judges were arrested based on papers filed in court. However, the official and the newspaper were held to be at fault for not correcting their previous damaging reports when the judges were acquitted.

b. Government-issued documents?

Yes. Government documents or decisions may be relied upon, and their contents need not be reported with absolute accuracy, as noted above with respect to opinion and fair comment. Official newspapers, at least, have been granted some latitude, especially in reporting on behavior that the government seeks to curb. The *Liberation Army Daily*, for example, won a lawsuit over an article that claimed a young man had changed his identity to hide prior crimes of gang rape and theft.[32] Police records revealed that he had been involved in theft and hooliganism, which the court held were close enough to gang rape and theft, considering that the point of the story was that he had changed his identity to hide his police record.

Similarly, the *Wenzhou Daily* prevailed in a suit brought by a singer whom the paper had called a convicted rapist.[33] He had actually been convicted of hooliganism, not rape, but the court found that the two crimes were equally serious in the public eye. (His additional argument that he had served his sentence and should no longer be identified as an ex-convict was also rejected.) Another newspaper won a case brought by a Hong Kong businessman in 1988 over an article that criticized him for *zhapian* (a criminal offense of deception or fraud) when he had in fact been held liable for *qipian* (misrepresentation, which is not a criminal offense).[34] It remains to be seen whether foreign or nonofficial news outlets and individual defamation defendants can benefit from the same degree of latitude these newspapers have enjoyed, with their official sanction and supervision.

c. Quasi-governmental proceedings?

Government agencies, social organizations (such as the branches of the China Youth League or Women's Protection Association), enterprises (including businesses), and other institutions may not be held liable for defamation for decisions they make regarding their internal operations. For instance, the Hunan Institute of Foreign Language and Foreign Trade disciplined six students for drunkenness and sexual conduct and announced that disciplinary decision to all of its students. The court of first instance accepted the defamation case the six students filed, ruled in favor of them, and awarded them more than 200,000 yuan (US$28,502) for the harm to their reputations. An appellate court reversed, holding that the case should never have been accepted in the first place because it challenged an internal decision of the Institute. (The Case Receipt Office of a Chinese court screens all cases submitted and is responsible for rejecting cases that do not assert legitimate causes of action, before any further proceedings take place.)

If a business or institution disseminates false statements about its internal disciplinary proceedings to outsiders, however, it may be sued. Whether newspapers that correctly report those statements may be held liable remains an open question, but the result would probably depend on the degree of care shown by the publisher.

11. Is there a privilege for republishing statements made earlier by other, bona fide, reliable publications or wire services?

No. Under Chinese law, not only publishers but also republishers generally have the obligation to examine the truth of the articles they publish or republish. If a republisher does not independently examine the truth of statements or otherwise republishes them with some fault, the republisher may be held liable. However, due to the special position of the government-run Xinhua News Agency, statements issued by Xinhua may be redistributed without liability.

A 1985 case illustrates the general rule. The journal *Women's Literature* first published a news story and three other journals later republished the same story. An individual filed suit for defamation against the author, *Women's Literature,* and the three other journals.[35] The court determined that the article defamed the plaintiff and that all four journals had committed defamation by publishing or republishing it without adequately examining the truth of the story.

However, a recent decision indicates that Chinese courts may be reconsidering or abandoning the traditional rule. Golden Paper Electronic Publication Center (Golden Paper) was sued for an article on its website about the photographic work "Mao Zedong and Li Na (Mao Zedong's daughter)" because the article identified the wrong person as the author of the work, instead of naming the plaintiff's father, who was the actual author and whose reputation was allegedly harmed by the error.[36] In its defense, Golden Paper asserted that the article was a republication of an article previously published by *South Daily*, which Golden Paper had not altered, and that it should not be held liable for *South Daily*'s mistake. The trial court and the appellate court ruled that Golden Paper should not be held liable for libel for republishing the article without verifying its truth.

12. Are there any restrictions regarding reporting on:

a. Ongoing criminal investigations?

There is no statute or regulation that prohibits reporting on ongoing criminal investigations, except to the extent that such reporting may reveal State secrets. However, information published about criminal investigations must come directly from a police official authorized to share it with reporters.

b. Ongoing criminal prosecutions?

Access to courtrooms is not specifically guaranteed to reporters. The public has a right of access to judicial proceedings, except in cases involving State secrets, trade secrets, divorce, individual privacy, or crimes committed by minors, but reporters are required to request permission, in writing, to attend public court proceedings. If they are discovered taking notes or making recordings without permission, reporters may be removed from courtrooms and their notebooks, tape recorders, and video cameras may be confiscated.

Reporters often do not attend court proceedings because the courts have public relations departments that issue summaries of proceedings for the purpose of public education. If a reporter requests permission to attend a trial and report on it, permission may be granted (on the condition that the reporter report without bias and not tendentiously), but the court may also have one of its own reporters prepare a summary. Newspapers may reprint the official summaries, but courts expect to approve any revisions the newspaper may make to that summary.

c. Ongoing regulatory investigations?

There are no express restrictions, except that reporting on matters involving State secrets, which may be defined broadly, is firmly proscribed.

d. Ongoing civil litigation, or other judicial proceedings?

No, except as noted above. However, news reports of criminal or civil cases involving foreign individuals, foreign companies, or foreign subject matter are not supposed to be published before the embassy or consulate of the foreign country has been informed of a case. The relevant court or government agency should notify the embassy or consulate.

13. Are prior restraints or other prepublication injunctions available on the basis of libel or privacy, and if so, what are the standards for obtaining such relief?

No statute or regulation specifically addresses this issue. However, injunctions to cease publication of material that has been found defamatory are available, and it is reasonable to anticipate that a court may grant a prior restraint if the plaintiff proves before publication that the material is defamatory. Tight internal controls exercised by press entities generally prevent such cases from reaching the courts, and prepublication review and censorship by various State and Chinese Communist Party media agencies also help prevent the dissemination of actionable content.

Some other possible remedies for defamation in China are noted in the Appendix below, as are restrictions on publishing material on certain sensitive topics or expressing certain impermissible views.

14. Is a right of privacy recognized (either civilly or criminally)?

a. What is the definition of "private fact"?

The term "private fact" has not been defined by the law. Judges and lawyers identify private facts by applying the common meaning of the words in light of prevailing concepts of morality endorsed by society at large. The most widely accepted definition of "private facts" in China is facts of private life that a person would be not willing to have disclosed and that have nothing to do with the person's public life. What a reasonable person would deem private would probably be found private. Generally, an individual's health status, disease, disability, family life, private diary, private letters, and the like are regarded as private facts.

One category of private facts that the Supreme Court has specifically addressed resembles the old *per se* libel category of "loathsome disease." Medical and health care institutions violate the law protecting reputation if they disclose that a person suffers from gonorrhea, syphilis, AIDS, or Hansen's disease (leprosy), but they may notify relatives of such illnesses.

b. Is there a public interest or newsworthiness exception?

No public interest or newsworthiness exception is recognized. In China, unlike many Western legal systems, the right of privacy is included within the right of reputation. It is unlawful to publicly disclose private facts about an individual in oral or written form, or to publish private materials without permission, if the disclosure or publication does harm to the reputation of the party concerned. If the person's reputation is not harmed, the right of privacy will not be found to have been violated, even if private information was published.

In a 1998 case, a transsexual individual agreed to be interviewed by a news reporter and provided certain information about why he chose transsexuality.[37] However, during the visit, the individual repeatedly told the reporter that he could write a news story about him but that the report should not disclose his real name and photo. The reporter ignored those requests and published an article in a newspaper with the individual's real name and photo. The individual filed and won a lawsuit against the reporter and the newspaper that published the article.

Businesses do not have privacy rights, but they may be able to protect confidential information as trade secrets. Information about executive compensation, for instance, may be published if it is available from public filings. If the information comes from a source with a duty to keep it confidential, however, some form of trade secret protection may apply. A publisher may face liability for publishing a trade secret if the publisher knew, before publishing it, that the information was obtained by theft, threat, promise of gain, or some other unlawful or inappropriate means. As a matter of practice, when publishers receive documents disclosed without authorization, they generally contact the business entity involved and do not publish the information without its consent.

c. Is the right of privacy based in common law, statute, or constitution?

The right to privacy is based upon statutes and the Constitution. China employs the civil law system and does not recognize the concept of common law.

15. May reporters tape-record their own telephone conversations for note-taking purposes (not rebroadcast) without the consent of the other party?

There is no law prohibiting reporters from taping their own telephone conversations. However, ethical guidelines issued by the All-China Journalists Association call for journalists to use only lawful and proper means to gather news, and to respect requests made by interviewees.[38] The guidelines do not have the force of law, but courts may refer to them in deciding claims against journalists and news organizations. Reporters are therefore advised to identify themselves as reporters during telephone interviews and to honor reasonable requests made by interviewees. A recording may then serve as proof of a reporter's ethical conduct as well as evidence of the truth of what is ultimately reported and of the care the journalist exercised. Television reporters should note that there is a general government policy disfavoring hidden-camera videotaping.[39] Videotaping in public places rather than private homes or businesses presumably reduces the risk of a claim for invasion of privacy.

16. If it is permissible to record such tapes, may they be broadcast without permission?

There is no express prohibition on broadcasting secretly recorded tapes of interviews, but, as noted above, hidden-camera recordings are risky. News reports using hidden-camera footage may be censored from domestic broadcasts, although such footage is sometimes included in official news reports, often orchestrated in conjunction with law enforcement activities. If nothing that is broadcast will harm anyone's reputation and the statements broadcast are true, there should be no liability. But both the taper and the broadcaster may be held liable if material that is broadcast is found to violate the right of reputation. A legal interpretation issued by the Supreme Court provides that a news source is liable as well as the publisher if the source actively provides news material or expressly permits it to be published and the material is defamatory.

17. Is there a recognized evidentiary privilege preventing the disclosure of confidential sources relied upon by reporters?

There is no such provision in Chinese law.

18. In the event that legal papers are served upon the newsroom (such as a civil complaint), are there any particular warnings about accepting service of which we should be aware?

In the event that a civil complaint is served, the newsroom may accept it or refuse it. If the newsroom wishes to accept it, the chairman, legal representative, or other person authorized to receive documents from outside the organization on behalf of the newsroom must sign the receipt in his or her name and record the date of service. The delivery person may be told if the newsroom does not wish to accept service. However, documents will still be deemed to have been served if the delivery person records the refusal to accept service and leaves them at the newsroom's registered business address before a witness who signs the service sheet to attest that service was made.

If the complaint names the news organization as defendant, not accepting service would probably be useless. If, on the other hand, the complaint names only an individual employee or independent contractor, it is not necessary for the news organization to accept service on the individual's behalf. Accepting service for the employee or independent contractor will not make the organization a defendant, but there is usually no reason for an organization to accept service on an employee's or contractor's behalf, especially if the organization itself is not a party. An individual employee may also refuse to accept service. However, a complaint will be deemed to have been served if the refusal is properly witnessed and documented.

In the event that a request for cooperation in an administrative or criminal investigation is served, you should make sure that there are two investigators present and check their identity certificates to see whether the certificates identify the particular investigators and whether the identity certificates are properly sealed. You should also check whether the legal request for cooperation is properly signed and chopped. If you have any questions, you may make a call to the investigators' bureau chief for confirmation. If everything is genuine, you must cooperate with the investigation.

19. Has your jurisdiction applied established media law to Internet publishers?

Yes. The same rules have been applied to Internet publishers, as a 2001 case illustrates.[40] The plaintiff and the defendant met each other at a party held by the users of chat rooms. Afterward, the defendant began to post articles in one of the chat rooms that insulted and defamed the plaintiff, using one of his screen names and the plaintiff's screen name. The plaintiff sued, and the court held that, although the space on the Internet may be virtual, the actions taken by people on the Internet are real. The plaintiff's reputation was damaged in the chat room and among people the plaintiff and defendant knew, who knew their real names. The defendant was held liable for defamation and was ordered to post an apology in the chat room and on its website and to pay 1,000 yuan ($140) for the plaintiff's mental anguish, as well as court costs.

In addition to applying established media law principles to Internet publishers, the Chinese government has promulgated several new laws to regulate Internet content specifically. The Ministry of Information Industry and the State Council issued Provisional Rules for the Administration of Online Publishing, which became effective in 2002. Regulations governing Internet news information services were promulgated in 2005, and new regulations governing the broadcast of news or other audio or video content through the Internet (State Administrative Rules on Internet Video/Audio Services) went into effect in January 2008.

The regulatory scheme requires Internet service providers and online publishing entities to monitor political, social, and security-related content, filter users' searches, block various websites, delete objectionable content, and monitor e-mail traffic. The government also employs a sophisticated firewall system, through which it monitors Internet content and blocks access to websites deemed dangerous or offensive.

20. If established media law has been applied to Internet publishers, are there any ways in which Internet publishers (including chat room operators) have to meet different standards?

Much like the regulations governing the content of newspapers and other periodicals (see Appendix, below), the Internet regulations prohibit, among other things, the posting or transmission of content that harms the honor of the nation, spreads rumors or disturbs the social order, defames or insults third parties, or incites illegal assemblies, associations, or gatherings that disturb the social order.[41] An online publisher must immediately delete any content that violates these provisions, retain relevant records, and provide them to the State if there is an investigation into the publication of the offending Web activity. The regulations likewise require online publishers to retain copies of all content and the Internet addresses of all sources of news information that they post and transmit.[42]

Operators of websites or bulletin-board or chat-room services are expected to delete any material posted by third parties that is insulting or defamatory on its face. If an operator is notified of defamatory material that it did not previously identify as defamatory, and is provided with evidence to prove that the content is unlawful, the operator must delete the material or risk liability for defamation.

A 2007 case illustrates the application of these principles.[43] Shangtou Yi Xun Network Co., Ltd. (Yi Xun) operates a bulletin-board service (BBS) on which a user posted an article that allegedly contained false statements about a GPS product manufactured by the plaintiff, Shantou Sai Ge Che Sheng Navigation Equipment Co., Ltd. (Che Sheng). Che Sheng notified Yi Xun, the BBS operator, about the disparaging article, but it did not provide any evidence to support its claim. After Yi Xun failed to take down the article, Che Sheng filed suit. The court found for Yi Xun because the challenged article was not disparaging on its face, and Yi Xun simply operated the website on which the offending article was posted by someone else. Even after Yi Xun was notified of the article's potentially defamatory character, the court held, it was under no obligation to delete the article absent evidence that the article was false.

21. Are there any cases where the courts enforced a judgment in libel from another jurisdiction against a publisher in your jurisdiction?

None have been found. Chinese courts may enforce judgments rendered in jurisdictions with which China has entered into treaties providing for the enforcement of judgments on a reciprocal basis.

Appendix

Navigating Media Law in China

Because the Chinese media and legal system are so different from media and legal systems elsewhere, many basic principles and practices in Chinese journalism differ significantly from those of the rest of the world. The following are some differences worth keeping in mind.

1. Parties

In China, civil defamation claims may be asserted on behalf of individuals who are deceased. Suits may be filed by spouses, parents, children, siblings, grandparents, or grandchildren. Criminal charges may not be pursued to protect the reputation of someone who is deceased.

In media cases, both author and publisher may be sued, unless the author is employed by or is under the administrative control of the publisher, in which case the Supreme Court has indicated that only the publisher may be named as a defendant. News sources may be sued as well as media outlets, but only if the sources have authorized the media to publish the news the sources provided.

2. Remedies

In addition to awards of damages and injunctions to cease publication, courts may order defendants to apologize and to publish retractions, clarifications, and apologies to the same extent that the original statements were published, in order to restore the reputation of the defamed party. Pursuant to the 1998 interpretation of the Supreme Court, courts will examine and approve retractions, clarifications, and apologies before they are published. If a defendant fails or refuses to print a correction or clarification, the court may publicly announce its decision to help remedy the damage the defamation caused. The regulations governing Chinese newspapers and periodicals, for instance, provide that, "[w]here the lawful rights and interests of a citizen, a legal person, or some other organizations are infringed upon due to the false and untruthful contents of a newspaper [or periodical], its publishing unit shall make public correction, eliminate the effects, and bear civil liabilities according to law."[44] Private parties may sue, or State media regulators may require the publication of corrections to protect the public interest.[45]

3. Regulation of Domestic Media

Media organizations may not operate in China without government permission. Prior authorization and a license from the appropriate State agency are required for publishing, printing, copying, or distributing books, newspapers, periodicals, or audio-visual publications.[46] The publication of a work without a license is considered an illegal publication. Similarly, only entities and individuals with prior State approval to publish information over the Internet may do so.[47]

Three primary State agencies—the General Administration of Press and Publication (GAPP), which regulates periodicals and books; the Press and Publication Administration (PPA), which specifically supervises newspaper publishing; and the State Administration of Radio, Film and Television, which regulates radio, television, satellite, and Internet broadcasts in China—are responsible for promulgating regulations for the media, issuing the mandatory operating licenses, and censoring and regulating content.[48] The Central Propaganda Department of the Communist Party is also responsible for monitoring the content of Chinese print, radio, and television media, and it issues weekly faxes and other bulletins that delineate banned topics for domestic media agencies. The Ministry for Information Industry is responsible for licensing and regulating Internet service providers, and the State Council Information Office also reviews online content.

Chinese reporters and editors must hold press cards issued by the PPA or the GAPP, which must be renewed every five years.[49] A press card may be revoked if a reporter or publisher fails to "respect and follow government-issued laws, regulations, and professional journalist ethics." Professionals working in the media must also meet certain occupational requirements, and directors and editors in chief of publications must pass State examinations.[50]

Many media organizations in China are directly owned or controlled by the State or the Communist Party. The Xinhua News Agency, which is controlled by the Communist Party's Central Propaganda Department, operates as the spokesperson for the central government and is the primary source of official news. China Radio International, China Central Television, *Guangming Daily*, and *People's Daily* are also directly controlled by the Central Publicity Department and communicate official government news. Xinhua News Agency has the additional responsibility of supervising the release of news and information in China by foreign news agencies.

4. Regulation of Foreign Media

a. Foreign News Agencies

If news or information from a foreign news agency is used in a publication, broadcast, or electronic transmission in China, the user must clearly indicate the source of the information. This requirement of attribution is apparently intended to warn the reader that the information comes from a foreign source.[51]

The activities of foreign news agencies in China are governed by the Regulations Concerning Foreign Journalists and Permanent Offices of Foreign News Agencies (1990) and Measures for the Administration of the Release of News and Information in China by Foreign News Agencies (2006). Foreign news agencies may establish offices in China subject to the approval of the News Administration Office of the Ministry of Foreign Affairs. As mentioned above, Xinhua controls the release and distribution of news and information from foreign news agencies in China, but it may do so indirectly. Xinhua may approve a Chinese agent to distribute a foreign agency's news and information in China. The approved local agent becomes responsible for daily editorial oversight, but Xinhua may work directly with foreign news agencies itself and retains the right to censor materials disseminated by any foreign news agency in China.

In addition to establishing a structure of control over foreign news agencies, the 2006 Measures also restate some of the general restrictions on content described in Section 5, below, which apply to all publications in China.[52]

In April 2007, in its first review of foreign news agencies since the promulgation of the 2006 Measures, Xinhua authorized four foreign news agencies to release news and information in China: Reuters Asia/Pacific Limited, JiJi Press of Japan, ET Net Limited of Hong Kong, and NNA China Ltd. In September 2007, three additional overseas news agencies were authorized to release news and information in China: RIA of Russia, Sipa of France, and EYEDA of Japan.[53]

b. Foreign Journalists

Foreign journalists are permitted to enter China for news collection and reporting, subject to certain approval requirements and restrictions.[54] To stay in China for more than six months, a journalist must obtain a J-1 visa, for a foreign resident correspondent. For a visit of less than six months for the purpose of reporting a news story, taking professional photographs, creating a documentary, or shooting a film, a J-2 visa is required. Both J visas require the prior approval of a Chinese embassy, Chinese consulate, or other competent Chinese government authority. The journalist may be required to present a CV, an itinerary, a description of the project planned, a list of any equipment to be imported, and an invitation or assignment letter from the entity that has commissioned the work in China, which can be the journalist's foreign employer.

Foreign journalists are subject to restrictions on their travel and other activities in China. They may have to obtain prior permission from the

Information Department of the Ministry of Foreign Affairs or other authorities to travel outside the areas where they are based, to visit certain restricted areas, or to conduct interviews.[55] The Chinese government may also monitor the movements and communications of foreign correspondents. Hotel clerks may notify local public security bureaus when guests with J visas check in.[56]

All foreign journalists (and news agencies) are required to "observe journalistic ethics" and are forbidden to engage in activities incompatible with their status or detrimental to China's national security, reputation, or social and public interest. Their journalistic activities in China may be suspended for violations, and their visas and licenses may be revoked.[57]

Foreign journalists who want to travel to China for a personal vacation and apply for tourist visas may be asked to provide letters from their employer attesting to the fact that they will not be doing any reporting during the visit.

5. Sensitive Topics

The media in China are subject to direct government censorship, but many news organizations are able to operate without day-to-day supervision because the government has established lists of "restricted" and "prohibited" topics to guide their treatment of sensitive issues.

The list of outright prohibitions, summarized below, is directed generally at preventing the expression of particular views. Editors in chief are responsible for ensuring that "prohibited" articles are not published. The penalties for publishing prohibited items may include large fines, suspension or revocation of the license to publish, and criminal prosecution.

"Restricted" topics, also outlined below, are general subjects on which views the government considers dangerous could be expressed. Articles about such subjects are not banned outright, but publishers are required to submit the articles to be reviewed and "recorded" through the local branch of the Press and Publication Administration prior to publication. The approval and "recording" of an article protects the publisher from punishment for statements made on a potentially perilous topic and also serves as surveillance radar for the government and the Communist Party. Publishers make their own decisions about which articles to submit for review and recording, but the rules require approval and recording before publishing on one of the restricted topics.

a. Prohibited articles

The State Council, in its Regulations on the Administration of Newspaper Publishing (2005) and Regulations on the Administration of

Periodical Publishing (2005), has listed the following types of articles that may not be published:

- Articles that oppose basic principles set out in the Constitution of the PRC. An example might be an article asserting that men are superior to women and therefore should have greater rights. (Equal rights and status are guaranteed by the Constitution.)
- Articles that may do harm to the integrity, sovereignty, and completeness of the dominion of the PRC. Calling for the independence of Taiwan, for instance, is forbidden. Articles about the debate over independence for Taiwan may be published, but they may not reach the conclusion that independence for Taiwan is appropriate.
- Articles that disclose State secrets or harm the safety of the PRC (see above).
- Articles that may do harm to the glory and interests of the PRC. Insulting generalizations about the Chinese people, government, and military are prohibited. However, criticism of particular individuals or institutions with regard to particular matters is not.
- Articles that promote divisions between peoples in China, destroy solidarity, and harm the customs of minority groups. China has many ethnic minority groups, including Tibetan, Uigher, and Miao peoples. Criticism of minority groups is not permitted, nor is the advocacy of independence or greater autonomy for them.
- Articles that promote sex, superstition, false science, murder, or violence.
- Articles that harm the morality of society and negate or erode respected cultural traditions. For instance, an article exhorting young people not to feel obligated to take care of elderly parents would not be permitted.
- Articles that defame or insult anyone (see above).
- Articles that deny the need for society to be guided by Marxism, Leninism, the system of thought of Mao Zedong, and the theories of Deng Xiaoping.
- Articles that depart from the strategies and policies of the Chinese Communist Party.
- Articles that conflict with official policy on religions in a way that affects social stability. The Chinese government is officially neutral on religion, and articles that discriminate against particular religions are not allowed. On the other hand, religion may not be exalted as a source of authority superior to the Communist Party.
- Articles that promote vulgarity, base tastes, or incorrect political views. For the most part, this prohibition is intended to restrict

communications that could promote sex, drug use, drinking, or Western democracy.

- Articles that spread rumors or false news and interfere with the work of the Communist Party and the government. This prohibition could be broadly applied.

b. Restricted topics

The Press and Publication Administration, in its Rules on Recording of Sensitive Subjects Selected for Books, Journals, Videotapes and Electronic Publications (1997), set out the following list of "restricted" topics on which official approval should be sought for publication:

- The important documents of the Communist Party and the State
- The work and life of current and former important leaders of the Communist Party and the government
- State secrets and confidential information of the Communist Party
- The structure of the government and its Communist Party and administrative leadership
- The various peoples and religions of China
- National defense and the campaigns, battles, lives, and important figures of the People's Liberation Army in every historical period
- The Cultural Revolution
- Important events and figures in the history of the Chinese Communist Party
- Figures at high levels of the Kuomintang (the Nationalist Chinese Party, which established the current government on Taiwan) and other parties defeated by the Communist Party in China. Chiang Kai-shek is the most prominent example. Articles reflecting somewhat favorably on his patriotism have probably been officially vetted.
- Important events and leaders of the former Soviet Union, Eastern Europe, communist parties, and other friendly parties in other countries
- Maps of the territory of China
- Books published in the Hong Kong Special Administrative Region, Macao, and Taiwan
- Translations of ancient novels into contemporary language
- Imported comic books or videotapes
- Lists containing contact information for individual enterprises

Although articles on such topics are not forbidden, the government has put publishers on notice that they should be submitted for review.

Publishers therefore proceed at some risk, though guidance can be drawn from precedents established by other publishers.

Chapter Notes

1. Constitution of the People's Republic of China (PRC), Art. 38.

2. Opinions of the People's Supreme Court of China on Several Issues in Implementing the General Principles of Civil Law of China (1990), Art. 140.

3. See cases collected at H.L. Fu & R. Cullen, *Media Law in the PRC* (1996), 193; see also H.L. Fu & R. Cullen, "Defamation Law in the People's Republic of China," *The Transnational Lawyer*, vol. 11, no. 1 (Spring 1998); B. Liebman, "Innovation Through Intimidation: An Empirical Account of Defamation Litigation in China," *Harvard International Law Journal*, vol. 47, no. 1 (Winter 2006).

4. Criminal Law of the PRC, Art. 246.

5. Committee to Protect Journalists, "Falling Short: As the 2008 Olympics Approach, China Falters on Press Freedom" (August 2007), at 37; D. Pugh, "On the Zhengzhou Four's Conviction," available at http://lists.ilps-news.com/pipermail/info-bureau/2005-February/000918.html.

6. See Criminal Law of the PRC, Art. 246.

7. Replies of the People's Supreme Court of China to Several Questions in Hearing Defamation Cases (1993), Reply 7.

8. *Li Guzhen v. Tuan Jie News Press for Defamation*, Ref. No. 115212000014, Intermediate People's Court of Miao Autonomous Prefecture (September 11, 2000), Laws and Regulations of China (CD available from China National Information Center).

9. Chen Xiaoyan, *China Journalist*, June 2000.

10. Interpretations of the People's Supreme Court of China on Several Questions in Hearing Defamation Cases (1998), Reply 9.

11. *Beijing Baidu Network Communication Technology Co., Ltd. v. Beijing San Ji Xian Network Technology for Unfair Competition and Libel* (2007), Hai Min Chu Zi No. 17564.

12. Replies of the People's Supreme Court of China to Several Questions in Hearing Defamation Cases (1993), Reply 9.

13. *Hu Jichao, Zhou Kongzhao and Shi Shucheng v. Liu Shouzhong and Zunyi Evening News for Defamation*, Ref. No. 113216199202, Intermediate People's Court of Zunyi (June 20, 1992), Laws and Regulations of China (CD published by China National Information Center).

14. *News and Media Torts* (Cao Ruilin, ed.), in *Theory and Legal Practice of Compensation for Damages* (Zhu Mingshan, gen. ed.) (Publishing House of the People's Court, 2000).

15. Cited in Fu & Cullen, *supra,* at 199.

16. *Li Haifeng, et al. v. Yeji Police, Anhui TV Station, et al. for Libel and Right of Privacy,* Hefei Intermediate Court (March 15, 2006).

17. See, e.g., Fu & Cullen, *supra,* at 200–201, 204–07.

18. *News and Media Torts, supra,* at 113.

19. *Li Haifeng, supra.*

20. China Trial Review (1994), cited in Fu & Cullen, *supra,* at 200.

21. Jia Hepeng, "'Science Cop" Faces Backlash," *China Daily* (12/14/2006), available at http://www.chinadaily.com.cn/cndy/2006-12/14/content_758362.htm.

22. *Id.*; Wu Min Er Zhong Zi No. 817 (2006), available at http://edu.qianlong.com/34001/2007/04/19/3182@3794948.htm.

23. Jia Hepeng, *supra.*

24. *Id.*

25. Order of the State Council No. 492 (04/05/2007); "New Rules Issued to Require Government Transparency," Xinhua (4/25/2007), available at http://www.chinadaily.com.cn/china/2007-04/24/content_858745.htm, and "Landmark Decree to Encourage Gov't Transparency" Xinhua (4/24/2007), available at http://www.chinadaily.com.cn/china/2007-04/24/content_857930.htm.

26. *News and Media Torts, supra,* at 146.

27. Wei Yongzhen, *Bei Gao Xi Shang de Ji Zhe* (Reporter as Defendant), 52 (Shanghai People's Publishing House, 1994).

28. *Id.*

29. Wei, *supra,* at 14.

30. Interpretations of the People's Supreme Court of China on Several Questions in Hearing Defamation Cases (1998), Reply 6.

31. *Huang Shiguan and Huang Xinde v. Guangxi Legal News Press and Fan Baozhong for Defamation* (Guangxi High Court 2001), in *Disputes on Defamation* (Zhu Mingshan, ed.), 219 (China Legal Publishing House, 2003).

32. Hu & Cullen, *supra,* at 202.

33. Wei, *supra,* at 52.

34. *Id.,* at 61–62.

35. *Wang Faying v. Liu Zhen, Women's Literature (and three other magazines) for Defamation,* Ref. No. 113216198901, Hebei High Court (July 5, 1989), Laws and Regulations of China, *supra.*

36. Appeal of the Judgment for the Dispute of Copyright Infringement and Libel Between Wu Zhuqing and Golden Paper Electronic Publication Center (2007), Er Zhong Min Zhong Zi No. 13085.

37. *Li X (anonymous) v. Hao Dongbai for Defamation,* Ref. No. 115211999067, Lanzhou Intermediate People's Court (November 17, 1999), Laws and Regulations of China, *supra.*

38. All-China Journalists Association, Professional Ethical Principles for Journalists (1994, rev. 1997).

39. Central Propaganda Department, General Administration of Broadcasting, Film and Television, Implementation Rules Regarding the Enhancement and Improvement of Media Supervision (2005) (news interviews and reports should not be conducted in an illegal or immoral way, and reporters should not conduct hidden videotaping or voice recording). Another potential risk is posed by Article 21 of the National Security Law, which prohibits the possession of instruments for surreptitious video recording or wiretapping that are suitable for the purposes of spying.

40. *Zhang Jing v. Yu Lingfeng for Defamation on the Internet,* Ref. No. 113216200103, Nanjing Gulou District Court (July 16, 2001), Laws and Regulations of China, *supra.*

41. Regulations Governing Internet News Information Services, Art. 19. Compare to Regulations on the Administration of Newspaper Publishing (RANP) (2005) and Regulations on the Administration of Periodical Publishing (RAPP) (2005).

42. *Id.*, Art. 21.

43. *Shantou Se Ge Che Sheng Navigation Equipment Co., Ltd. v. Shantou Yi Xun Network Co., Ltd. for Defamation* (2006), Long Min Yi Chu Zi No. 61.

44. RANP and RAPP, Arts. 26.

45. *Id.*

46. RANP, Arts. 2, 4, 41; RAPP, Arts. 2, 5, 39.

47. Provisional Rules for the Administration of Online Publishing (2002), Article 6; Administrative Rules on Internet Video/Audio Program Services (2008), Arts. 8, 9.

48. RANP Art. 48; RAPP Arts. 5, 46; Regulations for the Administration of Radio and Television (1997) Art. 31.

49. RAPP Art. 39; RANP Art. 41.

50. RANP Arts. 56–57; RAPP Arts. 54–55.

51. *Id.*, Art. 13.

52. Regulations Concerning Foreign Journalists and Permanent Offices of Foreign News Agencies, Art. 11.

53. "3 more foreign news agencies OKed to release financial info, photos in China" Xinhua (Sept. 26, 2007) available at http://www.chinadaily.com.cn/china/2007-09/26/content_6136604.htm.

54. Regulations Concerning Foreign Journalists and Permanent Offices of Foreign News Agencies (1990).

55. See Regulations Concerning Foreign Journalists and Permanent Offices of Foreign News Agencies (1990), Art. 15; J. Yardley, "China Plans Temporary Easing of Curbs on Foreign Journalists," *New York Times* (Dec. 2, 2006), available at http://www.nytimes.com/2006/12/02/world/asia/02china.html?_r=1&oref=slogin. The Chinese government temporarily relaxed various restrictions on foreign reporters around the time of the 2008 Beijing Summer Olympics. The Regulations on Reporting Activities in China by Foreign Journalists During the Beijing Olympic Games and Their Preparatory Period, which came into effect January 1, 2007, provide that foreign journalists are not required to obtain advance permission from provincial authorities for interviews or visits outside Beijing and permit foreign journalists to bring in their own equipment, including radio communication equipment. The regulations are set to expire on October 17, 2008, after the Olympic Games have concluded.

56. *Id.*

57. Regulations Concerning Foreign Journalists and Permanent Offices of Foreign News Agencies (1990), Arts. 14, 19; Measures for the Administration of the Release of News and Information in China by Foreign News Agencies (2006), Arts. 11, 16.

CHAPTER 6

Hong Kong

EDWARD J. DAVIS
Davis Wright Tremaine LLP

WITH DOREEN WEISENHAUS
AND RICK GLOFCHESKI
University of Hong Kong

Davis Wright Tremaine LLP
1633 Broadway
New York, NY 10019 USA
Phone: 212-489-8230
Fax: 212-489-8340
www.dwt.com
eddavis@dwt.com

Introduction to the Hong Kong Legal System

As a consequence of its historical status as a British colony, Hong Kong relies heavily on English decisions as a source of law and as a touchstone for the development of legal principles, including those in the area of tort. Decisions of courts in other Commonwealth common law jurisdictions, such as Australia, are also influential. The Hong Kong Constitution—the Basic Law, in force since 1997, when Hong Kong returned to China—provides that the decisions of "other common law jurisdictions" may be relied on as precedents. Hong Kong is a Special Administrative Region of the People's Republic of China, and national laws of the PRC, including media regulations, are not applied in Hong Kong, with the exception of some laws governing defense and foreign affairs.[1]

Although defamation is the only area of civil law in which there may be trial by jury in Hong Kong, there have been few such trials, most of them in recent years.

1. What is the locally accepted definition of libel?

Courts in Hong Kong generally look to English sources for the basic principles of libel law, including the elements of the tort and defenses. One Hong Kong court has referred to the English treatise, *Gatley on Libel and Slander* (Gatley) as the "leading textbook" and applied the following "working definition of defamation" from *Gatley:* "Defamation is committed when the defendant publishes to a third person words or matter containing an untrue imputation against the reputation of the plaintiff."[2]

Words may be considered to have a defamatory meaning not only if they expose the plaintiff to "hatred, ridicule or contempt," but also if they have the effect of causing members of society to "shun and avoid" the plaintiff, or if they "tend . . . to lower the plaintiff in the estimation of right-thinking members of society generally," according to a textbook on Hong Kong tort law, citing various English authorities.[3]

When ridicule can amount to defamation is a controversial issue in most legal systems, but ridicule has been successfully relied on in Hong Kong, notably in the case of *Li Yau-wai v. Genesis Films Ltd.*[4] The plaintiff's photograph had been used in a bawdy movie to represent a deceased fictional character. Another character in the movie used the picture as a focus for entreaties to send his mother (the deceased character's wife) erotic dreams. This elicited mirth from the audience, teasing from the plaintiff's friends, and embarrassment for him. Without extensive analysis, the court held that this exposed the plaintiff to ridicule "of such a nature as to amount to defamation."[5]

Allegedly libelous words are considered in their "ordinary and natural meaning."[6] Consistent with English cases, Hong Kong courts have held that the court must view the statements as would the "hypothetical reasonable reader" who is "not naïve but . . . is [also] not unduly suspicious."[7] In a recent decision, the court held that the "hypothetical reader" is:

> a reasonable, fair-minded man or woman, of ordinary intelligence, with the ordinary person's general knowledge and experience of worldly affairs and knowledge of the Chinese language, both its literary and colloquial usage. He is not naïve but not unduly suspicious. He can read between the lines, can read in an implication more readily than a lawyer and may indulge in a certain amount of loose thinking, but not as being avid for scandal. This reader just reads the report once. He would not engage in an over-elaborate analysis of the material as though he were examining a contract document or a scientific journal.[8]

In distinguishing between libel and slander, Hong Kong courts have generally followed English cases, treating defamatory statements as libel whenever they are published in permanent form (for example, in books and newspapers). Section 22 of Hong Kong's Defamation Ordinance (Cap. 21) clarifies that "[f]or the purposes of the law of libel and slander, the broadcasting of words shall be treated as publication in permanent form." Accordingly, radio and television broadcasts containing defamatory statements would be considered libelous.

2. Is libel-by-implication recognized, or, in the alternative, must the complained-of words alone defame the plaintiff?

Hong Kong courts effectively recognize the concept of libel-by-implication. However, they generally distinguish between two types of innuendo: "popular" innuendo and "true" or "legal" innuendo.

The first refers to secondary meanings of words that require no special knowledge for an understanding of that secondary meaning; the second requires that the audience for the allegedly libelous statement know of some circumstances that make superficially innocent words defamatory or that add a further defamatory meaning to words that are defamatory in their natural meaning. As Lord Denning explained in the case of *Beijing Television v. Brightec Ltd. and Others,*[9] the distinction between the two categories has ramifications for the pleading requirements imposed on the plaintiff:

> First, the cause of action based on popular innuendo. If the plaintiff relies on the natural meaning of the words . . . he must, in his statement of claim, specify the person or persons to whom they were published; save in the case of a newspaper or periodical which is published to the world at large, when the persons are so numerous as to go without saying—or book, I would add.
>
> Secondly, the cause of action based on a legal innuendo. If the plaintiff relies on some special circumstances which convey (to some particular person or persons knowing these circumstances) a special defamatory meaning other than the natural and ordinary meaning of the words . . ., then he must in his statement of claim specify the particular person or persons to whom they were published and the special circumstances known to that person or persons [and] there is no exception in the case of a newspaper: because the words would not be so understood by the world at large; but only by the particular person or persons who know the special circumstances.[10]

Beijing Television offers a somewhat unusual application of the concept of innuendo. The plaintiff television company sued for libel over a statement that it had "met with bad luck . . . [T]he Television's popular lady program-in-charge [sic] Du Yu and the Deputy Minister of Broadcast . . . had their adulterous affair exposed, and they were caught at the scene during their adulterous acts in bed. This scandal caught the leaders of Beijing Television with great embarrassment." The plaintiff pleaded as "special circumstances" supporting a defamatory innuendo (*inter alia*) the "type of the programme, the expected clean image of Du Yu in a programme for personal, family emotional life and relationships, the PRC audience it catered for, . . . the expectation of its audience and advertisers and the stricter moral and social standards observed in the Mainland." Based on these facts, the court declined to dismiss the action at the pleading stage. However, facts such as the type of program and general characteristics of its audience do not add a hidden meaning to the statement complained of; they may affect how harshly a particular audience would judge the plaintiff, rather than what that audience would take the particular words about the plaintiff to mean.

3. May corporations sue for libel?

Yes. It is well established that corporations may sue for libel, that is, for statements that damage their trade or business reputation. Media companies have even sued each other for libel.[11] Non-business entities may also sue. For instance, a charity and a university have been found to have standing to sue.[12]

4. Is product disparagement recognized, and if so, how does that differ from libel?

Yes. This tort differs from libel in various ways. The plaintiff must prove that the statement was untrue, that it was primarily motivated by malice—that is, by a desire to injure the plaintiff—and, unless one of two conditions applies, that actual, provable damage resulted. Under the common law, actual damage always had to be proved, but the common law has been changed to some extent by Section 24(1) of the Defamation Ordinance, which created two exceptions. There is no need to establish actual damage if either (a) the statement was "calculated" (which means likely) to cause pecuniary damage and was published in written or permanent form; or (b) the statement was "calculated" to cause such damage to the plaintiff in connection with any office, profession, calling, trade, or business.

5. Must an individual be clearly identified (by name or photograph) to sue for libel? Can a group of persons sue for libel, even though not named?

A plaintiff need not be explicitly identified by name or image to sue for libel. Hong Kong courts have held that veiled references to plaintiffs in fictional works and newspapers (even using a fictitious name or nickname) may be sufficient to identify the plaintiff.[13]

Hong Kong courts also recognize some forms of "group libel" if the words complained of can be reasonably understood to refer to the plaintiff(s). For example, in *Sin Cho Chiu v. Tin Tin Publication Development Ltd. and Another,*[14] the defendant newspaper reported that a "delegation of elders of the securities industry" had gone to Beijing, and it added—without referring specifically to the plaintiff—that "most of the members of the delegation are 'tainted elements.'" The plaintiff was identified elsewhere in the article as a member of the delegation, and the court held that since the "ordinary reader" would naturally look elsewhere in the article to discover the identity of the "tainted" members and would have little difficulty in concluding that the plaintiff was one of them, the plaintiff could sue.

6. What is the fault standard(s) applied to libel?

a. Does the fault standard depend on the fame or notoriety of the plaintiff?

No. Consistent with its roots in the English common law, libel in Hong Kong is a strict liability tort. Once the plaintiff has proved that a defamatory statement was made about him or her, the burden shifts to the defendant to prove that one of the applicable defenses applies.

b. Is there a heightened fault standard or privilege for reporting on matters of public concern or public interest?

A heightened fault standard may apply if any of the defenses listed below, which take into account the degree of the defendant's fault, can be invoked.

1. ***Innocent Dissemination.*** This can be viewed as a defense or as a plea of "not published." Booksellers, libraries, and distributors may rely on a defense of innocent dissemination, but not printers or publishers, who can be presumed to have the opportunity to read what they are disseminating. The defense amounts to saying that the defendant played a part in disseminating the publication but had no actual knowledge of the defamatory nature of any of the published material and was not negligent with respect to whether it contained defamatory matter.[15]

2. ***Lack of Malice.*** Although malice is not an element of the plaintiff's cause of action, the absence of malice is a common element of several defenses at common law. If a defendant has successfully invoked a defense that is vitiated by a showing of malice, malice must generally be proved by the plaintiff.[16]

3. ***The Qualified Privilege.*** The qualified privilege long recognized in England is commonly said to arise where the defendant is under a

duty to communicate or has an interest in communicating the allegedly defamatory statement to the recipient of the statement and the latter also has a reciprocal duty or interest in receiving it. It is well established that certain reports are privileged at common law—for instance, reports of judicial proceedings and reports of parliamentary proceedings.

The qualified privilege is defeated where the defendant has acted with "malice"—i.e., either what U.S. lawyers would call "common law malice" ("ill will or spite") or something closely approximating "*New York Times*" or "constitutional" malice, in the sense of reckless disregard for truth or falsity. Thus, mere carelessness or unreasonable belief in the truth of the statement will not qualify as malice,[17] but recklessness in making the statement, not caring whether it was true, will qualify.[18] Malice can also be proved where, on an otherwise privileged occasion, the defendant's dominant motive in making the statement is improper—for instance, to attack the plaintiff or gain some advantage.[19] For purposes of defeating the qualified privilege, it makes no difference whether the plaintiff is a public or otherwise well-known figure.

According to Hong Kong practitioners, the privilege described by the the House of Lords in *Reynolds v. Times Newspapers Ltd.*[20] has been considered in Hong Kong on only two occasions thus far (see below), and the privilege recognized by the High Court of Australia in *Lange v. Australian Broadcasting Corporation*[21] has not been argued in the Hong Kong courts. In *Lange,* the court held that a qualified privilege protects the publication of information, opinions, and arguments concerning governmental and political matters, subject to the publisher proving the reasonableness of its conduct. In *Reynolds,* Lord Nicholls insisted that there be no special rule for political and governmental matters, but that the privilege be available, more broadly, for statements on matters of serious public concern.

Whether or not the *Reynolds* privilege can be successfully invoked depends on a number of nonexclusive factors identified by Lord Nicholls, including:

1. The seriousness of the allegation. The more serious the charge, the more the public is misinformed and the individual harmed, if the allegation is not true.
2. The nature of the information and the extent to which the subject is a matter of public concern.
3. The source of the information. (Some informants have no direct knowledge of the events. Some have their own axes to grind, or are being paid for their stories.)
4. The steps taken to verify the information.

5. The status of the information. (The allegation may have already been the subject of an investigation that commands respect.)
6. The urgency of the matter. (News is often a perishable commodity.)
7. Whether comment was sought from the plaintiff. (He may have information others do not possess or have not disclosed. An approach to the plaintiff will not always be necessary, but it will almost always help.)
8. Whether the article contained the gist of the plaintiff's side of the story.
9. The tone of the article. (A report may raise questions or call for an investigation. It need not adopt allegations as statements of fact.)
10. The circumstances of the publication, including the timing.[22]

The first Hong Kong decision to consider the *Reynolds* privilege, *Cutting de Heart v. Sun News Ltd. and Another,*[23] gave the *Reynolds* decision a very broad reading, in particular with respect to what constitutes subject matter of public interest, and the measures to be taken by the defendant to verify the story and seek a comment from the plaintiff. The *Reynolds* privilege was applied to protect an item in a newspaper's readers' complaints column about unsatisfactory hair treatment provided by the plaintiff's salon and the salon's alleged failure to honor its "satisfaction guarantee."

Subsequently, in *Jameel v. Wall Street Journal Europe,*[24] the House of Lords reinforced the *Reynolds* privilege and confirmed that it goes beyond conventional qualified privilege. The *Reynolds* privilege does not require proof of a reciprocal duty/interest relationship in the conventional sense because, according to Lord Hoffmann, it is the subject matter, not the occasion, that is privileged. Putting it another way, "if the publication is in the public interest, the duty and interest are taken to exist" (at 382). Moreover, "there is no question of the privilege being defeated by proof of malice because the propriety of the conduct of the defendant is built into the conditions under which the material is privileged" (per Lord Hoffmann at 381). What is important is whether the steps taken to gather and publish the information were responsible and fair. In this context, Lord Nicholls' ten non-exclusive factors identified in *Reynolds* "are not tests that the publication has to pass . . . but . . . must be applied in a practical and flexible manner" (per Lord Hoffmann at 384). For these reasons the defendant newspaper's otherwise libelous article, alleging that the Saudi Arabian plaintiffs' bank accounts were being monitored by Saudi authorities in cooperation with U.S. authorities for possible terrorism connections, was found to be privileged.

More recently, in Hong Kong, in *Abdul Razzak Yaqoob v. Asia Times Online Ltd.* [2008] HCA 1142 of 2006, the High Court of First Instance considered the *Reynolds* defense where an Internet news service published an article alleging money laundering, terrorist financing, and drug trafficking by a prominent Pakistani businessman and his companies based in

Dubai. The court found the defense not proved because, on consideration of Lord Nicholls' ten factors, it found that the defendant had not engaged in responsible journalism. In particular, sources had not been adequately checked, and the journalist's faxed questions to the plaintiff, which were written casually, directed to a corporate fax number, and focused on the plaintiff's gold-trading rather than the allegations of illegal activity, did not provide a real opportunity for the plaintiff to comment on the allegations as envisioned in *Reynolds*. *Reynolds* was treated by the court as the prevailing authority, not *Jameel*. Significantly, the court made no mention of the admonition in *Jameel* that Lord Nicholls' ten factors were not "tests that the publication has to pass." Rather, the court applied the ten factors one by one to the facts of the case in reaching its decision that the necessary standard for responsible journalism was not reached and that the defendant's publication was therefore not privileged.

4. ***Fair Comment.*** The defense of fair comment (see Question 8 below) is available in Hong Kong and is defeated by a finding of malice, although the inquiry is framed in a distinctive manner and, in this context, malice has a restricted meaning. Here, malice means that the defendant did not have an honest belief in the truth of the statement he or she made. As Lord Nicholls explained in the Hong Kong case *Cheng and Another v. Tse Wai Chun,*[25] one of the four elements of the defense is that "the comment must be one which could have been made by an honest person, however prejudiced he may be, and however exaggerated or obstinate his views." While the court in *Cheng*, following the English cases, emphasized that "a critic need not be mealy-mouthed in denouncing what he disagrees with," many of the English authorities (including *Reynolds*) warn that the privilege "cannot be used as a cloak for mere invective."

5. ***Statutory Defenses.*** Under Section 4 of the Defamation Ordinance, a newspaper may plead as a defense to libel that it acted without actual malice or gross negligence and that it promptly published an apology and paid "amends" into Court. The defense is available if the defendant establishes that:

> The libel was inserted in the newspaper without actual malice and without gross negligence, and that before the commencement of the action, or at the earliest opportunity afterwards, [the defendant] inserted in the newspaper a full apology for the libel, or if the newspaper in which the libel appeared is ordinarily published at intervals exceeding 1 week, had offered to publish the said apology in any newspaper to be selected by the plaintiff in the action. . . .
>
> Provided that it shall not be competent to any defendant in such action to set up any defence without at the same time making a payment of money into court by way of amends, and every such defence so filed without such

> payment into court shall be deemed a nullity and may be treated as such by the plaintiff in the action.

A newspaper defendant unsuccessfully invoked Section 4 in *Chu Siu Kuk Yuen v. Apple Daily Ltd. and Others.*[26] The paper mistakenly named the plaintiff solicitor (attorney) in a report about a solicitor in the same building who disappeared with a large quantity of money. Because the newspaper had failed to perform simple fact-checking, it was unable to establish the absence of gross negligence, though neither actual malice nor defamation by deliberate intention was found. (The decision offers no detailed discussion of these concepts.)

Section 25 of the Defamation Ordinance provides a further statutory defense for "[u]nintentional defamation" that, like the Section 4 defense, calls for "an offer of amends." According to Hong Kong practitioners, it has not yet been relied upon. Section 25 states:

> (1) A person who has published words alleged to be defamatory of another person may, if he claims that the words were published by him innocently in relation to that other person, make an offer of amends under this section; and in any such case–
>
> (a) if the offer is accepted by the party aggrieved and is duly performed, no proceedings for libel or slander shall be taken or continued by that party against the person making the offer . . . (but without prejudice to any cause of action against any other person jointly responsible for that publication);
>
> (b) if the offer is not accepted by the party aggrieved, then, except as otherwise provided by this section, it shall be a defence, in any proceedings by him for libel or slander against the person making the offer . . ., to prove that the words complained of were published by the defendant innocently in relation to the plaintiff and that the offer was made as soon as practicable after the defendant received notice that they were or might be defamatory of the plaintiff, and has not been withdrawn.
>
> (2) An offer of amends under this section must be expressed to be made for the purposes of this section, and must be accompanied by an affidavit specifying the facts relied upon by the person making it to show that the words in question were published by him innocently in relation to the party aggrieved; and for the purposes of a defence under Subsection (1)(b) no evidence, other than evidence of facts specified in the affidavit, shall be admissible on behalf of that person to prove that the words were so published.
>
> (3) An offer of amends under this section shall be understood to mean an offer:

(a) in any case, to publish or join in the publication of a suitable correction of the words complained of, and a sufficient apology to the party aggrieved in respect of those words;
(b) where copies of a document or record containing the said words have been distributed by or with the knowledge of the person making the offer, to take such steps as are reasonably practicable on his part for notifying persons to whom copies have been so distributed that the words are alleged to be defamatory of the party aggrieved.

"Malice" also enters the analysis if an offer of amends is rejected. The publisher may not then rely on a defense of innocent publication unless the publisher can prove that the author acted without malice:

(6) Subsection (1)(b) shall not apply in relation to the publication by any person of words of which he is not the author unless he proves that the words were written by the author without malice.

7. Is financial news about publicly traded companies, or companies involved with a government contract, considered a matter of public interest or otherwise privileged?
Yes. Reports about such companies would fall within the general category of matters of public interest, and their affairs would generally be appropriate subjects for the defense of fair comment. But there is no blanket restriction that would prevent such companies from suing.

8. Is there a recognized protection for opinion or "fair comment" on matters of public concern?
Yes. The Hong Kong courts have largely followed the well-established English common law–qualified privilege for fair comment, mentioned in the response to Question 5 above. In the *Cheng* case, Lord Nicholls identified the following "noncontroversial" principles governing the privilege for fair comment:

1. "the comment must be on a matter of public interest [which is] not to be confined within narrow limits."
2. "the comment must be recognizable as comment, as distinct from an imputation of fact. If the imputation is one of fact, a ground of defence must be sought elsewhere, for example justification [i.e., the defense of truth]."
3. "the comment must be based on facts which are true or protected by privilege. . . . If the facts on which the comment purports to be founded are not proved to be true or published on a privileged occasion, the defence of fair comment is not available."

4. "the comment must explicitly or implicitly indicate, at least in general terms, what are the facts on which the comment is being made. The reader or hearer should be in a position to judge for himself how far the comment was well founded."
5. "the comment must be one which could have been made by an honest person, however prejudiced he might be, and however exaggerated or obstinate his views."

Despite Lord Nicholls' instruction that matters of public interest should not be narrowly construed, the concept of public interest applied by courts in Hong Kong may be surprisingly narrow.

In *Li Ching v. Koo Too Shing,*[27] the court held that the affairs of an organization of 200-odd clansmen in Yuen Long were "of supreme indifference to outsiders" and were therefore not a matter of public interest. However, a more recent decision, *Next Magazine Publishing Ltd. and Another v. Ma Ching Fat,*[28] held that the behavior of a major shareholder in a publicly listed company in selling his shares was a matter of public interest. The judge found that a prominent figure in the business community, who was the vice chairman of a public company that owned a daily newspaper with a very wide circulation in Hong Kong, and who was selling his entire shareholding in the company over a period of barely a week for approximately $143 million, was "plainly a matter of public interest, and worthy of comment by persons involved in the media." And in *Top Express Consultants Ltd. v. Tai Lo Ngan Ying,*[29] the court held that the proper operation of a learning institute preparing candidates for American professional examinations such as the CPA exam was a matter of public interest.

9. Are there any requirements upon a plaintiff, such as demand for retraction or right of reply, and if so, what impact do they have?

No. There are no provisions requiring a plaintiff to seek a retraction. If a defendant wishes to rely on the statutory defense contained in Section 4 of the Defamation Ordinance, which protects publishers who act without actual malice or gross negligence, the defendant must publish "a full apology for the libel" before an action is commenced or at the earliest opportunity thereafter, or, "if the newspaper in which the libel appeared is ordinarily published at intervals exceeding 1 week, [the defendant must offer] to publish the . . . apology in any newspaper to be selected by the plaintiff in the action . . ." and must satisfy the other conditions contained in Section 4, including the payment of amends into court. Similarly, the statutory defense in Section 25 of the Defamation Ordinance for "[u]nintentional defamation" requires an "offer of amends" as described in the response to Question 6 above.

A form of right of reply is included in the requirements for qualified privileges for fair and accurate reports of certain official or public proceedings. (See, e.g., the response to Question 10a below.)

10. Is there a privilege for quoting or reporting on:

a. Papers filed in court?

Reports of court proceedings are subject to a qualified privilege at common law, if the proceedings themselves are in public. Section 13 of the Defamation Ordinance contains a broad and presumably absolute privilege for the press in covering litigation. This is based on English legislation, and in England the privilege is treated as absolute. Hong Kong courts should follow suit:

> (1) A fair and accurate report in any newspaper or broadcast of proceedings publicly heard before any court shall, if published contemporaneously with such proceedings, be privileged: Provided that nothing in this section shall authorize the publication of any blasphemous or indecent matter.[30]

Section 14 of the Defamation Ordinance also provides a statutory qualified privilege, which may be defeated by a showing of malice, for certain specifically enumerated types of "fair and accurate" reports, including reports of proceedings of quasi-governmental bodies as well as many government tribunals and commissions (see the Schedule to the Defamation Ordinance for the full list of such reports). Fair and accurate reports of certain proceedings in this category are privileged unless they are published with "malice" or published without providing a sufficient "explanation or contradiction," if the plaintiff has requested one, i.e., "if it is proved that the defendant has been requested by the plaintiff to publish in the manner in which the original publication was made a reasonable letter or statement by way of explanation or contradiction, and has refused or neglected to do so, or has done so in a manner not adequate or not reasonable having regard to all the circumstances."[31]

Further, pursuant to Section 14(3) of the Defamation Ordinance, reports of such proceedings are *not* protected if the publication is otherwise "prohibited by law" or concerns a matter that is "not of public concern and the publication . . . is not for the public benefit." English courts have held that these last two requirements—"public concern" and "public benefit"—are separate and that both are necessary.

b. Government-issued documents?

Yes. Pursuant to Section 14 of the Defamation Ordinance and with reference to paragraph 12 of Part II of the Schedule, a copy or fair and accurate report or summary of any notice or other matter issued by or on behalf of any government department, or by or on behalf of the Commissioner of Police, for the information of the public is privileged. Publication of an extract or abstract of a document published by order of the Legislative Council is also protected, under Defamation Ordinance Section 12.

c. Quasi-governmental proceedings?

Yes. A fair and accurate report of the findings or decision of any of the following associations may be privileged, by virtue of Section 14 of the Defamation Ordinance and Part II of the Schedule to it:

1. an association formed in Hong Kong for the purpose of promoting or encouraging the exercise of or interest in any art, science, religion or learning, and empowered by its constitution to exercise control over or adjudicate upon matters of interest or concern to the association;
2. an association formed in Hong Kong for the purpose of promoting or safeguarding the interests of any trade, business, industry or profession, or of the persons carrying on or engaged in any trade, business, industry or profession, and empowered by its constitution to exercise control over or adjudicate upon matters connected with the trade, business, industry or profession, or the actions or conduct of those persons;
3. an association formed in Hong Kong for the purpose of promoting or safeguarding the interests of any game, sport or pastime to the playing or exercise of which members of the public are invited or admitted;
4. any public meeting held in Hong Kong, that is to say, a meeting bona fide and lawfully held for a lawful purpose and for the furtherance or discussion of any matter of public concern, whether admission to the meeting is general or restricted;
5. a report of the proceedings at a general meeting of any company or association constituted, registered or certified by or under any Ordinance or Act of Parliament or incorporated by Royal Charter, not being a private company within the meaning of the Companies Ordinance (Cap. 32);
6. a copy or fair and accurate report or summary of any notice or other matter issued for the information of the public by or on behalf of the Consumer Council;
7. a copy or fair and accurate report or summary of any report made or published under Section 16 or 16A of the Ombudsman Ordinance (Cap. 397);
8. a copy or fair and accurate report or summary of any report prepared and supplied for the purposes of Section 30 of the Mandatory Provident Fund Schemes Ordinance (Cap. 485) or prepared and published under

Section 32 of that Ordinance. The privilege also extends to findings of international courts, public registers, and any notices published pursuant to court order.

11. Is there a privilege for republishing statements made earlier by other, bona fide, reliable publications or wire services?

No. Hong Kong courts follow the common law rule that the republication of a libel gives rise to liability in the same way as publication of the original libel: "a person who publishes a rumor by repeating it, albeit stating it to be a rumor, cannot justify the libel contained in that rumor by proving the existence of the rumor."[32]

12. Are there any restrictions regarding reporting on:

a. Ongoing criminal investigations?

Yes. There are several statutory restrictions on reports of criminal investigations, including investigations for bribery, corruption, and drug trafficking.[33] Under the Prevention of Bribery Ordinance (Cap. 201) Section 30, reports that could tip off targets in bribery or corruption investigations are prohibited. Penalties for violations include a fine of up to HK$20,000 and imprisonment for up to one year. The Drug Trafficking (Recovery of Proceeds) Ordinance (Cap. 405) Section 24, criminalizes any disclosure likely to prejudice an investigation. Section 26 of the ordinance specifically bans the publication or broadcast of any information that would reveal or suggest that authorities have been informed that property was purchased with proceeds of drug trafficking or was used or is intended to be used in connection with drug trafficking, or that would reveal or suggest the identity of a person making such a disclosure. The Organized and Serious Crimes Ordinance (Cap. 455) Section 26, prohibits similar disclosures in connection with property funded by the proceeds of an indictable offense. Anyone who reveals information about the identity or location of a person in the witness protection program or being considered for the program, in violation of Witness Protection Ordinance (Cap. 564) Section 17(1), faces up to ten years in prison.

b. Ongoing criminal prosecutions?

Yes, there are a number of express statutory restrictions on reporting court proceedings. Some are temporary, until a case is concluded, and others are permanent.[34]

The Magistrates Ordinance (Cap. 227) Section 87A contains the general rule that written reports or broadcasts of "committal proceedings"—in which a magistrate decides whether there is sufficient evidence for a person to be sent for trial by indictment—are allowed to provide only certain narrowly defined details, such as the name of the court and the identities of the parties and witnesses:

(a) the identity of the court and the name of the magistrate;
(b) the names, addresses, occupations and ages of the parties and witnesses;
(c) the offense with which the accused is charged, or a summary thereof;
(d) the names of counsel and solicitors engaged in the proceedings;
(e) any decision of the magistrate to commit the accused for trial, and any decision of the magistrate on the disposal of the case of any defendants not committed;
(f) where the magistrate commits the accused for trial, the charge on which he is committed, or a summary thereof, and the court to which he is committed;
(g) where the committal proceedings are adjourned, the date and place to which they are adjourned; and
(h) whether legal aid was granted to the accused.

Those who may be held liable for violating these provisions include the owner, editor, publisher, or distributor of a newspaper or, in the case of a broadcast report, any person who transmits or provides the program in which the report is broadcast and any person whose functions correspond to those of the editor of a newspaper or magazine. Those responsible for violations may be found guilty of an offense, fined HK$10,000, and imprisoned for six months. There are similar restrictions on the reporting of bail applications under the Criminal Procedure Ordinance (Cap. 221) Section 9P(1) and restrictions on reporting the identities of complainants in connection with certain sexual offenses under the Crimes Ordinance (Cap. 200) Section 156 and of juvenile offenders under the Juvenile Offenders Ordinance (Cap. 226) Section 20A. Finally, there are limits on the publication of details of matrimonial cases under the Judicial Proceedings (Regulations of Reports) Ordinance (Cap. 287), Section 3.

c. Ongoing regulatory investigations?

None.

d. Ongoing civil litigation, or other judicial proceedings?

There are rather convoluted provisions concerning the publication of reports of court proceedings held in private. Generally, if the court orders that information shall not be published, publishing it is the offense of contempt of court. It is also an offense under the Judicial Proceedings (Regulation of Reports) Ordinance (Cap. 287) Section 5 to publish in certain situations (such as proceedings involving persons with mental disability), or if publication is likely to prejudice the proceedings of the court. There is an exception for innocent publication under Section 4.

13. Are prior restraints or other prepublication injunctions available on the basis of libel or privacy, and if so, what are the standards for obtaining such relief?

Yes. For libel:

> If there is a real possibility of the defendant repeating the defamatory statement, the court may be prepared to grant an injunction to order a stop to further publication. This is a discretionary remedy. It may be available on an interim (interlocutory) basis, pending trial, but this is rare, because it is viewed as a very serious infringement on freedom of speech. An interlocutory injunction will only be granted if it is clear that the statement is defamatory, that if the defendant intends to plead justification, the plaintiff can show that the words are untrue (this may be done on the basis of affidavits), and that there is no reason to take the view that prima facie the occasion of publication is or will be privileged.[35]

Similarly, in privacy cases involving the tort of breach of confidence, a court may issue an injunction to prevent further publication or disclosure of confidential information. In 2006, a court issued a preliminary injunction to prevent further publication of covert photographs taken of a Cantonese pop star undressing after a concert, which had been published in a local magazine.

14. Is a right of privacy recognized (either civilly or criminally)?

a. What is the definition of "private fact"?

According to a textbook on Hong Kong media law, "while there is no general right to privacy in Hong Kong, numerous laws address privacy in some aspect."[36] In line with the historical approach of the United Kingdom courts, those of Hong Kong have held that there is no common law tort of invasion of privacy. There is a tort of breach of confidence, which has been used to protect certain sorts of communications, and the courts have recognized it in Hong Kong.[37]

There is also limited legislative protection of privacy. To some extent this is based on the United Kingdom legislation protecting electronically held data, but in Hong Kong the law protects personal data that could identify an individual held in other forms, including photographs.[38] The legislation is the Personal Data (Privacy) Ordinance (Cap. 486). It essentially provides that data may be used only for the purposes for which it is collected. The persons to whom the data pertains have a right of access to it and a right to compensation for improper use.

In 2007, however, Hong Kong's Privacy Commissioner for Personal Data (whose office oversees implementation of the data ordinance) found that Yahoo! Hong Kong, an e-mail service provider, did not contravene the Hong Kong ordinance when its mainland Chinese subsidiary disclosed a subscriber's IP address and some e-mail account information to Chinese prosecutors. The Privacy Commissioner held that the information did not constitute "personal data" because it did not identify a specific individual and that there was "insufficient evidence" that Yahoo! Hong Kong turned over the data, as it did not control its subsidiary.[39] The subscriber, mainland journalist Shi Tao, was sentenced to ten years in prison for violating Chinese state secrets laws. The Hong Kong Administrative Appeals Board subsequently disagreed with the conclusion that Yahoo! Hong Kong did not control the information, finding that its mainland subsidiary was acting as "an agent." But the board dismissed the appeal, agreeing that the disclosed information was not personal data and adding that Shi had consented to disclosure when he accepted Yahoo's terms of service.

In 2008, the Privacy Commissioner recommended the creation of a new criminal offense for knowingly, without the consent of a data user, obtaining or disclosing personal data held or leaked by a data user or selling personal data so obtained. His recommendation came in response to highly controversial leaks on the Internet of personal graphic sexual images involving some of Hong Kong's most famous celebrities. In early 2008, singer and actor Edison Chen publicly admitted to taking videos of numerous female actresses and singers in what appeared to be acts of consensual sex. He said that the images had been stored on his notebook computer, which had been sent to a computer shop for repairs. Hong Kong authorities charged a shop employee with accessing a computer with criminal intent and charged several others with uploading obscene images onto the Internet. As of mid-2008, their cases were pending and no new privacy legislation had been introduced.

b. Is there a public interest or newsworthiness exception?

Section 61 of the Personal Data (Privacy) Ordinance provides certain exemptions for the collection and disclosure of data in the course of "news activity," which includes "any journalistic activity" and the gathering, preparation, and dissemination of news or articles, programs, or observations on news or current affairs, including exemptions for dissemination of data "in the public interest."

c. Is the right of privacy based in common law, statute, or constitution?

Apart from the limited common law tort of breach of confidence, some specific privacy rights are set forth in the Personal Data (Privacy) Ordinance described above. The Bill of Rights Ordinance (Cap. 383) Article 14 prohibits arbitrary or unlawful interference with a person's privacy by government action. General protections for privacy of the person, home and "other premises," and communications are set forth in the Basic Law, Articles 28–30. In 2006, the government was forced to enact a new covert surveillance law, the Interception of Communication and Surveillance Ordinance (Cap. 589), after being successfully challenged in court for violating Article 30's ban on unlawful interference with private communications and the Bill of Rights Ordinance Article 14.[40]

15. May reporters tape-record their own telephone conversations for note-taking purposes (not rebroadcast) without the consent of the other party?

Yes. There appear to be no restrictions on such recording.

16. If it is permissible to record such tapes, may they be broadcast without permission?

Yes. However, in certain circumstances such a broadcast could be challenged as an instance of the tort of breach of confidence.

17. Is there a recognized evidentiary privilege preventing the disclosure of confidential sources relied upon by reporters?

Yes. There is a recognized common law rule—known as the "newspaper rule"—that acts as a limitation on the normal principles permitting discovery of the identity of other participants in a tort. Depending on the public interest at stake (in the protection of confidential sources, for example), a court should not order the disclosure of the identity of the author of an item or the source of information. This rule has been applied in at least one Hong Kong case.[41]

18. In the event that legal papers are served upon the newsroom (such as a civil complaint), are there any particular warnings about accepting service of which we should be aware?

No, except that anyone who receives legal papers should know how and when they were received and should contact counsel promptly.

19. Has your jurisdiction applied established media law to Internet publishers?

In a small number of cases, ISPs or the publishers of material on the Internet have been sued in the Hong Kong courts. We can break the cases down into five categories:

1. ***Cases where a paper publication that also appears on the Internet has been the subject of litigation.*** In *Chu Siu Kuk Yuen v. Apple Daily Ltd. and Others,* a newspaper was sued for its online publication.[42] The court noted that because the circulation of the newspaper exceeded 415,000, the possible additional effect of the Internet publication was not relevant to either liability or damages.

2. ***Cases where the fact of publication on the Internet—and thus in Hong Kong—has been the basis for bringing an action in Hong Kong, even though the parties are not actually resident in Hong Kong.*** This was the situation in *Investasia Ltd. and Another v. Kodansha Co. Ltd. and Another.*[43] It was held that the plaintiff had established a sufficient connection with Hong Kong to be able to bring an action in Hong Kong; the main authority was the English case of *Berezovsky v. Michaels and Others (Forbes).*[44]

3. ***Cases where the subject of the litigation has been an e-mail.*** In *Drummond v. Atuahene-Gima,*[45] the subject matter of the action was an e-mail—but only the author was sued and the form of the communication made no difference to the legal analysis. In *Emperor (China Concept) Investments Ltd. v. SBI E-2 Capital Securities Ltd. and Another,*[46] an allegedly defamatory e-mail was sent from Hong Kong to a recipient in Singapore and downloaded there. The author and his employer were sued in Hong Kong. The Court applied general private international law principles and the principle from the Australian decision of *Gutnick v. Dow Jones & Co. Inc.,*[47] to the effect that publication occurs at the place where the content is downloaded, and granted the defendants' application for a stay of the proceedings in Hong Kong on the grounds of *forum non conveniens.* The case of *Wang Lin Jia v. Ng Kai Cheung,*[48] concerned defamatory e-mails sent by the defendant from Hong Kong to recipients in Hong Kong and Singapore. The plaintiff's application for an interlocutory injunction to bar the sending of further e-mails was granted. The court concluded that even the e-mails downloaded in Singapore were actionable in Hong Kong, citing *Boys v. Chaplin*[49] for the proposition that a tort committed abroad is actionable in Hong Kong if it is actionable in both the foreign jurisdiction and Hong Kong.

4. ***Cases where a website operator has been sued for chat room publications.*** Several actions have been commenced against the website IceRed.com., seeking the disclosure of names, addresses, and IP addresses of those who have posted allegedly defamatory messages. In one case, the company E-Silkroad Holdings, alleging that there were libelous messages

posted about it on the IceRed discussion board website, obtained a court order requiring IceRed to provide the IP addresses of the authors of the allegedly libelous messages.[50]

5. ***Cases where a news service based in Hong Kong published an article on the Internet but it was unclear whether the article had been downloaded in Hong Kong.*** In *Abdul Razzak Yaqoob v. Asia Times Online Ltd.* [2008] HCA 1142 of 2006, the defendant's online news service was based in Hong Kong but it was not clear whether the offending article, which concerned activities in Dubai and was available online for just one day, had been downloaded in Hong Kong or only overseas. The court found that the article was probably downloaded in Hong Kong as well as overseas, but even on the assumption that the publication was downloaded only outside Hong Kong, the court held that it had jurisdiction to hear the case because the defendant corporation was based in Hong Kong.

20. If established media law has been applied to Internet publishers, are there any ways in which Internet publishers (including chat room operators) have to meet different standards?

Hong Kong law does not provide a statutory immunity for ISPs or webmasters. Although the normal practice in Hong Kong courts is to follow UK cases quite closely, there is no equivalent in Hong Kong to the UK 1996 Defamation Act, with its special protection for ISPs.

21. Are there any cases where the courts enforced a judgment in libel from another jurisdiction against a publisher in your jurisdiction?

The general principles and rules of enforcement of foreign judgments in Hong Kong are that:

1. Under the common law, an action may be brought to enforce a foreign court judgment. The common law rules are the same as those of England and would include the rule that a foreign judgment is not enforceable if it is impeachable on certain grounds, for instance that it was obtained by fraud, or that enforcing it would amount to enforcing a foreign penal or tax law.[51]
2. The Foreign Judgments (Reciprocal Enforcement) Ordinance (Cap. 319) provides a statutory procedure for registration and enforcement of foreign judgments. No common law action is required. The procedure applies only to judgments from jurisdictions that have been determined to offer reciprocal enforcement treatment to Hong Kong judgments. Section 4 of the ordinance provides that a judgment may be registered in the Court of First Instance (the main court of unlimited jurisdiction in Hong Kong) within six

> years of the date of delivery of the judgment. Under Section 6 a registration may be set aside on the grounds, *inter alia,* "(v) that the enforcement of the judgment shall be contrary to public policy in the country of the registering court."

With respect to defamation, reported Hong Kong cases have not raised any issue regarding the enforceability of a foreign judgment. In view of the fact that Hong Kong tends to fall into that group of countries with a more generous (pro-plaintiff) view of liability and damages, it is unlikely that a Hong Kong court would refuse to enforce a judgment on the grounds upon which some U.S. courts have declined to recognize awards from countries with less forceful constitutional protection for freedom of speech.

Chapter Notes

1. D. Weisenhaus, *Hong Kong Media Law: A Guide For Journalists and Media Professionals* (Hong Kong University Press 2007) (hereafter, *Weisenhaus*), p. 11.

2. *Ling Ham Herbalist Koon v. Radio Television Hong Kong* [1998] HKEC 67 (High Ct. of HK Special Admin. Region) (quoting *Gatley*).

3. R. Glofcheski, *Tort Law in Hong Kong* (Sweet & Maxwell Asia, 2nd ed., 2007) (hereafter, *Glofcheski*) at 652 (citing, *inter alia, Parmiter v. Coupland* [1840] 6 M&W 105; *Youssoupoff v. Metro-Goldwyn-Mayer Pictures Ltd.* [1934] 50 Times Law Report 581; and *Sim v. Stretch* [1936] 2 All ER 1237 (HL)).

4. [1987] HKLR 711.

5. Id.

6. See, e.g., *Glofcheski* at 661 (citing *Next Magazine Publishing Ltd. & Others v. Oriental Daily Publisher Ltd.* [2000] 2 HKLRD 333).

7. See, e.g., *Peregrine Investments Holdings Ltd. v. The Associated Press* [1997] HKLRD 1073 (quoting *Skuse v. Granada, The Independent,* April 2, 1993 [1996] *Entertainment and Media Law Reports* 278, and *Yam Chi Ming v. Sing Pao Newspaper Company Limited* [2006] HCA 99 of 2005).

8. *Yam Chi Ming v. Sing Pao Newspaper Company Limited (id.).*

9. [1999] 2 HKC 665.

10. *Beijing Television v. Brightec Ltd. and Others* (*id.*) (quoting, in part, *Fullam v. Newcastle Chronicle and Journal Ltd.* [1977] 1 WLR 651 at 654H-655D (*per* Lord Denning MR)) (internal quotation marks omitted).

11. See, e.g., *Next Magazine Publishing Ltd. and Others v. Oriental Daily Publisher Ltd.* (note 5 above).

12. *China Youth Development Ltd. v. Next Magazine Publishing Ltd.* [2000] HCA 6206 of 1994; *Hong Kong Polytechnic University v. Next Publishing Ltd.* [1997] 7 Hong Kong Public Law Reports 286.

13. *Glofcheski* at 663–64.

14. [2002] 1 HKLRD A21. The court also cited and applied a potentially far-reaching statement of principle by Lord Atkin in the English case *Knuppfer v. London Express Newspaper Ltd.* [1944] AC 116 at 121–22.

15. As discussed in Subsection (5) of Question 6 b ("Statutory Defenses"), Section 25 of the Defamation Ordinance provides a distinct statutory defense for "[u]nintentional defamation" if an "offer of amends" (defined in the statute) is made by the defendant and rejected by the plaintiff.

16. Since actual malice is not an element of libel, it need be proved by the plaintiff only if it is an element of a defense that the defendant has otherwise successfully raised.

17. *Tsang Hon Chu v. Wong Kwok Leung,* [2005] DCCJ 3917 of 2003.

18. *Lee Man Kin v. Wang Mei Chun and Others* [2005] HCA 2876 of 2003.

19. See *Ho Ping Kwong v. Chan Cordelia* [1989] 2 HKC 415 for a full discussion.

20. [2001] 2 AC 127.

21. [1997] 189 CLR 520.

22. *Reynolds,* note 19 above, at 205.

23. [2005] 3 HKLRD 133.

24. [2007] 1 AC 359.

25. [2000] 3 HKLRD 418.

26. [2002] 1 HKLRD 1.

27. [1946–1972] HKC 414.

28. [2003] 1 HKLRD 751.

29. [2003] DCCJ 4065 of 2002.

30. Gatley has suggested that "contemporaneous" should be taken to mean "as nearly at the same time as the proceedings as is reasonably possible, having regard to the opportunities for preparation of the report and the time of going to press or making the broadcast."

31. Defamation Ordinance Section 14(2).

32. See, e.g., *Oriental Press Group Ltd. and Others v. Ted Thomas* [1995] HCA 5217 of 1995.

33. *Weisenhaus* at 153–156.

34. *Weisenhaus* at 78–83.

35. *Glofcheski* at 707–08, citing *Chan Shui Shing Andrew and Others v. Ironwing Holdings Ltd.* [2001] 2 HKC 376.

36. *Weisenhaus* at 106 (see also chapter on privacy at 103–125).

37. *Li Yau-wai v. Genesis Films Ltd.* [1987] HKLR 711; *Lam Tai Hing v. Koo Chih Ling, Linda* [1993] 2 HKC 1; *Nam Tai Electronics v. Pricewaterhouse Coopers* [2008] 1 HKLRD 666.

38. *Eastweek v. Privacy Commissioner* [2000] 1HKC 692.

39. *Weisenhaus* at 114, 179–80.

40. *Leung Kwok Hung and Another v. Chief Executive of HKSAR* [2006] HKEC 816.

41. *Sham v. Eastweek Publisher Ltd.* [1994] 2 HKLR 381.

42. Note 25 above.

43. [1999] 3 HKC 515.

44. [1999] EMLR 278.

45. [2000] 1055 HKCU 1 (reported as *Drummond v. Kwaku* [2000] 1 HKLRD 604).

46. [2005] 4 HKLRD L6.

47. [2002] 210 CLR 575.

48. [2008] HCA 113 of 2008.

49. [1969] 3 WLR 322.

50. D. Nairne, "Court Forces IceRed's Hand on Giving Names," Technology Post, *South China Morning Post*, May 22, 2001, at 3.

51. *Korea Data Systems Co. Ltd. v. Chiang Jay Tien* [2001] 3 HKC 239.

CHAPTER 7

India

JANMEJAY RAI, PHILLIP NINAN, AND JAYNE KURIAKOSE

Kochhar & Co.

Kochhar & Co.
S-454, Greater Kailash Part-II
New Delhi – 110-048
Phone: 91 11 2921 1606, 2921 5477
Fax: 91 11 2921 9656, 2921-4932
www.kocchar.com
delhi@kochhar.com

Introduction to the Indian Legal System

India's legal system is based on a Constitution that came into force in 1950 and is largely based upon English common law. India's judiciary is often receptive to important U.S. court decisions. The Constitution guarantees equal rights to all citizens and prohibits discrimination on the basis of race, gender, caste, ethnicity, and religion. The Constitution also states that "All citizens shall have the right (a) to freedom of speech and expression. Nothing . . . shall affect the operation of any existing law, or prevent the State from making any law, in so far as such law imposes reasonable restrictions on the exercise of the right conferred by the said sub-clause in the interest of the security of the State, friendly relations with Foreign States, public order, decency or morality . . . ."[1]

Although politically arranged on a federal system and maintaining delineated central and state laws, India has a unified court system that administers both federal and state laws. A criminal case is heard first by the court of a Judicial Magistrate or District and Sessions Judge depending upon the gravity of the offense and the punishment prescribed for the same. The court of first instance for a civil case is the court of a Munsif or Civil Judge depending upon the monetary value of the subject matter under dispute. Both trial courts are divided into judicial districts, and these courts' decisions are appealed to a High Court in each state or group of states. The Supreme Court of India hears final appeals. The twenty-one High Courts and the Supreme Court are charged with protecting fundamental rights and constitutional interpretation. Supreme Court decisions are binding precedent on all courts in India.

1. What is the locally accepted definition of libel?

Indian law treats libel in both criminal and civil form. The most widely and commonly accepted definition of defamation, which takes within its sweep both libel (defamation in some permanent form) and slander (defamation in a transient form), is "a false statement about a man to his discredit." Section 499 of the Indian Penal Code, 1860 (IPC) provides the following definition of defamation:

> Whoever, by words, either spoken or intended to be read, or by signs or by visible representation, makes or publishes any imputation concerning any person intending to harm, or knowing or having reason to believe that such imputation will harm, the reputation of such person, is said, except in the cases hereinafter excepted, to defame that person.

The IPC goes on to provide no less than ten exceptions to the above definition. However, broadly speaking, in order to maintain a criminal action for libel, the following ingredients must be present:

1. The imputation must be published;
2. The imputation must have been made by words intended to be read or by other visible representations in permanent form; and
3. The imputation must have been made with the intention to harm or with the knowledge or having reason to believe that it will harm the reputation of the person concerned.

Under the Indian civil law of torts (based on various decided cases), a defamatory statement is one that:

> Directly or indirectly, in the estimation of others, lowers the moral or intellectual character of that person, or lowers the character of that person in respect of his caste or of his calling, or lowers the credit of that person, or causes it to be believed that the body of that person is in a loathsome state, or in a state generally considered as disgraceful.

It may be pertinent to note that law of torts is neither codified nor a very well-developed branch of law in India, and most of its principles emanate from common law (decided English cases). Some illustrations with respect to a tortious view of defamation are as follows: To say that a person built his fortune on the backs of the uneducated masses is not defamatory, but to refer to a person as a "Godse" (Gandhi's assassin) was held to be defamatory because it asserted that the subject would resort to murder.[2] To say that a person is the type who would commit a crime has also been found to be defamatory.[3]

2. Is libel-by-implication recognized, or, in the alternative, must the complained-of words alone defame the plaintiff?

Libel-by-implication is recognized under Indian law. However, words that are *prima facie* innocent would not be actionable unless the plaintiff proves their secondary or latent defamatory meaning. Where the words alleged to be defamatory do not appear to be such on their face, the plaintiff is required to make out the circumstances that made such words actionable by innuendo. Courts recognize that a defamatory innuendo may be put forward by way of a question, exclamation, conjecture, or irony.

3. May corporations sue for libel?

Yes, corporations have standing to sue for libel.

4. Is product disparagement recognized, and if so, how does that differ from libel?

Product disparagement is recognized under Indian law, and it is illegal for a tradesman in India to disparage the products of a rival.[4] Courts in India have also found generic disparagement of rival products, without direct reference to the competitor, objectionable and have passed orders restraining such disparagement. In the recent case of *Glaxo Smith Kline Consumer Health Care Limited v. Heinz India Private Limited and Ors*,[5] the High Court of Calcutta held that the advertisement of Heinz for their product Complan was wrong and offending as it sought to project Glaxo Smith Kline Consumer Health Care Limited's (GSK's) competing product Horlicks as inferior. The case revolved around a storyboard. The storyboard projected in Heinz's TV advertisement sought to project GSK's product Horlicks as lacking in the supply of an adequate quantity of protein and other nutrition to help the growth of children. The comparison was sought to be made by pouring two liquids, one of brown color (which was also the color of Complan) in a white cup of the same size, and another liquid of white color (which was also the color of Horlicks) being poured in a murky brown cup of equal size with an indication of the letter *H*. The market survey report conducted by an expert body stated that every consumer in the public at large who was a regular customer of the Horlicks, and for that matter other consumers as well, got the clear impression that the letter *H* represented Horlicks. It was held that the comparison was harmful because it sent the message that GSK's product Horlicks does not help in the growth of children, whereas use of the Heinz product Complan does result in significant growth of children.

The essential difference between libel and product disparagement is that libel must contain an element of malice whereas there is no such requirement in the case of product disparagement.

5. Must an individual be clearly identified (by name or photograph) to sue for libel? Can a group of persons sue for libel, even though not named?

In order to sue for libel under Indian law, it is not necessary that an individual be clearly identified by way of name or photograph. If plaintiffs can show that they were specially referred to, it is immaterial whether the words complained of described the plaintiffs by their own names or initial letters or by a fictitious name or even by somebody else's name. Further, it is also immaterial whether or not the defendant intended the defamatory statement to apply to the plaintiffs or knew of the plaintiffs' existence (if the statement might reasonably be understood by those who knew the plaintiffs to refer to them).

Indian law has rejected a "group libel" approach. The relevant rule in this regard is that for an imputation to be held as defamatory for a group of persons, it must be directed against a definite and specified group of persons.[6]

It may amount to defamation to impute anything to a deceased person, if the imputation would harm the reputation of that person if living, *and* is intended to be hurtful to the feelings of the family or other near relatives of the deceased.

6. What is the fault standard(s) applied to libel?

a. Does the fault standard depend on the fame or notoriety of the plaintiff?

To a certain degree, yes. Under Indian law, the following elements are weighed in a finding of liability: (1) the nature and character of the libel; (2) the extent of circulation of the libelous imputation; (3) the position in life of the parties; and (4) the other surrounding circumstances of the case.

b. Is there a heightened fault standard or privilege for reporting on matters of public concern or public interest?

Indian libel law is dotted with a number of substantive defenses and privileges. Courts have also applied a broadly read public interest privilege, which protects a good faith opinion respecting the conduct of public servants in the discharge of their public functions, or respecting their character, so far as their character appears in that conduct, and no further.[7]

The public interest privilege has also been read to immunize speech addressing the conduct of any person touching any public question. Again, the opprobrium must be limited to the subjects' character in direct relationship to the public issue conduct in question. The Supreme Court of India has to a considerable extent adopted the "actual malice" standard as elucidated in the U.S. case of *New York Times v. Sullivan,* and suits brought by public officials must show that at least with regard to statements confined to that person's public conduct, a claim cannot succeed absent the plaintiff establishing that the statement was made with "reckless disregard for the truth."[8]

Truth is an absolute defense in civil claims,[9] but criminal defense in libel must include a showing that the statement at issue serves the public interest.

7. Is financial news about publicly traded companies, or companies involved with a government contract, considered a matter of public interest or otherwise privileged?

Financial news about publicly traded companies or companies involved with government contracts per se may not be considered a matter of public interest and consequently may not be privileged. However, there may be cases where news regarding publicly traded companies or companies involved with government may be considered to be in the realm of public interest but at the same time would depend upon the peculiar facts and circumstances of each case.[10]

8. Is there a recognized protection for opinion or "fair comment" on matters of public concern?

Yes. Under Indian law, a qualified privilege exists for "fair and bona fide comment on a matter of public interest."[11] However, the word "fair" embraces the meaning of honest and also of relevancy to the matter of public interest. Courts will reject this defense if there is a credible allegation that the reporter's error was not in good faith, as malice (knowing falsity) will defeat the privilege. Under Indian law, a statement is said to have a qualified privilege when no action lies for it, even though it is false and defamatory, unless the plaintiff proves malice.

The following matters have been found to be considered in the "public interest": affairs of the state; public acts of ministers and officers of the state; the administration of justice; public institutions and local authorities; ecclesiastical matters; books, pictures, and works of art; theaters, concerts, and other public entertainment; and appeals to the public, e.g., a medical person bringing forward some new method of treatment and advertising it or a person appealing to the public by writing letters to a newspaper.

Indian law has also broadly interpreted a "common interest" privilege, wherein "It is not defamation to convey a caution, in good faith, to one person against another, provided that such caution be intended for the good of the person to whom it is conveyed, or of some person in whom that person is interested, or for the public good."

For purposes of criminal defamation, a mere belief in the statement made will not suffice to establish a "good faith" privilege. Under courts' reading of the IPC, "the accused must show that he had a rational basis, had acted with due care, and was satisfied that the imputation was true."[12]

9. Are there any requirements upon a plaintiff, such as demand for retraction or right of reply, and if so, what impact do they have?
No. Indian law does not require that a plaintiff demand retraction prior to proceeding with a libel claim. However, if the defendant tenders an apology that is accepted by the plaintiff, the defendant can resist the plaintiff's action for damages for defamation in the court of law. There is no statutory right of reply under Indian law.

10. Is there a privilege for quoting or reporting on:

a. Papers filed in court?
Yes. Quoting or reporting of a true, accurate, and bona fide account of papers (pleadings, applications, and affidavits) filed in court may be privileged if they relate to matters of public interest. Papers filed in court enjoy an absolute privilege whereby no action lies even though they are false and defamatory or made falsely and maliciously or made without any reasonable or probable excuse. A statement is absolutely privileged when no action lies for it, even though it contains false or defamatory allegations, without regard to whether the reporter has knowledge of its falsity.

b. Government-issued documents?
Under the Indian law of torts, quoting or reporting of a true, accurate, and bona fide account of any governmental/official documents or publications is also absolutely privileged, provided that the documents contain matters of public interest. Because the Indian definition of "public interest" includes governmental affairs and the administration of justice, the privilege is widely construed.

Statements made during parliamentary proceedings, judicial proceedings, or state proceedings are also protected by absolute privilege.

c. Quasi-governmental proceedings?

Yes. Disciplinary proceedings are generally deemed to be in the nature of quasi-judicial proceedings in India, and thus privileged. Also, quoting or reporting of true, accurate, and bona fide accounts of the same may be privileged if they contain matters of public interest.

11. Is there a privilege for republishing statements made earlier by other, bona fide, reliable publications or wire services?

No. Although such reports may be subject to a public interest defense, there is no specific immunity for the republication of defamatory material from other publications or wire services. For this reason, when defamatory material is considered for republication, reporters and editors should make some bona fide effort to ascertain the truth of the matter reported, and determine whether the article serves the public interest.

12. Are there any restrictions regarding reporting on:

a. Ongoing criminal investigations?

Yes. Reporting of an ongoing criminal investigation should be such that the report should not malign the character and conduct of the person or body of persons being investigated without sufficient or reasonable excuse. Further, the report should not be judgmental so as to create a prejudice in the minds of the general public and also the investigating agency.

b. Ongoing criminal prosecutions?

Reporting on ongoing criminal prosecutions is allowed subject to the restriction that such report is impartial, bona fide, and gives a fair and substantially accurate account of such proceedings. Indian law also imposes certain restrictions on reporting criminal investigations, such as where: (1) the reporting or publication is contrary to the provisions of any statute in force; (2) the court has expressly prohibited reporting or publication of all information relating to the proceeding; (3) the court sits in camera for reason connected with public order or the security of the state; or (4) the information relating to a secret process, discovery, or invention is an issue before the court.

Indian law also proscribes violation of reporting restrictions above with punishment under the Contempt of Courts Act, 1971.[13] Reporters should be aware that courts can, by application or on their own initiative, institute publication bans without notice to the press.

c. Ongoing regulatory investigations?

The same restrictions would apply as for ongoing criminal investigations (in Question 12a above).

d. Ongoing civil litigation, or other judicial proceedings?

The same restrictions would apply as for ongoing criminal prosecutions (in Question 12b above).

13. Are prior restraints or other prepublication injunctions available on the basis of libel or privacy, and if so, what are the standards for obtaining such relief?

Yes. Prepublication injunctions are available on the basis of libel or invasion of privacy. However, the court will only interfere if the plaintiff satisfies the court that: (1) the statement about to be published is demonstrably false; and (2) there is some likelihood of immediate and pressing injury to person or property or trade of the plaintiff.[14]

Further, prepublication restraint on a publication may also be obtained by demonstrating to the court that the publication is being made for the sole purpose of harming the plaintiff. An injunction could also be obtained by establishing that the intention behind the publication is to blackmail the plaintiff.

14. Is a right of privacy recognized (either civilly or criminally)?

Yes. The right to privacy is recognized in India under the Supreme Court of India's reading of Article 21 of the Constitution, which guarantees "the right to life and personal liberty."

However, fundamental rights under the Constitution (such as those found in Article 21) can only be enforced against the State or statutory bodies formed under a specific legislation, and cannot be enforced against private individuals or entities. In the event a breach of privacy claim is brought against a private citizen, the same would need to be brought as a civil suit to obtain damages or an injunction. Recently, these claims are being looked at favorably by the courts even though a right to undisturbed privacy is not recognized in the common law in India.

a. What is the definition of "private fact"?

There is no statutory definition of "private fact." However, it is surmised that a private fact must include all aspects of personal intimacies of the home, the family, marriage, motherhood, procreation, religion, health, sexuality, etc. A private fact can, at best, have an inclusive definition and cannot be defined with a catalog approach.

b. Is there a public interest or newsworthiness exception?

The Press Council of India has framed "Norms for Journalistic Conduct," which lay down general rules to be followed by all journalists. The Norms categorically provide that the press shall not intrude or invade the privacy of an individual unless outweighed and warranted by larger public interest. Provision 13 of the Norms states that:

> The Press shall not intrude or invade the privacy of an individual unless outweighed by genuine overriding public interest, not being a prurient or morbid curiosity. So, however, that once a matter becomes a matter of public record, the right to privacy no longer subsists and it becomes a legitimate subject for comment by Press and media among others.

India has recognized a newsworthiness exception to privacy claims. In the case of Auto Shankar, a convicted felon who brought claims in privacy after newspapers published details from his life available from public records, the court held that even without authorization, such use was permitted.[15] It is generally held that persons who voluntarily thrust themselves into the public light or raise a controversy may not have a cause of action for privacy, at least as far as such private facts related to the controversy being reported upon.

One of the latest and prominent judgments passed by the Delhi High Court recently relating to the newsworthiness exception is in the matter of *Indu Jain v. Forbes Inc.*[16] Indu Jain had filed a suit against Forbes Inc. seeking, *inter alia*, a decree of permanent injunction restraining *Forbes* from publishing her name in *Forbes* magazine's feature on the wealthiest people in the world. Jain was featured in the *Forbes* list of billionaires, both in the Asia list and in the world list. In this landmark case, the Court laid down the law relating to right to privacy in India. The Court held that the disputed publication has to be judged as a whole and news items, advertisements, and published matter cannot be read without the accompanying message that is purported to be conveyed to the public. The Court further held that unless it is established that the publication has been made with reckless disregard for truth, the publication shall not normally be prohibited. In the instant case, the Court refused to grant permanent injunction against the publication of the feature on many grounds including, *inter alia*, that (i) Jain was a prominent public figure, (ii) Jain was aware of the previous editions of such publications featuring her, (iii) Forbes had explained the nature of its publication and methodology used to arrive at the financial figures, (iv) various communications on the subject matter were exchanged between Forbes and Jain, and (v) there was no damage or irreparable loss or injury suffered by Jain. As of 2008, this judgment has not been overruled by a judgment of a superior court.

c. Is the right of privacy based in common law, statute, or constitution?

The right to privacy as an independent and distinctive concept originated under common law and the law of torts, under which a new cause of action for damages resulting from unlawful invasion of privacy was recognized. In recent times, however, the said right has acquired a constitutional status by virtue of a galaxy of Supreme Court judgments, which have held that the right to privacy is implicit in the right to life and personal liberty enshrined under Article 21 of the Constitution of India.

New technological advances have spurred on the legislative growth of privacy law in India and provisions relating to the protection of an individual's privacy rights have been incorporated in recently enacted legislation such as the Information Technology Act, 2000 (IT Act). The IT Act provides remedies against the breach of confidentiality and privacy.[17]

A study of recent case law relating to the right to privacy reveals the following two elements as the main ones that would make up a claim for breach of privacy:

(1) the existence of facts of which there is a reasonable expectation of privacy; and
(2) the publicity given to those private facts that would be considered highly offensive to an objective, reasonable person.[18]

Citizens have a right to privacy of their own selves, family, marriage, procreation, motherhood, child-bearing, and education, among other matters.[19] Under Indian law, no individual or entity can publish anything concerning the above matters without a party's consent, regardless of whether the material reported is truthful, laudatory, or critical.[20]

It may also be noted that India is a signatory to the International Covenant on Civil and Political Rights, 1966 (the Covenant). Article 17 of the Covenant provides for the "right to privacy." India is also a signatory to the Universal Declaration of Human Rights, 1948 (the Declaration). Article 12 of the Declaration is almost similar in terms to Article 17 of the Covenant.

15. May reporters tape-record their own telephone conversations for note-taking purposes (not rebroadcast) without the consent of the other party?

Persons are generally not permitted to tape-record their telephone conversations with anyone, without the knowledge or consent of all parties to the call. However, Provision 16 of the Norms states that tape-recording a telephone conversation may be allowed where such recording is "necessitated for protecting the journalist in a legal action or for other compellingly good reasons."

16. If permissible to record such tapes, may they be broadcast without permission?

No. Even if a compellingly good reason exists for recording such, the same may not be broadcast without the permission of the other party.

17. Is there a recognized evidentiary privilege preventing the disclosure of confidential sources relied upon by reporters?

Yes. It is known as the "newspaper rule," and reporters may not be compelled to disclose the confidential source of their information at an interim stage in a court proceeding.[21] However, there is no privilege protecting reporters from disclosing their source of information if the court requires such a disclosure in the interest of justice, such as the prevention of a crime or a threat to public health or safety.

18. In the event that legal papers are served upon the newsroom (such as a civil complaint), are there any particular warnings about accepting service of which we should be aware?

In case of a civil action, if service of summons is rejected by a reporter (the defendant) at the workplace (the newsroom) and if the process server affixes such summons at a conspicuous place in or outside the newsroom, the service would be deemed to have been effected.[22] If the defendant does not appear before the court after such deemed service, the court would proceed to hear the matter *ex parte.*

In case of a criminal proceeding for defamation, if a reporter (the accused) rejects the service of summons, he can have an arrest warrant issued against him.

19. Has your jurisdiction applied established media law to Internet publishers?

There have been no reported judgments thus far wherein an Internet publisher has been held liable for defamation, libel, or violation of the right to privacy. However, under the IPC's statutory definition of defamation, it would appear that the Indian law of torts is broad enough to include Internet publishers within its sweep for purposes of defamation and privacy actions.

However, in India's first cyber defamation case filed in the Delhi High Court,[23] an employee of a company was injuncted from sending anonymous and highly derogatory e-mails to his employers and subsidiaries of the company where he worked.

20. If established media law has been applied to Internet publishers, are there any ways in which Internet publishers (including chat room operators) have to meet different standards?

There are no substantive differences. Internet publishers (including chat room operators) have to comply with all the aforesaid prescribed standards.

The only exception to the aforesaid has been provided in Section 79 of the IT Act. Under Section 79 of the IT Act, Internet publishers including chat room operators (both of which fall within the definition of an "intermediary" under the IT Act) are not liable for an offense under or contravention of the IT Act in respect of any third party information or data made available by them if they prove that (a) the offense or contravention was committed without their knowledge; and (b) they had exercised all due diligence to prevent the commission of such offense or contravention.[24]

21. Are there any cases where the courts enforced a judgment in libel from another jurisdiction against a publisher in your jurisdiction?
There are no reported cases where a court in India has enforced a foreign judgment for libel against a publisher in India.

Chapter Notes

1. Article 19(1)(a) and 19(2) of the Constitution of India.

2. *Purshottam Sayal v. Prem Shanker* AIR 1966 All. 377 (1519).

3. *S.M. Narayanan v. S.R. Narayana Iyer,* AIR 1961 Mad. 254 (257).

4. *Dabur India Limited v. Emami Limited 2004 (29) PTC1 (Del); Pepsi Co. Inc. and Ors v. Hindustan Coca Cola Limited and Anr (2003 (27) PTC 305 (Del) (DB); Hindustan Lever v. Colgate Palmolive (I) Limited, 1998 (1) SCC 720).*

5. 2007(2) CHN 44.

6. *G. Narasimhan, G. Kasturi & K. Gopalan v. T.V. Chokkappa: (1972)* 2 Supreme Court Cases *680.*

7. *Sewakram Sobhani v. R.K. Karanjiya* AIR 1981 SC 1514 (1519).

8. *R. Rajgopal v. State of Tamil Nadu* (1994) 6 SCC 632.

9. *Nellikka Achuthan v. Deshabimani Printing and Publishing House Ltd.,* AIR 1986 Ker. 41 (43).

10. For example, substantiated reports alleging financial mismanagement in a publicly traded company or corruption in the award of a government contract to a particular company may fall within the realm of public interest.

11. *Dainik Bhaskar v. Madhusudan Bhargava,* AIR 1991 MP 162 (166).

12. *Sukra Mahto v. Basudeo Kumar Mahto,* AIR 1971 SC 1567 (1569).

13. Section 12 of the Contempt of Courts Act, 1971, provides that a Contempt of Court may be punished with simple imprisonment for a term which may extend to six (6) months or with a fine which may extend to Rupees Two Thousand (Rs. 2000/-) or with both. However, the accused may be discharged or the punishment awarded may be remitted on an apology being made to the satisfaction of the court.

14. *Reliance Petrochemicals Ltd. v. Indian Express Newspapers Bombay Pvt. Ltd.*, AIR 1989 SC 190 (195).

15. *R. Rajgopal v. State of Tamil Nadu* (1994) 6 SCC 632.

16. 2007 Delhi High Court Judgment (unreported).

17. Section 72 of the IT Act.

18. *Govind v. State of M.P.*, (1975) 2 SCC 148; *R. Rajgopal v. State of Tamil Nadu* (1994) 6 SCC 632; *Indu Jain v. Forbes Incorporated*, 2007 Delhi High Court Judgment (Unreported); *Ajay Goswami v. UOI & Ors*, (2007) 1 SCC 143; *Khushwant Singh v. Maneka Gandhi*, AIR 2002 Delhi 58; *Kaleidoscope (India) (P) Ltd. v. Phoolan Devi*, AIR 1995 Del 316; *People's Union of Civil Liberties v. Union of India* (1997), 1 SCC 301.

19. *Govind v. State of M.P.*, (1975) 2 SCC 148; *R. Rajgopal v. State of Tamil Nadu* (1994) 6 SCC 632.

20. *Govind v. State of M.P.*, (1975) 2 SCC 148; *R. Rajgopal v. State of Tamil Nadu* (1994) 6 SCC 632.

21. *Nishi Prem v. Javed Akhtar* AIR 199 Bom. 222.

22. Order V Rule 17 of the Code of Civil Procedure, 1908 (as amended till date) lays down the procedure for service of summons when defendant refuses to accept service or cannot be found.

23. *SMC Pneumatics (India) Pvt. Ltd. v. Jogesh Kwatra* Delhi High Court—Because this was only an interim injunction passed by the Delhi High Court and not the final order, the same has not been reported.

24. The Ministry of Information Technology is contemplating issuing a model "Code of Conduct and Practices to be adopted for the functioning of Cyber Cafes/Chat Room Centers." In this regard, a draft code is being prepared by the Asian School of Cyber Laws (ASCL) under the supervision of the Ministry of Information Technology. http://www.financialexpress.com/fe_archive_full_story.php?content_id=42771, *Financial Express* dated September 26, 2003.

CHAPTER **8**

Japan

YOSHIO ITEYA, TOMOYA FUJIMOTO,
AND AKIRA MARUMO
Mori Hamada & Matsumoto

Mori Hamada & Matsumoto
Marunouchi Kitaguchi Building
1-6-5 Marunouchi, Chiyoda-ku
Tokyo 100-8222, Japan
Phone: (81) (3) 5223-7777
Fax: (81) (3) 5223-7666
www.mhmjapan.com
yoshio.iteya@mhmjapan.com

Introduction to the Japanese Legal System

The Japanese system is a nonfederalist organization with four court levels: summary courts, district and family courts, high courts, and the Supreme Court. The Japanese system was reconstructed in 1946, at the end of World War II. The Japanese Bill of Rights (1946), with thirty-one articles related to human rights and many other laws emphasizing human rights, is modeled after the U.S. legal system. It is considered a civil law system with customary differences.

The decision-making process in Japan is unique. The Japanese legal system is divided among six codes: the Constitution, the civil code, the code of civil procedure, the penal code, the code of criminal procedure, and the commercial code. Japanese courts examine and consider both Japanese laws and international laws to determine what a fair resolution might be. The system includes a single Supreme Court, eight high courts, fifty district and family courts, and forty-eight summary courts for small criminal and small civil actions. With easily accessible court records, out-of-court settlements are very common in the Japanese system.

1. What is the locally accepted definition of libel?

In Japan, there is both civil and criminal liability for libel and related offenses. Libel (*meiyo-kison*) under the Civil Code (Articles 709 and 710) constitutes a tort, and has been interpreted to mean a statement that injures "the social reputation that a person enjoys due to his or her personal merits such as personality, character, fame and credibility."[1] The standard applied in determining whether a statement has damaged a person's social reputation is that of the average reader, giving a normal reading and attention to the statement.[2]

Under the Criminal Code, there are three offenses that are relevant to libel:

1. damage to honor (*meiyo-kison*), which is defined as the injuring of a person's social position or reputation through publicly alleging facts (Article 230);
2. insult (*bujoku*), which is defined as the injuring of a person's reputation in public without alleging facts (Article 231); and
3. damage to credit (*shinyo-kison*), which is defined as the injuring of a person's credit by delivering false rumors or employing deceptive measures (Article 233).

The definition of libel under the Civil Code includes the three offenses under the Criminal Code.

The criminal penalty for both damage to honor (*meiyo-kison*) and damage to credit (*shinyo-kison*) is imprisonment for as long as three years and/or a fine of up to 500,000 yen. The penalty for insult (*bujoku*) is imprisonment of up to thirty days and/or a minor fine (1,000 yen to 10,000 yen). Imprisonment is rarely ordered and fines are the customary punishment.

A defendant who is found to have committed libel under the Civil Code would be liable to pay damages to the plaintiff. The amount of these damages, of course, will depend upon the circumstances of each case and the severity of the defamation. The amount of damages awarded by the court in the case of newspaper and news reports is mostly in the range of 10,000 yen to 500,000 yen, with a small number of awards in egregious cases on the order of 2–4 million yen, although there has been recent discussion about increasing the amount of damages awarded by courts to a range of 5,000,000 yen to 10,000,000 yen. The courts have the authority to also demand that the publisher place a notice of apology or revocation, and in very rare cases, to delete the report altogether. However, the Supreme Court denied the right of a person whose social reputation was injured by a television report to require a rebroadcast of a modified report.[3]

2. Is libel-by-implication recognized, or, in the alternative, must the complained-of words alone defame the plaintiff?

Under Japanese law, libel-by-implication is not recognized as a separate legal concept, but given Japan's very broad interpretation of defamatory meaning, libel may occur in a statement that does not allege any false facts. Given the central role of "face" or "honor" in Japanese culture, the test applied is whether the average person would consider that the reputation of the plaintiff has been damaged. Therefore, if the average person would consider a statement that is defamatory only by implication to have injured the plaintiff's reputation, then the statement will fall within the definition of libel, despite the fact that no direct statement has been made.

3. May corporations sue for libel?

Yes. Corporations are also recognized as having reputations of their own that can be injured. The Supreme Court has held that political parties, companies, and other legal entities may also have social reputations that can be injured.[4]

In addition, local municipal entities constitute legal entities that can be sued for libel.[5]

4. Is product disparagement recognized, and if so, how does that differ from libel?

Under Japanese law, product disparagement is not recognized as a separate legal concept. However, to the extent that any product disparagement falls within the above definition of libel, it would be actionable in Japan. One such example is a case where false statements made in respect of a dictionary sold by the plaintiff company were held to constitute libel.[6]

5. Must an individual be clearly identified (by name or photograph) to sue for libel? Can a group of persons sue for libel, even though not named?

In principle, an individual must be clearly identified to be able to sue for libel. It is not necessary that the statement actually name the plaintiff, rather that the plaintiff be sufficiently identifiable as a result of the report. Therefore, defamatory reports in respect of a large class of people (e.g., residents of Tokyo, members of a business community) will not constitute libel. However, in the event the class is sufficiently small, and the members of that class are specified or identifiable, a report may constitute libel of the members of that class, but not of the class itself.

6. What is the fault standard(s) applied to libel?

a. Does the fault standard depend on the fame or notoriety of the plaintiff?

No. The fame or notoriety of the plaintiff is not considered in applying the test for determining whether libel has been constituted, which is whether the plaintiff's reputation in society has been injured. However, as mentioned below, there is a defense available to a defendant in Japan that the report was a matter of public concern or in the public interest. The fame or notoriety of the plaintiff will only be a factor taken into consideration when determining whether or not a report constitutes an invasion of privacy.

b. Is there a heightened fault standard or privilege for reporting on matters of public concern or public interest?

In Japan there is only one fault standard that is applied in libel cases. This analysis is generally described as:

1. whether the report relates to a matter in the public interest (including a benefit or loss to the public's understanding of an important issue);
2. whether the report is made mainly to promote that public interest; and
3. whether the report is true or the reporter had adequate basis to believe that the report is true.[7]

Unlike law in certain U.S. cases, the fact that the reporter may have believed that the report was true is not sufficient to mount the defense. All three of the above criteria must be met. The defendant must present to the court evidence upon which the report was based, and it will be adjudged on an objective standard.

7. Is financial news about publicly traded companies, or companies involved with a government contract, considered a matter of public interest or otherwise privileged?

There is no case law in Japan that has held, as a general principle, that financial news in relation to a public company is a matter of public interest. Whether financial news about publicly traded companies is in fact in the public interest will depend on the coverage of the report and the facts of each case. For example, a report about companies involved in a government contract may be considered to be in the public interest, provided that the coverage of that report is relevant to the government contract.

8. Is there a recognized protection for opinion or "fair comment" on matters of public concern?

Yes, a protection for "fair comment" will be available where:

1. the opinion or comment is relevant to matters of public concern;
2. it is made mainly to promote the public interest;
3. a substantial portion of the facts upon which the opinion or comment is made are true or the reporter had adequate basis to believe that the facts are true; and
4. the report is not an extreme personal attack.[8] However, that opinion or comment cannot be beyond what is a reasonable opinion or comment in tone or tenor, and may constitute actionable insult (*bujoku*).[9]

The statement is treated as an opinion or comment when facts alleged in the statement regarding other entities cannot be proved by evidence, and the statement is treated as an allegation of facts when the facts can be proved by evidence.[10]

9. Are there any requirements upon a plaintiff, such as demand for retraction or right of reply, and if so, what impact do they have?

Under Japanese law, the plaintiff does not have any statutory right of reply, such as the right to require the defendant to place a counterargument. However, under Article 723 of the Civil Code, a plaintiff can ask the court to require a defendant to take measures to remedy the damage to the plaintiff's reputation, such as placing a notice of apology or a notice of retraction in the defendant's publication. In very rare cases the defendant has been ordered to delete the defamatory report altogether. An order to place such a notice is usually made where the court regards the payment of damages alone as insufficient to remedy the damage to the plaintiff's reputation or honor.

Westerners are reminded here that apologies have a special meaning in Japanese culture, and in the event that a publication is inaccurate or otherwise potentially actionable, the offer of a very prominent and sincere public apology may resolve impending litigation.

10. Is there a privilege for quoting or reporting on:

a. Papers filed in court?

There is no special privilege for reporting on court documents under Japanese law. The fact that a statement was made in court papers does not relieve reporters of their responsibility regarding the accuracy of that statement. The fact that the relied-upon papers come from the court may go a long way in convincing a judge that the reporter had a good faith basis upon which to base the statement; however, journalists should be cautioned that there is no "absolute" privilege. Thus, reporters have the burden of seeking out and reporting information that might be contrary to the assertions made in court papers.

Article 230-2(2) of the Criminal Code gives some assistance to a defendant in strictly deeming (i.e., there can be no exceptions or rebuttal) that reporting on criminal actions before public prosecution is in the public interest.

b. Government-issued documents?

The same will apply for government-issued documents and quasi-governmental proceedings. Provided that papers filed in court are a matter of public record (some courts may be closed), there will be no problem with respect to breach of privacy in disclosing the content of the papers.

c. Quasi-governmental proceedings?

There is no particular privilege for this type of material.

11. Is there a privilege for republishing statements made earlier by other, bona fide, reliable publications or wire services?

No. In Japan, the republishing of statements subjects the repeating party to claims of libel. However, the fact that the republishing is based on the report of a bona fide, reliable publication or wire service will be regarded as one factor in favor of the defendant's determination or belief that the facts alleged in the report are true, which is one of the elements of the defense to libel outlined in 6b above.

Reporters and editors must be judicious in their reliance upon other publications and wire services. The fact that it was published elsewhere is not enough: the court will examine the general reliability and expertise of the first publisher. In this regard, there is at least one Supreme Court case holding that a newspaper publisher did not have a reasonable basis to believe the truth of news it sourced from a news agency the court found lacking in such reliability.[11] "Gossip" or "rumor" Web pages popular throughout Asia should not be blindly relied upon.

12. Are there any restrictions regarding reporting on:

a. Ongoing criminal investigations?

There are no particular restrictions on reporting any of the matters above in addition to the general principles of libel already mentioned.

Article 230-2(3) of the Criminal Code provides a defense to any libel claim pursuant to that Code where (1) the defendant was reporting in respect of a public official or a candidate for public office; and (2) the report was true. Please note, however, that any comments should be made carefully in accordance with the principles of "fair comment" mentioned above.

b. Ongoing criminal prosecutions?
None.

c. Ongoing regulatory investigations?
None.

d. Ongoing civil litigation, or other judicial proceedings?
None.

13. Are prior restraints or other prepublication injunctions available on the basis of libel or privacy, and if so, what are the standards for obtaining such relief?

Prior restraints and prepublication injunctions are available under Japanese law on the basis of libel and breach of privacy. The standard to obtain such relief in respect of libel is as follows:

1. the matters alleged in the report are not true or the report is clearly not made in the public interest; and
2. there is a risk that the victim will incur serious damage that cannot be remedied.

The standard to obtain such relief in respect of breach of privacy is as follows:

1. the report is clearly not in the public interest; and
2. there is a risk that the victim will incur serious damage that cannot be remedied.

14. Is a right of privacy recognized (either civilly or criminally)?

a. What is the definition of "private fact"?

Violation of the right of privacy can be the basis for civil action in tort under the Civil Code. A "private fact" is a fact that:

1. concerns the private life of a person or matters deemed to relate to the private life of a person;
2. the person would not want to have disclosed, judged on the standard of the average person; and
3. has not yet been disclosed.

b. Is there a public interest or newsworthiness exception?

Yes. As mentioned in our response to 6a above, the privacy of celebrities or people in the public eye, such as politicians and well-known entertainers, is acknowledged by the courts to be more limited than the average "person in the street."[12] The extent to which the privacy of such people is limited will depend on the extent of their fame and the nature of their activities in society.

c. Is the right of privacy based in common law, statute, or constitution?

There is a right of privacy that is recognized under both the Japanese Constitution and the Civil Code. Under the Constitution, a right of privacy is derived from a general right to the pursuit of happiness under Article 13. The Supreme Court has generally defined this right as one that precludes the reckless or arbitrary disclosure of information about an individual's private life.

This right has been further construed by scholars to include a right to control one's personal information, although the Supreme Court has not specifically elaborated further on the definition of the constitutional "right to privacy." Article 709 of the Civil Code also provides for a tort action in connection with a breach of a right of privacy, as discussed in 14a above.

The discussion of privacy rights has most recently been focused on protection of personal information in connection with the maintenance and use of information databases. Under the Law Concerning Protection of Private Information, "Private Information" is defined as information relating to a living individual's name, date of birth, and other matters that could identify specific individuals (including items of information that may be easily collated with other information to identify specific individuals). Private Information Handling Entities (i.e., entities who maintain databases of Private Information) are under certain obligations with respect to the use and protection of Private Information in their possession.

15. May reporters tape-record their own telephone conversations for note-taking purposes (not rebroadcast) without the consent of the other party?

This area of the law is unclear in Japan, and there are several different views as to whether reporters can tape-record their telephone conversations with another party without the consent of that party.

One view is that this action would be immoral but not illegal, as the other party has the ability to control his or her side of the conversation. A second view is that the recording could be illegal as a violation of the party's reasonable expectation of privacy. The third view attempts to resolve the two by reasoning that the legality of the action will depend on a fact-based analysis of whether the complaining party should reasonably have expected the privacy of the conversation to be maintained in the circumstances. Generally, if a person clearly identifies herself on the telephone as a journalist or reporter to the person, then it could be reasonable to assume that the conversation will be "on the record."

16. If permissible to record such tapes, may they be broadcast without permission?

The legality of broadcasting a tape-recorded conversation without explicit consent is unclear under Japanese law. Although not statutorily proscribed, there is some scholarly consensus that broadcasting the visual image of an individual requires the individual's consent, as this entails issues involving an individual's "right of portrait." While it is possible that a voice recording may not rise to the same level of legal protection as a visual image, we believe that, in the absence of legal precedent, the prudent course would be to obtain explicit consent prior to broadcasting a tape-recorded conversation.

17. Is there a recognized evidentiary privilege preventing the disclosure of confidential sources relied upon by reporters?

No. There is no statutory or common law "shield law" and confidential sources relied upon by reporters must be disclosed in legal proceedings. A reporter is not under any obligation to disclose a source prior to the proceedings.[13]

18. In the event that legal papers are served upon the newsroom (such as a civil complaint), are there any particular warnings about accepting service of which we should be aware?

If legal papers are sent to you in respect of proceedings in Japan, a court-appointed agent will serve the papers, and no issue can be taken regarding the validity of the service. In this case, therefore, we recommend that you accept service of the documents and contact your legal advisers immediately.

19. Has your jurisdiction applied established media law to Internet publishers?

As discussed in Question 20 below, Japanese libel law has been applied to statements published on the Internet. There is, however, no case testing the jurisdictional limits of Japanese libel law in connection with Internet publications. Thus, there remains a question as to whether Japanese courts would apply its law to statements published on a server located outside of Japan. It is likely that Japanese libel law would apply in such case if, at a minimum, the libelous statement was published in Japanese and reasonably directed at an audience in Japan.

20. If established media law has been applied to Internet publishers, are there any ways in which Internet publishers (including chat room operators) have to meet different standards?

In a case involving libelous statements published on an Internet bulletin board, the Tokyo High Court has held that the system operator operating the bulletin board is under a duty to delete the libelous statements where:

1. the system operator knows about the libelous statements; and
2. the system operator has necessary authority to delete the statements.[14]

Internet service providers, including those called *keiyu providers* that just provide services enabling access to Internet sites, enjoy a "safe harbor" from liability for defamatory or infringing material under the Law Concerning Limitation of Damages to Specific Telecommunications Service Providers and Disclosure of Sender Information, which provides that liability is limited to cases where (1) it is technologically possible for the ISP to prevent the distribution of the defamatory or infringing material, and (2) either the ISP knows that the material is defamatory or infringing or had reasonable cause to know that the material is defamatory or infringing. No case law has yet tested the meaning of "reasonable cause" in this context.

21. Are there any cases where the courts enforced a judgment in libel from another jurisdiction against a publisher in your jurisdiction?

There is no reported case of a foreign libel judgment being enforced in Japan. However, there is no reason to believe that the general principles for enforcement of foreign civil judgments in Japan should not be applied the same for a judgment in a libel case as for a case based on any other cause of action.

In general, the requirements for enforcement of a foreign civil judgment without reconsideration of the merits are as follows:

1. the foreign judgment concerned is duly obtained and is final and conclusive;
2. the jurisdiction of the foreign court is recognized under Japanese law or international treaty;
3. service of process has been duly effected other than by public notice or the defendant has appeared in the relevant proceedings without receiving service thereof;
4. the foreign judgment (including the court procedure leading to such judgment) is not contrary to public policy or doctrines of good morals in Japan; and

5. judgments of Japanese courts receive reciprocal treatment in the courts of the foreign jurisdiction concerned.The Supreme Court has denied enforcement of a foreign judgment granting punitive damages, ruling that the Japanese legal system regarding civil liability does not adopt the concept of punitive damage and enforcing such foreign judgment would be contrary to public or good morals doctrines in Japan. [15]

Chapter Notes

1. Supreme Court, May 27, 1997, Minshu 51-5-2024.
2. Supreme Court, July 20, 1956, Minshu 10-8-1059.
3. Supreme Court , November 25, 2004, Minshu 58-8-2326.
4. Supreme Court, January 28, 1954, Minshu 18-1-136.
5. Tokyo Hight Court, February 19, 2003.
6. Tokyo High Court, October 2, 1996.
7. Supreme Court, June 23, 1966, Minshu 20-5-1118.
8. Supreme Court, April 24, 1987, Minshu 41-3-490.
9. Supreme Court, September 9, 1997.
10. Supreme Court, July 15, 2004, Minshu 58-5-1615.
11. Supreme Court, March 8, 2002.
12. Tokyo High Court, December 25, 2000; Tokyo District Court, February 29, 2000.
13. Supreme Court, March 6, 1980.
14. Supreme Court, September 5, 2001 (*Nifty Serve* Case).
15. Supreme Court, July 11, 1997, Minshu 51-6-2573.

CHAPTER 9

Korea

D.S. CHOI, CHRISTINA LEE
AND J.H. KIM
Kim & Chang

Kim & Chang
Seyang Building, 223 Naeja-dong
Jongno-gu
Seoul 110-720, Korea
Phone: (822) 3703-1114
Fax: (822) 737-9091/3
www.kimchang.com
lawkim@kimchang.com

Introduction to the Korean Legal System

The Korean legal system is a civil law system derived procedurally from the European civil law system and substantively from the Japanese legal system. After the Republic of Korea was established in 1948, many Japanese laws remained, and much American jurisprudence was imported during the U.S. military occupation of 1945–1948. The democratization movement by the Korean public brought significant changes to the Constitution in 1987, and with the inauguration of the first civilian government in 1993, the legislative reform activity continued to adopt more democratic reform and to improve the legal system.

The Korean Constitution is the founding document, and it defines the government as a democratic republic, with three branches; the executive, the legislative, and the judiciary. All laws are weighed against constitutional principles. Laws are enacted by the legislative branch. The executive branch also has the authority to issue laws, as well as to submit bills to the National Assembly. The Constitution also allows the president to make emergency orders in time of internal turmoil, external menace, natural calamity, or a grave financial or economic crisis. The National Assembly, the Supreme Court, and the Constitutional Court have authority to enact regulations relating to proceedings and internal rules and the conduct of business. The Constitution provides legislative procedures during times of national emergency.

Also, "customary law" is to be relied upon as the basis for deciding civil cases. The Korean judiciary system is three-tiered: the Supreme Court, the highest court; the High Courts, the intermediate appellate courts; and the trial courts (District Courts) which include the specialized Patent Court, Family Court, and Administrative Courts. There are five High Courts and thirteen District Courts, divided into geographic districts. The chief justice of the Supreme Court is appointed by the president with the consent of the National Assembly, for a single six-year term of office. The Supreme Court justices are appointed by the president on the recommendation of the chief justice with the consent of the National Assembly. Their term of office is six years, and they may be reappointed. All other judges are appointed by the chief justice with the consent of the Conference of Supreme Court Justices. Their term of office is ten years, and they may be reappointed.

In addition, Korea maintains a Constitutional Court, formed in September, 1988. This Court is not part of the regular judicial structure. It has jurisdiction over the following areas: (1) the constitutionality of an act upon the request of the courts; (2) impeachment; (3) dissolution of a political party; (4) disputes about the jurisdictions between state agencies, between state agencies and local governments, and between local governments; and (5) petitions relating to the Constitution as prescribed by an act. The Constitutional Court consists of nine justices qualified to be court judges. They are appointed by the president for a six-year term and may be reappointed. For matters involving impeachment, three judges are appointed from persons selected by the National Assembly, and three are appointed from persons nominated by the chief justice of the Supreme Court.

Supreme Court decisions are important in interpreting the contents of the relevant acts and subordinate statutes. Article 8 of the Court Organization Act states that a judgment rendered in the judicial proceedings of a superior court shall take precedence over the judgment of a lower court with respect to a particular case, thereby denying the generally recognized doctrine of *stare decisis* and demonstrating a significant difference between the Korean legal system and Anglo–American legal systems. There is no American-style system of judicial precedent, and a decision of the Supreme Court does not have the binding force of precedent in subsequent cases of a similar nature. It merely has a persuasive effect. The interpretation of a law rendered in a particular case by the Supreme Court, however, does have a binding effect on the lower courts when the case is remanded.

1. What is the locally accepted definition of libel?

Generally speaking, libel may be described as public disclosure of information resulting in injury to another's reputation. The information may be true or false. If, however, (1) the information is proven to be true, or (2) the defendant exercised due care and had good reason to believe that the information was true (although it is later proven to be false), liability may be avoided if the intention behind the disclosure was solely to benefit the general public under Article 310 of the Korean Criminal Code. If the information is proven to be false and the defendant fails to make a showing that upon exercise of due care, there would have been good reason to believe that the information was not true more severe sanctions may be imposed.[1] If the information, whether true or untrue, is made public by newspapers, magazines, radio, or other publications for the purpose of libeling a particular person and the reputation of the person is injured as a result, the penalty will be raised. However, a libel suit cannot be filed against the express will of the injured party.

The following are examples of statements that have been found to be defamatory:

- *Hanguk Nondan*[2] published a report that citizen movement groups threatened conservative groups with violence and threatened to blackmail *chaebols* or other companies. Four citizen movement groups initiated a damages suit, and the Korean Supreme Court held that, although the report dealt with a matter of public interest, it severely harmed the social status of the victims and appeared to have been motivated by a sense of vengeance or the purpose of slander.[3]
- MBC[4] aired a false news report that public prosecutors in Daejeon received bribes from attorneys.[5]
- *Hanguk Nondan* reported that a producer of KBS,[6] who produced a documentary titled *Who Caused the Korean War,* is a follower of Kim Il Sung, the former leader of North Korea.[7]
- MBC aired a news report that an attorney's malpractice resulted in a court decision disadvantageous to his client, describing the attorney as "a man not worthy to be called a man" and "disheartening and vexing." The Supreme Court held that the news was based on truth, but the above expressions are tortious personal attacks beyond the limitation of freedom of expression of opinion.[8]

The following statements have been found to be not defamatory:

- The Supreme Court held that the sentence "The Jeju Resistance Movement of April 3, 1948 was suppressed with relentless slaughter under an illegal declaration of martial law, which was directed by ex-President Syngman Rhee" is not defamatory regarding Syngman Rhee.[9]

- An editorial cartoon depicted people who were blamed for the 1997 financial crisis purchasing airplane tickets and discussing how to fly to foreign countries. The court held that the cartoon should not be interpreted to specifically confirm that the plaintiffs are actually committing or planning a flight to foreign countries.[10]

2. Is libel-by-implication recognized, or, in the alternative, must the complained-of words alone defame the plaintiff?

Indirect, implied libel is possible, even if the complained-of words, in and of themselves, do not defame the plaintiff. Even if the plaintiff is not specifically named, and even if the injurious information is not specifically attributed to the plaintiff, if the disclosure can reasonably be deemed to be injurious to the plaintiff's reputation, libel may be implied.[11]

3. May corporations sue for libel?

Yes, any natural person or corporate or other entity may sue for libel. The infringement on the social status of an entity, in case such infringement has a detrimental effect on the accomplishment of the entity's objectives, constitutes a tort.[12]

4. Is product disparagement recognized, and if so, how does that differ from libel?

Yes, product disparagement is recognized, and there appears to be no requirement that the parties be competitors. This cause of action was allowed to proceed in a case where a TV news channel reported that automobile mileage enhancement devices do not actually work and that the producer of such devices made an exaggerated advertisement.[13] In the advertisements of a powdered milk maker, the milk maker called competitors' milk products "pus milk."[14] In the foregoing case, the Supreme Court held that the expense of counter-advertisement should be included in the total amount of damages.

Product disparagement that deceives or misleads consumers, and therefore possibly frustrates fair competition, may also be subject to administrative sanctions (corrective measures or surcharge fines) by the Fair Trade Commission or to criminal sanctions under the Act on Fair Labeling and Advertisement.

5. Must an individual be clearly identified (by name or photograph) to sue for libel? Can a group of persons sue for libel, even though not named?

As indicated above, an individual need not be specifically identified in order to sue for libel, since implied libel is possible. Group libel is recognized, even if the individual persons are not specifically named in the complained-of words. The plaintiffs to the lawsuit must be specifically identified in pleadings.

Individual members of a group may be defamed by the name of a group they belong to, even though they cannot be the subject of the defamation on their own. However, if the allegedly defamed group has such a small membership that group libel can affect the reputation of its individual members, or if the indicated group may be deemed to refer to its individual members, considering the circumstances of that time, individual members of the group may be deemed to be the victims. Specific conditions of libeling individual members include the size and nature of an indicated group, the status of a victim in the group, etc.

However, if libel can hardly be seen as targeting a particular person in the group and criticism becomes diluted for its members, not affecting their reputation, it cannot constitute an individual libel.

For example, if a TV news report indicated the "XX district mobile patrol police squad," the police officers who were working in the squad at the time of reported investigation will be deemed to be victims of libel.[15] However, simple indication of Seoul citizens or Gyeonggi-do citizens alone does not constitute a libel.[16]

6. What is the fault standard(s) applied to libel?

a. Does the fault standard depend on the fame or notoriety of the plaintiff?

The law does not provide any detailed guidance as to the fault standard applicable to libel, and in theory, the fault standard should not change depending on the fame or notoriety of the plaintiff.

It should be noted that the heightened public status of the plaintiff may actually result in higher-than-ordinary damages: the fame or notoriety of the plaintiff will naturally have some bearing on the determination of the degree of injury suffered by such plaintiff. Since the injury to reputation may become more serious in the case of famous persons (e.g., public figures), extra care may need to be taken when dealing with information pertaining to such persons.

b. Is there a heightened fault standard or privilege for reporting on matters of public concern or public interest?

Yes. The Supreme Court held that a fault standard should differ, depending on whether the plaintiff is a public figure, or whether the expression is about matters of public concern, and that restrictions on freedom of the press should be eased when it comes to matters of public concern and social significance.[17]

If due care is taken and there is good reason to believe that the information being disclosed is true, the defendant may be protected from liability for libel on the grounds that disclosure benefits the general public.[18] For example, MBC aired a news report that a public prosecutor mistakenly filed a double indictment for one wrongdoing, describing such action as "illegal imprisonment," "unprecedented in the history of the Korean judiciary system," and with a caption "shameful public prosecutor." The Supreme Court held that on the facts presented, even if the above information were not true, MBC exercised due care and had good reason to believe that the information was true.[19]

In particular, in the event facts closely related to public activities of a public figure are disclosed, it is deemed, in principle, that there exists evidence proving that the disclosure benefits the public interest. Insofar as the main purpose or motive behind the disclosure is for public interest, it should be appropriate to deem the disclosure as benefiting public interest, even though other personal purpose or motive is incidentally implied.[20]

For example, there was a case where a politician held a press conference and made a protest against a criminal case and a personal tax investigation. The Supreme Court held that the main purpose of the press conference was not for a personal problem, but to unveil the prosecution's unfair handling of election criminals and alleged political oppression, and the content was for public interest. The Supreme Court, therefore, ruled that if the content is true or there is a good reason to believe it is true, the politician's defamatory expression shall not be illegal.[21]

Another example concerns the privacy of drunk driving. It can't be said drunk driving is a private matter, because it takes place in a public place and anyone may become a victim of a drunk-driving accident, which is a criminal act subject to the Road Traffic Act. If the drunk driver is an ordinary person, the act itself is a matter of concern and it does not attract attention who the drunk driver is. However, if the drunk driver is a public figure, it will be a matter of concern who the public figure is. Therefore, in such cases involving public figures the media is free to report on the matter.[22]

7. Is financial news about publicly traded companies, or companies involved with a government contract, considered a matter of public interest or otherwise privileged?

No special privilege is granted to financial news reporting about publicly traded companies or companies involved with government contracts.

Absent other circumstances, such reporting may not necessarily be considered a matter of public interest.

8. Is there a recognized protection for opinion or "fair comment" on matters of public concern?

There is no statutory protection for opinion or "fair comment" on matters of public concern. In practice, however, Korean courts generally recognize protection for fair comments on matters of public concern based on the freedom of the press principle under the Constitution. The Supreme Court has held that expression or disclosure of matters that have "public or social value (especially with regard to the morality or integrity of public officials) must be more highly protected in light of freedom of speech rights."[23] At the same time, note that extra care may need to be taken when reporting on matters of public concern or public interest (e.g., public figures), because the injury may be more severe.

Indication of facts is needed for a libel. "Indication of facts" is opposite to "expression of views," based on evaluation or assessment. It means a report or a statement of specific past or present facts, which can be proven by evidence. Simple expression of political views, not indication of facts, does not constitute libel.[24]

For example, for a statement such as "[h]e is heretic and never studied theology in a systematic way," the Supreme Court decided that this is an expression of defendants' pure opinion or comment, based on their subjective analysis of religion, and does not constitute libel.[25]

9. Are there any requirements upon a plaintiff, such as demand for retraction or right of reply, and if so, what impact do they have?

Yes. Article 764 of the Korean Civil Code provides that a victim of libel may demand that "relevant measures" be taken as necessary for the restoration (to the best extent possible) of such victim's reputation. Such relevant measures would include correction or retraction of the report.

Under the Act on Press Arbitration and Damages Remedy that went into effect on July 28, 2005, one may directly file a claim for the right of reply without undergoing the press arbitration procedure. The exercise of such rights does not preclude the victim's separate right to sue for damages.

10. Is there a privilege for quoting or reporting on:

a. Papers filed in court?

As a general matter, there is no special privilege for quoting or reporting on such material. To the extent the aforementioned documents are intended for public disclosure, accurate quotes with proper attributions and reports prepared with due care will likely benefit from the privilege afforded to disclosure of true information, because the substance of the report will likely be deemed to benefit the general public.

The decision of the tribunal under the relevant church denomination to expel a church's senior pastor will become known to the church or its believers in time, and the distribution of copies of the tribunal decision to those who come to the church to attend the service should not be unconstitutional, although defamatory to the pastor himself. The decision, based on true facts and for the benefit of the church or its believers, or at least in no violation of social norms, is on the premise of disclosure.[26]

b. Government-issued documents?

Similarly, although there is no stated privilege, the exercise of due care in reporting a matter of public concern will in most cases avoid liability. Reporters are advised to provide an opportunity for a subject to respond to potentially defamatory allegations, and to carefully consider the authenticity of any relied-upon documents.

c. Quasi-governmental proceedings?

No reported case law speaks to this specific issue. However, the greatest degree of protection will depend on the degree to which the public interest is served by the reporting on any such material.

11. Is there a privilege for republishing statements made earlier by other, bona fide, reliable publications or wire services?

No. For instance, if the daily press uses an inadequate method to contact the persons concerned, and in reliance upon other press reports, makes a report without any further effort to verify the facts, such press cannot be exempted from damages liability.[27]

12. Are there any restrictions regarding reporting on:

a. Ongoing criminal investigations?

There are restrictions regarding the publication of the identity of persons under investigation. The Supreme Court has held that, for the report of ongoing criminal investigations: (1) the press must adequately and sufficiently collect news materials supporting the authenticity of the investigated facts; (2) the content of the report must be objective and just; (3) the report may not use such terms or expressions that may give readers an impression that the concerned person is guilty; and (4) the reporter must use anonyms as far as possible, if the concerned person is not a public figure, and must take other necessary measures not to disclose the identity of the concerned person.[28]

In one case, a daily press reporter made a false report of an ongoing criminal case, and he based his report only on other news reports and a copy of the writ of arrest. The Supreme Court held that the reporter did not pay sufficient attention to verifying the content to be reported.[29]

Since the Constitution embodies the concept of "innocent until proven guilty" (Article 27(4)), due care should be exercised when reporting on any criminal investigations or prosecutions so as not to inadvertently injure another's reputation by implying guilt.

If a defamatory newspaper report is just for public interest and the reported fact is proven to be true, it should not constitute an illegal act. Even if the report cannot be proven to be true, but there is good reason for the reporter to believe it is true, the report shall not constitute an illegal act, due to lack of reason attributable to the reporter. Considering the significant impacts of newspapers on society, the report shall not be based simply on rumors or speculation, but on reasonable materials or basis, before it can be said there is good reason for the reporter to believe it is true. Any report of the information, as provided by the source, shall not protect the reporter from liability for the illegal act. Only when there is good reason to believe the information is true, based on reasonable data and materials, can the reporter be protected from liability for the illegal act.[30]

b. Ongoing criminal prosecutions?

There are no express statutory restrictions regarding reporting on ongoing criminal prosecutions.

c. Ongoing regulatory investigations?

There are no express statutory restrictions regarding reporting on ongoing regulatory investigations.

d. Ongoing civil litigation, or other judicial proceedings?

There are no express statutory restrictions regarding reporting on civil litigation or other judicial proceedings.

13. Are prior restraints or other prepublication injunctions available on the basis of libel or privacy, and if so, what are the standards for obtaining such relief?

Yes. If the requesting party is able to make a *prima facie* showing of: (1) its right to be protected (e.g., that the information in question is of a private nature which should not be disclosed), and (2) the urgent need for the preliminary injunction (e.g., that there will result immediate and irreparable damage once such information is disclosed), preliminary injunction may be obtainable under Korean Civil Enforcement Procedure Law, Article 300(2).

14. Is a right of privacy recognized (either civilly or criminally)?

a. What is the definition of "private fact"?

The concept of "private fact" is not expressly defined in any statute, but the right of privacy is legally recognized and entitled to protection under both the Constitution and the Korean Criminal Code. Although various provisions of the laws do not provide a simple definition of what constitutes a "private fact," a person's personal life, including any and all information not generally known to the public, would be deemed to be included within the concept of "privacy."[31] For infringement on privacy, the disclosed facts should be what the relevant person does not want to be disclosed from an ordinary person's point of view, and at the same time the disclosed facts should be what are not known to the general public yet, and the disclosure might make the person feel uncomfortable or uneasy.[32]

In one case, a TV program aired the silhouette of the face of a victim of failed plastic surgery on her breast, and the voice of the victim was aired without any computer alteration, which would have masked the identity of the victim. The Supreme Court held that this was an infringement of privacy beyond the scope of approval originally given by the victim, and therefore triggered damages liability.[33]

b. Is there a public interest or newsworthiness exception?

In contrast to the public interest exception in libel, newsworthiness alone would not entitle the defendant to take such an exception.[34] As discussed above, if (1) the disclosed information is proven to be true, or (2) the defendant exercised due care and had good reason to believe that the information was true (although it is later proven to be false), it may be possible to avoid liability if the defendant is able to demonstrate that the intention behind the disclosure was solely to benefit the general public.

c. Is the right of privacy based in common law, statute, or constitution?

This right is based in the Constitution.

15. May reporters tape-record their own telephone conversations for note-taking purposes (not rebroadcast) without the consent of the other party?

Yes. Tape-recording a telephone conversation by a party to the conversation is not illegal even if it is done without the consent of the other party.

In the case of a three-way telephone conversion, tape-recording of a telephone conversation by a party to the conversation is not illegal, because conversation with the other two parties can't be said to be a "conversation with others."[35]

Please note, however, that tape-recording a telephone conversation between two parties without the consent of both parties may be a breach of the Act on Protection of Communications Secrets and may trigger criminal punishment.[36]

16. If permissible to record such tapes, may they be broadcast without permission?

Even though there is no court precedent on this point, we believe that broadcasting the recording without permission in the case above would not breach the Act on Protection of Communications Secrets.

17. Is there a recognized evidentiary privilege preventing the disclosure of confidential sources relied upon by reporters?

There is no statutory "Shield Law," and to date, there have been no court precedents granting such evidentiary privilege to reporters. We note, however, the Civil Procedure Law provides for some basis for a reporter's refusal to disclose its sources as "professional secrets" entitled to protection, in cases where the reporter is called to testify as a third-party witness.[37]

18. In the event that legal papers are served upon the newsroom (such as a civil complaint), are there any particular warnings about accepting service of which we should be aware?

In Korea, service of process will be made through the relevant court office, and not directly on the defendant(s). The defendant(s) would receive notice from the court, and as such, there should be no particular procedural concerns relating to the service of process issue.

19. Has your jurisdiction applied established media law to Internet publishers?

Yes. On November 12, 2003, the Seoul District Court handed down a decision finding the president and reporters of an Internet newspaper, *OhMyNews,* liable for defamation and holding that they must compensate victims for damages.

20. If established media law has been applied to Internet publishers, are there any ways in which Internet publishers (including chat room operators) have to meet different standards?

Not in particular.

However, please note that under Article 61 of the Act on Promotion of Use of Information Network and Information Protection, the maximum sanction is increased for defamation through the Internet. Those who intentionally disclose facts through the information and communication network for the purpose of slandering a person and injuring the person's reputation as a result, could be sentenced to up to three years of imprisonment or fined up to 20 million won, while those who intentionally disclose false facts through the information and communication network for the purpose of slandering a person and injuring the person's reputation as a result, could be sentenced to up to seven years of imprisonment or disqualified for up to ten years, or fined up to 50 million won.

However, those who intentionally disclose facts and injure a person's reputation as a result could be sentenced to up to two years of imprisonment or fined up to 5 million won, while those who intentionally disclose false information and injure the reputation of a person could be sentenced to up to five years of imprisonment, or disqualified for up to ten years, or fined up to 10 million won.

21. Are there any cases where the courts enforced a judgment in libel from another jurisdiction against a publisher in your jurisdiction?
There are no such cases to the best of our knowledge.

Chapter Notes

1. Korean Civil Code, Articles 751(1), 764; Korean Criminal Code, Articles 305(1) and 309(2).
2. A conservative Korean periodical.
3. Supreme Court decision dated January 24, 2003, 2000 *Da* 37647.
4. Munhwa Broadcasting Corporation, a Korean broadcaster.
5. Supreme Court decision dated September 2, 2003, 2002 *Da* 63558.
6. Korea Broadcasting System, a Korean broadcaster.
7. Supreme Court decision dated December 24, 2002, 2000 *Da* 14613.
8. Supreme Court decision dated March 25, 2003, 2001 *Da* 84480.
9. Supreme Court decision dated January 19, 2001, 2000 *Da* 10208.
10. Supreme Court decision dated July 28, 2000, 99 *Da* 6203.
11. Supreme Court decision dated December 27, 2007, 2007 *Da* 29379; Supreme Court decision dated January 1, 2003, 2000 *Da* 37647; Supreme Court decision dated May 14, 1991, 91 *Do* 420; Supreme Court decision

dated April 12, 1994, 93 *Do* 3535; Supreme Court decision dated November 9, 1982, 82 *Do* 1256; and Supreme Court decision dated November 14, 1989, 89 *Do* 1744.

12. Supreme Court decision dated October 22, 1999, 98 *Da* 6381.

13. Supreme Court decision dated October 8, 1999, 98 *Da* 40077.

14. Supreme Court decision dated April 12, 1996, 93 *Da* 40614, 40621.

15. Supreme Court decision dated May 12, 2006, 2004 *Da* 35199.

16. Supreme Court decision dated November 26, 1960, 4293 *Hyungsang* 244.

17. Supreme Court decision dated July 22, 2003, 2002 *Da* 62494.

18. Supreme Court decision dated October 11, 1988, 85 *Da Ka* 29.

19. Supreme Court decision dated February 27, 2004, 2001 *Da* 53387.

20. Supreme Court decision dated October 13, 2006, 2005 *Do* 3112.

21. Supreme Court decision dated July 22, 2003, 2002 *Da* 62494.

22. Seoul District Court decision, dated September 3, 1997, 96 *Gahap* 82966.

23. Supreme Court decision dated February 27, 2004, 2001 *Da* 53387.

24. Seoul Central District Court decision, dated October 11, 2006, 2005 *Gahap* 11173.

25. Supreme Court decision, dated October 26, 2007, 2006 *Do* 5924.

26. Supreme Court decision, dated February 14, 1982, 88 *Do* 899.

27. Supreme Court decision dated May 28, 1996, 94 *Da* 33828.

28. Supreme Court decision dated January 26, 1999, 97 *Da* 10215, 10222.

29. Supreme Court decision dated May 10, 2002, 2000 *Da* 50213.

30. Seoul Civil District Court decision, dated August 17, 1990, 90 *Gahap* 35265.

31. Constitution, Article 17; Korean Criminal Code, Article 316; Supreme Court decision dated September 4, 1998, 96 *Da* 11327.

32. Supreme Court decision, dated December 22, 2006, 2006 *Da* 15922.

33. Supreme Court decision dated September 4, 1998, 96 *Da* 11327.

34. Supreme Court decision dated September 4, 1998, 96 *Da* 1132.

35. Supreme Court decision, dated October 12, 2006, 2006 *Do* 4981.

36. Supreme Court decision dated October 8, 2002, 2002 *Do* 123.

37. Korean Civil Procedure Law, Article 315(1).

CHAPTER 10

Malaysia

H.R. DIPENDRA

Tengku Hishamudin Ram Dipendra

Tengku Hishamudin Ram Dipendra
48-2, Second Floor
Jalan Medan Setia 2 Plaza Damansara
Bukit Damansara
50490 Kuala Lumpur
Phone: +603 2095 6505
Fax: +603 2095 7505
www.thrd.com

Introduction to the Malaysian Legal System

The civil court system in Malaysia is divided into the subordinate courts and the superior courts. Briefly, the superior courts consist of the appellate courts (Federal Court, the Court of Appeal) and the High Court, while the subordinate courts consist of the Sessions Court and the Magistrates Court. The jurisdictions of the courts are mainly separated by the monetary value of the claim, and the High Court has an unlimited jurisdiction to hear all civil claims.[1] The subordinate courts, on the other hand, can hear civil claims where the amount claimed or damages awarded does not exceed RM250,000.00 (approximately US$77,000.00).[2] Further, the subordinate courts have no ability to grant interlocutory relief like injunctions or restraining orders, which must be initiated at the High Court.

The Federal Court is the highest court in Malaysia. The Federal Court may hear appeals of civil decisions of the Court of Appeal only if the Federal Court grants leave to do so. The Court of Appeal generally hears all civil appeals arising from the High Court except where against judgment or orders made by consent. The High Courts in Malaysia have general supervisory and revisory jurisdiction over all the subordinate courts, and jurisdiction to hear appeals from the subordinate courts in civil matters.

Malaysia, like many Commonwealth nations, adopts a common law system. As such, decisions from Commonwealth jurisdictions such as the United Kingdom, Australia, India, and Singapore can be used as "persuasive authorities."[3]

1. What is the locally accepted definition of libel?

There is no universal test applied as to what is defined as libel. An objective standard will be used to determine if a word or statement is deemed defamatory[4] and it includes the following:

(a) if the word or statement tends to lower the claimant in the estimation of right-thinking members of society generally;[5]

(b) if the word or statement exposes the claimant to public hatred, contempt, or ridicule;[6] or

(c) if the word or statement causes the claimant to be shunned or avoided.[7]

2. Is libel-by-implication recognized, or, in the alternative, must the complained-of words alone defame the plaintiff?

Defamation of a person by implication is recognized in Malaysia. The Malaysian courts will ascertain whether a reasonable person would understand the natural or ordinary meaning of the implication. Such a meaning is not confined to the literal or strict meaning of the words but includes any inferences that can reasonably be drawn by such persons. Any evidence, however, must be confined to the particular character of the person's life or that the person's character has suffered irreparable damage.[8]

Some examples include words, satire, fantasy, or fictional creations that clearly referred to the claimant,[9] implying that a woman has a contagious disease or leads an unchaste life[10] or words disparaging the claimant in any office, profession, or business.[11]

3. May a corporation sue for libel?

A corporation may sue or be sued for libel.[12] In the case of a corporation suing, it must be brought under its own name.

4. Is product disparagement recognized, and if so, how does that differ from libel?

Any statement disparaging a claimant's property, goods, or product may give rise to an action for malicious falsehood. The words or statement complained of must cause pecuniary damage to the claimant personally.[13] The inclusion of the term "malice" is taken to mean that the words complained of must reveal a wrongful act done intentionally and without just cause and excuse.[14] If the word or statement complained of also disparages the owner of said person's property, goods, or products, the owner can equally opt for an action for libel. However, the owner will not be allowed to recover damages twice for the same loss.

An essential ingredient in a claim for malicious falsehood is proof of special damage.[15] Therefore, if there is loss of reputation but no pecuniary loss suffered, an action for malicious falsehood will not succeed. This is subject to the exception in Section 6(1) of the Defamation Act, [16] which states that:

> In any action for slander of title, slander of goods or other malicious falsehood, it shall not be necessary to allege or prove special damage:
> (a) if the words upon which the action is founded are calculated to cause pecuniary damage to the plaintiff and are published in writing or other permanent form; or
> (b) if the said words are calculated to cause pecuniary damage to the plaintiff in respect of any office, profession, calling, trade or business held or carried on by him at the time of the publication.

In libel, there is no need to show special damage before the statement becomes actionable. Another difference is that for malicious falsehood, the words must be published maliciously. There is no such requirement for libel. Also, for malicious falsehood, it is not necessary for the statement to injure the reputation of the claimant.

5. Must an individual be clearly identified (by name or photograph) to sue for libel? Can a group of persons sue for libel, even though not named?

The short answer is no, but an action for libel can be brought by any person not so named. Ultimately, it is a question of fact especially where ordinary, sensible readers with special knowledge could and did understand that the facts referred to the claimant.[17]

6. Please describe the fault standard(s) applied to libel?

(a) Does the fault standard depend on the fame or notoriety of the claimant?

In general, Malaysian law has presumed that a consistent standard of fault is applicable to all claimants. As such, fame or notoriety of the claimant at best affects only the amount of damages awarded by the court, if indeed the claimant was defamed.

(b) Is there a heightened fault standard or privilege for reporting on matters of public concern or public interest?

There is no statutory definition of what amounts to "public concern" or "public interest" and Malaysian law does not allow a higher fault standard when reporting matters of public interest. What matters is how the statement was expressed and whether such statements were for the benefit of the public at large. The defendant may avail himself or herself of the test adopted in *Reynolds v. Times Newspapers Ltd.*,[18] which states the following:

(a) Was the publisher under a legal, moral or social duty to whom the material was published?
(b) Did those to whom the material was published have an interest to receive that material?
(c) Were the nature, status and source of the material, and the circumstances of the publication, such that the publication should in the public interest be protected in the absence of proof of express malice?

Very broadly, political or state matters (including management of public institutions) have all been considered to be matters of public interest. If the claimant can show some form of malice, then the defense of privilege cannot be relied on at all. It is also a question of law whether an occasion is privileged.[19]

Section 12 of the Defamation Act[20] also provides for specific occasions when the defense of qualified privilege is available to a newspaper. The section states:

(1) Subject to this section, the publication in a newspaper of any such report or other matter as is mentioned in the Schedule shall be privileged unless the publication is proved to be made with malice.
(2) In an action for libel in respect of the publication of any such report or matter as is mentioned in Part II of the Schedule, this section shall not be a defense if it is proved that the defendant has been requested by the plaintiff to publish in the newspaper in which the original publication was made a reasonable letter or statement by way of explanation or contradiction, and has refused or neglected to do so, or has done so in a manner not adequate or not reasonable having regard to all the circumstances.
(3) Nothing in this section shall be construed as protecting the publication of any blasphemous, seditious or indecent matter or of any matter the publication of which is prohibited by law, or of any matter which is not of public concern and the publication of which is not for the public benefit.

(c) What are the traditional defenses to a libel claim?

There are statutory defenses under the Defamation Act 1957, which are traditionally used in a claim for libel. These include:

(a) *Fair Comment*[21]—where the defendant has to show that the facts were truly stated, did not contain any imputation of a corrupt/dishonorable motive to the person whose conduct or work is criticized, and is an honest expression of legal opinion.

(b) *Justification*[22]—this is an absolute defense and the ingredients include that the statement complained of is true and its imputation in the complaint can be justified.

(c) *Privilege*[23]—includes absolute privilege and qualified privilege. In the instance of an absolute privilege, it must refer to a complete and unrestricted forum[24] (e.g., parliamentary proceedings, judicial proceedings, and military proceedings).

Qualified privilege, on the other hand, requires that the defendant show that the statement was not published falsely or maliciously and that such publication can be shielded by qualified privilege.[25] If a statement was made on grounds of public policy, made in an interest (legal, social, moral, etc.), done legitimately with no express malice and with an honest belief, then qualified privilege may be relied upon. Also note the test adopted in *Reynolds* above.

(d) *Defence of Accord & Satisfaction/Offer to Amend*[26]—where the defendant can settle a claim for defamation on the terms the claimant sees fit.

(e) *Unintentional Defamation/Innocent Dissemination.*[27]

(f) *Defence of Duress*[28]—this is strictly dependent on the facts and circumstances of the case in question.

7. Is financial news about publicly traded companies, or companies involved with government contracts considered a matter of public interest or otherwise privileged?

Financial news on publicly listed companies would be a matter of public interest.

8. Is there a recognized protection for opinion of "fair comment" on matters of public concern?

The defense of fair comment is available under Malaysian law. In order to succeed, the defendant needs to establish the following elements:

(a) the words complained of are comments, though they may consist of or include inference of facts;

(b) the comment is on a matter of public interest;

(c) the comment is based on facts;
(d) the comment is one which a fair-minded person can honestly make on the facts proved; and
(e) the statement was not published maliciously.

9. Are there any requirements upon a claimant such as a demand for retraction or right of reply, and if so, what impact do they have?

In Malaysia, there is no requirement that the claimant must first demand a retraction or a right of reply (which is not acceded to) before a right of action accrues, although in practice, it is normal for a claimant to first ask that the intended defendant issue an apology to the claimant's satisfaction.

Under Section 7 of the Defamation Act,[29] a person who claims to have published the libel innocently may make an offer of amends by way of an affidavit. It is also important that the offer must include the manner in which a suitable correction or apology should be made and practicable steps to notify those who may have received the defamatory statement.

If the claimant accepts the offer of amends, the claimant may no longer sue for libel. If such an offer to amend is rejected, the fact that an offer to amend was made may be used as a defense for the defendant to show that the information had been published innocently, that the offer was made as soon as practicable, and that the offer has not been withdrawn.

Under Section 10 of the Defamation Act,[30] defendants may, in mitigation of damages, give evidence that they had made or offered an apology to the claimant as soon as they had an opportunity to do so.

10. Is there a privilege for quoting or reporting on:

(a) Papers filed in court?

Yes, as long as it available to the public, such as the statement of claim, defense, and other court documents.[31] This has also been provided for under item 2 of Part I of the Schedule to the Defamation Act.[32] The copy or extract must be fair and accurate and the publication must be made without malice.

In relation to judicial proceedings, Section 11(1) of the Defamation Act provides for the protection of such publication. That is, it says, "a fair and accurate and contemporaneous report of proceedings publicly heard before any court lawfully exercising judicial authority within Malaysia and of the judgment, sentence or finding of any such court shall be absolutely privileged, and any fair and bona fide comment thereon shall be protected, although such judgment, sentence or finding be subsequently reversed, quashed or varied, unless at the time of the publication of such report or comment the defendant who claims the protection afforded by this section knew or ought to have known of such reversal, quashing or variation."[33]

(b) Government-issued documents?

The answer is the same as (a) above. Documents issued in accordance with or under the circumstances contemplated in the Schedule to the Defamation Act, e.g., a notice, advertisement, or report issued by a public officer in accordance with the requirements of any written law (item 3 of Part I), or a copy or a fair and accurate report or summary of any notice issued for the information of the public by or on behalf of the government (item 5 of Part II) is also covered by absolute privilege.

The Houses of Parliament (Privileges and Powers) Act[34] allows for reports, papers, and journals that are published directly under the authority of Parliament to be protected by absolute privilege. Further, any persons who are subject to any civil or criminal proceedings on account of the publication by such persons or their employee, by order or under the authority of Parliament or any committee, of any reports, paper, or journals, have the statutory protection of a summary stay of proceedings.[35]

(c) Quasi-governmental proceedings, such as those by professional associations (for example disciplinary proceedings)?

Yes, so long as the reporting complies with the requirements of item 3 of Part II of the Schedule to the Defamation Act,[36] where it must be a fair and accurate report of proceedings at a meeting of a commission, tribunal committee, or board appointed for the purpose of an inquiry, being a meeting to which admission is not denied to representatives of newspapers or other members of the public.

11. Is there a privilege for republishing statements made earlier by other, bona fide reliable publications or wire services?

No such privilege is available under Malaysian law. If there is republication of a libelous statement, it is deemed to be a new libel. The publisher cannot rely on a defense that the publication was based on a previously published statement. The same would apply if the published statement is posted on the Internet.[37]

12. Are there any restrictions regarding:

(a) Reporting on ongoing criminal investigations?

Only information released by the investigating authority or publicly available may be published. The Official Secrets Act 1972 will apply to documents classified under this Act.

(b) Reporting on ongoing criminal prosecutions?

Under section 3 of the Judicial Proceedings (Regulation of Reports) Act,[38] it is unlawful to print or publish:

(a) in relation to any judicial proceedings any indecent matter or indecent medical, surgical or physiological details being matter or details the publication of which would be calculated to injure public morals; or

(b) in relation to any judicial proceedings for divorce, dissolution of marriage, nullity of marriage, judicial separation or restitution of conjugal rights, any particulars other than the following:

  (i) the names, addresses and occupations of the parties and witnesses;

  (ii) a concise statement of the charges, the defenses and counter charges in support of which evidence has been given;

  (iii) submissions on any point of law arising in the course of the proceedings and the decision of the court thereon; and

  (iv) the decision of the court and any observations made by the court in giving it.

Further, under Section 5A of the Juvenile Courts Act 1947,[39] restrictions are placed on the publication of information relating to court proceedings that could lead to the identification of any child or young person concerned with the proceedings.

Similarly under Section 15 (2) of the Courts of the Judicature Act 1964[40] and Section 101 (2) of the Subordinate Courts Act 1948,[41] the courts may enjoin any person from publishing sensitive details about any witness or anything likely to lead to the identification of the witness in the proceedings.

(c) Reporting on ongoing regulatory investigations?

No such restrictions under Malaysian Law other than 12 (a) and (b) above.

(d) Reporting on ongoing civil litigation or other judicial proceedings?

No such restrictions under Malaysian law other than 12 (a) and (b) above.

13. Are prior restraints or other prepublication injunctions available on the basis of libel or privacy, and if so, what are the standards for obtaining such relief?

Restraints and prepublication injunctions are available under Malaysian law. The High Court has the power to grant interlocutory injunctions to restrain the publication or repetition of defamatory statements.[42]

The court is generally slow in granting an interlocutory injunction unless it can be shown that:

(a) the statement is unarguably defamatory;
(b) there are no grounds for concluding the statement may be true;
(c) there is no other defense that might succeed; and
(d) there is evidence of an intention to repeat or publish the defamatory statement.

Absent such a showing, no interlocutory injunction will be granted. The burden of proof falls upon the claimant.[43]

14. Is a right to privacy recognized (either civilly or criminally), and if so:

(a) What is the definition of "private fact"?
There is no general right of privacy under Malaysian law.

(b) Is there a public interest or newsworthiness exception?
No such right exists in Malaysia.

15. May reporters tape-record their own telephone conversations for note-taking purposes (not rebroadcast) without the consent of the other party?
Yes. However, if relied upon in court proceedings, the strength of such evidence may be challenged.

16. If permissible to record such tapes, may they be broadcast without permission?
Although there are no specific restrictions on a subsequent broadcast, restrictions in the form of a potential breach of confidence may limit the scope of broadcast without permission.

17. Is there a recognized evidentiary privilege preventing the disclosure of confidential sources relied upon by reporters?
No such special privileges are accorded to confidential sources under Malaysian law. However reporters may choose to withhold such confidential sources on ethical grounds and ask that the courts not require such disclosure unless the information requested is critical in the determination of the case. Reporters may be held in contempt of court if they do not reveal their sources when directed by the courts, although this is rare.

18. In the event that legal papers are served upon the newsroom (such as a civil complaint), are there any particular warnings about accepting service of which we should be aware?

There are no particular warnings about accepting service of court process in Malaysia. Legal process (e.g., a Writ of Summons) has to be served personally in Malaysia and at the registered address of the intended defendant. Where the defendant is an individual, the legal process has to be served on the individual personally (whether at home, in the office, or at any other place), unless an order for substituted service is obtained, whereby such legal process may be served through an advertisement in the newspapers or posted at the last known address of the reporter. Defendants will usually have eight days after service to file a memorandum of appearance in court if they wish to defend the claim, failing which the plaintiff will be at liberty to enter a judgment in default of appearance against the defendant.[44]

19. Has your jurisdiction applied the above law to Internet publishers?

Yes, where the form of publication of the defamatory statement was publication on the Internet.

20. If so, are there any ways in which Internet publishers (including chat room operators) have to meet different standards?

No. However, it is worthwhile to note that Section 263 of the Malaysian Communications and Multimedia Act 1988 states that Internet publishers or Internet service providers (ISPs) must use their best endeavors to ensure that their network facilities are not being used in relation to the commission of any offense in Malaysia.

21. Are there any cases where the courts enforced a judgment in libel from another jurisdiction against a publisher in your jurisdiction?

No such cases have been reported yet.

Chapter Notes

1. Rules of the High Court 1980.
2. Subordinate Court Rules 1980, Subordinate Courts Act 1948.
3. The Civil Law Act 1956.
4. *Keluarga Communications Sdn Bhd v. Normala Samsuddin* (2006) 8 MLJ 700.
5. *Abdul Rahman Talib v. Seenivasagam & Anor* (1965) 1 MLJ 142.

6. *Syed Husin Ali v. Syarikat Perchetakan Utusan Melayu Bhd* (1973) 2 MLJ 56; *JB Jeyaratnam v. Goh Chok Tong* (1985) 1 MLJ 334.

7. *Youssoupoff v. MGM Pictures Ltd.* (1934) 50 TLR 581.

8. *Karpal Singh v. DP Vijandran* (2001) 4 MLJ 161.

9. *Ummi Hafilda Ali v. Ketua Setiausaha Part Islam SaMalaysia* (2006) 4 MLJ 761.

10. Section 4 Defamation Act 1957; *Luk Kai Lam v. Sim Ai Leng* (1978) 1 MLJ 214.

11. Section 5 Defamation Act 1957.

12. *Great One Coconut Products Industries (M) Sdn Bhd v Malaysian banking Berhad* (1985) 2 MLJ 469; *Triplex Safety Glass Co. Ltd. v. Lancegaye Safety* (1930) 2 KB 395.

13. Section 3 and 6 (1) (b) Defamation Act 1957, *Fielding v. Variety Incorporated* (1967) 2 All ER 497.

14. *S Pakianathan v. Jenni Ibrahim* (1988) 2 MLJ 173; *Institute of Commercial Management United Kingdom v. New Straits Times Press (Malaysia) Berhad* (1993) 1 MLJ 408.

15. *Joyce v. Sengupta* [1993] 1 WLR 337; *Tjanting Handicraft Sdn Bhd v. Utusan Melayu Sdn Bhd & Ors* (2000) 2 MLJ 574.

16. Act 286.

17. *JB Jeyaratnam v. Lee Kuan Yew* (1979) 2 MLJ 282.

18. (1988) 3 WLR 863 (CA).

19. *Kian Lup Construction v. Hong Kong Bank Malaysia Bhd* (2002) 7 MLJ 283.

20. Act 286.

21. Section 9 Defamation Act 1957 (Act 286).

22. Section 8 Defamation Act 1957 (Act 286), *Abdul Rahman Talib v. Seenivasagam & Anor* (1965) 1 MLJ 142.

23. Sections 11 and 12 Defamation Act 1957 (Act 286).

24. *Trapp v. Mackie* (1979) 1 WLR 377.

25. *Adam v. Ward* (1917) AC 309.

26. Section 7 Defamation Act (Act 286), *Vincent Tan Chee Yioun v. Hj Hamzah & Ors* (1995) 1 MLJ 39, Misliha bin *Lignan v. Linguaphone* (2003) LNS 598, and *Gaunder v. Melinda Alison Monteiro* (2006) MLJU 301.

27. Section 7 Defamation Act (Act 286).

28. *Lee Kuan Yew v. Chee Soon Juan* (2003) SGHC 78.

29. Act 286.

30. Act 286.

31. *Coopers & Lybrand v. Singapore Society of Accountants* (1988) 3 MLJ 134.

32. Act 286.

33. It does not, however, authorize the publication of any statement that is blasphemous, seditious, or indecent matter or of any matter the publication of which is prohibited by law.

34. 1952 (Act 347).

35. Section 27 of Act 347.

36. Act 286.

37. *Ummi Hafilda Ali v. Karangkraf Sdn Bhd & Ors* No.2 (2000) 6 MLJ 532.

38. Act 114.

39. Act 90.

40. Act 91.

41. Act 92.

42. Order 29 Rule 1 Rules of the High Court 1980 and section 25 (2) Courts of the Judicature Act 1964 (Act 91).

43. *Ngoi Thiam Who v. CTOS Sdn Bhd* (2001) 4 MLJ 510.

44. Rules of the High Court, 1980.

CHAPTER 11

The Middle East

CHARLES J. GLASSER JR.
Bloomberg News

WITH AVA MACALPIN
Princeton University

Introduction to Media Law in the Middle East

Publishing in the Middle East presents a unique set of challenges for journalists, broadcasters, and publishers. The two most significant problems are that, first, the scant Press Law that there is offers few if any meaningful guarantees for a free and robust media: at the same time it prescribes severe criminal penalties for vaguely defined forms of defamation.[1] Second, there is a strong Islamic undercurrent in any approach to publication or broadcast. Even in those nations that may not describe themselves as theocracies, the political and cultural power of fundamentalist Islam permeates the legal foundation.

Lacking the legal resources to fully detail specific press laws from all nations in this region, we have in this chapter endeavored to describe the political culture, the legal system, and recent media-related incidents in Iran, Iraq, Lebanon, Syria, the UAE, Egypt, and Saudi Arabia.

In addition, because of the strong Islamic cultural underpinning in media relating to these areas, we have included below a brief summary of potentially defamatory topics in *sharia* (Islamic religious law). Reporters and editors are advised to take these issues into account when reporting in or about this part of the world. Recent events stemming from publications touching and concerning Islam and its adherents have exposed a raw nerve, with various news organizations coping in different ways.

The most well-known of these instances is the September 2005 publication by a Danish newspaper, *Jyllands-Posten*, of a series of twelve satirical cartoons ("The Mohammed Cartoons") that depicted the Prophet Mohammed. The cartoons did not attack the personality of Mohammed, or even the tenets of Islam, but were rather commentary about the violent and bloody acts committed in his name: pure, simple, and fair commentary in any rational world about the meaning of religion itself. But Islamic law forbids graphic depiction of the Prophet, and the publication of the cartoons—in a non-Arab language newspaper a half a world away—so allegedly outraged Muslims that riots in Iran, Saudi Arabia, and Syria followed, with calls for boycotts of Danish goods. The cartoons became an excuse for widespread and violent attacks on Western embassies and properties. (The Iranian government responded by installing an anti-Semitic art exhibit in a Teheran museum.)

The *Jyllands-Posten* later apologized for offending Muslims, but not for publishing the cartoons. The riots and inflammatory reaction by Muslims worldwide in turn provoked a reticence among Western publishers to republish the cartoons, even in the context of news about the violent reactions. For example, *The New York Times* chose not to reprint the cartoons in any form. In statements made through then-Public Editor Barney Calame's column,[2] Executive Editor Bill Keller said that the decision was based on:

> . . . abundant evidence that a significant number of people—some of them our readers—consider these cartoons deeply offensive and inflammatory . . . . Indeed, to publish them after seeing the outrage and violence across the Islamic world could be perceived as a particularly deliberate insult.[3]

Even when straight reporting about events that touch and concern Islam is involved, reactions in the Muslim world can be unfathomably incendiary. In early May 2005, *Newsweek* published an anonymously sourced article by investigative journalist Michael Isikoff that alleged that American interrogators at Guantanamo Bay, Cuba, had flushed a Koran down a toilet to humiliate and emotionally abuse their Muslim detainees. The Pentagon reportedly had ample prepublication opportunity to confirm or deny the report, but did not wave off the reporter from publishing. Within days of publication and in response to the article, Islamic fundamentalists in the Arab world staged mass protests that often turned to riots. These also included mob attacks on Western consulates, and at least fifteen people were killed and sixty injured in the rioting.[4] Two weeks after the publication and the riots, *Newsweek* retracted the article when investigation of the reporter's work determined that the confidential source, allegedly a government official, said he could not be certain whether the story was true.[5]

Defamation in the Islamic Context

The *Jyllands-Posten* and the *Newsweek* incidents underscore the need to at least be aware of the volatility of religious issues in the Middle East. At this stage, some discussion of general points about *sharia* and its overlap into defamation are warranted. Below are the most likely instances of defamatory meaning in the Islamic context:

- Accusing Muslims of violating the prohibition on *riba*. Riba, likened to usury, is basically the profit from speculative and/or interest-bearing investments. Islamic companies retain cleric/accountants to review investments, most of which must be asset-backed. Trading in pure debt is forbidden.
- Accusing Muslims of selling shoddy goods to/defrauding another Muslim. This is accusing them of sinning against certain *hadith* (The Prophet's sayings) that prohibit dishonest conduct.
- The accumulation of wealth without charity (tithing, or *zakah*).
- Conspicuous or wasteful consumption (*israj*).
- Making forbidden investments in or having business relationships in certain industries, funds, or companies such as those involving alcohol, gambling, weapons production, meat packing with pork, or pornography.

Iran

Iran is a constitutional Islamic Republic, a theocracy whose political system is laid out in the 1979 constitution called *Qanun-e Asasi*. Iran's makeup has several intricately connected governing bodies, some of which are democratically elected and some of which are determined by religious leaders. The concept of *velayat-e faqih* (guardianship of the jurist) plays an influential role in the governmental structure.[6]

There are four civil courts: first level civil courts, second level civil courts, independent civil courts, and special civil courts. The latter attend to matters related to family laws and have jurisdiction over divorce and child custody. Criminal courts fall into two categories: first and second level criminal courts. The first level courts have jurisdiction over prosecution for felony charges, while the second level courts try cases that involve lighter punitive action. The Constitution requires all trials to be open to the public unless the court determines that an open trial would be detrimental to public morality or public order, or in case of private disputes, if both parties request that open hearings not be held. Most journalists are tried in closed sessions and often without their attorneys being allowed to attend.

The Constitution provides for freedom of the press as long as published material accords with Islamic principles. The publisher of every newspaper and periodical is required by law to have a valid publishing license. Any publication perceived as being "anti-Islamic" is not granted a publication license. In practice, the criteria for being anti-Islamic have been broadly interpreted to encompass all materials that include an anti-government sentiment. Noteworthy is the fact that criminal penalties in Iranian Press Law often include the death sentence.

The major daily newspapers for the country are printed in Tehran. The leading newspapers include *Jumhori-yi Islami, Resalat, Kayhan, Abrar,* and *Ettelaat.* The *Tehran Times* and *Kayhan International* are two English-language dailies in Tehran. While all these newspapers are considered to be appropriately Islamic, they do not endorse every program of the central government. For example, *Jumhori-yi Islami,* the official organ of the IRP before its dissolution in 1987, presents the official government line of the Prime Minister. By contrast, *Resalat* is consistently critical of government policies, especially those related to the economy.[7]

It appears that the government is only slightly tolerant of measured criticism of official policies as long as such criticism does not challenge authority of leadership or conflict with religious edicts.[8] Nonetheless, extended pretrial detention of reporters and editors under criminal law is common in Iran.[9] As of this writing, AFP reported that the Iranian Parliament is drafting legislation that criminalizes websites "establishing web logs and sites promoting corruption, prostitution and apostasy." The specific sentences journalists face for improper publication include "hanging, amputation of the right hand and then the left foot as well as exile."[10]

Notable Media Events

In June of 2008, five online journalists were arrested after they planned publication of a story commemorating a 2005 public demonstration organized by feminists. The five online journalists were Jila Bani Yaghoub of the daily *Sarmayeh* and the *Canon Zeman Iran,*[11] Jelveh Javaheri of *Change for Equality*[12] (who was previously arrested at the end of 2007), Aida Saadat of the daily *Etemad* and *Change for Equality*, and Farideh Ghayb and Sara Loghmani of *Canon Zeman Irani* and *Change for Equality*. Their lawyer, Nasrine Satoudeh, was also arrested.[13]

In May of 2008, Said Matinpour, a reporter for *Yarpagh*, an Azeri-language weekly based in Tehran, faced an eight-year suspended sentence by a Tehran revolutionary court for "maintaining relations with foreigners" and "publicity against the Islamic Republic." According to Reporters

Without Borders, the trial was conducted behind closed doors and without his lawyer being allowed to attend.[14]

Iranian officials often use licensing provisions as a form of censorship and suspend the publication of journals that challenge too closely government policies or otherwise engage in "advocacy journalism." According to Reporters Without Borders, the reformist daily *Hambasteghi* and the weekly *Paygam Borujerd* were ordered to cease publication by the Ministry of Culture and Islamic Orientation in April of 2008. The shutdowns were allegedly related to the publication of articles about the son of a leading religious figure and viewed as "offensive and insulting towards the people."[15]

Iraq

After the Gulf War, the Coalition Provisional Authority (CPA) was established in 2003 under Multi-National Force–Iraq protections. On June 28, 2004, the CPA transferred sovereignty to the Iraqi Interim Government. A four-year, constitutionally based government took office in March 2006, and a cabinet was installed in May 2006.

Iraq is a constitutional democracy with a federal system of government. The 2005 Iraqi Constitution guarantees all Iraqis basic rights in many areas. The executive branch consists of the Presidency Council (one president, two deputy presidents) and a Council of Ministers (one prime minister, two deputy prime ministers, and thirty-four cabinet ministers). The President is the Head of State, protecting the Constitution and representing the sovereignty and unity of the state, while the Prime Minister is the direct executive authority and commander in chief. Beginning in 2006, the military and police began transitioning from being under the operational control of the Multi-National Forces–Iraq command to Iraqi command and control.[16]

Iraqi courts are divided into two major divisions: Civil and Criminal. Personal Status courts, which form a third division, mainly deal with matters of personal status similar to Family Courts in the West, such as marriage, divorce, custody of children, inheritance, endowments, and similar matters. Litigation in all of these courts is generally provided in three stages, namely, courts of first instance, appeal, and cassation. State security matters and serious criminal offenses are usually referred to special courts. Judges are usually appointed by the Ministry of Justice.

As of this writing, reorganization of the administrative entities controlling media is still underway. The current regulator is the Iraqi Communications and Media Commission, ostensibly to be augmented by a Higher Media Commission. The current public broadcaster is the Iraqi Media

Network, which is a successor to the Coalition Provisional Authority's radio stations and several other radio and television stations. The Iraqi Media Network currently operates the Radio of the Republic of Iraq and the government-supported *al-Iraqiya* TV station. Many private TV stations are available, such as *Al Sharqiya*.[17]

According to the Stanhope Centre for Communications Policy Research, a Temporary Code regulating media has been in place since 2004. English text of that Code is difficult to obtain. According to a July 2004 press release from the Committee to Protect Journalists, that Temporary Code empowers the government to "impose sanctions, including closure, against outlets that cross 'red lines' in their coverage" including "banning certain criticisms of the prime minister."

Notable Media Events

Due to the relatively new formation of government and the very recent liberation from Saddam Hussein's tightly controlled media, there have been no reported developments in libel or privacy. Sadly, due to political instability and terrorist insurgencies, the greatest number of notable media events relate not to publishing but to the safety of reporters in Iraq. All Westerners—even journalists—are considered fair game for Islamic terrorists. Although it is sad but not unreasonable to expect some casualties among journalists covering formal combat,[18] the Committee to Protect Journalists reports that as of this writing 129 journalists have been killed on duty in Iraq since 2003.[19]

In addition to challenges from insurgents, journalists have also faced difficulties from Iraqi and Coalition forces and administrators for alleged involvement with insurgents. Iraqi journalist Bilal Hussein, an Associated Press stringer photographer, was arrested by U.S. military authorities in April 2006 on the basis of his close relationship with insurgents. Hussein was released in 2008 under a general amnesty program without a finding of his guilt or innocence.[20]

Syria

An authoritarian military-dominated regime, Syria was established by the League of Nations mandate on 1946. In November 1970, Hafiz al-Asad, a member of the Socialist Ba'th Party and the minority Alawite sect, seized power in a bloodless coup and brought a degree of political stability to the country. Following the death of Asad, his son Bashar was approved as president by popular referendum in July 2000.[21]

The legal system is predicated on a combination of French and Ottoman civil law; Islamic law is used in the family court system. Judges are appointed (and removed) by a Supreme Judicial Council, which answers to the President. There is a Supreme Constitutional Court as well as a Court of Cassation, Appeals Courts, and trial courts consisting of Magistrate Courts or Courts of First Instance. There are also specialized jurisdictional courts, such as Juvenile Courts; Personal Status (or Family) Courts; Customs Courts; Economic Security Courts (which hear cases related to economic crimes); and most noteworthy to journalists, a Supreme State Security Court, which asserts jurisdiction over issues related to state security.[22]

Although there is a Constitutional guarantee of free expression, in practice Syria's Emergency Law ("The Revolution Protection Law") and Penal Code—and its vague definitions of "crimes against state security"—allow the Government broad discretion in restricting reportage.[23] The Emergency Law also prohibits the publication of "false information" that opposes "the goals of the revolution."

The Penal Code also prohibits "attempting to illegally change the Constitution," "preventing authorities from executing their responsibilities," and "acts or speech inciting confessionalism." In August 2001, the government amended the Press Law to permit the reestablishment of publications that were circulated prior to 1963 and established a framework in which the National Front Parties, as well as other approved private individuals and organizations, would be permitted to publish their own newspapers.

Notably, Articles 285 and 286 of the Syrian Penal Code punish "any person who disseminates information considered false or exaggerated and which is liable to undermine national morale." These amendments also provide for imprisonment and severe financial penalties for the publication of "inaccurate" information, particularly if it "causes public unrest, disturbs international relations, violates the dignity of the state or national unity, affects the morale of the armed forces, or inflicts harm on the national economy and the safety of the monetary system."[24]

Persons found guilty of publishing such information are subject to prison terms ranging from one to three years and fines ranging from $10,000 to $20,000 (500,000 to 1 million Syrian pounds). The amendments also impose strict punishments on reporters who do not reveal their government sources in response to government requests.

Notable Media Events

Because of state ownership of traditional media and the controls the government has on these outlets' content, Internet-based critics now appear to bear the main force of the government's suppression. As of June 2008, Kareem Arbaji, a young business consultant who posted criticism of the government in a chat forum, has been held without trial for more than a year because of comments he allegedly posted on the online discussion forum *Akhawia.*[25]

In May of 2008, Tariq Biassi was sentenced to three years in prison for posting an article criticizing the Syrian secret services. According to Reporters Without Borders, the authorities identified Biassi by tracing the origin of the Internet connection. Telecommunications minister Amr Salem ordered owners of websites to keep personal details on all authors of articles and columns. The country's two biggest access providers, Syria Telecommunication Establishment (STE) and Aloola, are state owned.[26]

The government has also taken precautionary action against journalists who are in the prepublication process of investigating fraud or corruption. In December of 2007, the Information Ministry wrote to the state radio and TV broadcaster and to the editors of the government newspapers, including *Tishrin*, *Al-Thawra,* and the *Syria Times*, notifying them that they had decreed a ban on publishing any story written by Waddah Muhyiddin, a well-known investigative print journalist. Muhyiddin was accused of spreading false information by the Central Commission for Control and Investigation, the official body that investigates fraud in state agencies.[27]

United Arab Emirates

Established in 1971, the United Arab Emirates is a federation of seven states (Abu Dhabi, Ajman, Dubai, Fujairah, Ras Al Khaima, Sharjah, and Umm Al Quwain) with a federal system responsible for foreign affairs, security and defense, nationality and immigration issues, education, public health, currency, and postal, telephone, and other communications services.[28] Dubai and Ras Al Khamina maintain their own judicial systems while the other emirates participate in a single federal judicial system. The Federal UAE courts are composed of two main divisions (civil and criminal) and are striated into three stages of litigation (First Instance, Appeal, and the Federal Supreme Court (colloquially referred to as Court of Cassation)). In addition, the UAE maintains *sharia* courts, which review matters of personal status, and in certain Emirates such as Abu Dhabi also includes serious criminal cases, labor, and other commercial matters. Important cases with a security aspect are referred to special courts.[29]

The UAE Constitution includes a press freedom clause, which is supplemented by Federal Law No. 15 (The Publication Law) of 1980. That law criminalizes certain statements, including criticism of the president of the state or of rulers of the Emirates; distributing journalistic materials or information offending Islam and religious holy matters or public morals and ethics; criticizing the governing system of the state and its interests, the Arab civilization, personal or family privacy, Arab and Islamic states, and its president; and any publication or broadcast that might harm the national currency or might cause disorder to the national economy.[30]

As strict as the Publication Law is, some leeway for western news organizations is enjoyed in the existence of "Dubai Media City" in Dubai. Created by His Highness Sheikh Mohammed Bin Rashid Al Maktoum, (UAE Vice President, Prime Minister, and the Ruler of Dubai), the DMC offers physical space in which news and other media organizations can operate, provided they comply with The Dubai Technology and Media Free Zone Codes of Guidance (2003). That Code purports to promote fairness and protection of privacy while not impinging upon the "concept" of Freedom of Expression.[31]

Notable Media Events

In November 2007, a Dubai appeals court overturned the convictions of the former editor of the English-language *Khaleej Times*, Shimba Kassiril Ganjadahran, and one of his reporters, Mohsen Rashed, on charges of libel. The two journalists had been sentenced to two months in prison for a story about a Dubai woman's lawsuit against her husband that led to his imprisonment. The appellate court decision came after Sheikh Mohammed Bin Rashid Al Maktoum had publicly declared that he believed it was not proper to imprison reporters for press crimes.[32]

Egypt

The Federal Research Division of the Library of Congress describes modern Egypt as the product of state-building efforts of its founding leaders, Gamal Abdul Nasser and Anwar as-Sadat. Researchers add that Egypt's centuries of subordination to foreign rule, long struggle for independence, and its continuing dependency on other countries have combined to generate a powerful nationalistic thread in the political culture.[33]

The legal system is based on a mixture of Islamic and civil law (particularly French codes). A national Constitution was adopted in September 1971, of which Article 2 affirms Islam as the state religion. Separate *sharia* courts were integrated into the national court system in 1956. The Constitution was amended in 1980 to add recognition of the principles of Islamic jurisprudence as the principal source of legislation. Appeals are heard by regular judges in the Courts of Appeal and, ultimately, the Court of Cassation.[34] Regarding transactions between natural persons or legal entities, "the most important legislation is the Egyptian Civil Code of 1948 (the ECC) which remains the main source of legal rules applicable to contracts."[35] Much of the ECC is based upon the French Civil Code and, to a lesser extent, upon various other European codes and upon Islamic law (especially in the matters of personal status). Although a codified and not a common-law system, Egyptian courts are guided by the principles and precedents of the Court of Cassation (for civil, commercial, and criminal matters) and the Supreme Administrative Court (for administrative and other public law matters).

Prior to Anwar Sadat's ascendancy to power, all broadcast media remained government controlled, and even after his rise, "government-appointed newspaper editors were still expected to 'self-censor' their product and were subject to removal when they did not."[36] After Sadat's murder and in the reforms of Hosni Mubarak's leadership, secular media gained a degree of operational and editorial liberty, including the tolerated publication of small opposition newspapers and weeklies. Nonetheless, various sections of Egyptian law criminalize "putting out false news harming the reputation and interests of the country" or "incitement to hatred of Islam."[37] According to Reporters Without Borders, constitutional reforms approved by Parliament in March 2007 included an amendment to Article 179 that gives authorities power to arrest people suspected of terrorism, search their homes, intercept their mail, and tap their phones without a court order.

Notable Media Events

In June of 2008, the Egyptian courts heard several media- and speech-related trials. Attempts to silence or at least control criticism over the Internet grabbed the lion's share of prosecutors' attention and resources. According to Menassat (a Middle-Eastern media watchdog group funded by the Ministry of Foreign Affairs of The Netherlands through the Dutch media advocacy group *Free Voice*), a group of fifty-one Egyptian websites criticized a local judge for using their material in his book about freedom of information and intellectual property rights without proper attribution. In turn, the judge filed a suit before the Administrative Judicial Court against the fifty-one websites, claiming that they were "defamatory for the reputation of Egypt." Although the trial court dismissed the judge's case, he has appealed that dismissal and the matter is as of this writing *sub judice*.[38]

In the same month, Menassat also reported about raids and seizure of broadcasting equipment at the Cairo News Company (CNC), a multimedia production company that hires its services out to more than forty satellite channels working in Egypt. In April 2008, using CNC's services, several satellite channels, including *al-Jazeera*, broadcast footage of Egyptian protesters ripping up pictures of Egyptian President Hosni Mubarak during riots against high prices. Two days later, the CNC building was raided by government agents and CNC's satellite broadcasting equipment was confiscated. CNC was accused of owning broadcasting equipment without a license.[39]

The physical and legal intimidation of reporters appears to be a commonly used technique to control content in Egypt. According to Reporters Without Borders, police in the Delta region city of Rahmanya physically attacked Kamal Murad of the weekly newspaper *Al-Fajr* in June 2008. Murad was arrested while using his mobile phone to take photos of police beating peasants. According to Murad, the police had been called by a landlord who was trying to force the peasants to sign leases. Murad is now being prosecuted on the basis of allegations brought against him by the police. Murad was held for two days and then charged with assuming a false identity, assaulting the police, inciting violence, and defamation. He faces between six months and three years in prison on the charges. Meanwhile, he has not been able to recover his mobile phone, SIM card, or notes. The matter is *sub judice*.[40]

In March of 2008, Ibrahim Issa, the editor of the weekly *Al Dustour* newspaper, was sentenced to a six-month prison term after being convicted under Articles 171 and 188 of the Criminal Code of publishing false information "liable to harm the general interest and the country's stability." According to the BBC, the publication that led to the arrest was an article Issa edited about a legal case against President Mubarak, allegedly accusing him of misusing public money during the privatization of state-owned companies. Issa was also fined 200 pounds (30 euros).[41]

Foreign newspapers distributing editions to Egypt are also subject to "gazetting": the practice of having circulation banned in a country by executive or administrative order. In February of 2008, after publishing photographs containing images of the infamous "Mohammed Cartoons," the *Frankfurter Allgemeine Zeitung*, *Die Welt*, the London-based *Observer*, and the *Wall Street Journal* had their Egyptian distribution cut off by the Information Ministry. The ministry issued a statement saying that "any newspaper or magazine that publishes something offensive towards the Prophet. . . . or the three monotheistic religions will be banned."[42]

Lebanon

Lebanon is an independent republic established pursuant to a Constitution promulgated in 1926. Executive power is vested in a president (elected by the legislature for six years) and a prime minister and cabinet, chosen by the president but responsible to the legislature. This political structure is informed by the ethic and religious sensitivities so common in the region: The Constitution requires that the president must be a Maronite Christian, the prime minister a Sunni Muslim, and the president of the National Assembly a Shi'a Muslim. Decisions by the president must be countersigned by the prime minister and concerned minister(s) after approval by the National Assembly. Legislative power is exercised by a 128-member National Assembly elected for a four-year term by universal adult suffrage. All adult males have the right to vote, while only women over twenty-one years of age with a grade school education may participate in the electoral process.[43]

The judiciary in Lebanon is divided horizontally into four main court systems, each having a multilevel hierarchical structure: the civil court (*kadaa' dli*); the administrative court system (*Majlis al-Shura*); the military court system; and the religious court systems.[44] In the civil courts, original jurisdiction is normally found in the courts of first instance, followed by courts of appeal, and finally the Cassation Court. The administrative courts' jurisdiction is limited to matters involving or arising from administrative decisions issued by the state or any of its agencies and institutions. The military courts have a specialized criminal jurisdiction restricted to arms and ammunitions (other than for hunting), crimes against national security, crimes committed in a military facility, or certain specific crimes involving members of the military forces. Finally, the religious court's jurisdiction is limited to matters of personal status and family law.[45]

The Sûreté Générale (Security Directorate) is authorized to approve all foreign materials, including magazines, plays, books, and films. According to Menassat, the law prohibits attacks on the dignity of the head of state or foreign leaders. Lebanon also maintains a Publication Court through which the Security Directorate is authorized to approve all foreign materials, including magazines, plays, books, and films. Legislation prohibits attacks on the dignity of the head of state or foreign leader. A 1991 security agreement between Lebanon and Syria effectively prohibits the publication of any material deemed harmful to either state.

As of 1999, Lebanon saw a rebuilding of its communications infrastructure. Government-controlled Radio Lebanon broadcasts in Arabic, and Tele-Liban broadcasts on three channels in Arabic, French, and English. By 2001 there were thirty-six radio stations and seven television stations. The government owns one radio and one television station, and the rest are privately owned. As of 2001, there were 300,000 Internet subscribers served by twenty-two service providers.[46] Even during the civil war, some twenty-five newspapers and magazines were published without restriction. Newspapers freely criticize the government but refrain from criticizing political groups that have the power to retaliate forcibly. As of 2002, the largest Arabic dailies included *An-Nahar* (*The Day*, circulation 77,600), *Al-Anwar* (*Lights*, 58,675), *As-Safir* (*The Ambassador*, 50,000), *Al-Amal* (*Hope*, 35,000), *Al Hayat* (*Life*, 31,030), *Al-Sharq* (36,000), and *Al-Liwa*

(*The Standard*, 15,000). Also influential are the French-language papers *L'Orient–Le Jour* (23,000), *Le Soir* (16,500), and *Le Réveil* (10,000).[47]

Journalists can be fined up to 200 million LL (about 1,100 euros) for defamation of the president or other heads of state under a 1994 media law. Inciting sectarian strife can lead to similar fines under the Penal Code. There is no institutionalized precensorship in Lebanon but random prepublication checks by the authorities often take place. The audiovisual media law bans the live broadcasting of unauthorized political gatherings and some religious events.[48] It also prohibits commentaries deemed damaging to the nation's economy. The Ministry of Information can shut down broadcasters or publishers deemed not conforming to the law but it has not done so since the Syrian withdrawal in 2005. Journalists in Lebanon exhibit a high degree of self-censorship and are keenly sensitive to local taboos, such as Lebanon's relations with Israel. Lebanon is still officially at war with Israel, and it is illegal for any Lebanese citizen, including journalists, to enter into contact with an Israeli citizen.

Notable Media Events

Lebanon may enjoy the most press freedom among Arab states in the region, with rare judicial prosecutions for publishing statements arguably damaging to the reputation of the government or against the vaguely defined interests of state stability.

A present and more difficult threat is the repeated attempts of Islamic fundamentalists to intimidate or even kill journalists. In January of 2008, Reporters Without Borders reported that a car bomb exploded at the residence of Aziz El-Metni, the publisher of the *Al Anbaa* Socialist weekly newspaper.[49] Other attacks on the press have proved more costly in human terms: in May of 2008 the Iranian-sponsored Hezbollah fired rockets into the offices of three moderate position outlets: the daily newspaper *Al-Mustakbal*, the radio station Radio Orient, and the television station Future News, killing at least ten and wounding another twenty people in the attacks.[50]

Saudi Arabia

Saudi Arabia is a religiously based monarchy in which the sovereign's dominant powers are regulated according to *sharia*, tribal law, and custom. There is no written constitution; laws must be compatible with Islamic law. In a decree of March 1992, the king was granted exclusive power to name the crown prince his successor. The Council of Ministers, first set up in 1953, is appointed by the king to advise on policy, originate legislation, and supervise the growing bureaucracy. The post of prime minister has been reserved for the king, and the crown prince has been appointed first deputy prime minister. Most other important posts in the cabinet are reserved for members of the royal family. In 1992, King Fahd announced the creation of the *Majlis al Shura*, an advisory body that would provide a forum for public debate. The king appointed sixty male citizens not belonging to the royal family to four-year terms on this body, which held its first meeting in 1992.

Because the Saudi Arabian legal system is based on *sharia* in strict accordance with the interpretation of the *Hanbali* school of Sunni Islam, judges must be *qadis*, men who have spent years studying the accepted sources of *sharia*: the Koran and the authenticated traditions (*hadith*) of the Prophet Muhammad's rulings and practices. Historically, the decisions of *qadis* were subject to review only by the ruler; the judiciary is not an independent institution but an extension of the political authority. The Ministry of Justice, established by King Faisal in 1970, is responsible for administering the country's more than 300 courts. The minister of justice is the de facto chief justice. The Supreme Judicial Council supervises the courts, reviews all legal decisions referred to it by the minister of justice, expresses legal opinions on judicial questions, and is required to approve all sentences of death, amputation, and stoning.[51]

The Ministry of Information effectively supervises all periodicals through the Press Law of 1964. This law requires a fifteen-member committee to assume financial and editorial responsibility for all privately owned newspapers. The members of these committees are approved by the Ministry of Information. According to Menassat, the government may appoint and discharge editors and can fire journalists who publish articles considered morally or politically inappropriate. The government routinely censors newspapers and self-censorship among local journalists (who are required to be licensed) is widespread. The Saudi Press Agency establishes the editorial line to be followed by the print media.[52] Foreign publications are heavily censored before being permitted into the kingdom. The objective of the censors is not only to remove politically sensitive materials but also to excise advertisements deemed offensive to public morality.[53]

Article 39 of the Basic Law of Government declares that "information, publication, and all other media shall employ courteous language and the state's regulations, and they shall contribute to the education of the nation and the bolstering of its unity. All acts that foster sedition or division or harm the state's security and its public relations or detract from man's dignity and rights shall be prohibited. The statutes shall define all that."[54]

While there are about twenty-two Internet Service providers, all connections are routed through a state server. The Telecommunication and Information Technology Authority is responsible for licensing Internet service providers, filtering the Internet, and registering Saudi domains. The Internet Service Unit routinely blocks access to nearly 400,000 websites with the aim of protecting citizens from content that is deemed morally or politically inappropriate. Some Internet users have turned to Internet services providers in surrounding countries in order to circumvent the restrictions on the Internet in Saudi Arabia.[55]

Notable Media Events

As elsewhere in the Arab world, the tight controls on traditional media have pushed dissidents, contrarian columnists, and investigative reporters into cyberspace. In May of 2008, blogger Fouad Al Farhan had been held for at least four months by authorities after he published commentary about the "advantages" and "disadvantages" of being a Muslim.[56] Print reporters do not entirely escape the attention of censors and government officials. In April 2006, Rabah Al-Quwai, who writes for the Saudi daily newspapers *Okaz* and *Chams,* was arrested and held for more than two weeks after the online version of his column criticized religious extremism in Saudi Arabia.[57]

Chapter Notes

1. See, generally, "*The Internet In the Arab World: A New Space of Repression?*" published by The Arabic Network For Human Rights Information, available at http://www.hrinfo.net/en/reports/net2004/index.shtml.

2. http://publiceditor.blogs.nytimes.com/2006/02/04/the-times-wont-publish-cartoons/#more-45. A number of Western news organizations, including the *Wall Street Journal* and Bloomberg News, did publish photographs of people reading or burning the cartoons in the context of current event reporting. See http://en.wikipedia.org/wiki/List_of_newspapers_that_reprinted_Jyllands-Posten%27s_Muhammad_cartoons#Ordered_by_country.

3. Some critics noted that although fearful of offending Muslims, the *New York Times* made no such soul-searching analysis when it published photographs of conceptual artist Andres Serrano's "Piss Christ," an installation comprised of a crucifix complete with a figure of Jesus attached, submerged in a flask of the artist's own urine. See, e.g., http://michellemalkin.com/2007/07/30/which-of-these-is-a-crime-in-america/.

4. "*Newsweek* Says It Is Retracting Koran Report," the *New York Times*, May 17, 2005, http://query.nytimes.com/gst/fullpage.html?res=9E02E5DF1639F934A25756C0A9639C8B63&sec=&spon=&pagewanted=3.

5. See "*Newsweek* Apologizes: Inaccurate Report on Koran Led to Riots," *Washington Post*, May 16, 2005, at http://www.washingtonpost.com/wp-dyn/

content/article/2005/05/15/AR2005051500605.html; "How a Fire Broke Out" at http://www.msnbc.msn.com/id/7857407/site/newsweek/print/1/displaymode/1098/; "*Newsweek* Retracts Koran-Desecration Story" at http://www.foxnews.com/story/0,2933,156612,00.html.

6. http://www.nyulawglobal.org/globalex/iran.htm#_The_Court_System.

7. United States Library of Congress Country Studies, at http://lcweb2.loc.gov/frd/cs/cshome.html.

8. "Conservative Daily Banned For Insulting Sunni Muslims", Reporters Without Borders, Feb. 7, 2007, at http://www.rsf.org/article.php3?id_article=20958.

9. Afghan journalist Ali Mohaqiq Nasab, the editor of the monthly *Haqoq-e-Zan* (Women's Rights), was held for eighty-six days before final release, and Mohammad Sadegh Kabovand, the publisher of the weekly *Payam-e Mardom-e Kurdistan* has been held for more than ten months as of this writing.

10. http://technology.iafrica.com/news/technology/1010080.htm.

11. http://www.irwomen.com.

12. http://www.we4change.info.

13. "Nine Women, Including Five Journalists, Arrested In Latest Attempt To Intimidate Cyber-Feminists," Reporters Without Borders, June 13, 2008, at http://www.rsf.org/article.php3?id_article=27472.

14. "Two Journalists Get Suspended Jail Terms For 'Publicity' Against The Government," June 11, 2008, at http://www.rsf.org/article.php3?id_article=27446.

15. According to Reporters Without Borders, at least seventeen publications have been banned or shut down in 2008 alone. See "Ministry Of Culture And Islamic Guidance Suspends More Newspapers," at http://www.rsf.org/article.php3?id_article=26500.

16. United States Department of State, Bureau of Near Eastern Affairs, at http://www.state.gov/r/pa/ei/bgn/6804.htm.

17. http://www.iraqimedianet.net/.

18. See, generally, "War Reporting" section at http://www.rsf.org/rubrique.php3?id_rubrique=741.

19. http://www.cpj.org/Briefings/Iraq/Iraq_danger.html.

20. http://www.rsf.org/article.php3?id_article=26602; see also "Iraq Orders U.S. Military to Free Jailed Photographer," 4/10/2008 at http://www.nytimes.com/2008/04/10/business/media/10photog.html?_r=1&ref=business&oref=slogin.

21. https://www.cia.gov/library/publications/the-world-factbook/geos/sy.html#Govt.

22. *Id.*

23. United States Dep't of State, "Country Reports on Human Rights," available at http://www.state.gov/g/drl/rls/hrrpt/2002/18289.htm.

24. See http://www.shrc.org/data/aspx/d4/254.aspx.

25. http://www.akhawia.net. Most dissident websites are filtered and blocked by the government.

26. http://www.rsf.org/article.php3?id_article=26986.

27. http://www.rsf.org/article.php3?id_article=24861.

28. http://www.emirates.org/gov.html.

29. http://gulf-law.com/uae_judicial.html.

30. http://www.dubai-law.org/.

31. The complete code is available at http://www.tecom.ae/law/law_8.htm.

32. http://www.rsf.org/article.php3?id_article=24342.

33. http://countrystudies.us/egypt/.

34. http://www.law.emory.edu/ifl/legal/egypt.htm.

35. http://www.nyulawglobal.org/globalex/Egypt.htm.

36. http://countrystudies.us/egypt/116.htm.

37. http://www.rsf.org/article.php3?id_article=25429.

38. http://www.menassat.com/?q=en/news-articles/3973-egypt-s-courts-inundated-media-trials-week.

39. *Id.* See also "Egyptian Censor Inflicting Pain on Media," *Middle Eastern Times*, 7/13/2008 at http://www.metimes.com/International/2008/06/19/egptian_censor_inflicting_pain_on_media/4898/.

40. http://www.rsf.org/article.php3?id_article=27778.

41. http://news.bbc.co.uk/2/hi/middle_east/5118876.stm.

42. http://www.rsf.org/article.php3?id_article=25860.

43. http://www.nationsencyclopedia.com/Asia-and-Oceania/Lebanon-GOVERNMENT.html.

44. http://www.loc.gov/law/help/lebanon.html.

45. *Id.*

46. http://www.nationsencyclopedia.com/Asia-and-Oceania/Lebanon-MEDIA.html.

47. *Id.*

48. http://www.menassat.com/?q=en/media-landscape/1154-state-media.

49. http://www.rsf.org/article.php3?id_article=25175.

50. "Hezbollah Seizes Large Chunks of Beirut," *Sydney Morning Herald*, 05/09/08 at http://www.smh.com.au/news/world/hezbollah-seizes-large-chunks-of-beirut/2008/05/09/1210131249414.html.

51. http://countrystudies.us/saudi-arabia/51.htm.

52. http://www.menassat.com/?q=en/media-landscape/state-media-15.

53. http://countrystudies.us/saudi-arabia/56.htm.

54. *Id.*

55. *Id.*

56. http://www.hrinfo.net/en/reports/2008/pr0426-2.shtml.

57. http://www.hrinfo.net/en/reports/2008/pr0426-2.shtml.

CHAPTER 12

Singapore

TAY PENG CHENG

Wong Partnership LLP

Wong Partnership LLP
One George Street #20-01
Singapore 049145
Phone: (65) 6416 8000
Fax: (65) 6532 5722
www.wongpartnership.com.sg
pengcheng.tay@wongpartnership.com.sg

Introduction to the Singapore Legal System

The Singapore legal system has evolved since the attainment of independence from the Federation of Malaysia in 1965. Although there are areas of Singapore law with roots in Indian, Australian, and New Zealand legislation, the foundation of the Singapore legal system is largely English in origin. In the early days, during the evolution of the Singapore legal system, the principles and rules of English common law and equity were applied in Singapore by way of general reception. There was also specific reception of English law when a local statute or provision thereof provided for such application.

The Application of English Law Act, which was enacted in 1993, clarified the application of English law in Singapore. Under this Act, English enactments after November 12, 1993 do not form part of Singapore law, except those specifically set out in the First Schedule of the Act and any other English enactment that applies to or is in force in Singapore by virtue of any written law. English enactments listed in the First Schedule of the Act (which also provides for the extent of application of each enactment) include the Partnership Act, the Misrepresentation Act, the Sale of Goods Act, and the Unfair Contract Terms Act.

The Singapore judiciary system is broadly divided into two levels: The upper tier comprises the Supreme Court, which consists of the Court of Appeal and the High Court. The subordinate courts follow, which comprise the District and Magistrate Courts (with a civil jurisdictional limit of S$250,000 and S$60,000, respectively) and other specialist courts including the Juvenile Court, Coroner's Courts, and the Small Claims Tribunal (with a civil jurisdictional limit of S$10,000). The Supreme Court of Judicature Act governs the structure of the Supreme Court and the Subordinate Courts Act that of the subordinate courts. All proceedings are tried before a judge (or a panel of judges, in the Court of Appeal). There are no juries in the Singapore legal system, and the judge in both civil and criminal matters undertakes the fact-finding.

The Court of Appeal is the highest appellate court in Singapore and hears both civil and criminal appeals. The High Court exercises both original as well as appellate civil and criminal jurisdiction. The subordinate courts exercise both civil and criminal jurisdiction.

1. What is the locally accepted definition of libel?

There is no exhaustive definition of what constitutes defamation in Singapore. A statement is defamatory of the person about whom it is published if it:

1. tends to lower him in the estimation of right-thinking members of society generally;[1]
2. exposes him to public hatred, contempt, or ridicule;[2] or
3. causes him to be shunned or avoided.[3]

There are two categories of defamation—libel and slander. For there to be libel, the statement must be made in writing or some other permanent form. Where the words are published orally or in some other transient form, it is termed slander.

Examples of statements that have been found to be defamatory include allegations that a politician is spreading lies and defaming the defendant and that a police report will be lodged against the politician for a criminal offense.[4] An advertisement asserting that a competitive retailer is lying to the public as to the source of parts used in his or her products,[5] and allegations that a company has a "poor credit rating,"[6] are further examples.

2. Is libel-by-implication recognized, or, in the alternative, must the complained-of words alone defame the plaintiff?

Yes, it is possible to defame a person by implication. When the court determines the meaning of the words, it seeks to ascertain what reasonable persons would collectively understand as the natural or ordinary meaning of the words. Such a meaning is not confined to the literal or strict meaning of the words but includes any inferences that can reasonably be drawn by such persons.[7]

Even if the ordinary meaning of the words is not defamatory, it may become so when the words are coupled with special facts that the readers know.[8]

3. May corporations sue for libel?

Yes, a corporation, as a legal entity, is entitled to mount a claim for libel. In this regard, Section 19(5) of the Companies Act[9] provides that a corporation shall be capable of suing and being sued.

4. Is product disparagement recognized, and if so, how does that differ from libel?

A cause of action is available for a statement disparaging property or goods, under the separate tort of "malicious falsehood."[10] If, however, a statement disparaging property also implies some defamatory meaning about the owner and is made in writing or some other permanent form, an action for libel may be possible (although the law will ensure that a plaintiff does not recover damages twice for the same loss).

The primary difference between the tort of malicious falsehood and libel is that an essential ingredient of the former is proof of special damage.[11] Hence, if there is loss of reputation but no pecuniary loss, an action for malicious falsehood will not succeed. This is subject to the exception in Section 6(1) of the Defamation Act,[12] which states that:

> In any action for slander of title, slander of goods or other malicious falsehood, it shall not be necessary to allege or prove special damage:
> (a) if the words upon which the action is founded are calculated to cause pecuniary damage to the plaintiff and are published in writing or other permanent form; or
> (b) if the said words are calculated to cause pecuniary damage to the plaintiff in respect of any office, profession, calling, trade or business held or carried on by him at the time of the publication.

In libel, there is no need to show special damage before the statement becomes actionable.

Another difference is that for malicious falsehood, the words must be published maliciously. There is no such requirement for libel. Further, for malicious falsehood, it is not necessary for the statement to injure the reputation of the plaintiff, which is a requirement for libel.

5. Must an individual be clearly identified (by name or photograph) to sue for libel? Can a group of persons sue for libel, even though not named?

There is no requirement that the subject of a story be expressly named. Even if an individual is not expressly named or identified, an action may proceed if ordinary, sensible readers with their general knowledge and common sense could and did understand the story to refer to the plaintiff.[13]

A class of persons cannot generally be defamed as a class, nor can an individual be defamed by a general reference to the class to which he belongs.[14] However, if the words, combined with the relevant circumstances, refer to some persons individually, those who were referred to can sue.[15]

6. What is the fault standard(s) applied to libel?

a. Does the fault standard depend on the fame or notoriety of the plaintiff?

The fame or notoriety of the plaintiff does not affect the actionability of the words, although it would have an impact on the damages recoverable. However, it may be more difficult for the plaintiff to prove that the words were defamatory (in that they caused others to think lowly of him), if he already has a poor reputation to begin with.

b. Is there a heightened fault standard or privilege for reporting on matters of public concern or public interest?

There is no higher fault standard when reporting matters of public interest. There are, however, more defenses available to the defendants if they are reporting a matter of public interest. A subject is considered a matter of public interest if it is such as to affect people at large, so that they may be interested in, or concerned with, what is going on or what may happen to them or others.

Some examples of matters of public interest include political or state matters, church and religious matters, and the management of public institutions and public performances. Matters of public interest are not privileged solely for that reason, but may form the basis of two defenses—qualified privilege and fair comment. It is important to note that both defenses are defeated if the plaintiff can show that the publication was done maliciously.

A privileged occasion is an occasion where the person who makes a communication has an interest or a legal, social, or moral duty, to make such communication to the person to whom it is made, and the person to whom the communication is so made has a corresponding interest or duty to receive it.[16]

Having said that, there is no general "media privilege" at common law. The law does not recognize an interest in the public strong enough to give rise generally to a duty to communicate in the press; such a duty may only exist on special facts.[17] Along with the duty to communicate is a corresponding interest to receive such information on the part of the public.[18] In addition, the duty must be a duty to publish to the public at large and an interest must exist in the public at large to receive the publication; it is insufficient if only a segment of the public is concerned with the subject matter of the publication.[19]

Section 12 of the Defamation Act also provides for specific occasions when the defense of qualified privilege is available to a newspaper. These provisions, however, do not limit or abridge any privilege subsisting at common law before the commencement of the Defamation Act.[20]

7. Is financial news about publicly traded companies, or companies involved with a government contract, considered a matter of public interest or otherwise privileged?

In the same context, financial news about publicly listed companies would be a matter of public interest. There may be greater difficulty in making the same contention for private companies involved with a government contract.

8. Is there a recognized protection for opinion or "fair comment" on matters of public concern?

There is a defense of fair comment available under Singapore law. In order to succeed in the defense, the defendant needs to establish the following four elements:[21]

1. the words complained of are comments, though they may consist of or include inference of facts;
2. the comment is on a matter of public interest;
3. the comment is based on facts; and
4. the comment is one which a fair-minded person can honestly make on the facts proved.

The defense is only available if the statement was not published maliciously.

9. Are there any requirements upon a plaintiff, such as demand for retraction or right of reply, and if so, what impact do they have?

There is no requirement that the plaintiff must first demand a retraction or a right of reply before a suit is filed. A right of reply, commonly offered by a newspaper to an allegedly defamed person, is not necessarily of legal significance, since it does not show that the newspaper accepts that the earlier statement was in fact defamatory.

Section 7 of the Defamation Act provides that a person who claims to have published the libel innocently may make an Offer of Amends. If such an offer is accepted by the plaintiff, Section 7(1)(a) provides that the plaintiff may not sue for libel after that. If such an offer is rejected, Section 7(1)(b) provides that it may be a defense for the defendant to show that the information had been published innocently, that the offer was made as soon as practicable, and that the offer has not been withdrawn.

Section 10 of the Defamation Act also provides that a defendant may, in mitigation of damages, provide evidence that he had made or offered an apology to the plaintiff, as soon as he had an opportunity to do so.

10. Is there a privilege for quoting or reporting on:

a. Papers filed in court?

There is qualified privilege attaching to such reports, under Item 2 of Part I of the Schedule to the Defamation Act, read with Section 12 of the Defamation Act. The copy or extract must be fair and accurate and the publication must be made without malice.

As for reports of judicial proceedings, under Section 11(1) of the Defamation Act, "a fair and accurate and contemporaneous report of proceedings publicly heard before any court lawfully exercising judicial authority within Singapore and of the judgment, sentence or finding of any such court shall be absolutely privileged, and any fair and bona fide comment thereon shall be protected, although such judgment, sentence or finding be subsequently reversed, quashed or varied, unless at the time of the publication of such report or comment the defendant who claims the protection afforded by this section knew or ought to have known of such reversal, quashing or variation."

However, Section 11(2) states the qualification that nothing in Section 11 shall authorize the publication of any "blasphemous, seditious or indecent matter or of any matter the publication of which is prohibited by law."

b. Government-issued documents?

This depends on the nature of the document, and the circumstances under which it was issued. Qualified privilege will attach to documents issued in accordance with or under the circumstances contemplated in the Schedule to the Defamation Act, e.g., a notice, advertisement, or report issued by a public officer in accordance with the requirements of any written law (Item 3 of Part I), or a copy of a fair and accurate report or summary of any notice issued for the information of the public by or on behalf of the government (Item 5 of Part II).

Under Section 7 of the Parliament (Privileges, Immunities and Powers) Act,[22] reports, papers, and journals that are published directly under the authority of Parliament are protected by absolute privilege and any persons who are subject to any civil or criminal proceedings on account of the publication by such person or their employee, by order or under the authority of Parliament or any committee, of any reports, papers, or journals, have the statutory protection of a summary stay of proceedings. By comparison, those who publish extracts from or abstracts of any such parliamentary report, paper, or journal are given only a qualified privilege under Section 8 of the Parliament (Privileges, Immunities and Powers) Act, and they have to prove that the extract or abstract was printed or published bona fide and without malice. Part II of the Act also enumerates a wide range of circumstances subject to a qualified privilege.

c. Quasi-governmental proceedings?

Possibly, provided it satisfies the requirements of Item 3 of Part II of the Schedule to the Defamation Act, e.g., that it must be a fair and accurate report of proceedings at a meeting of a commission, tribunal committee, or board appointed for the purpose of an inquiry, being a meeting to which admission is not denied to representatives of newspapers or other members of the public.

11. Is there a privilege for republishing statements made earlier by other, bona fide, reliable publications or wire services?

Under common law, every republication of a libel is a new libel and each publisher is answerable as if it originated with him.[23] Thus, it is no defense to claim that the defendant's publication was based on a previously published statement.

12. Are there any restrictions regarding reporting on:

a. Ongoing criminal investigations?

For ongoing criminal investigations, if information on such investigations is released by the investigating agency, these can be published. (See answers to Question 10b above.) Restrictions may, however, be placed on the publication of information that is protected by the Official Secrets Act (OSA).[24]

It would be a contravention of the OSA for a person to receive information knowing, or having reasonable grounds to believe, that such information was, at the time of receipt, communicated to him in contravention of the OSA.[25]

b. Ongoing criminal prosecutions?

The Judicial Proceedings (Regulation of Reports) Act[26] (JPA) places some restrictions on the reporting of judicial proceedings. Under Section 2 of the JPA, it is unlawful to print or publish:

(a) in relation to any judicial proceedings any indecent matter or indecent medical, surgical or physiological details being matter or details the publication of which would be calculated to injure public morals; or
(b) in relation to any judicial proceedings for divorce, dissolution of marriage, nullity of marriage, judicial separation or restitution of conjugal rights, any particulars other than the following:
    (i) the names, addresses and occupations of the parties and witnesses;
    (ii) a concise statement of the charges, the defenses and countercharges in support of which evidence has been given;
    (iii) submissions on any point of law arising in the course of the proceedings and the decision of the court thereon; and
    (iv) the decision of the court and any observations made by the court in giving it.

    Provided that nothing in this paragraph shall be held to permit the publication of anything contrary to paragraph (a).

The Children and Young Persons Act[27] (CYPA) also places restrictions on the publication of information relating to court proceedings. Sections 35(1) and (2) of the CYPA state as follows:

(1) Subject to Subsection (2), no person shall—
    (a) publish or broadcast any information relating to any proceedings in any court or on appeal from any court that reveals the name, address or school or that includes any particulars that are calculated to lead to the identification of any child or young person concerned in the proceedings, either as being the person against or in respect of whom the proceedings are taken or as being a witness therein; or
    (b) publish or broadcast any picture as being or including a picture of any child or young person so concerned in any such proceedings.
(2) The court or the Minister may, if satisfied that it is in the interests of justice so to do, by order dispense with the requirements of Subsection (1) to such extent as may be specified in the order.

There may also be restrictions dictated by the Court in respect of a particular matter.

c. Ongoing regulatory investigations?

Generally, the prohibitions on material prescribed in Questions 12a and 12b above.

d. Ongoing civil litigation, or other judicial proceedings?

Generally, the prohibitions on material prescribed in Questions 12a and 12b above.

13. Are prior restraints or other prepublication injunctions available on the basis of libel or privacy, and if so, what are the standards for obtaining such relief?

The Court has the power to grant interlocutory injunctions to restrain the publication or repetition of defamatory statements.[28] However, as freedom of speech is a constitutional liberty,[29] the jurisdiction will be exercised sparingly and only in clear cases.[30]

The cases show that the Court may grant such an interlocutory injunction where:

1. the statement is unarguably defamatory;
2. there are no grounds for concluding the statement may be true;
3. there is no other defense that might succeed; and
4. there is evidence of an intention to repeat or publish the defamatory statement.

14. Is a right of privacy recognized (either civilly or criminally)?

a. What is the definition of "private fact"?

There is no general right of privacy under Singapore law. There is also no specific legislative protection in Singapore with regard to privacy.

b. Is there a public interest or newsworthiness exception?

Not applicable.

c. Is the right of privacy based in common law, statute, or constitution?

Not applicable.

15. May reporters tape-record their own telephone conversations for note-taking purposes (not rebroadcast) without the consent of the other party?

There are no restrictions against the taping of conversations in such context. However, in the defense of a libel suit, the probative value of such taped conversations may be challenged if the publisher seeks to rely on the tape in evidence.

16. If permissible to record such tapes, may they be broadcast without permission?

As there is no general right of privacy in Singapore, there is no restriction on the grounds of privacy against broadcasting such tapes without permission. However, there may be restrictions on other grounds—for example, that the broadcast may be a breach of confidence. If the tape contains defamatory remarks, such broadcast may result in publication of the remarks.

17. Is there a recognized evidentiary privilege preventing the disclosure of confidential sources relied upon by reporters?

There are no such special privileges accorded to confidential sources under Singapore law.

Where a report is published based on information obtained from unnamed or confidential sources, and justification is pleaded as a defense, the publisher must be prepared to call those sources as witnesses in trial. This creates difficulties for a publisher, as it involves balancing the successful defense of a claim against journalistic principles. Ultimately, a commercial decision will have to be made as to whether a defense can be mounted without the necessity of calling such witnesses.

18. In the event that legal papers are served upon the newsroom (such as a civil complaint), are there any particular warnings about accepting service of which we should be aware?

Legal process (e.g., a Writ of Summons) has to be served personally in Singapore. Hence, if the defendant is a Singapore company, the legal process has to be served personally[31] on the registered office address of the company.

Likewise, if the defendant is a reporter, the legal process has to be served on the reporter personally (whether at home, in the office, or at any other place), unless an order for substituted service[32] is obtained. In that case, the legal process may be served through an advertisement in the newspapers, or be posted at the last known address of the reporter.

The defendant will have eight days after service to file a memorandum of appearance with the Court if he wishes to defend the claim brought against him.[33] It is important that this deadline be adhered to, as the plaintiff will be entitled to enter judgment in default of appearance if the defendant does not take the necessary steps within the stipulated time frame.[34]

19. Has your jurisdiction applied established media law to Internet publishers?

There have been cases where one of the forms of publication of the defamatory statement was publication on the Internet.[35] However, to the best of our knowledge, in these cases, the publication on the Internet was not an issue.

20. If established media law has been applied to Internet publishers, are there any ways in which Internet publishers (including chat room operators) have to meet different standards?

The cases so far have not dealt with Internet publication in detail.

There has however been academic debate in recent years, on the related issue of liability of Internet Service Providers (ISPs). The debate stems from the interpretation of S10 of the Electronic Transactions Act,[36] which states that,

> (1) A network service provider shall not be subject to any civil or criminal liability under any rule of law in respect of third-party material in the form of electronic records to which he merely provides access if such liability is founded on
> (a) the making, publication, dissemination or distribution of such materials or any statement made in such material; or
> (b) the infringement of any rights subsisting in or in relation to such material.
>
> (2) Nothing in this section shall affect
> (a) any obligation founded on contract;
> (b) the obligation of a network service provider as such under a licensing or other regulatory regime established under any written law; or
> (c) any obligation imposed under any written law or by a court to remove, block or deny access to any material.
>
> (3) For the purposes of this section "provides access," in relation to third-party material, means the provision of the necessary technical means by which third-party material may be accessed and includes the automatic and temporary storage of the third-party material for the purpose of providing access; "third-party," in relation to a network service provider, means a person over whom the provider has no effective control.

At the outset, it is observed that there is no definition of a "network service provider." There is thus some uncertainty as to whether an ISP would in fact be covered by this section. Even if ISPs are covered under this section, the section has been criticized for having too broad an exclusion of both civil and criminal liability,[37] as this exclusion would apply as soon as a network service provider is able to prove that it merely provided access for the making, publication, dissemination, or distribution of the materials or the infringement of any rights of the same.

Further, on the plain reading of the section, this defense of having "merely provided access" seems to be available to the ISPs irrespective of whether they had knowledge that the statements may attract some form of civil or criminal liability.[38] In addition, the section does not expressly provide for circumstances where the ISP may in fact have some form of editorial control or power to remove the contents. Having said that, if an ISP has such control and power, this could be evidence against the defense of having "merely provided access."[39]

While these views are purely academic, they do demonstrate that this area of law remains highly uncertain and it will be interesting to see how the Court would deal with this in due course.

21. Are there any cases where the courts enforced a judgment in libel from another jurisdiction against a publisher in your jurisdiction?
To the best of our knowledge, there have been no such cases as yet.

Chapter Notes

1. *Sim v. Stretch* [1936] 2 All ER 1237 followed in *Aaron v. Cheong Yip Seng* [1996] 1 SLR 623 and *Oei Hong Leong v. Ban Song Long David and Others* [2005] 1 SLR 277.

2. *Sim v. Stretch* [1936] 2 All ER 1237; *Lee Kuan Yew v. Davies* [1989] 1 SLR 1063.

3. *Youssoupoff v. Metro-Goldwyn-Mayer Pictures Ltd.* [1934] 50 TLR 581, as accepted locally in *Oei Hong Leong v. Ban Song Long David and Others, supra,* note 1.

4. *Tang Liang Hong v. Lee Kuan Yew and Another and Other Appeals* [1998] 1 SLR 97.

5. *Cristofori Music Pte Ltd. v. Robert Piano Co. Pte Ltd.* [2000] 3 SLR 503.

6. *L.K. Ang Construction Pte Ltd. v. Chubb Singapore Private Limited* [2003] 1 SLR 635.

7. *Aaron v. Cheong Yip Seng* [1996] 1 SLR 623.

8. *Rubber Improvement Ltd. v. Daily Telegraph Ltd.* [1964] AC 234; *DHKW Marketing & Anor v. Nature's Farm Pte Ltd.* [1999] 2 SLR 400.

9. Cap. 50.

10. *Kaye v. Robertson* [1991] FSR 62, followed in *Challenger Technologies v. Dennison Transoceanic Corporation* [1997] 3 SLR 582.

11. *Joyce v. Sengupta* [1993] 1 WLR 337, which was cited with approval in *Integrated Information Pte Ltd. v. CD-Biz Directories Pte Ltd. & Ors* [2000] 3 SLR 457.

12. Cap. 75.

13. *Lee Kuan Yew v. Davies, supra,* note 2.

14. *DKHW Marketing & Anor v. Nature's Farm Pte Ltd., supra,* note 7.

15. *Knupffer v. London Express Newspaper Ltd.* [1944] AC 116.

16. *Supra,* note 5.

17. *Supra,* note 7.

18. Ibid.

19. Ibid.

20. *Supra,* note 12, Section 12(4).

21. *Chen Cheng v. Central Christian Church* [1999] 1 SLR 94.

22. Cap. 217.

23. *Supra,* note 6; *Lee Kuan Yew v. Chee Soon Juan* [2003] 3 SLR 8.

24. Cap. 213.

25. Ibid., Section 5(2).

26. Cap. 149.

27. Cap. 38.

28. In the exercise of its equitable jurisdiction under Section 3(a) of the Civil Law Act (Cap. 43) and Section 18(2) of the Supreme Court of Judicature Act (Cap. 322) read with para. 14 of the First Schedule thereto. The District Courts have the power to grant injunctions under Section 31(2) of the Subordinate Courts Act (Cap. 321).

29. Article 14, Constitution of the Republic of Singapore.

30. *Kwek Juan Bok Lawrence v. Lim Han Yong* [1989] 1 SLR 655.

31. Rules of Court, O 10 r 1.

32. Rules of Court, O 62 r 5.

33. Rules of Court, O 12 r 2 read with O 12 r 4.

34. Rules of Court, O 13 rr 1 and 2.

35. For example, *Tang Liang Hong v. Lee Kuan Yew and Another and Other Appeals, supra,* note 4, and *T J Systems (S) Pte Ltd. and Others v. Ngow Kheong Shen* [2003] SGHC 73.

36. Cap. 88.

37. Ang Peng Hwa,"Chapter 8: Legal and Regulatory Hurdles to E-Commerce in Singapore," *Impact of the Regulatory Framework on E-Commerce in Singapore* (1, 2002)

38. Tan Ken Hwee, "Breaking New Ground: The Electronic Transactions Act," (1998) *AsiaBusiness Law Review.*

39. Lesley Chew SC, "The Law's Response to Defamation on the Web," *A Comparison Law Gazette,* May 2001 (4).

CHAPTER 13

Thailand

SINFAH TUNSARAWUTH
Attorney at Law

97/101 Moo 4 Moo Ban Lak Si Land
Vibhavadi Rangsit Road
Sigan, Don Muang
Bangkok 10210
Thailand
Phone: ++662 503 7861
sinfah@hotmail.com

Introduction to the Thai Legal System

Despite being a country that enjoys the greatest freedom of expression in Asia and being among a small number of countries in the region that provide statutory guarantee of access to government information, Thailand still treats defamation as a criminal offense. Offenders can be sued for criminal and/or civil cases for a defamatory act. Criminal lawsuits seek imprisonment for the offenders, while civil lawsuits seek monetary or any other kind of compensations.

Thailand has a civil law system. Its fundamental law is included in the four main codes, namely, the Penal Code, Civil and Commercial Code, Criminal Procedure Code, and Civil Procedure Code. Course syllabuses for undergraduate law students in universities mainly deal with provisions in these four codes.

In terms of its news media landscape, Thailand's terrestrial radio and television stations are owned by the state and seen as more conservative in their news reporting compared to newspapers, which are all owned by private companies. Therefore, Thai radio and television have never been sued for defamation or libel. Defamation and libel are more often the concern of newspapers. This chapter on Thailand, hence, will discuss only defamation and libel cases concerned with Thai newspapers.

The recent enactment of Press Registration Act A.D. 2007 will be likely to change the way defamation cases are filed against Thai newspapers. The Act, which came into effect on December 19, 2007 and replaced the previous draconian Press Act A.D. 1941, has made it easier for Thai nationals to start a newspaper. Now Thai nationals who want to start a newspaper can simply "notify" the authorities rather than seek a permit. Under the new law, Thai authorities can no longer censor or close newspapers under any circumstance. However, the new Act, which deals with print media and newspapers, still allows the country's police chief to bar importation of any publication that deems to be *lèse majesté* or contrary to public order or good morals. For instance, the police chief still can bar anyone from bringing into Thailand the book *The King Never Smiles.*

For cases related to defamation, the new law relieves newspaper editors and publishers of the liability of a defamatory offense committed by authors or reporters of the newspaper. In the 1941 act, the editor and the author of a defamatory article had to share the liability as principals of the offense, and if the author could not be located, the publisher had to become a principal of the offense as well. Now it seems only reporters or columnists would be sued for defamatory offenses in newspapers. In early 2008, retail giant Tesco Lotus, the local trade name of multinational Tesco of the United Kingdom, sued a freelance columnist and another staff reporter of the same newspaper in two separate libel cases in civil court without naming the editor of the newspaper as a defendant. Both cases are still pending in court.[1]

The Structure of the Civil Court System

Thailand's system of court of justice, both civil and criminal, has three levels—namely, the court of first instance, the appeal court, and the Dika[2] court (or supreme court as known in Western countries). After the court of first instance announces its verdict, the defendant may appeal his case to the appeal court, and then to the Dika court. A verdict passed by the Dika court is the final judgment of any case.

The civil and criminal courts have their own separate proceedings in each of the three levels. Bangkok has a number of courts of first instance, but each of the other provinces has at least one court of first instance for civil and criminal cases. Thailand has seventy-six provinces including Bangkok, the capital. Appeal courts are located at a regional level. There is only one Dika court for both civil and criminal cases in the country and it is located in Bangkok.

Thailand also has separate specialized courts—such as the constitutional court, administrative court, labor court, bankruptcy court, intellectual property, and international trade court—each of which has its own governing legislation, and case filing and hearing proceedings. These specialized courts usually have two levels—first instance, and supreme. The constitutional court, however, has only one sitting located in Bangkok and examines cases or disputes regarding provisions in the constitution only.

1. What is the locally accepted definition of libel?

Defamation is an offense under Chapter 3 of Title 11 in Thailand's Penal Code. Title 11 deals with offenses against liberty and reputation, and Chapter 3, Sections 326–333, deal specifically with defamation. The Penal Code does not provide a definition of defamation, but Section 326, which is the main provision of the offense, defines what constitutes a defamatory act:

> Section 326—Whoever imputes anything to the other person before a third person in a manner likely to impair the reputation of such other person or to expose such other person to hatred or contempt is said to commit defamation, and shall be punished with imprisonment not exceeding one year or fine not exceeding twenty thousand baht, or both.

Thailand's Civil and Commercial Code makes no distinction between slander and libel, and the legislation does not have any chapter that deals specifically with civil defamation. Slander and libel are included in provisions on wrongful acts or torts under the Civil and Commercial Code. A "wrongful act" is defined in Section 420, Chapter 1 of Title 5 of the Code:

> Section 420—A person who, willfully or negligently, unlawfully injures the life, body, health, liberty, property or any right of another person, is said to commit a wrongful act and is bound to make compensation therefore.

A slander or libel must be a wrongful act that injures the reputation of a person. Section 423 of the Civil and Commercial Code deals with what could be seen as slander or libel:

> Section 423—A person who, contrary to the truth, asserts or circulates as a fact that is injurious to the reputation or the credit of another or his earnings or prosperity in any other manner, shall compensate the other for any damage arising therefrom, even if he does not know of its untruth, provided he ought to know it.
>
> A person who makes a communication the untruth of which is unknown to him does not thereby render himself liable to make compensation, if he or the receiver of the communication has rightful interest in it.

The key difference between what constitutes defamation in the Penal Code and slander or libel in the Civil and Commercial Code is the effect of truth as a defense. Newspapers can still be found guilty of defamation in a criminal court if the court finds the statement at issue true, but as a personal matter pertaining to the injured person. By contrast, in a civil court, if what has been reported is true, the newspapers will not be deemed to have committed any wrongdoing.

Usually, plaintiffs, when taking legal action against journalists or publishers, will file for defamation in criminal court in hope of seeking jail terms for the defendants and will seek monetary damages in civil court if they are seeking compensation. Because Thailand's Penal Code sets limits on the amount of the fine the court can award for an offense, the plaintiffs will not receive high monetary compensation in criminal cases. The civil court will usually await judgment of the defamation case in the criminal court and often make its verdict in agreement. The civil court will then set the amount of monetary compensation and/or other remedies for the defendants to comply with.

The Thai criminal court tends to see statements reaffirming a fact as defamatory but statements expressing opinion as not defamatory. Cursing or swearing is also seen not to be defamatory by Thai court. For instance, the accusation of "corruption" or "cheating," such as an allegation that someone has favored another person in a bidding process, is defamatory.[3] A statement saying that a lawyer took money but did not give it to the party concerned has been found defamatory.[4] Accusing a man of being a "womanizer" has been held not defamatory.[5]

2. Is libel-by-implication recognized, or, in the alternative, must the complained-of words alone defame the claimant?

Yes, it is possible to defame a person by implication. The Thai court usually determines the meaning of words, first, by applying the meaning provided for in the dictionary of the Royal Institute, the official reference for Thai-language words. However, the court also takes into consideration the social and cultural implication of the words. When a man was alleged to be a womanizer, the court said "womanizer" means, according to the Royal Institute's dictionary, "a person who longs for sexual relationship" and that "since the plaintiff is a man, in the opinion of the society or ordinary persons who hear the words said by the defendant, it cannot be incurred that it is an imputation to the plaintiff in a manner likely to impair the reputation of the plaintiff or to expose the plaintiff to hatred or contempt. It is normal that men will long for sexual relationship. Therefore, the words said by the defendant are not defamatory to the plaintiff."[6]

On the other hand, when a woman was alleged to have a sexual relationship with the husband of another woman, the defendant was found to be guilty of defamation.[7]

The Thai court also takes into consideration the context of the words in the article in which such words are published. A journalist wrote a newspaper column comparing the plaintiff to another schoolteacher who had the "real spirit of being a teacher" and wrote that the plaintiff should rather be called "a person hired for teaching" because the plaintiff had acted very differently from the other teacher. The Dika court ruled that the comparison allowed those who heard the words to think that the plaintiff had bad behaviors and was unsuited to be a teacher.[8]

3. May a corporation sue for libel?

Under Thai law, a corporation or a limited company is a juristic person and is entitled to enjoy the same rights as a natural person. Therefore, a corporation can sue for defamation or libel and can be a defendant in such a lawsuit as well. Thailand's Civil and Commercial Code defines the rights of juristic persons in Section 67.

> Section 67—Subject to Section 66, a juristic person enjoys the same rights and is subject to the same duties as a natural person, except those who, by reason of their nature, may be enjoyed or incurred only by a natural person.

Many corporations have sued Thai newspapers for defamation. One of the recent internationally known cases was the defamation lawsuit filed by Shin Corporation Public Company Limited (plaintiff), at the time stilled owned by the family of former Thai prime minister Thaksin Shinawatra, v. Ms. Supinya Klangnarong, Thai Journal Group Company Limited (publisher of the Thai-language *Thai Post* daily), two authorized directors of the company, and the newspaper's managing editor (altogether five defendants). Shin Corp. filed its lawsuit with the Criminal Court in Bangkok on October 2, 2003.[9]

Tesco Lotus, the Thai subsidiary of multinational retailer Tesco in the United Kingdom, has also sued for criminal defamation against a Thai official of the Thai Chamber of Commerce and has two other libel lawsuits in civil court against one Thai freelance columnist and one staff reporter of a Thai-language daily. Tesco Lotus is the local trade name, while the company filed in the lawsuits as the plaintiff is Ek-Chai Distribution System Company Limited, the company name that is registered under Thai law.[10]

4. Is product disparagement recognized, and if so, how does that differ from libel?

Thai law does not specifically recognize product disparagement, but product disparagement could be seen as asserting or circulating false statements that injure "earnings or prosperity" of the plaintiffs as stipulated in Section 423 of the Civil and Commercial Code cited above.

5. Must an individual be clearly identified (by name or photograph) to sue for libel? Can a group of persons sue for libel, even though not named?

No. Even though a person is not expressly identified, he or she still can sue for defamation if the context of published statements can be traced back to indicate the plaintiff without any doubt. Thai newspapers have the practice of naming people in the news using the initials of their names rather than their full first and family names, but then they provide details about the person to the extent that readers can easily guess who he or she is.

In 2006, former national police chief San Sarutanon filed ten lawsuits against seventeen defendants who included a senior police officer, journalists, publishers, editors, and newspapers, in libel charges in civil court. The plaintiff alleged that the defendants made statements that he was a womanizer and had sexually harassed a female reporter, though the defendants did not mention him by name or position.[11]

On July 10, 2003, a Thai-language newspaper reported that a local official in Nan province in the north of Thailand was an influential person, that he was elected to his office because of his influence, and that he was involved in illegal logging. The story used an initial to refer to the official but said he died in March 2003 because of heart failure. The son of the official filed defamation charges with the police against the newspaper on behalf of his father. The police helped settle the dispute because it went to court.[12]

Under Thai law, two or more persons may be parties to the same case as joint-plaintiffs or joint-defendants if it appears that there exists between them a common interest in the subject matter of the case,[13] but each of the plaintiffs and defendants must be expressly identified in the complaints.[14] There have been defamation cases in Thai courts in which the prosecuting party included more than one plaintiff. But each member in the party was clearly named in the complaint.

Thai court has dismissed cases in which the plaintiff's identity was unclear. For instance, the Dika court has ruled that the term "armed forces" did not refer to any particular force, and that the defendant in the case could not be seen as specifically imputing anything to the army. The act of the defendant, therefore, did not defame the army.[15]

6. Please describe the fault standard(s) applied to libel, particularly:

(a) Does the fault standard depend on the fame or notoriety of the plaintiff?

Under the Penal Code, there is no regard to the fame or notoriety of the plaintiff as the maximum penalty stipulated in the Code is applicable to everybody. However, in civil court, a famous plaintiff could certainly argue for higher compensation on the grounds that the defamatory statements hurt his or her earnings or prosperity more than those of an ordinary plaintiff.

(b) Is there a heightened fault standard or privilege for reporting on matters of public concern or public interest?

Thailand's Penal Code and Civil and Commercial Code do not clearly set a privilege for reporting on matters of public concern or public interest. The matter is very much left to the discretion of the court. However, defendants usually cite public concern or public interest in their defense.

But if the subject matter deals with listed companies or public officials, a Thai court would tend to regard it as a matter of public concern or public interest.

In 2005, Picnic Corporation Public Company Limited, which is listed in the Thai stock market, sued a Thai-language newspaper for publishing defamatory statements about the company's accounting system. The court ruled that because Picnic Corporation was a public company, which could offer its shares to sell to the public, members of the public who were shareholders of the plaintiff were entitled to receive information and performance results of the plaintiff. Reporting such information in accordance with its profession was the direct duty of the newspaper, which could be carried out under the law.[16]

In 2001, an official of a local administration sued the defendant for alleging that he had embezzled a public plot of land. This case went to the Dika court, which ruled that because the plaintiff was running in an election, it was justified that the defendant disclosed information about the plaintiff to the public "for the protection of a legitimate interest" and "by way of fair comment on any person or thing subjected to public criticism."[17]

However, in 2006, the Dika court ruled that the headlines in a Thai-language newspaper using the terms "cruel" and "tyranny" were defamatory in describing then Thai Prime Minister Chuan Leekpai. The report published in 2003 was about a crackdown on antigovernment protestors while Chuan was the Prime Minister.[18]

(c) What are the traditional defenses to a libel claim?

Thailand's Penal Code allows for the defendant to prove to the court that what he or she has said in impairing someone's reputation is true. But the court will not allow such proof if the defendant defames the plaintiff on personal matters and if such proof will not benefit the public. This provides some key strategies for the defense in a criminal court trial. Newspapers will have to prove to the court that what they have published is true and it is what the public needs to know and thereby is not a personal matter of the plaintiff. This defense is provided for in Section 330 of the Penal Code.

> Section 330—In the case of defamation, if the person prosecuted for defamation can prove that the imputation made by him is true, he shall not be punished.
>
> But he shall not be allowed to prove if such imputation concerns personal matters, and such proof will not be benefit to the public.

Traditional defense of defamation charges is also provided in Section 329 of the Penal Code.

> Section 329—Whoever, in good faith, expresses any opinion or statement:
> (1) by way of self justification or defense, or for the protection of a legitimate interest;
> (2) in the status of being an official in the exercise of his functions;
> (3) by way of fair comment on any person or thing subjected to public criticism; or
> (4) by way of fair report of the open proceedings of any Court or meeting, shall not be guilty of defamation.

In applying the provisions provided in Section 329, the most widely applied defense by a Thai newspaper is fair comment in good faith on persons or issues subjected to public criticism.

7. Is financial news about publicly traded companies, or companies involved with government contracts considered a matter of public interest or otherwise privileged?

Companies listed in the Thai stock market, formally known as the Stock Exchange of Thailand or SET, are required by law to publish their financial statements and performance results, which are accessible to members of the public. Thai courts usually regard this information as a matter of public interest. (See Item 6 (b) on the court case about Picnic Corporation Public Company Limited.)

Companies involved with government contracts are also seen as a matter of public interest and journalists or members of the public can apply the Official Information Act A.D. 1997 in acquiring information about such contracts from the government. This Act, which allows access to information held by state agencies, will be discussed more in Item 14 of this chapter.

8. Is there a recognized protection for opinion of "fair comment" on matters of public concern?

Yes. Section 329 of Thailand's Penal Code recognizes as not defamatory "fair comment made in good faith on persons or things subjected to public criticism." (See Item 6(c).)

9. Are there any requirements upon a plaintiff such as a demand for retraction or right of reply, and if so, what impact do they have?

Thailand's Penal Code, Civil and Commercial Code, and the Press Registration Act A.D. 2007 do not provide for any demand for retraction or right of reply.

10. Is there a privilege for quoting or reporting on:

(a) Papers filed in court?

Section 329 of the Penal Code stipulates that a "fair report in good faith of the open proceedings of any court" shall not be held as defamatory. (See Item 6(c) for complete citation of Section 329.)

Statements and/or opinions made by parties in court proceedings or by their lawyers are also protected by law. This protection is provided for in Section 331 of the Penal Code.

> Section 331—A party in a case or his lawyer who expresses opinion or statements in the proceedings of the Court in favor of his case shall not be guilty of defamation.

The Dika court ruled that a newspaper that published reports quoting complaints on criminal charges filed in court without adding any word to it did not commit any defamatory offense. Rather, it was a fair reporting of open-court proceedings in good faith.[19]

(b) Government-issued documents?

To this author's best knowledge, Thai newspapers have never been sued for defamation for quoting or reporting on government-issued documents. Thailand is among a small number of countries in Asia that has an Official Information Act, which requires government agencies to make accessible to the public a great deal of information held by the government.

(c) Quasi-governmental proceedings, such as those by professional associations (for example disciplinary proceedings)?

Thai law does not provide privilege for quoting or reporting on proceedings of professional associations. But if Thai newspapers report proceedings of, for instance, the Medical Council of Thailand, which is taking disciplinary action against a physician, the newspapers could apply the defense of "fair comment in good faith on any person or thing subjected to public criticism."

11. Is there a privilege for republishing statements made earlier by other, bona fide reliable publications or wire services?

Thai law does not specifically provide any privilege for republishing statements made earlier by other, bona fide reliable publications or wire services. However, if a person is being sued for defamation in court for statements that had earlier been made by the same person in other publications but which the plaintiff had not taken action against, that person can cite such no action by the plaintiff for those previous publications as a defense in the current court case.

In *Shin Corporation Public Company Limited v. Supinya Klangnarong and four other defendants*, Supinya's statements that were sued for defamation in this case had earlier been published in a journal, and she had also made similar statements in another earlier press conference. But Shin Corporation did not rebut the allegations made in the journal or at the press conference. Nor did the company take any action against her on those two earlier occasions. Supinya's lawyer used this as a defense in court, and the court cited this lack of action by Shin Corporation in those two cases in its judgment to dismiss the case.[20]

12. Are there any restrictions regarding:

(a) Reporting on ongoing criminal investigations?
(b) Reporting on ongoing criminal prosecutions?
(c) Reporting on ongoing regulatory investigations?
(d) Reporting on ongoing civil litigation or other judicial proceedings?

Generally speaking, there is no restriction on reporting on any ongoing criminal investigations, criminal prosecutions, regulatory investigations, civil litigation, or other judicial proceedings. For criminal prosecutions, civil litigation and other judicial proceedings, this is already explained in Item 10(a). For criminal investigations and regulatory investigations, newspapers shall be protected if they make their reports by quoting the investigators or documents issued from such investigations.

13. Are prior restraints or other prepublication injunctions available on the basis of libel or privacy, and if so, what are the standards for obtaining such relief?

Under Thai law or any practice known, there are no prior restraints or other prepublication injunctions available on the basis of libel or privacy. Under the Press Registration Act A.D. 2007, government officials under no circumstances can order any prepublication censorship of any Thai newspapers on any basis. Thai court has never been known to ever issue any prepublication injunctions on the basis of libel or privacy either.

14. Is a right to privacy recognized (either civilly or criminally), and if so:

(a) What is the definition of "private fact"?

A person's dignity, reputation, and privacy are protected under Section 35 of the Constitution A.D. 2007.

> Section 35—A person's family rights, dignity, reputation or the right of privacy shall be protected.

The assertion or circulation of a statement or picture in any manner whatsoever to the public, which violates or affects a person's family rights, dignity, reputation or the right of privacy, shall not be made except for the case which is beneficial to the public.

> A person is entitled to be protected from unlawful use of personal information related to him as provided by law.

More specifically, personal information is currently protected under Official Information Act A.D. 1997, which deals with both government and personal information held by state agencies. Personal information held by private entities, such as commercial banks or private hospitals, is not dealt with in this Act. The Official Information Act does provide for a definition of personal information.

"Personal Information" means information relating to all the personal particulars of a person, such as education, financial status, health record, criminal record or employment record, which contain the name of such person or contain a numeric reference, code or such other indications identifying that person as fingerprint, tape, or diskette in which a person's sound is recorded, or photograph, and shall also include information relating to personal particulars of the deceased.

Chapter Three of the Act, which deals with personal information, also gives a definition of a person.

> Section 21—For the purpose of this Chapter, "person" means a natural person who is of Thai nationality and a natural person who is not of Thai nationality but has a residence in Thailand.

Therefore, personal information about a foreigner who does not have a residence in Thailand is not protected under this Act.

(b) Is there a public interest or newsworthiness exception?

The Official Information Act stipulates that state agencies shall not disclose personal information in their control to other state agencies or other persons without prior or immediate consent given in writing by the person who is the subject thereof except for, among other circumstances, the disclosure to state officials for the purpose of preventing the violation of law or non-compliance with the law, conducting investigations and inquiries, or instituting legal actions of any type whatsoever; or the disclosure necessary for the prevention or elimination of hazards to the life or health of persons. The provisions contained in Section 24 of the Official Information Act can be seen as providing for disclosing personal information for public interest.

15. May reporters tape-record their own telephone conversations for note-taking purposes (not broadcast) without the consent of the other party?

Yes. Thai reporters may tape-record their own telephone conversations for note-taking purposes without the consent of the other party. In an off-the-record interview, the interviewee can assume that the reporter will not quote him by name and/or position. In an on-the-record interview, the interviewee can assume that the interview will be recorded. Usually in a long conversation, part will be on the record and part will be off the record. Thai interviewees usually will not mind having the entire conversation recorded. But the reporters should bear in mind which part of the conversation is on the record and which is background and should handle them differently in their report.

16. If permissible to record such tapes, may they be broadcast without permission?

Usually, if an interviewee agrees to have an interview recorded, he will not have any problem with broadcasting the interview. Many Thai-language dailies now collaborate with broadcasting companies to do news programs on radio. They usually use the tapes recorded by their newspaper reporters for broadcasting on radio. For interviews by broadcasting journalists, usually the interviewees are aware that what they say will be broadcast even though the journalists may not specifically ask for their permission.

17. Is there a recognized evidentiary privilege preventing the disclosure of confidential sources relied upon by reporters?

Under Thai law, there is no provision preventing the disclosure of confidential sources relied upon by reporters. To this author's best knowledge, there has rarely been any court case involving disclosure of information sources of Thai reporters. Most Thai newspapers have been sued for defamatory statements made by editorial staff themselves or by interviewees expressly identified in the articles published.

18. In the event that legal papers are served upon the newsroom (such as a civil complaint), are there any particular warnings about accepting service of which we should be aware?

Copies of complaints filed by plaintiffs in court are usually delivered by hand, by court officials, to the residence or office of defendants named in the complaints. If no one is present to accept the complaints, the plaintiffs can request a court order to have the complaints posted on the door or gate of the residence or office of the defendants. In civil cases, the defendants will usually have fifteen days to give their answer to the court.

19. Has your jurisdiction applied the above law to Internet publishers?

There is no law that directly deals with Internet publication either. The law that Thai authorities apply to deal with communications via the Internet is the Computer-Related Offenses Commission Act of 2007, which mainly deals with computer hacking, fraudulence, and forgery of computer information, and posting pornography on the Internet.

Generally speaking, Thai authorities have been lenient with information flow on the Internet as long as there is no offense against national security or members of the royal family.

20. If so, are there any ways in which Internet publishers (including chat room operators) have to meet different standards?

None.

21. Are there any cases where the Courts enforced a judgment in libel from another jurisdiction against a publisher in your jurisdiction?

No. Thai courts have never enforced a judgment in libel from another jurisdiction against a publisher in Thailand. Libel or defamation, in the case of Thailand, is not a serious offense, and it would be unlikely for Thai courts to enforce a judgment of such an offense from another country in Thailand.

Section 333 of the Penal Code sets defamation as a compoundable offense, meaning that if the injured person does not press charges or decides to drop the charges later, the state cannot take the case against the offender. Therefore, it is unlikely that Thai courts will punish an offender in Thailand when the injured person does not file the case in the country.

Chapter Notes

1. Phra Khanong court in Bangkok. Black Case Number 2327/2551. Minburi court in Minburi province. Black Case Number Por 312/2551.

2. *Dika* literally means petitions submitted to the King.

3. Dika court. Dika Judgment Number 3520/2543.

4. Dika court. Dika Judgment Number 3086/2522.

5. Dika court. Dika Judgment Number 3015/2543.

6. Dika court. Dika Judgment Number 3015/2543.

7. Dika court. Dika Judgment Number 3725/2538.

8. Dika court. Dika Judgment Number 1724/2543.

9. Criminal court in Bangkok. Black Case Number 3091/2546. Red Case Number 685/2549.

10. Black Case Numbers 4228/2550, 2327/2008, and Por 312/2551.

11. Appeal court in Bangkok. Black Case Number 2292–2301/2549. Red Case Number 10542–10551/2550.

12. Interview with in-house lawyer of Thai-language *Khom Chad Luek* daily.

13. Section 59 of the Civil Procedure Code.

14. Section 67 of the Civil Procedure Code.

15. Dika court. Dika Judgment Number 3954/2539.

16. Samut Sakorn court in Samut Sakorn province. Black Case Number 4971/2548. Red Case Number 5244/2549.

17. Dika court. Dika Judgment Number 4563/2544.

18. Dika court. Dika Judgment Number 7038/2549.

19. Dika court. Dika Judgment Number 3654/2543.

20. Criminal court in Bangkok. Black Case Number 3091/2546. Red Case Number 685/2549.

PART **THREE**

Europe

Belgium

England and Wales

France

Germany

Italy

Netherlands

Poland

Russian Federation

Spain

Switzerland

CHAPTER **14**

Belgium

STEVEN DE SCHRIJVER
Van Bael & Bellis

Van Bael & Bellis
Louizalaan 165 Avenue Louise
B-1050 Brussels, Belgium
Phone: 32-2-647-73-50
Fax: 32-2-640-64-99
www.vanbaelbellis.com
sdeschrijver@vanbaelbellis.com

Introduction to the Belgian Legal System

The Belgian judicial system resembles the civil law system of its neighbor, France. There are two court branches within the Belgian system: the administrative courts and the ordinary courts. The administrative courts deal with matters relating to administrative law, i.e., the organization, the functioning, and the control of the executive. The ordinary courts have jurisdiction over civil and criminal actions. In view of the territorial organization of its court system, Belgium is divided into more than two hundred counties (*kantons/cantons*), twenty-six districts (*arrondissementen/ arrondissements*), and five judicial areas (*rechtsgebieden/ressorts*).

At the county level, which is the lowest level, a distinction must be made between the Police Court (*Politierechtbank/Tribunal de police*) and the Justice of the Peace (*Vredegerecht/Justice de paix*). A Justice of the Peace is, in general, empowered to hear all cases involving claims of up to 1,860 euros. In addition to this general competence, a Justice of the Peace has exclusive jurisdiction over certain specific claims regardless of the amount involved in the claim (e.g., real property leases). Appeals against judgments of the Justice of the Peace are, depending on the subject matter, heard by the Court of First Instance or the Commercial Court of the district in which the Justice of the Peace is located. The Police Courts are empowered to hear all cases involving civil consequences of road accidents and cases involving misdemeanors (*overtredingen/contraventions*); these are mostly minor traffic offenses. Appeals against judgments of the Police Court are heard by the Criminal Court (*Correctionele Rechtbank/Tribunal correctionnel*), which is a division of the Court of First Instance.

At the district level, each of Belgium's twenty-six judicial districts has three different courts resolving different matters. There is a Court of First Instance composed of three divisions: one dealing with civil law (Civil Court—*Burgerlijke Rechtbank/Tribunal civil*), one dealing with criminal law (Criminal Court—*Correctionele Rechtbank/Tribunal correctionnel*), and one dealing with juvenile matters (Juvenile Court—*Jeugdrechtbank/Tribunal de la jeunesse*). Furthermore, there is a Commercial Court (*Rechtbank Van Koophandel/Tribunal de commerce*) empowered to hear commercial cases. Finally, the Labor Court (*Arbeidsrechtbank/Tribunal du travail*) specializes in labor matters.

At the judicial level, Belgium has five Courts of Appeal and five Labor Courts of Appeal. Appeals against judgments rendered by the Courts of First Instance and the Commercial Courts are brought before the Court of Appeal (*Hof van Beroep/Cour d'appel*). Appeals against judgments rendered by the Labor Courts are brought before the Labor Court of Appeal (*Arbeidshof/Cour du travail*) of the judicial area in which the Labor Court is located. In the area of criminal law, the Assize Courts (*Hoven van Assisen/ Cours d'assises*) and the military courts should also be cited.

Belgium has one Supreme Court (*Hof van Cassatie/Cour de cassation*), which is located in Brussels. The principal task of the Supreme Court is to review judgments that can no longer be appealed on the merits. The review by the Supreme Court is limited to issues of law. The Supreme Court will only verify whether the judgment that is being reviewed has applied the law correctly and has respected mandatory procedural rules.

Finally, Belgium also has a Court of Arbitration (*Arbitragehof/Cour d'arbitrage*) and a Council of State (*Raad van State/Conseil d'Etat*). Both courts have constitutional and administrative law competences.

1. What is the locally accepted definition of libel?

Criminal Libel

Law recognizes libel in both criminal and civil jurisprudential spheres. Under Articles 443 *et seq.* of the Belgian Criminal Code, libel consists of "viciously and publicly attributing to a given person a fact, the legal proof of which may not or cannot be established and which is likely to harm that person's honor or to expose that person to public contempt."

The Belgian Criminal Code distinguishes between cases where the author of the allegations is not able to prove the veracity of the allegations, even though allowed to do so[1] (*laster/calomnie*), and cases where the law does not allow the author of the allegations to bring such proof or where such proof is impossible (*eerroof/diffamation*). Criminal liability requires the satisfaction of various conditions.

First, there must be intent to harm the person who is the subject of the allegations (*animus iurandi*).[2] The intent to harm is not presumed and must be duly demonstrated by the public prosecutor. The intent to harm can simply be inferred, however, from the statement at issue.[3] Criminal libel is not simply constituted by the false facts put forth in the complained-of statement, but rather by the purely subjective and particularly insulting quality attributed by the author of the allegations to the acts of the article's subject.[4] In this regard, it does not matter whether the author of the allegations knew, at the time of making the allegations, that the allegations were false.[5]

Second, the complained-of statement must be sufficiently precise for criminal liability to lie. Indeed, Articles 443 *et seq.* of the Belgian Criminal Code require the imputation of a precise fact about the subject, i.e., not merely a general character failing about the subject.[6]

Third, the allegation must be the object of a real and actual publication. Pursuant to Article 444 of the Belgian Criminal Code, the allegations must have been made: (1) in public meetings or public places; or (2) in the presence of several individuals in a place open to a certain number of persons; or (3) in any place, in the presence of the offended person and in front of witnesses; or (4) on written documents or images which have been distributed, sold, or exposed to the public; or (5) on written documents which have not been publicized but which have been addressed to several persons.

Libel committed by journalists in the printed press is adjudicated in accordance with the laws governing the press. Pursuant to Article 150 of the Belgian Constitution, violations of the laws governing the press (*persmisdrijf/délit de presse*) must be prosecuted before the Assize Court[7] *(Hof van Assisen/Cour d'assises)*. There is an exception for complaints about articles motivated by racism and xenophobia. In those instances, the criminal court *(Correctionele Rechtbank/Tribunal correctionnel)* has jurisdiction under the Law of 7 May 1999.[8]

The Belgian Supreme Court has held that four elements must be present for there to be a violation of the laws governing the press:[9] (1) a criminal offense; (2) an abuse in the expression of one's opinions (in this regard, "opinion" must be construed broadly and includes any thought); (3) the use of printed material (i.e., the laws governing the press can only be violated when the author has manifested his or her opinion in the printed press); and (4) publicity (i.e., the litigious statement must have been really and effectively publicized).[10]

In practice, prosecution before the Assize Court for violations of the laws governing the press is rare[11] because the procedure is costly, requires a jury, and usually gives the sued-upon statements further publicity.

It should finally be noted that the Belgian Supreme Court has held that libel broadcast via radio or on television is not covered by Article 150 of the Belgian Constitution and must therefore be prosecuted before lower criminal courts *(Correctionele Rechtbank/Tribunal correctionnel).*[12] In one case, the Belgian Supreme Court applied Article 150 of the Belgian Constitution to the broadcasting of a television show because it was accompanied by the publication of a book on the same subject matter, thus considering that the defamatory statements were associated.[13] The question of whether libel committed on the Internet is a violation of the laws governing the press has not yet been addressed by the Belgian Supreme Court.

Civil Libel

Pursuant to Articles 1382 *et seq.* of the Belgian Civil Code, libel plaintiffs can seek vindication in tort, without regard to whether the conditions set out by Articles 443 *et seq.* of the Belgian Criminal Code are fulfilled.[14] This is the case where, for instance, there is no *animus iurandi.*[15]

Under Belgian law, the civil libel plaintiff is required to establish the existence of the following three elements: (1) a negligent act or omission (a fault);[16] (2) an injury that has been sustained; and (3) a causal relationship between the negligent act or omission and the injury.

The fault standard in libel is no different from that in other torts. A fault may have been committed by journalists where they have breached a legal provision or where they have not acted as reasonably prudent journalists would have, if placed in similar circumstances. A breach of the provisions of the Belgian Criminal Code on libel is considered a *per se* fault for the application of Article 1382 *et seq.* of the Belgian Civil Code.

Belgian courts have found the following statements to be defamatory: allegations that the manager of a co-ownership had been previously laid off from his activities as manager of another enterprise and that his mistakes in the management of the joint ownership had cost 100,000 Belgian francs to the joint owners;[17] precise allegations that a journalist is a member of the Israeli secret service, thus casting doubt as to his objectivity;[18] allegations that sexual abuses are statistically more often committed by Catholic priests than by "normal" persons and statements that the number of Catholic priests that have been prosecuted are just the "visible part of the iceberg";[19] allegations that a security company did not have the required special license from the Council of Ministers and that the company was in fact a private militia;[20] the publication of pictures with sensationalized or catchy titles in order to discredit a person;[21] defamation of former NATO secretary-general Mr. W. Claes in relation to his involvement in the Agusta helicopter scandal;[22] false allegations that Finance Minister D. Reynders possesses a secret bank account in Luxembourg.[23]

Belgian law is unique insofar as it has a strict specificity requirement, and statements of a vague or generalized nature are generally rejected as the basis for a libel claim. Belgian courts have found the following statements not to be defamatory: vague allegations relating to the bad management of a co-ownership;[24] allegations that a person shows a lack of civic spirit;[25] allegations that a person is crazy;[26] allegations that a person is a racist or a fascist.[27]

2. Is libel-by-implication recognized, or, in the alternative, must the complained-of words alone defame the plaintiff?

Libel-by-implication is not expressly recognized by the Belgian Criminal Code as a separate offense. Nonetheless, if an implied statement fulfills the conditions set out by the Belgian Criminal Code or if an implied statement fulfills the conditions set out by Articles 1382 *et seq.* of the Belgian Civil Code, it will trigger the application of the aforementioned provisions. In this respect, it does not matter that the allegations are formulated in the form of insinuations or requests for explanations.[28]

For instance, the Court of First Instance of Brussels ordered a Belgian newspaper to pay damages to a plaintiff for having published, under catchy and provocative headlines, statements that a reasonable reader would interpret as the plaintiff's involvement in a widely covered pedophilia and murder case.[29] It was held that journalists must only use data which they have controlled, to the reasonable extent of their means, and that the use of smart quotes or the conditional tense does not exempt them from liability in this respect.[30]

In another case, the Court of First Instance of Brussels held that the statement, made at a conference, that a journalist is a member of the Israeli secret service, without providing any proof thereof, must be considered to be defamatory. Although there is nothing defamatory on its face about being a member of this unit, the court found that such a statement could engender, in the minds of both the employer of the journalist and the readers, doubts as to the objectivity of that journalist's information.[31]

In a judgment of March 10, 1998, the Court of First Instance of Brussels considered that a press article creating confusion in the minds of the readers between two series of house searches, leading the general public to believe that the two series of searches related to the same individuals and the same companies, were defamatory. The Court of First Instance considered that those insinuations harmed the reputation of the companies, even though the conditional tense had been used in the article, as the plaintiffs were still considered, in the minds of the readers, to have participated in the illegal activities described in the article.[32]

3. May corporations sue for libel?

Yes, both civilly and criminally. Pursuant to Article 443 *et seq.* of the Belgian Criminal Code, any corporation can file a complaint with the public prosecutor if it considers that a person viciously and publicly attributed a fact to the corporation, likely to harm that corporation's honor or reputation or to expose that corporation to public contempt. Indeed, the victim of any allegation may be a natural person or a legal entity,[33] whether private or public.

As a criminal procedure is not likely to bring relief to a corporation that has been the victim of libelous allegations, the corporation will usually sue the author of the allegations for libel before the civil courts on the basis of the legal provisions governing tort liability. As mentioned above, the corporation will have to demonstrate fault on the part of the author of the allegations, an actual damage it has suffered, and a causal link between the fault and the damage.[34]

4. Is product disparagement recognized, and if so, how does that differ from libel?

Disparagement is recognized under Belgian law and consists in making a declaration that contains an element or an allegation likely to harm, in the minds of third parties, the creditworthiness or the reputation of an economic operator, or the products or services it offers, or its activities.[35] Under Belgian law, disparagement is thus considered to be a very prejudicial attack on a trader, which harms that trader's reputation, by means of a libelous act or simply by means of a critique that enables third parties to identify that trader.[36] It is an allegation likely to discredit the trader.[37]

Pursuant to the Law of 14 July 1991 on Unfair Trade Practices and the Information and the Protection of the Consumer (the Law on Unfair Trade Practices),[38] any advertising that contains elements that are disparaging about another trader, its products, its services, or its activities, is prohibited.[39] Product disparagement is thus considered, under Belgian law, to be an unfair trade practice, even if it only takes place by allusions or insinuations.[40] It does not matter whether the declaration is true or false or whether the declaration was made in good or bad faith.[41]

It should furthermore be noted that any advertising that contains misleading or disparaging comparisons or comparisons that unnecessarily allow the possibility of identifying one or more other traders is also prohibited.[42] Finally, any comparative advertising that disparages or discredits trademarks, commercial names, other distinctive signs, products, services, or activities of a competitor is forbidden.[43] For instance, a trader may not give the impression that the producer or the importer of products is guilty of counterfeiting products and selling counterfeited products, absent a judicial ruling on the matter.[44]

For a disparaging statement to be contrary to the Law on Unfair Trade Practices, some publicity must be given to the statement. A written statement that has only been sent to a small number of recipients will therefore not be considered to constitute disparagement, even if it contains, for instance, a tendentious description of legal proceedings against another trader.[45]

It should finally be noted that a critique in which a trader may be identified may constitute disparagement.[46]

5. Must an individual be clearly identified (by name or photograph) to sue for libel? Can a group of persons sue for libel, even though not named?

In order to sue for libel, a natural person or a legal entity must be clearly designated and, if the person is not named, should at least be identifiable. Any attack on a group of people or on a legal entity that does not have legal personality (such as a family)[47] does not constitute a violation of the law. Nonetheless, in such a case, any identifiable members of such entity could sue for libel if their honor has been harmed or if they have been subjected to public contempt.[48]

Criminal law contains exceptions allowing some form of group libel. Under Articles 446 and 447 of the Belgian Criminal Code, libel toward constituted bodies (such as, for example, legislative chambers, universities, and certain religious communities) is punished in the same way as libel toward individuals. Similarly, there is specific legislation that authorizes certain associations to file claims to defend their members or certain interests they promote. For example, the Law of July 30, 1991 on the Repression of Acts Inspired by Racism or Xenophobia[49] provides, in its Article 5, that human rights associations may go to court to defend the rights of their members or the interests that they protect.

6. What is the fault standard(s) applied to libel?

As mentioned above, in order for Articles 1382 *et seq.* to apply, any injured person must establish the existence of the following three elements: (1) a negligent act or omission (a fault); (2) an injury that has been sustained; and (3) a causal relationship between the negligent act or omission and the injury.

There is a fault on the part of the journalist who has breached a legal provision or who has not acted as a reasonably prudent journalist should have, in similar circumstances. In this regard, if a journalist breaches the provisions on libel contained in the Belgian Criminal Code or breaches Article 10 of the European Convention for the Protection of Human Rights and Fundamental Freedoms of the Council of Europe (the "Convention"), that journalist will also be considered to have committed a fault for tort liability purposes. It should be noted that if criminal proceedings are pending, the outcome of which is likely to contradict the judgment of the civil court or to have an influence on the outcome of the case, the civil judge must postpone its decision until the criminal judge has rendered a judgment.[50]

The appreciation of the fault must be made *in concreto,* i.e., the judge must consider the alleged fault of the journalist in its context.[51] This implies that the judge must balance the appreciation of the fault with the conditions of dissemination of the sued-upon statements, in particular the particularities of the medium used and the possibilities of a plaintiff's reply that were available on such a medium.[52]

In this balancing, the judge must take into account the behavior of a reasonably competent and diligent journalist.[53] The judge must also take account of the behavior of the average reader, listener, or viewer, i.e., a reasonably intelligent and attentive public.[54] Regard must also be given to the type of media and the nature of the information.[55]

Belgian case law has established the following practical guidelines that journalists should keep in mind at all times:

1. Journalists should behave as "normal, careful, and circumspect" journalists. It is not required that the information published have scientific accuracy or absolute reliability. However, journalists' publications cannot be based on rumors or unreliable information. Journalists are not entitled to publish articles that are manifestly incorrect or not supported by any evidence;[56]
2. Journalists' publications should be based on verified sources to the extent that this is reasonably possible. Absolute objectivity is, however, not required;[57]
3. Journalists should act carefully and their information should be reliable and verified;[58]
4. Journalists should prove their allegations.[59] It is not sufficient to publish defamatory allegations in a conditional manner or to place

them between quotation marks[60] or to formulate them as a question.[61] Journalists cannot hide behind the confidentiality of their sources to avoid the obligation to prove their allegations.[62] However, if certain allegations are based on rumors, publication may not be illegal to the extent that the requisite reservations have been made;[63]

5. In satiric press articles, allegations may be formulated more sharply or critically.[64]

a. Does the fault standard depend on the fame or notoriety of the plaintiff?

Yes. Belgian case law considers that the fault standard varies with the fame or the notoriety of the plaintiff. In this regard, it has been held that a politician, artist, or litigant must be able to withstand more severe criticism than a mere citizen.[65] The limits of the criticism must therefore be considered more loosely for a politician in his capacity of politician than for a private person, because those who decide to publicly lead a political action must accept that their speeches, statements, and actions might be the object of controversies, during which the usual means of communication may lead to the use of an aggressive or excessive language.[66] This view is supported by the European Court of Human Rights (ECHR). According to the ECHR, public figures must endure more criticism than private persons in order for political debate, essential in democracy, to properly function. Libel laws must honor this distinction. Therefore, a person's right to protection against defamatory or slanderous speech should be analyzed in relation to his or her societal duties.[67]

Nonetheless, those extended boundaries are not limitless. The press is not entitled to harm the honor and reputation of a person by creating, in the minds of the general public, "malevolent suspicions or unjust assumptions."[68] There are restrictions, among which stands an obligation of strict veracity regarding the facts,[69] the interdiction of libelous or injurious statements,[70] or the imputation of facts, decisions, or statements that are not accurate or not established.[71] A journalist therefore commits a serious offense when accusing a person without seeking confirmation from that person[72] or where the journalist only has weak information.[73]

b. Is there a heightened fault standard or privilege for reporting on matters of public concern or public interest?

Although there is no express privilege granted to journalists for reporting on matters of public concern, journalists nonetheless benefit from a certain heightened fault standard in reporting on matters of public interest. When ruling upon a case, Belgian courts and tribunals usually balance, on the one hand, the interests of the press and, on the other hand, the rights of the individual concerned. Nonetheless, Belgian law requires that publications must be accurate, complete, and objective. The fault standard is addressed in the following spheres.

Political sphere.[74] As mentioned above, it is accepted that speeches, statements, and actions in the political sphere may be the justifiable object of controversies.[75]

Judicial sphere. It is also judicially recognized that the press is entitled to report on the functioning of justice or the work of judges, which includes reporting on sentences pronounced in public. It is usually considered that the fact that a case is definitively ruled upon does not imply that the case may not be the object of future criticism.[76] Moreover, even though the Belgian Criminal Procedure Code provides for the secrecy of criminal investigations, it was likewise considered that the publishing of a book on a case that had not yet been ruled upon by the Assize Court could not be forbidden. In this case, the judge considered that he could see no reason why jurors would be influenced by the sued-upon book rather than by the precise and detailed information that they would obtain during the trial.[77]

Economic sphere. Considerable latitude is also given to reports of economic activities.[78] Nonetheless, when reporting on such matters, one must have recourse to serious methods of investigation and only use information the accurateness of which has been duly verified.[79] It was thus held that consumer protection reporting must be neutral, objective, and conducted by qualified persons. The information must be collected with prudence and must be scrupulously controlled with the most serious methods of investigation.[80] The rights of the producer whose products are the subject matter of the study must be safeguarded.[81]

The public interest is addressed in other areas from time to time. In three cases regarding an information campaign organized by public authorities to warn the general public about the danger of sects, it was considered that the public authority had an obligation to provide information that is accurate, as complete as possible, and objective.[82]

7. Is financial news about publicly traded companies, or companies involved with a government contract, considered a matter of public interest or otherwise privileged?

Financial news about publicly traded companies or companies involved with government contracts is not specifically considered as a matter of public interest or otherwise privileged. There are no specific rules or privileges with regard to the protection of financial information of publicly traded companies or companies involved with government contracts. Therefore, journalists are in principle free to publish financial news about publicly traded companies as long as that information is gathered and published in a legally acceptable manner.

Pursuant to Article 6 of Directive 2003/6/EC of the European Parliament and of the Council of 28 January 2003 on Insider Dealing and Market Manipulation ("Market Abuse"),[83] EU Member States should ensure that there are appropriate regulations in place to ensure that persons who produce or disseminate research concerning financial instruments or issuers of financial instruments and persons who produce or disseminate other information recommending or suggesting investment strategy, intended for distribution channels or for the public, take reasonable care to ensure that such information is fairly presented and disclose their interests or indicate conflicts of interest concerning the financial instruments to which that information relates. Similar provisions are contained in the Law of 2 August 2002 on the Supervision of the Financial Sector and Financial Services.[84]

8. Is there a recognized protection for opinion or "fair comment" on matters of public concern?

Yes. Opinions or fair comment on matters of public concern are legally protected in Belgium. This protection is based on Article 19 of the Belgian Constitution[85] as well as Article 10 of the Convention, both dealing with the freedom of expression. The Convention, which constitutes a minimum level of protection in addition to the protection granted by the Belgian Constitution (see Article 53 of the Convention), has a direct effect in the legal system (i.e., it can be invoked in legal proceedings before a Belgian court).[86] As a result, the Convention and the case law of the ECHR are particularly important in Belgium.

ECHR Case Law and Fair Comment

The ECHR has interpreted the freedom of expression in Article 10 of the Convention in a broad way. The following examples demonstrate what may fall within the scope of protection in Article 10 of the Convention:

1. ***Reporting on pending litigation***—The *Sunday Times* (1979): The *Sunday Times* published an article in relation to the thalidomide disaster that formed the background to pending litigation (parents of children who were victims of the drug thalidomide sued Distillers, the manufacturers of the drug, for negligence).[87]
2. ***Criticism of politicians***—*Lingens* (1986): The ECHR held that a government official accused of holding an "accommodating attitude" toward the Nazis had to endure more criticism as a result of his public position.[88]

3. ***Criticism of the government***—*Castells* (1992): Spain sued Senator Castells for insulting the government in a magazine article about violence in the Basque Country. According to the Spanish Criminal Code, insulting, falsely accusing, or threatening the government is punishable by imprisonment from six months to twelve years. Finding for Castells, the ECHR ruled that a democratic government should accept more criticism than private individuals and politicians.[89]

4. ***Nonpolitical issues of public interest***—*Thorgeirson* (1992): Iceland had charged writer Thorgeirson with defamation of unspecified police officers after he published two articles about police brutality. Iceland's Criminal Code called for punishing anyone who "vituperates or otherwise insults a civil servant" with fines or up to three years' imprisonment. The government argued that such defamatory expression should not be protected because it did not relate to the democratic political process. The ECHR however ruled that there is no warrant in its case law for distinguishing between political discussion and discussion of other matters of public concern. The ECHR also discussed the value of the press as a provider of information and a "public watchdog."[90] See also: *De Haes and Gijsels v. Belgium*[91] (defamation of judges); *Thoma v. Luxembourg*[92] (criticism on civil servants); *Colombani and Others v. France*[93] (insulting a foreign head of state); *Amihalachioaie v. Moldavia*[94] (criticism on judges); and *Yasar Kemal Gökçeli v. Turkey*[95] (criticism on government policy).

Significantly, the ECHR also acknowledged in *Handyside v. UK* (1976) that the freedom of expression applies not only to information or ideas that are favorably received or regarded as inoffensive or as a matter of indifference, but also to those that offend, shock, or disturb the state or any part of the population.[96]

The case law of the ECHR and the principles developed by the ECHR are equally applied in cases involving the freedom of expression decided by the Belgian courts. According to the Belgian courts, a wider degree of criticism, that could otherwise possibly be considered as defamatory, is accepted when:

(i) the criticism or polemic in the press concerns matters of public concern or facts which are the object of public debate or actual public discussion;
(ii) the criticism or defamatory allegations are directed against a politician or a publicly known person or his or her public function.

The following examples demonstrate what has been accepted as an opinion or fair comment on a matter of public concern;[97] criticism of a local politician;[98] a press article on certain share transactions by former president Mobutu of the Congo;[99] criticism of well-known politician S. Moureaux in relation to the Dutroux case;[100] a critical biography of a well-known person;[101] a press article on the relationship and contacts between politicians and persons convicted or suspected of certain crimes;[102] criticisms of a well-known Belgian politician named Jean Gol;[103] criticism of police and civil servants;[104] and criticism of a governmental institution.[105]

In some cases, it has been decided that criticism of politicians may go further than criticism of judges.[106] Furthermore, case law demonstrates that Belgian courts are more flexible if the defamatory allegations or criticisms are expressed by means of a moderated use of language or nonexcessive use of language.[107] The same applies if the defamatory allegations or critical judgments are based on reliable and carefully collected factual material.[108] Belgian case law also acknowledges that journalists are not only entitled to be critical, but also even provocative, and that the press should be regarded as a "public watchdog" of the democracy.[109]

Both Article 19 of the Belgian Constitution and Article 10 of the Convention provide that freedom of expression may be limited. Pursuant to the second paragraph of Article 10 of the Convention, the right to freedom of expression may be subject to restrictions and conditions in accordance with the following threefold test: an interference has to (1) be prescribed by law (i.e., statutory law or case law, in general law which is accessible and foreseeable); (2) have a legitimate aim (e.g., the territorial integrity, the impartiality of the judiciary, and the reputation or rights of others); and (3) be necessary in a democratic society (i.e., there has to be a pressing social need; it is not sufficient to be merely indispensable, desirable, or useful). In Belgium, these limitations are to be found in criminal as well as civil law.

Belgian Criminal Libel Law and Fair Comment

Examples of criminal laws that constitute limitations to opinions or fair comment on matters of public concern are contained in specific legislation in relation to the press (e.g., Press Decree of 20 July 1831); Criminal Code: e.g., provisions on libel and slander (Article 443 *et seq.* of the Belgian Criminal Code); offenses against the public order and public decency (Article 383 *et seq.* of the Criminal Code), etc. There is also specific criminal legislation that may restrict comment: e.g., limitations in relation to racism and xenophobia (Law of 30 July 1981 in relation to Racism and Xenophobia;[110] Law of 23 March 1995 in relation to the World War II Genocide,[111] etc.); specific limitations contained in, e.g., the Law of 8 April 1965 on the Protection of the Youth.[112]

"Fair Comment" Under Belgian Civil Libel Law

Civil law restrictions on opinions or fair comment on matters of public concern are based upon Articles 1382 *et seq.* of the Belgian Civil Code, which are the core provisions of Belgian tort law. Under Articles 1382 *et seq.* of the Belgian Civil Code, "a person who causes injury to the interests of another person must compensate that other person."

As mentioned above, Belgian law limits fair comment to avoid what it deems "unnecessarily offensive language" or "excessively critical or defamatory" allegations, solely aimed at causing damage. The following examples can be found in Belgian case law in relation to allegations and criticism that were considered to be unnecessarily offensive or excessively critical:[113] allegations against former Belgian prime minister P. Van Den Boeynants in relation to drug traffic, murder, and crime against the security of the State;[114] defamation of former NATO secretary-general W. Claes in relation to his involvement in the Agusta helicopter scandal;[115] and criticism based on inaccurate facts about Finance Minister D. Reynders in relation to the possession of a secret bank account in Luxembourg.[116]

9. Are there any requirements upon a plaintiff, such as demand for retraction or right of reply, and if so, what impact do they have?

Yes. Pursuant to Article 1 *et seq.* of the Law of 23 June 1961 on the Right of Reply[117] (the Law of 23 June 1961), any person has the right to request a reply if quoted by name or implicitly indicated in a "periodic writing." Articles 7 to 15 of the Law of 23 June 1961 also provide for a right of reply in broadcast or "periodic audio-visual programs," but this system differs in many aspects, in particular with regard to the conditions of admissibility and the recourse envisaged in the event of refusal of the insertion of the right of reply. For example, for the audiovisual press, contrary to the newspaper industry, the procedure is dealt with by the civil courts (which in a preliminary injunction procedure is ruled on the substance of the case) whose judgment cannot be appealed.[118]

Significantly, Articles 1 and 7 of the Law of 23 June 1961 explicitly provide that the right of reply does not deprive the persons concerned of the right to initiate legal proceedings. Legal scholars generally accept that the persons concerned are not obliged to make use of the right of reply prior to commencing legal proceedings. Similarly, to the extent a right for retraction exists, it does not prevent the persons concerned from initiating legal proceedings. Finally, it should be noted that although there are no specific requirements upon plaintiffs, such individuals are, in accordance with the general principles of tort law, nevertheless obliged to limit their own damage.

10. Is there a privilege for quoting or reporting on:

a. Papers filed in court?

Private persons are in principle free to provide information on legal proceedings in which they are involved. An important exception, however, applies in the framework of criminal investigations. Pursuant to Article 460*ter* of the Belgian Criminal Code, the use by a suspected party or a plaintiff claiming damages (*burgerlijke partij/partie civile*) of information obtained in the framework of an access to a (criminal) file is illegal and gives rise to criminal sanctions if that use hampers the investigation or violates the privacy rights, the physical or moral integrity, or the property of a person mentioned in the file.

For example, in June 2003, the Ghent Court of First Instance condemned a journalist of a Belgian newspaper for complicity in an abuse of access to file in accordance with Article 460*ter* of the Belgian Criminal Code.[119] The journalist published excerpts of a statement made by a suspect in a pedophilia case. The journalist received these documents from the plaintiff claiming damages. The Court ruled that the journalist violated the privacy rights and moral integrity of the defendant, some minors, as well as the husband of the suspect. The Ghent Court of Appeal confirmed the judgment of the Ghent Court of First Instance.[120] An appeal lodged by the journalist with the Belgian Supreme Court was unsuccessful.[121]

b. Government-issued documents?

We are not aware of any specific rules or restrictions in this respect. The restrictions set out in Question 10a equally apply. Some government-issued documents may be copyright protected.

c. Quasi-governmental proceedings?

We are not aware of any specific rules or restrictions in this respect. Some Belgian case law indicates that the rules applicable to criminal investigations also apply to disciplinary proceedings.[122]

11. Is there a privilege for republishing statements made earlier by other, bona fide, reliable publications or wire services?

Yes. In principle, journalists are entitled to republish statements made earlier by other, bona fide, reliable publications or wire services. The ECHR ruled in its *Thoma v. Luxembourg* judgment[123] that a radio journalist was allowed to refer to an article concerning a scandal that was published earlier in a newspaper. The ECHR stated that punishing a journalist for assisting in the dissemination of statements made by another person would seriously hamper the contribution of the press to the discussion of matters of public interest and should not be envisaged unless there were particularly strong reasons for doing so. In the case at hand, the Luxembourg appellate court had explained that journalists who merely quoted from an article that had already been published would only escape liability if they formally distanced themselves from the article and its content. The ECHR went further and explained that a general requirement for journalists to distance themselves from a libelous quotation was not reconcilable with the press's role of providing information on current events, opinions, and ideas. In the case at hand, the summary of the program showed that in any event the applicant had consistently taken the precaution of mentioning that he was beginning a quotation and of citing the author, and that in addition he had described the entire article by his fellow journalist as "strongly worded" when commenting on it. He had also asked a third party whether he thought what the author of the newspaper article had written was true.

Nonetheless, journalists in Belgium should be careful if they republish defamatory statements. Pursuant to Article 451 of the Belgian Criminal Code, journalists cannot avoid a conviction for libel by arguing that they simply reiterated what another person previously said. The case law on this issue is ambiguous and any factual situation should therefore be assessed on a case-by-case basis. Indeed, some courts decided that the fact that an analogue defamatory allegation has been published in other publications against which no complaint has been filed does not deprive the republication of its tortious character.[124] In other cases, however, the Belgian courts have taken into account the fact that the same allegations had been previously published in other media channels.[125]

In light of the above, when republishing statements made earlier by other persons or publishers, journalists may wish to take some precautions such as clearly mentioning the source, using conditional language, and consulting with local counsel.

12. Are there any restrictions regarding reporting on:

a. Ongoing criminal investigations?

There are no specific rules with respect to civil proceedings. Journalists do not have a presumptive right to access papers filed in court. However, parties are in principle free to provide information in relation to civil proceedings to the press. If journalists use this information, they should comply with the generally applicable limits to the freedom of expression as described above. Particularly, they should not (1) infringe the provisions on libel and slander; (2) violate the principles of public order or public decency; (3) publish incorrect or careless allegations; (4) use unnecessarily offensive language or excessively critical or defamatory allegations, solely aimed at causing damage; or (5) violate a person's privacy rights. In addition, journalists should be aware that the rules on copyright may apply.

Reporting on ongoing criminal investigations is restricted by the principle of secrecy. Article 28 *quinquies,* §1 *juncto* Article 57, §1 of the Belgian Criminal Procedure Code provides that, except for the exceptions provided for by law, [criminal] investigations are secret. Any person who is obliged, for professional reasons, to cooperate with such an investigation (such as civil servants employed by the Ministry of Justice, judges, police officers, judicial personnel, etc.) is bound by this principle of secrecy. Persons violating this obligation shall be punished with criminal sanctions (Article 458 of the Belgian Criminal Code).

Notwithstanding this general rule, information may sometimes be provided "in the public interest." Article 28 *quinquies,* §3 *juncto* Article 57, §3 of the Belgian Criminal Procedure Code state that a designated member of the court may provide information on ongoing criminal investigations to journalists if such is "in the public interest."

Any articles published in reliance thereupon should pay particular attention to the principles of the presumption of innocence, the rights of defense of the suspect, the sensitivities of the victim and third parties, as well as the privacy rights and dignity of all persons involved. In addition, the identity of the persons involved in the case should be kept secret to the extent that this is possible. This exception is further clarified in a circular letter of the Minister of Justice of April 30, 1999. For example, if information on ongoing criminal investigations is provided, this may occur under the following conditions set by the court officer acting as a source:

1. ***provision of information "on the record":*** the court member may be cited officially;
2. ***provision of information "off the record":*** the information provided by the court member may be used, but the court member may not be cited. Such information should enable journalists to publish "on the record" information correctly;
3. ***provision of "background information":*** this information may not be published by the journalist, but should allow journalists to expand their knowledge and understand the framework;
4. ***"embargo":*** agreement between the member of the court and the journalists that the journalists keep the information silent for a while (delay of publication);
5. ***"information stop" or "black-out":*** this is a temporary refusal to communicate information to the press.

Some specific provisions apply to trials of members of the police,[126] on reporting on minors (Article 80 of the Law of 8 April 1965 on the

Protection of the Youth[127]), and on victims of sexual violence (Article 378*bis* of the Belgian Criminal Code).

Journalists who publish information that they know to be provided by persons committing a violation of their confidentiality and professional secrecy obligations may be subject to criminal prosecutions (e.g., complicity in violation of professional secrecy obligations) or deontological sanctions (by the Algemene Vereniging van Beroepsjournalisten in België [AVBB]/Association Générale des Journalistes Professionnels Belges [AGJPB]).

Aside from obtaining information from the court or law enforcement officers, the press may reasonably rely upon counsel for litigants. Attorneys-at-law are entitled to provide information to the press if this is in the interest of the client. They should, however, take into account the presumption of innocence and the rights of defense of all parties involved, their privacy and dignity rights, as well as some professional rules. To the extent that this is possible, an attorney-at-law should keep secret the identity of the persons involved in the case (Article 28 *quinquies,* §4 *juncto* Article 57, §4 of the Belgian Criminal Procedure Code).

b. Ongoing criminal prosecutions?

Both the Belgian Constitution and the Convention allow reporting on ongoing civil and criminal litigation. For example, Article 148 of the Belgian Constitution as well as Article 6 of the Convention guarantee the right of public access to court hearings. Article 149 of the Belgian Constitution and Article 6 of the Belgian Convention include the obligation to publicly pronounce court decisions. Articles 19 and 25 of the Belgian Constitution as well as Article 10 of the Convention include the right of the press to report on ongoing court cases and other court-related matters.

These principles are limited, however, by the existence of other fundamental Belgian law rules, such as the protection of public policy, public order, and public decency. Rights of defense, the right to privacy, and the proper functioning of the judicial system may also impose restrictions on the basic principles set out above.

In addition, specific limitations apply with regard to:

1. ***divorces:*** the publication of the judicial debate in relation to divorces is prohibited (Articles 1270, 1306, and 1309 of the Belgian Judicial Code);
2. ***the protection of minors:*** reporting on the judicial debate in youth courts as well as publishing pictures or other images allowing third parties to identify the prosecuted minor is prohibited (Article 80 of the Law of 8 April 1965 on the Protection of the Youth);

3. ***victims of sexual offenses:*** the publication of information, without the consent of the victim of sexual offenses or the judicial authorities, allowing third parties to identify the victims is prohibited (Article 378*bis* of the Belgian Criminal Code).

c. Ongoing regulatory investigations?

We are not aware of any specific rules in relation to reporting on ongoing regulatory investigations. However, regulatory investigations by public authorities (e.g., antitrust) will often involve the collection of confidential data. The civil servants are in principle subject to a duty of secrecy and discretion in respect of such information. The publication or release of such confidential data may constitute a fault under civil law that may create a claim for compensation. In addition, the general restrictions to the freedom of expression and fair comments apply.

d. Ongoing civil litigation, or other judicial proceedings?

Both the Belgian Constitution and the Convention allow reporting on ongoing civil litigation (see, *inter alia,* Articles 19, 25, 148, and 149 of the Belgian Constitution as well as Articles 6 and 10 of the Convention). However, as mentioned above, journalists should comply with the generally applicable restrictions on freedom of expression. Particularly, they should not: (1) infringe the provisions on libel and slander; (2) violate the principles of public order or public decency; (3) publish incorrect or careless allegations; (4) use unnecessarily offensive language or excessively critical or defamatory allegations, solely aimed at causing damage; or (5) violate someone's privacy rights. In addition, other rules such as copyright may apply to briefs filed by parties.

13. Are prior restraints or other prepublication injunctions available on the basis of libel or privacy, and if so, what are the standards for obtaining such relief?

Yes, but although legally possible, it is rarely granted. Prepublication restraints are, in principle, available under Belgian law on the basis of libel or privacy. The president of the Court of First Instance may, pursuant to Articles 584 and 1039 of the Belgian Judicial Code, hear cases in summary proceedings (*kortgeding/référé*) and order interim measures in all matters deemed to be urgent. Urgency is usually defined as a situation where an immediate decision is desirable in order to avoid damage of some magnitude or serious inconvenience.[128] With respect to the press in particular, account must be taken of the impact on the general public of messages disseminated on the radio or on television. The president of the Court of First Instance has substantial discretion when deciding whether a given matter is urgent. Summary proceedings are handled in an expedited way and orders given by the president of the Court of First Instance in such cases may be appealed before the Court of Appeal.

Pursuant to Article 25 of the Belgian Constitution, the press is free and censorship may never be established. Moreover, Article 10 of the Convention guarantees freedom of expression, the exercise of which may only be subject to restrictions as are prescribed by law and are necessary in a democratic society. In this regard, the ECHR states that "the dangers inherent in prior restraint are such that they call for the most careful scrutiny on the part of the Court. This is especially so as far as the press is concerned, for news is a perishable commodity and to delay its publication, even for a short period, may well deprive it of all its value and interest."[129]

In Belgium, some courts held that Article 25 of the Belgian Constitution precluded the prohibition of the publication of information relating to comparative tests carried out by a consumer protection association,[130] the publication of information relating to criminal investigations,[131] the announced publication of a book on sects in Belgium and Luxembourg,[132] or the publication of a book on Flemish misses and models.[133] However, despite the constitutional prohibition, some judges increasingly imposed prepublication restraints, as is evidenced by the number of cases where cease-and-desist orders have been issued,[134] which have usually been confirmed by appeal courts.[135] For example, it was held that the publication of notes taken by an examining judge (*onderzoeksrechter/juge d'instruction*), i.e., the magistrate examining a criminal case, which had been released following the violation of the secrecy of a parliamentary investigation, could be forbidden.[136] It was also held that a temporary prohibition to broadcast a television show where the television show appears to harm manifestly and unnecessarily the honor and the reputation of a plaintiff was justified.[137]

The Belgian Supreme Court partly settled the controversy in the *Leempoel* case[138] and considered that the prohibition of censorship only applies to judicial interventions prior to any diffusion of a written media but does not encompass interim judicial measures that occur after this diffusion, which restrict the *prima facie* abusive use of the freedom of expression. In this case, the issue of the magazine in question had already been widely distributed.

It should finally be noted that some of the case law considers that since, according to the Belgian Supreme Court, Article 25 of the Belgian Constitution does not apply to audiovisual media, nothing prevents the adoption of provisional measures preventing the broadcasting of television programs.[139]

14. Is a right of privacy recognized (either civilly or criminally)?

The Belgian Supreme Court explicitly ruled that the protection of privacy is a legitimate restriction to the freedom of the press.[140] Importantly, case law also confirms that public persons also have a right to the protection of their privacy.[141] However, a critical biography of a public person is not on its face unlawful if the privacy rights of the person concerned are not violated.[142] On the contrary, revealing the sexual orientation of the members of a music band without their consent constitutes a violation of their privacy rights.[143]

a. What is the definition of "private fact"?

There is no generally accepted definition of what constitutes a "private fact." As Article 8 of the Convention, protecting a person's private life, has direct effect in Belgium, the interpretation of this provision by the ECHR is crucial to determine what constitutes a "private fact" under Belgian law. The ECHR has not formulated an exhaustive definition of "private life."[144]

However, it is clear that the concept of private life goes further than the mere right to privacy in the sense of seclusion. It concerns a sphere within which all persons can freely pursue the development and fulfillment of their personality. It follows from extensive case law of the ECHR that the following elements, activities, or measures *inter alia* concern a person's private life:[145] a person's name[146] and forename(s);[147] a person's picture;[148] a person's physical and moral integrity, including sexual life;[149] a person's right to develop relationships with other persons and the outside world;[150] a person's sexual life[151] and relationships between homosexuals and their partners with or without children;[152] compulsory medical treatment, including blood and urine tests imposed on prisoners to check for drugs,[153] compulsory vaccination, dental treatment, TB tests, or X-rays for children,[154] or compulsory administering of food;[155] a person's social life—the effective enjoyment of a social life that involves the capacity by reason of cultural and linguistic familiarity to enter into social relationships with others;[156] a person's personal relationships in business contexts;[157] the use of covert technological devices to intercept private communications; business or private conversations by telephone as well as the use of an office telephone;[158] and the collection of information by officials of the State about persons without their consent (e.g., the recording of fingerprinting, photography, and other personal information by the police even if the police register is secret).

Belgian legal scholars and case law often refer to the case law of the ECHR in order to determine what constitutes a "private fact." In any event, in Belgium, a private fact is a very broad concept. Some legal scholars include the following elements in their list of private facts: sex life, marriage and divorce, friendship, illness, religion, health, pregnancy, and political preferences. Other legal scholars also mention a person's physical and psychological integrity; moral and intellectual freedom; the right to be protected against defamation and the use of one's name, identity, or picture; the right to be protected against taking pictures, recording, taping and tape recordings; and the violation of professional secrecy.[159]

Finally, reference should be made to the Belgian Law of December 8, 1992, on the Protection of Privacy with regard to the Processing of Personal Data on the Protection of Data[160] (the "Data Protection Law") that regulates the "processing of personal data." Under the Data Protection Law, "personal data" is defined as any information relating to an identified or identifiable natural person. A person will be identifiable as soon as there is an objective possibility of identifying him or her directly or indirectly by any reasonable means (e.g., through a third person, a social security number, etc.), be it by the holder of the data or by any other person. Conversely, data that does not make the identification of the natural person possible (i.e., anonymous data) will fall outside the scope of the Data Protection Law. The notion of "processing" is very comprehensive. It encompasses any operation or set of operations involving personal data, whether or not by automatic means, such as the collection, recording, organization, storage, adaptation, alteration, retrieval, consultation, use, disclosure by transmission, dissemination, or otherwise making available, alignment, combination, as well as blocking, erasure, or destruction of personal data. The same regime applies to all these uses of personal data.

b. Is there a public interest or newsworthiness exception?

It is generally accepted that the privacy rights of persons having a public function (e.g., politicians, judges) and persons deliberately looking for or attracting public attention are more limited than those of "regular citizens." According to the ECHR, it is clear that the more public the location in which an activity takes place, the more difficult it is for applicants to establish that their right to respect for their private life is involved, although whether such an activity falls within the concept of private life or not must be judged on the basis of the nature of the activity itself.[161] Whether the privacy rights of private persons who become involved in public events or matters of public concern or facts which are the object of public debate or actual public discussion may be limited is, however, still subject to debate.

The absence of protection against press intrusions or the disclosure in the media of highly intimate, nondefamatory details of private life has not yet been subject to significant challenge before the ECHR. Some complaints, such as in the Irish case where the applicant complained that an insurance company taking photographs of the applicant outside his house constituted an infringement of the applicant's private life,[162] and the case introduced by Earl and Countess Spencer concerning press coverage of their private lives[163] have been declared inadmissible for failing to exhaust domestic remedies. As noted above, the determination of whether issues might arise under private life in relation to press intrusion might be influenced by the extent to which the person concerned courted attention, the nature and degree of the intrusion into the private sphere, and the ability of diverse domestic remedies to provide effective and adequate redress.

Furthermore, as far as the Data Protection Law is concerned, the processing of personal data carried out solely for journalistic purposes or for the purpose of artistic or literary expression is exempted from several important provisions of the Data Protection Law. For example, the prohibition to process personal data revealing racial or ethnic origin, political opinions, religious or philosophical beliefs, and trade-union membership, as well as data concerning sex life, health-related personal data, and personal data relating to judicial and administrative proceedings (Articles 6 to 8 of the Data Protection Law) does not apply to journalists. Significantly, this information should relate to data that was made public by the persons concerned or is closely related to the public character of the persons involved or the fact to which they are involved.

c. Is the right to privacy based in common law, statute, or constitution?

The right to privacy is based on Article 8 of the Convention (as interpreted by the ECHR), Article 22 of the Belgian Constitution (as interpreted by the Belgian courts), as well as the Data Protection Law (as interpreted by the Belgian courts).

Article 8 of the Convention provides that "everyone has the right to respect for his private and family life, his home and his correspondence." It is important to note that the right to respect for these aspects of privacy under Article 8 is qualified. This means that interferences by the state are permissible, but only if they satisfy the following conditions: any interference with the right should be (1) in accordance with the law; (2) in pursuit of one of the legitimate objectives spelled out in Article 8(2) of the Convention; and (3) proportionate (i.e., serve a pressing social need).

Similarly, Article 22 of the Belgian Constitution provides that "everyone has the right to the respect of his or her private and family life, except in the cases and conditions determined by law."[164]

15. May reporters tape-record their own telephone conversations for note-taking purposes (not rebroadcast) without the consent of the other party?

Yes. It is accepted that reporters may tape-record their own telephone conversations for note-taking purposes without the consent of the other party.[165] Article 314*bis* of the Belgian Criminal Code imposes important criminal sanctions on any persons who (1) either deliberately use any equipment, monitors, take cognizance of, record private communication or telecommunication, in which they do not participate, during its transmission, without consent of all persons participating in that communication or has this communication monitored, taken cognizance or recorded; (2) or with intent to commit one of the criminal offenses mentioned above, installs equipment or has it installed.[166]

Journalists should be advised that if the conversation is confidential in character and the other party has explicitly highlighted the confidential nature of the conversation, the disclosure of certain facts might give rise to tort liability as a breach of confidence.

16. If permissible to record such tapes, may they be broadcast without permission?

Although the case law on this issue is scarce, one court ruled that it is prohibited to broadcast tapes without the consent of the parties involved in the conversation on the tape recording.[167] In addition, broadcasting tapes without the permission of the other party may also constitute a violation of copyright.

17. Is there a recognized evidentiary privilege preventing the disclosure of confidential sources relied upon by reporters?

Until recently, Belgium had no specific law protecting a journalist's sources. However, journalists in Belgium could invoke Article 10 of the Convention in order to protect their journalistic sources. In its landmark judgment *Goodwin v. United Kingdom,*[168] the ECHR ruled that "without such protection, sources may be deterred from assisting the press in informing the public on matters of public interest. As a result, the vital public watchdog role of the press may be undermined and the ability of the press to provide accurate and reliable information may be adversely affected."

The protection of journalistic sources under Article 10 of the Convention is, however, not absolute. The ECHR has decided that an order of source disclosure is possible in certain circumstances, namely if interests are involved that are more imperative and more important than the freedom of expression. According to the ECHR, it is only when it is "justifiable by an overriding requirement in the public interest" that a disclosure order can be assumed to be in accordance with Article 10 §2 of the Convention. Furthermore, the ECHR underlines the idea that limitations on the confidentiality of journalistic sources "call for the most careful scrutiny by the Court."

In *De Haes and Gijsels v. Belgium,*[169] the ECHR applied the right of journalists to maintain secrecy of a source in a case in which journalists De Haes and Gijsels were held liable for defamation in criticizing some members of the judiciary. In its judgment, the ECHR held that Article 6 of the Convention does not allow national courts to reject an application from an accused journalist to consider alternative evidence besides the disclosure of the source of information by this journalist if such alternative evidence for the proof of the journalist's statements is available to the judiciary. The ECHR ruled that the journalists' concern not to risk compromising their sources of information by lodging the documents at stake themselves was legitimate. The rejection of the Belgian courts of analyzing at least the opinion of the three experts, whose reports had prompted De Haes and Gijsels to write their articles, was considered a breach of Articles 6 and 10 of the Convention.[170]

Notwithstanding the protection provided by Article 10 of the Convention, the Belgian legal framework in relation to the confidentiality of journalistic sources was not very well developed and gave rise to legal uncertainty. This was again demonstrated in the case initiated by Bourlard and NMBS/SNCB, the Belgian national railway company, against *De Morgen,* a Flemish newspaper. Upon request of a director of the NMBS/SNCB, two journalists of the newspaper *De Morgen* were ordered to submit a copy of an internal document they had referred to in an article criticizing the financial management of the NMBS/SNCB in a project relating to the construction of a new railway station for the TGV line in Liège. On May 29, 2002, the president of the Brussels Court of First Instance ordered the journalists of *De Morgen* (De Coninck and Vandermeir) to produce a copy of the document they referred to under forfeiture of a penalty payment of 25 euros per hour of delay. According to the president, the order could not be considered as a breach of professional secrecy of the journalists. De Coninck and Vandermeir appealed the order of the president of the Brussels Court of First Instance. Referring to the ECHR *Goodwin* judgment, the judge on appeal decided in favor of the journalists, stating that there was a risk that a protected source would be disclosed if the journalists had to submit a copy of the document.[171]

The existing legal uncertainty was taken away by the adoption of the Law on the Protection of Journalistic Sources (the "Law") on April 7, 2005.[172] Pursuant to Article 2, the Law applies to (1) "journalists" (defined as any person "who regularly and directly contributes to the processing, drafting, production or distribution of information to the public through a certain medium"); and (2) "editorial staff" (defined as any person "who in the execution of his or her function is obliged to become acquainted with information that may lead to the disclosure of a source, regardless of whether this happens through the processing, drafting, production or distribution of such information").

Article 3 of the Law provides that journalists and editorial staff have the right to refuse disclosing their information sources. Particularly, they cannot be forced to provide information, recordings, or documents that would, *inter alia,* reveal: (1) the identity of the source; (2) the nature or origin of the information; (3) the identity of the author of the text or audiovisual production; or (4) the content of the information or documentation.

Journalists and editorial staff may only be forced to reveal their sources where obliged to do so by a court order. Such a court order may be issued only if (1) the information is necessary to prevent acts threatening the physical integrity of one or more persons; (2) it is established that the information of the journalist or editorial staff is crucial to prevent these crimes; and (3) the information cannot be obtained in any other way.

Body searches, home searches, seizures, and telephone tapping may not relate to the data relating to the information sources of journalists or editorial staff, unless the aforementioned conditions apply.

18. In the event that legal papers are served upon the newsroom (such as a civil complaint), are there any particular warnings about accepting service of which we should be aware?

Accepting service of legal papers served upon the newsroom is a non-issue in Belgium. Article 43 of the Belgian Judicial Code states that persons to whom copies of legal papers are handed should sign the original to acknowledge receipt. If the addressee refuses to sign, the bailiff enters a note to that effect on the writ. As a result, in all cases, there will be proof in writing that the document has been served.

If a legal paper is served upon the newsroom, it is advisable that the company immediately contact a local attorney-at-law (*advocaat/avocat*) who will (1) verify whether the legal paper is served in accordance with the law (e.g., service at a registered office of the company; compliance with the requisite minimum period between the service date and the date of the introductory hearing; etc.); and (2) represent the company in court.

19. Has your jurisdiction applied established media law to Internet publishers?

As a general rule, it should be noted that the Belgian legal provisions also apply, subject to the private international law rules on jurisdiction and applicable law, to infringements committed on the Internet. Belgian courts have thus already applied the legal provisions on libel, privacy, disparagement, or racism to Internet publishers.

In a recent case, the Court of First Instance of Brussels held that libelous statements made on the Internet must be deemed to have been made in all places where those statements can be received and read and held that Belgian courts have jurisdiction to rule upon the matter.[173] A similar conclusion was reached by the Commercial Court of Mons, which thus considered, in application of Article 2 of the Convention of 27 September 1968 on jurisdiction and the enforcement of judgments in civil and commercial matters,[174] that it had jurisdiction to hear the case. In the latter case, the Court nonetheless held that Belgian law did not apply, as the act that was at the origin of the damage had been accomplished in the United States.[175]

As mentioned above, in order for the provisions on libel contained in the Belgian Criminal Code to apply, the sued-upon statements must have been made in public (e.g., mailing lists [but not private e-mails], newsgroups, discussion forums, and information on the World Wide Web).

A practical application of the provisions on libel was made in a case where the Bishop of Liège and his diocese sought a cease-and-desist order against the Raelian sect in order to have the contents of an Internet site accusing Catholic priests of being pedophiles removed and to prohibit the creation of any other Internet site having a similar content.[176] The Court of First Instance of Liège thus ordered the defendant as well as the Internet hosting service provider to delete the defamatory content from the Internet site and also ordered penalties in case of noncompliance.[177] This ruling was criticized as it did not distinguish the roles of the protagonists of the case: both the author of the Internet site and the hosting service provider were condemned. It was argued by some legal scholars that the hosting service provider was not actually able to *modify* the content of the Internet site, but could only delete or block access to the litigious Internet page.

Courts and tribunals do not always order the deletion of libelous statements from Internet pages. The Court of First Instance of Brussels considered it was sufficient to insert, next to the electronic version of the complained-upon article, a hyperlink referring the readers to the article mentioning the acquitting of the plaintiff.[178]

Belgian courts have also applied the legal provisions on product disparagement for infringements committed on the Internet. It was thus considered that a trader having, on its Internet site, a discussion forum on which the general public could share its opinion on a competitor was guilty of disparagement.[179]

In a ruling of December 22, 1999, the Brussels Criminal Court held that racist acts on the Internet amounted to a violation of the laws governing the press. In this case, an officer of the judicial police was prosecuted for having made racist statements in various Internet discussion groups.[180]

20. If established media law has been applied to Internet publishers, are there any ways in which Internet publishers (including chat room operators) have to meet different standards?

As the same legal provisions apply to publishers, whether they operate on the Internet or not, it can be considered that Internet publishers or chat room operators do not have to meet different standards than other publishers.

However, the Belgian Law of 11 March 2003 on Certain Legal Aspects of the Services of the Information Society (the "Law on Electronic Commerce")[181] provides immunity for hosting service providers if certain conditions are fulfilled. Article 20 of the Law on Electronic Commerce provides that a hosting service provider is not liable for information contained on Internet sites that it hosts, subject to the conditions that (1) it does not have knowledge of the illegal activity; (2) it acts promptly to render access to the information impossible or to remove the information, if ordered to do so by the public prosecutor.

It has also been held that a violation of the laws governing the press committed on the Internet should be considered as a "continuing offense" (*voortdurend misdrijf/délit continu*), as long as the statement in contention is easily accessible to any person surfing the Internet to find information on particular topics. Moreover, libelous statements that have been made in Internet discussion forums are archived and can thus easily be accessed with the use of search engines and hyperlinks. Such qualification as a "continuing offense" mainly has a bearing on limitation periods, the expiry of which precludes any criminal prosecution.

21. Are there any cases where the courts enforced a judgment in libel from another jurisdiction against a publisher in your jurisdiction?

We are not aware of any cases where Belgian courts enforced a judgment in libel from another jurisdiction against a publisher in Belgium.

Chapter Notes

1. Belgian Supreme Court, January 26, 1976, *Pas.*, 1976, I, 591.
2. Belgian Supreme Court, May 20, 1992, *Pas.*, I, 895; President of the Court of

First Instance of Brussels, March 2, 2000, not yet reported, RR 2000/77/C.

3. Belgian Supreme Court, July 10, 1916, *Pas.,* 1917, I, 191; Court of First Instance of Marche-en-Famenne, May 6, 1992, *J.L.M.B.,* 1993, 1066.

4. Brussels Court of Appeal, October 29, 1987, *Pas.,* 1988, II, 52.

5. Belgian Supreme Court, June 19, 1991, *Pas.,* 1991, I, 913.

6. Court of First Instance of Liège, October 22, 2004, not reported, available at http://www.barreaudeliege.be.

7. The Assize Court is the highest criminal court in Belgium, where jurors rule upon the guilt of the accused person. The Assize Court sits on an *ad hoc* basis. Its judgments cannot be appealed.

8. *Belgian Official Journal,* May 29, 1999.

9. Belgian Supreme Court, January 30, 1980, *J.T.,* 1981, 290.

10. Belgian Supreme Court, December 11, 1979, *Pas.,* 1980, I, 452; Belgian Supreme Court, October 21, 1981, *Pas.,* 1982, I, 259; Brussels Court of Appeal, April 1, 1982, *J.T.,* 1982, 636; Belgian Supreme Court, January 23, 1984, *Pas.,* 1988, 942; Brussels Court of Appeal, October 29, 1987, *Pas.,* 1988, II, 52.

11. There has only been one case since World War II (Assize Court of Mons, June 28, 1994, *J.L.M.B.,* 1994, 520).

12. Belgian Supreme Court, December 9, 1981, *Pas.,* 1982, I, 482.

13. Belgian Supreme Court, May 28, 1985, *Pas.,* 1985, I, 1219.

14. Brussels Court of Appeal, February 5,1990, *Pas.,* 1990, II, 154; Court of First Instance of Brussels, January 12, 1990, *J.L.M.B.,* 1990.

15. In this regard, it should be noted that the failure to observe the obligation of prudence of Articles 1382 *et seq.* of the Belgian Civil Code does not constitute the *animus iurandi* of Articles 443 *et seq.* of the Belgian Criminal Code (Belgian Supreme Court, November 18, 1992, *Pas.,* 1992, I, 1269). See also President of the Court of First Instance of Brussels, March 2, 2000, not reported, RR 2000/77/C.

16. The fault standard is further described under Question 6.

17. Court of First Instance of Liège, October 22, 2004, not reported, available at http://www.barreaudeliege.be.

18. Criminal Court of Brussels, April 11, 1991, *Rev. dr. étr.,* 1991, 214, *J.L.M.B.,* 1991, 804.

19. Liège Court of Appeal, November 28, 2001, *J.T.,* 2002, 308.

20. Brussels Court of Appeal, December 20, 1991, *Rev. dr. pén. crim.,*1992, 686.

21. Court of First Instance of Brussels, June 29, 1987, *J.T.,* 1987, 685.

22. Court of First Instance of Brussels, September 13, 1994, *A.J.T.,* 1994–95, 128.

23. Court of First Instance of Liège, May 7, 2002, *A&M*, 2002, 370.

24. Court of First Instance of Liège, October 22, 2004, not reported, available at http://www.barreaudeliege.be.

25. Criminal Court of Charleroi, March 13, 1954, *J.T.,* 1954, 334.

26. Criminal Court of Neufchâteau, May 13, 1993, *J.L.M.B.,* 1993, 965.

27. Court of First Instance of Liège, April 1, 1993, *J.L.M.B.,* 1993, 1144.

28. Court of First Instance of Brussels, July 2, 1993, *A&M,* 1996, 161.

29. Court of First Instance of Brussels, June 23, 1998, not reported, R.G. 96/10933/A.

30. Court of First Instance of Brussels, December 28, 1990, *J.L.M.B.,* 1991, 672.

31. Court of First Instance of Brussels, April 19, 1991, *J.L.M.B.,* 1991, I, 804.

32. Court of First Instance of Brussels, March 10, 1998, *A&M,* 1998, 377.

33. Belgian Supreme Court, February 5, 1900, *Pas.,* I, 141; Court of First Instance of Brussels, December 28, 1990, *J.L.M.B.,* 1991, 672.

34. Court of First Instance of Brussels, March 10, 1998, *A&M,* 1998, 377.

35. Brussels Court of Appeal, June 28, 2001, *J.T.,* 2002, 49.

36. President of the Commercial Court of Kortrijk, November 27, 2000, *Annuaire Pratiques du Commerce & Concurrence,* 2000, 217.

37. Brussels Court of Appeal, May 19, 1998, *Annuaire Pratiques du Commerce & Concurrence,* 1998, 118.

38. *Belgian Official Journal,* August 29, 1991.

39. Article 23.6 of the Law on Unfair Trade Practices.

40. Brussels Court of Appeal, June 28, 2001, *J.T.,* 2002, 49; Brussels Court of Appeal, June 26, 1998, *Annuaire Pratiques du Commerce & Concurrence,* 1998, 127.

41. Brussels Court of Appeal, June 28, 2001, *J.T.,* 2002, 49; President of the Commercial Court of Kortrijk, September 16, 2002, *Annuaire Pratiques du Commerce & Concurrence,* 2002, 650.

42. Article 23.7 of the Law on Unfair Trade Practices. Articles 23.6 and 23.7 of the Law on Unfair Trade Practices are mutually exclusive: if the disparagement is made in the framework of a comparison, Article 23.7 applies (President of the Commercial Court of Kortrijk, December 11, 2000, *Annuaire Pratiques du Commerce & Concurrence,* 2000, 238).

43. Article 23*bis*.5 of the Law on Unfair Trade Practices.

44. President of the Commercial Court of Antwerp, October 23, 2003, *Annuaire Pratiques du Commerce & Concurrence,* 2003, 660.

45. President of the Commercial Court of Tongeren, June 1, 1999, *Annuaire Pratiques du Commerce & Concurrence,* 1999, 616.

46. President of the Commercial Court of Kortrijk, November 27, 2000, *Annuaire Pratiques du Commerce & Concurrence,* 2000, 217.

47. Antwerp Court of Appeal, November 30, 1933, *R.W.,* 1934–35, col. 558.

48. Court of First Instance of Brussels, November 16, 1999, not reported, RG 98/7351/A.

49. *Belgian Official Journal,* August 8, 1981.

50. Article 4 of the Preliminary Title of the Belgian Criminal Procedure Code; Belgian Supreme Court, December 15, 1976, *Pas.,* I, 483.

51. Court of First Instance of Brussels, September 14, 1988, *J.T.,* 1989, 8.

52. President of the Court of First Instance of Brussels, March 2, 2000, not yet reported, RR 2000/77/C.

53. Court of First Instance of Brussels, January 12, 1990, *J.L.M.B.,* 1990, 424.

54. Commercial Court of Brussels, February 7, 1984, *J.T.,* 1984, 345.

55. Court of First Instance of Leuven, January 15, 1996, *A&M,* 1996, 460.

56. Court of First Instance of Brussels, September 21, 1999, *A&M,* 2000, 334; Court of First Instance of Brussels, April 26, 1991, *J.T.,* 1992, 315; Court of First Instance of Antwerp, September 22, 1997, *A&M,* 1997, 407.

57. Court of First Instance of Brussels, October 26, 2001, *A&M,* 2002, 88.

58. Ghent Court of Appeal, May 11, 1978, *R.W.,* 1977–78, 46; Court of First Instance of Brussels, June 23, 1998, *A&M,* 2000, 96; Court of First Instance of Brussels, March 30, 1999, *A&M,* 2000, 102; Court of First Instance of Brussels, December 23, 1999, *A&M,* 2000, 138; see also Court of First Instance of Brussels, November 9, 2001, *A&M,* 2002, 288.

59. Brussels Court of Appeal, February 5, 1990, *R.W.,* 1989–90, 1464; Ghent Court of Appeal, March 14, 1995, *A&M,* 1996, 159.

60. Court of First Instance of Brussels, December 28, 1990, *J.L.M.B.,* 1991, 672.

61. Court of First Instance of Brussels, September 13, 1994, *A.J.T.,* 1994–95, 128.

62. Brussels Court of Appeal, February 16, 2001, *A&M,* 2002, 282.

63. Court of First Instance of Brussels, November 21, 1990, *J.L.M.B.,* 1991, 24.

64. Court of First Instance of Brussels, May 4, 1999, *A&M,* 2000, 106; Brussels Court of Appeal, September 30, 1998, *R.W.,* 2000–01, 93.

65. Court of First Instance of Brussels, June 29, 1987, *J.T.,* 1987, 685.

66. President of the Court of First Instance of Antwerp, June 8, 1999, *A&M,* 1999, 388; President of the Court of First Instance of Brussels, March 2, 2000, not reported, RR 2000/77/C.

67. *Lingens v. Austria,* July 8, 1986. The judgments of the ECHR are available on the following Internet site: http://www.echr.coe.int and in this chapter will be referenced only by name and date on the basis of which they can be retrieved from the Internet site.

68. Court of First Instance of Brussels, June 29, 1987, *J.T.,* 1987, 685.

69. Court of First Instance of Neufchâteau, May 31, 1961, *J.L.,* 1961, 293.

70. Court of First Instance of Brussels, October 14, 1988, *J.L.M.B.,* 1988, 1224.

71. Court of First Instance of Brussels, December 28, 1990, *J.L.M.B.,* 1991, 673.

72. Court of First Instance of Brussels, April 2, 1996, *A&M,* 1997, 314.

73. Brussels Court of Appeal, September 25, 1996, *A&M,* 1997, 76.

74. See Question 6b.

75. President of the Court of First Instance of Antwerp, June 8, 1999, *A&M,* 1999, 388; President of the Court of First Instance of Brussels, March 2, 2000, not reported, RR 2000/77/C.

76. Court of First Instance of Brussels, June 29, 1987, *J.T.,* 1987, 685.

77. President of the Court of First Instance of Brussels, October 12, 1990, *Journ. Procès,* 1990, No. 181, 27.

78. Brussels Court of Appeal, June 25, 1969, *J.T.,* 1970, 155.

79. Brussels Court of Appeal, May 14, 1981, *J.T.,* 1981, 415.

80. Brussels Court of Appeal, June 25, 1969, *J.T.,* 1970, 153. See also Antwerp Court of Appeal, March 28, 1977, *R.W.,* 1977–78, 1445.

81. Brussels Court of Appeal, January 4, 1985, *J.T.,* 1985, 237.

82. President of the Court of First Instance of Brussels, April 23, 1999, *J.L.M.B.,* 1999, 1072.

83. OJ 2003 L96/16.

84. *Belgian Official Journal,* September 4, 2002.

85. Article 19 of the Belgian Constitution provides that the freedom to demonstrate one's opinions on all matters is guaranteed, except for the repression of offenses committed when exercising this freedom.

86. Belgian Supreme Court, March 6, 1986, *Arr. Cass.*, 1985–86; Belgian Supreme Court, May 10, 1985, *Arr. Cass.*, 1984–85, 1230.

87. *Sunday Times v. UK,* April 26, 1979.

88. *Lingens v. Austria,* July 8, 1986.

89. *Castells v. Spain,* April 23, 1992.

90. *Thorgeirson v. Iceland,* June 25, 1992.

91. February 24, 1997.

92. March 29, 2001.

93. June 25, 2002.

94. April 20, 2004.

95. March 6, 2003.

96. December 7, 1976. See also *Lopes Gomes da Silva v. Portugal,* September 28, 2000.

97. See also Court of First Instance of Neufchâteau, May 31, 1961, *J.L.*, 1960–61, 292; Liège Court of Appeal, November 30, 1951, *J.T.*, 1952, 400; Court of First Instance of Brussels, April 26, 1991, *J.T.*, 1992, 315.

98. Brussels Court of Appeal, June 25, 1986, *R.W.*, 1986–87, 804.

99. Court of First Instance of Kortrijk, November 17, 1989, *T.G.R.*, 1990, 116.

100. Court of First Instance of Brussels, September 21, 1999, *A&M,* 2000, 334.

101. Court of First Instance of Brussels, April 26, 1991, *J.T.*, 1992, 315.

102. Brussels Court of Appeal, September 25, 1996, *A&M,* 1997, 76.

103. Court of First Instance of Brussels, November 4, 1992, *Journ. Proc.*, 1992/228, 24.

104. Court of First Instance of Brussels, May 30, 2001, *A&M,* 2002, 291.

105. Court of First Instance of Brussels, October 26, 2001, *A&M,* 2002, 88.

106. Brussels Court of Appeal, February 5, 1990, *R.W.*, 1989–90, 1464. See also Brussels Court of Appeal, February 5, 1999, *A&M,* 1999, 274.

107. Court of First Instance of Brussels, October 26, 2001, *A&M,* 2002, 88.

108. Court of First Instance of Brussels, September 13, 1994, *R.W.*, 1994–95, 955; Court of First Instance of Brussels, June 30, 1994, *R.G.A.R.*, 1995, 12473; Brussels Court of Appeal, February 5, 1990, *R.W.*, 1989–90, 1464.

109. Court of First Instance of Brussels, March 21, 2000, *A&M,* 2000, 460.

110. *Belgian Official Journal,* August 8, 1981.

111. *Belgian Official Journal,* March 30, 1995.

112. *Belgian Official Journal,* April 15, 1965.

113. Court of First Instance of Brussels, October 26, 2001, *A&M,* 2002, 88.

114. Court of First Instance of Brussels, December 14, 1993, *A.J.T.,* 1994–95, 70; Brussels Court of Appeal, September 25, 1996, *A&M,* 1997, 76.

115. Court of First Instance of Brussels, September 13, 1994, *A.J.T.,* 1994–95, 128.

116. Court of First Instance of Liège, May 7, 2002, *A&M,* 2002, 370.

117. *Belgian Official Journal,* July 8, 1961.

118. On December 17, 2004, the Council of Europe's Committee of Ministers adopted a Recommendation on the right to reply in the new media environment. The Recommendation urges member states to extend the right to reply—which until now applied to the written press, radio, and television—to online communication services providing information edited in a journalistic manner. The right to reply is a particularly appropriate remedy in the online environment, as contested information can be instantly corrected and replies from those concerned can easily be attached.

119. Court of First Instance of Ghent, June 25, 2003, *A&M,* 2004, 79, err., *A&M,* 2004, 367.

120. Ghent Court of Appeal, May 25, 2004, not reported, referred to in: Belgian Supreme Court, December 7, 2004, not reported, available at: http://www.just.fgov.be/index_nl.htm.

121. Belgian Supreme Court, December 7, 2004, not yet reported, available at: http://www.just.fgov.be/index_nl.htm.

122. Ghent Court of Appeal, March 3, 1995, *R.W.,* 1996–97, 540.

123. March 29, 2001.

124. Brussels Court of Appeal, February 5, 1990, *R.W.,* 1990, 1464; Brussels Court of Appeal, February 16, 2001, *A&M,* 2002, 282; Court of First Instance of Brussels, December 14, 1993, *A.J.T.,* 1994–95, 70; Court of First Instance of Brussels, September 13, 1994, *A.J.T.,* 1994–95, 128.

125. Court of First Instance of Kortrijk, November 27, 1989, *T.G.R.,* 1990, 116.

126. See Article 4.3.3 of the circular letter of the Minister of Justice of April 30, 1999, as well as Article 35 of the Police Act as interpreted by a circular letter of October 10, 1995.

127. *Belgian Official Journal,* April 15, 1965.

128. Belgian Supreme Court, May 21, 1987, *Pas.,* 1987, 1160; Belgian Supreme Court, September 13, 1990, *Pas.,* 1991, 41.

129. *Observer en Guardian v. United Kingdom,* November 26, 1991; *Sunday Times v. United Kingdom,* November 26, 1991.

130. President of the Court of First Instance of Brussels, February 21, 1990, *R.W.,* 1990–91, 89.

131. President of the Court of First Instance of Brussels, January 9, 1997, *A&M,* 1997, 197; President of the Court of First Instance of Liège, January 12, 1999, *A&M,* 1999, 287.

132. President of the Court of First Instance of Antwerp, July 4, 1994, *A.J.T.,* 1994–95, 84.

133. President of the Court of First Instance of Antwerp, September 19, 1997, *A&M,* 1997, 408.

134. See, e.g., President of the Court of First Instance of Brussels, October 18, 1996, *A&M,* 1997, 83; President of the Court of First Instance of Brussels, October 24, 2001, *J.T.,* 2001, 780, confirmed on appeal: Brussels Court of Appeal, December 21, 2001, *J.L.M.B.,* 2002, 425–31 and Brussels Court of Appeal, April 22, 2002, *Journ. Procès,* 2002, No. 436, 26.

135. Brussels Court of Appeal, May 8, 1998, *J.L.M.B.,* 1998, 1046; Brussels Court of Appeal, December 21, 2001, *J.L.M.B.,* 2002, 425; Brussels Court of Appeal, April 22, 2002, *Journ. Procès,* 2002, No. 436, 26.

136. President of the Court of First Instance of Brussels, January 30, 1997, *J.L.M.B.,* 1997, 319 (confirmed on appeal). See also Belgian Supreme Court, June 29, 2000, *A&M,* 2000, 443.

137. Brussels Court of Appeal, March 22, 2002, *Journ. Procès,* No. 436, 26.

138. Belgian Supreme Court, June 29, 2000, *Journ. Procès,* 2000, No. 398, 25; *J.L.M.B.,* 2000, 1589.

139. President of the Court of First Instance of Brussels, October 24, 2001, *Journ. Procès,* 2001, No. 423, 20; Court of First Instance of Brussels, June 30, 1997, *A&M,* 1998, 264.

140. Belgian Supreme Court, September 13, 1991, *R.W.,* 1991–92, 464.

141. Brussels Court of Appeal, November 25, 1981, *J.T.,* 1982, 275 (re: privacy of the Royal family).

142. Court of First Instance of Brussels, April 26, 1991, *J.T.,* 1992, 315.

143. Court of First Instance of Ghent, November 22, 1999, *A&M,* 2000, 148, confirmed in Ghent Court of Appeal, June 12, 2001, *A&M,* 2002, 169. See also Brussels Court of Appeal, November 25, 1981, *J.T.,* 1982, 275; Antwerp Court of Appeal, January 18, 1984, *R.W.,* 1986–87, 2860; Court of First Instance of Ghent, December 16, 1981, *R.W.,* 1983–84, 2968.

144. *Costello-Roberts v. the United Kingdom,* March 25, 1993.

145. This list only includes some examples and is not exhaustive.

146. *Von Hannover v. Germany,* June 24, 2004; *Stjerna v. Finland,* November 25, 1994; *Burghartz v. Switzerland,* February 22, 1994.

147. *Guillot v. France,* October 24, 1996.

148. *Schüssel v. Austria,* February 21, 2002; *Friedl v. Austria,* judgment of January 31, 1995.

149. *X & Y v. the Netherlands,* March 26, 1986. While some interferences with the physical integrity of an individual may impinge on the private life of that person, not all such actions will do so. *Costello-Roberts v. the United Kingdom* (March 25, 1993) concerned the compatibility with Article 8 of the corporal punishment of a little boy. The ECHR noted that measures taken in the field of education may, in certain circumstances, affect the right to respect for private life but not every act or measure that may be said to affect adversely the physical or moral integrity of a person necessarily gives rise to such an interference. In the case at hand, the ECHR concluded that having regard to the purpose and aim of the Convention taken as a whole, and bearing in mind that sending children to school necessarily involves some degree of interference with their private lives, the ECHR considers that the treatment complained of by the applicant did not entail adverse effects for his physical or moral integrity sufficient to bring it within the scope of the prohibition contained in Article 8. Both the slight nature of the punishment and the fact that it had been imposed in the formal school environment were central to the ECHR's decision in this case.

150. *Niemietz v. Germany,* December 16, 1992.

151. *Dudgeon v. the United Kingdom,* October 22, 1981. However, not every sexual activity carried out behind closed doors necessarily falls within the scope of Article 8. In *Laskey, Jaggard & Brown v. the United Kingdom* (February 19, 1997), the applicants were involved in consensual sado-masochistic activities for the purposes of sexual gratification. While the ECHR did not formally have to determine the issue of whether the applicants' behavior fell within the scope of private life, it expressed some reservations about allowing the protection of Article 8 to extend to activities that involved a considerable number of people, the provision of specially equipped chambers, the recruitment of new members, and the shooting of videotapes that were distributed among the members.

152. *Kerkhoven v. The Netherlands,* May 19, 1992.

153. *Peters v. The Netherlands,* April 6, 1994.

154. Appl. No. 10435/83, July 12, 1978.

155. *Herczegfalvy v. Austria,* September 24, 1992.

156. See, e.g., *McFeeley v. United Kingdom,* May 15, 1980.

157. *Niemietz v. Germany,* December 16, 1992.

158. *Halford v. the United Kingdom,* June 25, 1997.

159. See, *inter alia,* B. Oversteyns, "Het recht op eerbiediging van het privéleven," *R.W.,* 1988–89, 490.

160. *Belgian Official Journal,* March 18, 1993.

161. *Tsavachidis v. Greece,* October 28, 1997.

162. *Appl. No. 18760/91 v. Ireland,* December 1, 1993.

163. *Spencers v. United Kingdom,* January 16, 1998.

164. See also Article 15 of the Belgian Constitution ("The domicile is inviolable; no visit to the individual's residence can take place except in the cases provided for by law and in the form prescribed by law") and Article 29 of the Belgian Constitution ("The confidentiality of letters is inviolable").

165. See, e.g., President of the Court of First Instance of Liège, October 9, 1992, *J.L.M.B.,* 1994, 235.

166. See also Article 109*ter* d of the Law of March 21, 1991 according to which it is prohibited to "willfully gaining knowledge of data relating to telecommunications which concerns another person."

167. President of the Brussels Commercial Court, March 21, 2000, *A&M,* 2000, 344.

168. March 27, 1996.

169. February 27, 1997.

170. See also *Ernst and others v. Belgium,* June 25, 2002.

171. President of the Court of First Instance of Brussels, June 7, 2002, *A&M,* 2002, 459.

172. *Belgian Official Journal,* April 27, 2005.

173. Court of First Instance of Brussels, February 19, 2004, not reported, R.G. No. 2004/622/A.

174. Convention of September 17, 1968, on jurisdiction and the enforcement of judgments in civil and commercial matters, replaced by the Council Regulation (EC) No. 44/2001 of December 22, 2000, on jurisdiction and the recognition and enforcement of judgments in civil and commercial matters (OJ 2001 L12/1).

175. Mons Commercial Court, June 15, 2001, not reported, R.G. No. A/00/2512.

176. Liège Court of Appeal, November 28, 2001, *J.T.,* 2002, 308.

177. See also President of the Court of First Instance, March 2, 2000, not reported, RR 2000/77/C, where an Internet service provider undertook to delete

and prevent, by all technical means, the publication of libelous statements on the Internet site of one of its customers.

178. Court of First Instance of Brussels, June 25, 2002, *A&M,* 2004, 367.

179. President of the Commercial Court of Antwerp, August 9, 2001, *Annuaire Pratiques du Commerce & Concurrence,* 2001, 666.

180. Brussels Criminal Court, December 22, 1999, not reported, available at http://www.droit-technologie.org/4_1.asp?jurisprudence_id=33.

181. *Belgian Official Journal,* March 17, 2003.

CHAPTER 15

England and Wales

MARK STEPHENS

Finer Stephens Innocent

Finer Stephens Innocent
179 Great Portland Street
London W1W 5LS
United Kingdom
Phone: +44 (0)20 7323 4000
Fax: +44 (0)20 7580 7069
www.fsilaw.co.uk
mstephens@fsilaw.co.uk

Introduction to the United Kingdom Legal System

The United Kingdom has three distinct legal jurisdictions: Scotland, Northern Ireland, and England and Wales. Although there are subtle differences among the three independent judicial systems, they share much of the same common law. This introduction will focus on fundamental court structure in England and Wales. The Scottish and Northern Ireland systems are similarly structured with separate branches for criminal and civil actions. Each branch has trial courts, known as county courts or high courts, appellate courts, magistrate courts, and a house of lords.

New laws in the UK common law system originate from either Parliament or common law through judicial decisions. Parliament, composed of the House of Commons and the House of Lords in a bicameral structure, has authority to pass various Acts of Parliament, also called statutes, to create new laws. Case law cannot overrule statutory law; however, case law does serve as a practical tool for determining contemporary application or enforcement of a statute. The hierarchical structure of the British court system demands that all lower courts must abide by any higher court's ruling.

Civil actions, depending on the financial magnitude of the claim and the societal implications of the legal issue at hand, are initially heard in either a county court or a high court. County courts, dispersed in counties throughout the country, are used to hear claims of marginal financial value or type of legal issue. County court decisions are binding solely to the county of that particular court; however, parties may appeal a county court decision, on questions of law only, to the Court of Appeal in the civil division. Appeals are then heard in the House of Lords—the highest court of appeal in England and Wales.

Criminal actions are handled in a similar fashion; less serious cases are heard in magistrate courts and are decided by magistrates with limited sentencing powers. More serious cases are sent to a higher crown court and are tried by a more established high court judge with a jury. Appeals from a magistrate court can go to a high court, and appeals from the high court must go to the House of Lords.

1. What is the locally accepted definition of libel?

Libel occurs when a defamatory statement is published about someone, in written or some other permanent form, or broadcast. A defamatory statement is simply one that damages a person's reputation or makes others think less of that person. It is possible for text, still or moving pictures, headlines, photographs, cartoons, jokes, and illustrations to be defamatory.

2. Is libel-by-implication recognized, or, in the alternative, must the complained-of words alone defame the plaintiff?

English law recognizes that, whereas some statements are not defamatory on their face or in their ordinary meaning, they may still carry discreditable implications to those with special (as opposed to general) knowledge, and thereby convey a defamatory imputation.

To cite a popular illustration, to say that someone was seen entering a particular house may be perfectly innocuous in its ordinary meaning, but would contain a defamatory imputation for anyone who knew that house to be a brothel. This is libel "by innuendo."

3. May corporations sue for libel?

Corporations and companies may sue for defamation but only for statements that damage them in their trade or business reputation. Partnerships and LLPs may also sue. Local authorities cannot. Trade unions and most unincorporated associations cannot sue for libel, but their members can.

It has become increasingly common, e.g., for senior executives responsible for the actions of a corporation to sue as its proxy.

4. Is product disparagement recognized, and if so, how does that differ from libel?

Where statements focus on the product, rather than on the actions of the producer, manufacturer, or supplier, there is less chance of a claim for libel. However, a claim may lie for malicious falsehood for product disparagement or "slander of goods." Such actions are rare and difficult. The producer has to prove a heavy burden: that the statement was false (contrast libel actions where falsity is presumed by law) and the maker of the statement was malicious (in other words, he or she made the statement knowing it to be false or recklessly published the statement); and the publication must cause financial loss or be likely to cause such loss.

5. Must an individual be clearly identified (by name or photograph) to sue for libel? Can a group of persons sue for libel, even though not named?

A person may bring a libel action if it is possible to identify an individual who is not named in a defamatory statement, but is discernable from the context in which the statement appears. Examples are photographs, clues given about the individual, or other information that tends to lead readers to identify the individual. The legal test is an objective one: whether reasonable readers would understand the statement to refer to the individual concerned (even where there are a number of other persons who might also be identified by the statement).

It is also possible to wrongly or unintentionally identify individuals who reasonable readers could conclude were the subject of the article. In the famous fictional story about Artemus Jones who was said to enjoy gambling, horse racing, and the company of French prostitutes, Jones was misidentified for a real-life Welsh Baptist who was most virtuous.

6. What is the fault standard(s) applied to libel?

a. Does the fault standard depend on the fame or notoriety of the plaintiff?

The law holds that a uniform standard of fault applies to plaintiffs regardless of their fame or notoriety or whether they are generally perceived as good or bad persons. It is presumed that the plaintiff has a good reputation. Practice may present a slightly different picture, however, because most libel actions are before juries who, when faced with someone who is famous, may have a difficult task in divorcing their own preconceptions about the celebrity from the facts at issue. Conversely, in extreme and rare cases, it might be reasonable to adduce evidence that a person has a bad reputation.

In relation to damages, the tendency is toward larger damages awards for celebrities than for ordinary people, and for derisory awards (e.g., £1, approximately $1.50) for plaintiffs who win—technically—but whose conduct finds disapproval with the jury.

b. Is there a heightened fault standard or privilege for reporting on matters of public concern or public interest?

Absent the sort of constitutional protection afforded by the First Amendment to the U.S. Constitution, English law has evolved in case law to a point where it can best be summarized as follows: Where matters of public interest are reported and the media has a legitimate duty/interest in doing so and the recipient has a corresponding duty/interest in receiving it, the report may attract the protection of the defense of "qualified privilege." A pair of cases, *Jameel (Mohammed) v. Wall Street Journal Europe Sprl* [2006][1] and the earlier *Reynolds v. Times Newspapers Ltd.*,[2] explain the application and evolution of this defense. Logically, the two cases are best read together as a two-step analysis. The first question, explained in detail by Jameel, is a "public interest" test: whether the allegedly defamatory speech in question is of a nature that the sued-upon statements vindicate the public interest by reference to subjects defined in Article 10 of the ECHR, such as those

> ". . . necessary in a democratic society, in the interests of national security, territorial integrity or public safety, for the prevention of disorder or crime, for the protection of health or morals, for the protection of the reputation or rights of others, for preventing the disclosure of information received in confidence, or for maintaining the authority and impartiality of the judiciary."[3]

It is only after the public interest test has been satisfied that the point-by-point criteria for abuse of the privilege will be applied, as detailed in the earlier *Reynolds v. Times Newspapers Limited.*

Those point-by-point criteria are:

1. ***the seriousness of the allegation.*** The more serious the charge, the more the public is misinformed and the individual harassed by the adverse impact on him or her if the story turns out to be false. Thus, the more serious the allegation, the weightier is the reporter's responsibility to be correct.
2. ***the nature of the information, and the extent to which the subject matter is a public concern.*** The more important the story is to the public's welfare, the more leeway for error will be granted.
3. ***the source of the information.*** Some sources have no direct knowledge of events. Some have their own axes to grind, or are

being paid for their stories. The credibility of the source, and the reporter's efforts to ascertain that credibility, will be examined.

4. ***the status of the information.*** The allegation may have already been the subject of an investigation that commands respect.
5. ***the steps taken to verify the information.*** Fact-finding, research, interviews, and investigation all combine to convince a judge that the qualified privilege should be applied.
6. ***the urgency of the matter.*** Whereas news is viewed by some as a perishable commodity, courts are less likely to be swayed by urgency arising from press-competitive pressures and more likely to be convinced by the public's immediate need for the information.
7. ***whether comment was sought from the claimant.*** He or she may have information others do not possess or have not disclosed. An approach to the claimant may not always be necessary. As a practical tip, because much litigation now centers on this area, it is often useful to have proof of contact and the matter put to the target, as well as showing that the target has a reasonable opportunity to inform himself or herself, respond meaningfully, and that response should be fairly included in the article.
8. ***whether the article contained the gist of the claimant's side of the story.*** Stories that unfairly edit a denial of wrongdoing may be found libelous.
9. ***the tone of the article.*** A newspaper can raise queries or call for an investigation. It need not adopt allegations as statements of fact.
10. ***the circumstances of the publication, including the timing.***

This is sometimes known colloquially as the defense of "responsible journalism." UK media defendants are faced with considerable legal presumptions to overcome at trial: both falsity and damage are presumed by law.

Truth (called "justification") is an absolute defense. In cases where an error has been made, or proving the truth is impossible, once a claimant has proved the words to be defamatory and to refer to him or her, the onus falls on the media defendant to prove that it acted "responsibly" (by reference to the above *Reynolds* and *Jameel* criteria).

Of course, substantial evidential difficulties can be faced. For example, where the media has relied upon confidential sources, it is impossible to prove the reliability of those sources without compromising that confidence in some way. There is a perception that the *Reynolds* Qualified Privilege is aimed at protecting investigative journalism rather than tabloid sensationalism, but very frequently it is investigative journalists who need to rely on confidential sources.

7. Is financial news about publicly traded companies, or companies involved with a government contract, considered a matter of public interest or otherwise privileged?

Owing to the importance of financial news to markets, this information will usually be of public interest, although there is little decided case law on the point. Such publications may fall within the protection afforded by:

1. Statutory qualified privilege, which extends to "fair and accurate" reports of: public meetings; proceedings at general meetings of UK public companies; copies of documents circulated to members of public companies in the United Kingdom/Channel Islands or Isle of Man and any findings or decisions by certain trade/business/industry/professional associations. Note that for this privilege to attach, the publication must not be prohibited by law or be malicious, and the subject matter must be of public concern.
2. *Reynolds* or *Jameel* Qualified Privilege (described in Question 6b above).

8. Is there a recognized protection for opinion or "fair comment" on matters of public concern?

The defense of fair comment protects statements of opinion or comment on matters of public interest. The defendant must be able to prove, in order to fall within this protection: that the statement was indeed comment (and not a statement of fact); that there is sufficient factual basis for the comment, i.e., the comment must be based on facts which are substantially true; that the comment is one which an honest person could hold (an objective test); and that the subject matter is of public interest. Fair comment will not apply if a claimant can prove that the source, author, or publisher was malicious.

9. Are there any requirements upon a plaintiff, such as demand for retraction or right of reply, and if so, what impact do they have?

No such steps are prescribed. It is for the claimant to specify to the defendant what remedies he or she is seeking, depending on the circumstances. Pursuant to the Pre-Action Protocol for Defamation, he or she must set out clearly the remedies he or she seeks when he first complains. Typical remedies sought are for publication of an apology and retraction (form and prominence to be agreed); an undertaking not to repeat the same or similar allegations; removal of an offending publication from a website; payment of damages; and payment of the claimant's legal costs.

There are currently legislative moves afoot to introduce a statutory right of reply. The practical difficulties with regard to implementation are presently proving most complex.

10. Is there a privilege for quoting or reporting on:

a. Papers filed in court?

Privilege will apply to documents filed at court that are "publicly available," e.g., the claim form, pleadings (now known as "statements of case"), and witness statements that have been read by the judge in a public hearing, judgments, and court notices.

In the case of any other documents concerned in the litigation that do not fall into the above category (such as papers drafted by litigants but not read by the judge), anyone who publishes their contents will be taken to have repeated any defamatory statements within them and may be vulnerable to a libel claim.

Absolute privilege attaches to statements made in "fair, accurate and contemporaneous" reports of judicial proceedings in open court in the United Kingdom.

Very limited documents are available directly from the Court Office. Increasingly, however, Masters (Junior Judges) are permitting journalists access to the Court file if they first explain their reasons for requesting it.

b. Government-issued documents?

Same as above.

c. Quasi-governmental proceedings?

Statements made by one officer of state to another in the course of duty are protected by privilege, as are "fair and accurate" copies/extracts/reports of any register kept by statute; government publications; matter published by international organizations and conferences; notices from governments; local authority meetings; inquiries, public meetings, parliamentary papers and proceedings; company meetings; and association meetings.

11. Is there a privilege for republishing statements made earlier by other, bona fide, reliable publications or wire services?

No. Anybody republishing or repeating defamatory statements will be treated for the purposes of a libel claim to have made those statements himself or herself. It is no defense to say you were merely repeating what you had been told, however reliable or reputable the source. Similarly, it will not aid a journalist to sprinkle a piece with words such as "allegedly" or "it is claimed"; he or she will be taken to have said the words himself or herself.

12. Are there any restrictions regarding reporting on:

a. Ongoing criminal investigations?

In terms of libel, in reporting criminal investigations and prosecutions, publishers should at all times have regard to the laws of libel. However, UK law is well known for restrictions of what reporters may or may not publish from court proceedings. At the heart of these "Contempt of Court" rules is the avoidance of publications that "create a substantial risk that the administration of justice will be seriously impeded or prejudiced." This is usually directed at the press prejudicing a jury by introducing facts or material not yet offered into evidence at trial that, if publicized, would prejudice that trial.

This is a strict liability offense. The journalist's intention is irrelevant and is not dependent on there being a specific court order in place.

In relation to criminal *investigations,* potential liability for contempt applies from when the proceedings become "active," meaning when a summons for the defendant's arrest is issued by a Court, or when the defendant is charged.

b. Ongoing criminal prosecutions?

Such risk of liability continues through the criminal *prosecution* and comes to an end when a defendant is acquitted or sentenced, or the action is otherwise discontinued. Serious prejudice is likely to arise from publication of the following matters: a defendant's previous convictions or details of his or her bad character; suggestions that a witness is unreliable; and details of evidence likely to be contested at trial. Note that revealing similar facts or evidence is a particularly fraught area, especially the closer it is to the date of the trial.

In addition to the general rule above, under Section 4(2) of the Contempt of Court Act 1981, a court may specifically order that publication of any report of the proceedings may be postponed if it appears necessary to avoid substantial risk of prejudice to the administration of justice in those proceedings or any other proceedings pending or imminent. These orders are general in nature; that is, they are directed to the press at large and not to specific publications.

In practice, Section 4(2) orders are often made to prevent the media from reporting on a particular piece of evidence that the judge in a libel case does not believe should be put before the jury. Such an order will, as a rule, be posted on the court door and notice-board for the attention of reporters attending.

Committal proceedings: Under the Magistrates' Courts Act 1980, reports of proceedings in which magistrates' courts commit an accused for trial and remand hearings may only cover the barest essentials, namely the name and address of the accused, the charges, any decision to commit, and arrangements for bail. Background information about the crime alleged should be kept distinct from any report of the proceedings. An accused may request reporting restrictions be lifted, but this is rare in practice. The reporting restrictions applied to the committed proceedings cease if the magistrates decide not to commit, or if they proceed to try the case themselves, or when the Crown Court trial itself is concluded.

Reporting of sexual offenses and young persons: Publishers must comply with statutory provisions, punishable by criminal sanction, prohibiting the identification of victims of certain sexual offenses such as rape, and the identification of young persons (under 18) in proceedings in which they are either defendants or witnesses.

Liability for prosecution costs: In a relatively recent development, the Courts Act 2003 empowers courts to impose costs upon third parties such as the media where there has been serious misconduct (whether or not amounting to contempt of court) by the media organization and where the court considers it appropriate. This provision was introduced after reporting by the *Sunday Mirror* led to the aborting of a criminal trial involving a number of Leeds footballers (*R v. Woodgate and others*),[4] necessitating a re-trial and where wasted costs were estimated at about £1 million. The media organization would potentially be liable for the wasted costs of the prosecution, defense, and court administration costs.

c. Ongoing regulatory investigations?

No specific restrictions apply but, as above, reporters must keep in mind the law of libel. Objectivity and balance in a story, rather than the taking of sides, are paramount if a publisher is to successfully raise the protection afforded by qualified privilege.

d. Ongoing civil litigation, or other judicial proceedings?

Contempt of court is a possibility. Civil proceedings become "active" when a matter is set down for trial (usually about halfway through the litigation process) and ends on judgment or discontinuance. However, in reality it is unlikely that in civil cases heard by a judge alone there will be a risk of strict liability contempt; judges are almost invariably presumed to be above influence by the media. However, jury trials are commonplace in libel actions and the media certainly needs to keep an eye on contempt of court in covering these.

Except where judgment or proceedings are held in open court, it is contempt to reveal reports of proceedings relating to children, family cases, mental health, national security, secret processes, and inventions or where there is a specific court order based on some proper source; note that this is not an unencumbered freestanding right.

Civil Procedure Rules: These rules govern the conduct of civil litigation and forbid parties from using, for any purpose other than the litigation itself, documents and witness statements disclosed by the parties. If the media come into possession of any such documents, great care needs to be exercised. Publication of such documents could amount to *contempt of court* where the documents or witness statements have not been read by the judge in a hearing in open court. The same applies to any pleadings that are not on the public court file. Thus, publishers should contact local counsel prior to basing reports on such documents.

13. Are prior restraints or other prepublication injunctions available on the basis of libel or privacy, and if so, what are the standards for obtaining such relief?

Yes, although there is a general rule against "prior restraint." Applications for prepublication injunctions on the basis of libel are very seldom successful because they can be defeated if the media organization asserts that it will defend any libel claim with a defense of truth/justification, or any other substantive defense such as fair comment or privilege. If a publisher has an arguable defense, the publication will not be restrained no matter how damaging the allegations may be: the Claimant may always seek damages after the publication.

As a general rule, the courts will be exceedingly slow to make interim restraint orders where the applicant has not satisfied the court that he or she will probably ("more likely than not") succeed at trial on privacy grounds. A number of considerations apply. Applications for injunctions arising out of privacy issues follow the general rules set out in the *American Cyanamid* case,[5] requiring the following criteria to be satisfied: there must be a serious issue to be tried which has some prospect of success at trial; the balance of convenience must favor the applicant; if at this stage the parties are equally balanced, the court will permit the status quo to prevail; or, should none of these tests succeed, the court will consider the merits of the case. Following the case of *Cream Holdings v. Banerjee,*[6] the court must be satisfied that the claimant has established that it is "likely" that the publication should not be allowed and that this threshold test was "a real prospect of success, convincingly established."

14. Is a right of privacy recognized (either civilly or criminally)?

Following the enactment of the Human Rights Act 1998, which enshrines the "right to respect for private and family life" (Article 8), the established common law cause of action in breach of confidence has developed into a modern concept of "misuse of private information" or "unjustified publication of personal information," now known colloquially as breach of privacy.

a. What is the definition of "private fact"?

No specific definition exists of "private fact" or "private information."

b. Is there a public interest or newsworthiness exception?

In *Naomi Campbell v. Mirror* (2002),[7] a breach of privacy was found after the tabloid published details of the supermodel's attendance at meetings of Narcotics Anonymous, accompanied by a photograph of her leaving a drug rehabilitation clinic. The court held that the photograph disclosed private facts (in this case medical information) about the model. It is suggested that a prudent approach by the media would involve identifying each element of arguably private information in the proposed publication; deciding whether in relation to each such element the subject of the article would have a reasonable expectation of privacy; considering whether in the case of any such element there is a public interest justification for the proposed publication (such as the correction of a false denial or disclosure of crime or other serious wrongdoing) and in relation to any element where there is no public interest justification weigh the value of the free speech right against the value of the privacy right. In the case of photographs, which have a particularly intrusive quality, these should be considered separately from the story by reference to the above criteria.[8]

The European Court of Human Rights decided in the 2004 *Princess Caroline* case[9] that there had been unauthorized publication of photographs of a princess engaging in everyday ordinary activities in public places. The ECHR held that the commercial interest of the press in publishing the photos had to yield to Princess Caroline's right to effective protection of her private life. This decision will have to be taken into account in future English cases in this area.

Examples of cases where "private facts" or "private information" have been at issue:

- *Beckham v. MGN* (2000)[10]—injunction granted: photographs of the interior of a footballer's house.
- *A v. B* (2002)[11]—injunction granted but overturned on appeal: details of a married footballer's affairs with two women.
- *Theakston v. MGN* (2002)[12]—injunction refused: written details of a night spent at a brothel by a television presenter. Injunction granted in relation to photographs of those same activities. Pictures are considered to be more intrusive and more likely to be subject to injunction.

15. May reporters tape-record their own telephone conversations for note-taking purposes (not rebroadcast) without the consent of the other party?

In theory, the United Kingdom is a one-party consent state, but E.U. legislation (Data Protection Acts and Regulation of Investigating Powers Act) has now effectively made this into a two-party consent state on pain of criminal sanction.

16. If permissible to record such tapes, may they be broadcast without permission?

The use of such one-party tapes may present a possible issue with breach of confidence if:

1. the information broadcast or published "has the necessary quality of confidence" (e.g., is private and secret); and
2. the source imparted the information in circumstances where, or where by making it clear, there would be a duty of confidence (e.g., employees giving information confidential to their employers; or evidence disclosed in litigation or official secrets); and
3. there has been unauthorized use of that information to the detriment of the person who communicated it.

17. Is there a recognized evidentiary privilege preventing the disclosure of confidential sources relied upon by reporters?

Section 10 of the Contempt of Court Act 1981 provides some limited protection for journalists to protect their confidential sources: "No court may require a person to disclose, nor is any person guilty of contempt of court for refusing to disclose, the source of information contained in a publication for which he is responsible, unless it is established to the satisfaction of the court that disclosure is necessary in the interests of justice or national security, or for the prevention of disorder or crime." In practice, the journalists' statutory protection is rarely challenged as it was reinforced by the European Court of Human Rights decision of *Goodwin v. UK.*[13]

The Police and Criminal Evidence Act (PACE) 1984 sets out the circumstances in which the police may apply to a judge, and a judge may grant disclosure of journalistic material. Before making an order, a judge has to be satisfied that there are reasonable grounds for believing that a serious offense warranting arrest has been committed; that the evidence would be admissible and of substantial value; that other methods to obtain the material have failed or are bound to fail; and that disclosure would be in the public interest.

Because failure to obey a court order is punishable by a contempt charge, reporters facing such demands should contact local counsel immediately.

18. In the event that legal papers are served upon the newsroom (such as a civil complaint), are there any particular warnings about accepting service of which we should be aware?

Strict procedural rules govern the service of papers commencing legal proceedings (e.g., a claim form, previously known as a writ), requiring service on either the registered office within the jurisdiction of the media company or on solicitors who act for the company and who have confirmed expressly that they have instructions to accept service. There may be valid and fundamental legal points to be raised in relation to the validity of service and a newsroom should not carelessly accept service of a claim; there is no obligation to do so.

An injunction is a mandatory court order requiring compliance under pain of fine or imprisonment, and is therefore a very different matter. It would be foolhardy in the extreme for a newsroom to ignore or reject an injunction that it receives as it will be taken to have been served with the injunction, and therefore have knowledge of its contents, from the moment it receives the document, even if it receives the injunction by way of a report from, e.g., a wire service. No longer do claimants have to serve each and every newsroom directly.

19. Has your jurisdiction applied established media law to Internet publishers?

Yes, especially in the areas of libel and confidential information. Recent reported libel cases involving publication on the Internet include the following: *Yousef Jameel v. Dow Jones & Co. Inc.* (2005 Court of Appeal)[14] (lawsuit brought on only five Internet hits held to be an abuse of process); *Don King v. Lennox Lewis* (2004 Court of Appeal)[15] (whether England was the correct forum in respect of defamation on the Internet); *Richardson v. Schwarzenegger* (2004 Queen's Bench Division)[16] (liability for republication in respect of a publication on the Internet, and *forum conveniens*); *Hewitt & Others v. Grunwald & Others* (2004 QBD)[17] (application to strike out a defense of qualified privilege failed in circumstances where publication of the press release was complained of on the Internet); *Vassiliev v. Frank Cass & Co. Ltd.* (2003 QBD)[18] (whether the defendant was protected by common interest privilege where there was publication on the Internet); and *Godfrey v. Demon Internet Ltd.* (1999 QBD)[19] (defendant was allowed to show other postings in news groups in mitigation of damages).

Confidential Information cases on the Internet in England include: *J. K. Rowling v. Persons Unknown* (2003 High Court)[20] (injunction granted restraining publication by the world at large of stolen Harry Potter manuscripts); *Covance Laboratories v. J* (2003 Chancery Division)[21] (whether Internet publication defeated a claim in confidence); *Attorney General v. Times Newspapers Ltd.* (2001 Court of Appeal)[22] (whether a publisher should be required to obtain prior approval from the Attorney General before publishing material that might be damaging to national security even where the information was already in the public domain as a result of Internet publication).

20. If established media law has been applied to Internet publishers, are there any ways in which Internet publishers (including chat room operators) have to meet different standards?

Generally the same standards apply as apply to publications in other forms, but an Internet service provider (ISP) may be able to avail itself of the safe-harbor defense of "unintentional publication" under Section 1 of the Defamation Act, 1996, where the ISP can show it was not author of the defamatory statement, that it took reasonable care in relation to the publication, and that it did not know, or had no reason to believe, that it had caused publication of a defamatory statement.

Following the *Godfrey v. Demon Internet* case (see Question 19 above), it seems that the prudent course for ISPs is that once they receive a complaint, they should consider temporarily removing the offending material immediately or they risk not being able to avail themselves of the unintentional publication defense. In practice, many ISPs ask for an indemnity from the claimant to abide the event of wrongful removal.

21. Are there any cases where the courts enforced a judgment in libel from another jurisdiction against a publisher in your jurisdiction?

This issue has arisen only rarely because of the ease with which reciprocal enforcement can be recognized by treaties among Commonwealth States and also among E.U. States.

It is possible to register money judgments from any jurisdiction which meets the UK's basic procedural standards. It is not possible to register foreign injunctive orders without commencing separate proceedings.

In any event, given that London is notoriously the "libel capital of the world" and a claimant-friendly environment in which to sue, most claimants come to the English courts to sue in the first place.

Chapter Notes

1. [2006] UKHL 44; [2007] 1 AC 359.
2. [2001] 2 AC 127; [1993] WLR 1010.
3. *Jameel* at ¶18.
4. *R v. Woodgate, Bowyer, Clifford and Others* (unreported).
5. *American Cyanamid Co v. Ethicon Ltd (No.3)* [1979] R.P.C. 215.
6. *Cream Holdings Ltd v. Banerjee* [2004] UKHL 44; [2004] 3 W.L.R. 918; [2004] 4 All E.R. 617; [2005] E.M.L.R. 1; [2004] H.R.L.R. 39; [2004] UKH.R.R. 1071; 17 B.H.R.C. 464; (2004) 101(42) L.S.G. 29; (2004) 154 N.L.J. 1589; (2004) 148 S.J.L.B. 1215.

7. *Campbell v. Mirror Group Newspapers Ltd, October 14, 2002* [2002] EWCA Civ 1373; [2003] Q.B. 633; [2003] 2 W.L.R. 80; [2003] 1 All E.R. 224; [2003] E.M.L.R. 2; [2003] H.R.L.R. 2; (2002) 99(42) L.S.G. 38; (2002) 146 S.J.L.B. 234.

8. *Campbell v. Mirror Group Newspapers Ltd* [2004] UKHL 22; [2004] 2 A.C. 457; [2004] 2 W.L.R. 1232; [2004] 2 All E.R. 995; [2004] E.M.L.R. 15; [2004] H.R.L.R. 24; [2004] UKH.R.R. 648; 16 B.H.R.C. 500; (2004) 101(21) L.S.G. 36; (2004) 154 N.L.J. 733; (2004) 148 S.J.L.B. 572.

9. *Von Hannover v. Germany* (59320/00) [2004] E.M.L.R. 21 (ECHR).

10. *Beckham v. MGN Ltd., QBD,* June 28, 2001 (unreported).

11. *A v. B Plc.* [2002] EWCA Civ 337; [2003] Q.B. 195; [2002] 3 W.L.R. 542; [2002] 2 All E.R. 545; [2002] E.M.L.R. 21; [2002] 1 F.L.R. 1021; [2002] 2 F.C.R. 158; [2002] H.R.L.R. 25; [2002] UKH.R.R. 457; 12 B.H.R.C. 466; [2002] Fam. Law 415; (2002) 99(17) L.S.G. 36; (2002) 152 N.L.J. 434; (2002) 146 S.J.L.B. 77.

12. *Theakston v. MGN Ltd.* [2002] EWHC 137; [2002] E.M.L.R. 22.

13. *Goodwin v. United Kingdom* (28957/95) [2002] I.R.L.R. 664; [2002] 2 F.L.R. 487; [2002] 2 F.C.R. 577; (2002) 35 E.H.R.R. 18; 13 B.H.R.C. 120; (2002) 67 B.M.L.R. 199; [2002] Fam. Law 738; (2002) 152 N.L.J. 1171.

14. *Dow Jones & Co. Inc. v. Jameel* [2005] EWCA Civ 75; (2005) 149 S.J.L.B. 181 *Times,* February 14, 2005; *Independent,* February 10, 2005.

15. *King v. Lewis* [2004] EWCA Civ 1329; [2005] E.M.L.R. 4.

16. *Richardson v. Schwarzenegger* (2004) EWHC 2422 (QBD).

17. *Hewitt v. Grunwald* [2004] EWHC 2959.

18. *Vassiliev v. Frank Cass & Co. Ltd.* (Defamation: Qualified Privilege) [2003] EWHC 1428; [2003] E.M.L.R. 33.

19. *Godfrey v. Demon Internet Ltd. (Application to Strike Out)* [2001] Q.B. 201; [2000] 3 W.L.R. 1020; [1999] 4 All E.R. 342; [1999] E.M.L.R. 542; [1998–99] Info. T.L.R. 252; [1999] I.T.C.L.R. 282; [1999] Masons C.L.R. 267; (1999) 149 N.L.J. 609.

20. *Bloomsbury Publishing Plc. (2) J K Rowling v. Newsgroup Newspapers Ltd. (2003)* [2003] EWHC 1087 Ch.

21. *Covance Laboratories v. J* (20 and 27 March 2003 Chancery Division), unreported.

22. *Attorney General v. Times Newspapers Ltd.* [2001] EWCA Civ 97; [2001] 1 W.L.R. 885; [2001] E.M.L.R. 19; (2001) 98(9) L.S.G. 38; (2001) 145 S.J.L.B. 30 *Times,* January 31, 2001; *Independent,* January 30, 2001.

CHAPTER 16

France

DOMINIQUE MONDOLONI
Willkie Farr & Gallagher LLP

Willkie Farr & Gallagher LLP
21-23, rue de la Ville l'Evêque
75008 Paris, France
Phone: +33.1.53.43.45.00
Fax: +33.1.40.06.96.06
www.willkie.com
dmondoloni@willkie.com

Introduction to the French Legal System

The French legal system, adhering to the principles of civil law, uses courts of first instance, appeals courts, and a court of last resort to resolve both civil and criminal actions. Proceedings are traditionally heard by a panel of magistrates, the parties being generally represented by attorneys who assist the plaintiff and/or defendant. With the notable exception of divorce and juvenile proceedings, all trials are open to the public.

Magistrates govern and enforce the French judicial system. The two kinds of magistrates are sitting magistrates and standing magistrates. Sitting magistrates serve as judges and deliver verdicts; standing magistrates represent state and public interests, prosecute criminal offenses, and ensure equitable and consistent enforcement of state law. Magistrates are assisted by clerks and ushers who record the verdict and ensure the sentence is served.

Civil and criminal actions, although handled in different courts, have similar progressions in the French system. Civil actions are initially tried in a court of first instance (*tribunaux de grande instance*). The proceedings are dominated by written submissions by the attorneys, and a verdict is often announced, in writing, by the panel of magistrates serving as judges, many weeks or months after the trial. Verdicts can be reevaluated by an appeals court (*Cour d'Appel*) and at the highest court, the Court of Cassation (*Cour de Cassation*). Unlike the civil *tribunaux de grande instance,* criminal tribunals, designated to hear criminal offenses, are organized into three groups. Police tribunals hear petty offenses, *tribunaux correctionnels* hear mid-level crimes, and the *cour d'assises* hears the most serious offenses. An appeals court, and possibly the Court of Cassation, can reevaluate the tribunal court's decision.

1. What is the locally accepted definition of libel?

Libel, and more generally defamation—French law does not distinguish between libel and slander—is statutorily defined as "any allegation or imputation of a fact which is contrary to honor or to the consideration in which is held a person or an institution."[1]

Defamation is an offense and as such is actionable in the criminal courts, but plaintiffs may choose to bring action exclusively in the civil courts. The essential elements of the offense are:

1. the making of a defamatory statement;
2. the publication of that statement;[2] and
3. the identification of the plaintiff as the person defamed.

1. *The Defamatory Statement*

The complained-of words must be such that they constitute a factual allegation as against the plaintiff or the imputation of a fact[3] to the plaintiff that is contrary to "honor" or is such that it injures the "consideration" in which that person is held by the community.

"Honor" is a concept common to all men and women and consists of the notion that one's conduct conforms to moral standards. A person of honor is one who accomplishes his or her duties and acts according to conscience. "Consideration" is the respect and esteem in which one is held by the community. To defame is to impute or allege conduct that is contrary to honor or that will damage someone's consideration. In general, defamation tends to involve charges that fall within the following categories: accusation of a crime; sexual impropriety or immoral behavior; disgraceful behavior; bankruptcy, financial irresponsibility, or dishonesty; or professional misconduct in one's business.

2. *Publication*

"Publication" means that the defamatory statement must have been made public. According to Section 23 of the Law of 29 July 1881, defamation is actionable if the defamatory statement was made orally in a public speech or declaration, or in print through the use of words, engravings, sketches, drawings, and generally any form of image, and was made public through any medium of mass communication including through the sale and distribution of printed material (e.g., books, newspapers, magazines), billboards, or any other support of the voice or images (e.g., radio, cinema, television, Internet).

3. *Identification*

The complained-of words must identify the plaintiff or be such that the plaintiff is identifiable. For example, if the complained-of words concern a small number of people, none of whom are identified individually in the statement but all of whom are nonetheless identifiable, then all those persons which form the group are entitled to act against the defendant. Such would be the case, say, of a statement to the effect that "the Board of Directors of Company X agreed with the CEO's decision to pay a kickback to the president of West Africa in order to obtain the contract for the construction of the capital's subway system."

2. Is libel-by-implication recognized, or, in the alternative, must the complained-of words alone defame the plaintiff?

Defamation is actionable even if the words in and of themselves are not libelous but, put in context, become defamatory.

3. May corporations sue for libel?

Yes.

4. Is product disparagement recognized, and if so, how does that differ from libel?

No, unless the denigration of a product is a means of injuring someone's reputation (e.g., "Butcher X's meat is rotten" can be defamatory for the plaintiff because it implies that Butcher X sells rotten meat, which is a statement that can damage his reputation. See also Supreme Court of France, 1st. Ch., 27 September 2005, *Légipresse,* 2006, III, p. 38).

However, whereas product disparagement in and of itself is not actionable as defamation, it can give rise to a civil action in tort between competitors on the basis of the theory of unfair competition. A medium that would publish or make public a denigrating statement by an economic operator of his competitor's goods would be actionable on the same grounds.[4]

5. Must an individual be clearly identified (by name or photograph) to sue for libel? Can a group of persons sue for libel, even though not named?

The plaintiff must be identified by name, photograph, or drawing or be identifiable (see discussion in Question 1 above). Group libel is possible in France. If a statement concerns a group of persons who are identifiable as a result of their membership in the group (e.g., the Town Council of City A, or the Board of Directors of Company X), then all can act against the defendant. The theory of *par ricochet* also allows a cause of action to lie when the unnamed plaintiff is closely associated with the subject of the story in such a manner that the story evokes the plaintiff's image in the mind of the reasonable reader.

6. What is the fault standard(s) applied to libel?

Defamation is an offense, so in principle it requires that the plaintiff demonstrate that the defendant acted in bad faith (i.e., with the knowledge that his or her statement was defamatory). However, Article 35*bis* of the Law of 29 July 1881 has instituted a notable exception to this principle of French criminal law by providing that the defendant's bad faith shall be presumed. The plaintiff only has therefore to establish the material elements of defamation. But the defendant shall be acquitted if he can reverse this presumption by proving good faith. The good faith defense is available to all defendants in an action for defamation and its success rests on four cumulative criteria: the objectivity of the presentation, the prudence in the expression (both of which include, for journalists, a careful verification of the sources), the absence of personal animosity towards the plaintiff, and the legitimacy of the goal pursued by the defendant (which includes public interest and artistic, literary, scientific, or historical critique).

a. Does the fault standard depend on the fame or notoriety of the plaintiff?

No.

b. Is there a heightened fault standard or privilege for reporting on matters of public concern or public interest?

There is no heightened fault standard from the perspective of the plaintiff (i.e., the fact that the plaintiff is a public figure does not place additional burden on the plaintiff). However, when reporting on matters of public interest or concern, certain defenses will be more readily available to the defendant. For example, truth of the defamatory statement is a defense that is available in most libel cases except, *inter alia,* when the facts alleged or imputed as against the defendant concern his or her privacy. Privacy will, however, be construed more restrictively when the defendant is a public figure. Matters that concern, e.g., a person's finances are generally considered to fall within the scope of privacy. Truth is therefore not an admissible defense in such an instance. But truth will be admitted as a defense if the defendant is a public figure where the aspects of his or her personal financial situation could have a bearing on the way that person will deal with public funds. Aspects of his or her intimacy (e.g., the existence of a liaison or the plaintiff's sexual preferences, etc.) will remain outside the scope of the *exceptio veritatis* defense.

Likewise, the good faith defense will be available to the defendant in matters of public interest (see 6 above).

In proving the truth of defamatory allegations, reporters may only rely upon material that they had actually acquired prior to publication. They may not use material learned through investigation after publication to justify the sued-upon article.

7. Is financial news about publicly traded companies, or companies involved with a government contract, considered a matter of public interest or otherwise privileged?

There is no particular privilege in relation thereto, but to the extent the information is of public concern, the defendant will be more readily believed in a good faith defense.

8. Is there a recognized protection for opinion or "fair comment" on matters of public concern?

To some extent, yes. An opinion *per se* is not actionable as a defamation. But there is a fine line between an opinion expressed by a journalist as to, say, the way a person manages his or her business, and defamation. Any factual allegation of impropriety in the management of a business, for example, would exceed the limits of opinion. The good faith defense to some extent resembles the "fair comment" defense known in common law jurisdictions (see 6 above).

9. Are there any requirements upon a plaintiff, such as demand for retraction or right of reply, and if so, what impact do they have?

French law does not provide that the plaintiff must address a demand for retraction before filing a complaint for libel nor does such a request, if made, have a bearing on the sanction that may ultimately be imposed on the defendant. But the Law of 29 July 1881 does provide for a "right of response," which is available to any person whose name was cited in an article, television program, or over the Internet.[5] This right of response is generally open to all persons whose name was cited, irrespective of whether the statements made in relation thereto are defamatory or not. There are, however, some notable exceptions (e.g., for television programs, the exercise of a right of response requires that the statements made are susceptible of being characterized as defamatory. Likewise, the right of response, being a right that is personal to the person who was cited, cannot in principle be exercised by anybody other than that person himself or herself. If that person is deceased, the heirs may exercise a right of response but only to the extent the statements made are defamatory towards the deceased.)

The right of response must be exercised within the three months that follow the first publication of the relevant person's name. It takes the form of a letter sent to the "director of publications"[6] requesting an insertion of its content at the same place and in the same font as those of the initial article. The "director of publications" is not entitled to refuse the request except if it exceeds the statutory length, is not in relation to the initial article (i.e., is not truly a response to the article), is defamatory in its content, or is such that it implicates third parties or the journalist. An illegitimate refusal or failure to print the response at the same place and in the same font as the initial article constitutes an offense that is actionable by the plaintiff.

The "right of response" is not a substitute for a complaint in defamation, and if the initial article is defamatory, plaintiffs are entitled to sue for defamation at the same time as they are entitled to exercise a right of response.

Section 65 of the Law of 29 July 1881 provides that criminal and civil actions in defamation are time barred within three months from the initial publication of the defamatory statement. The action must be introduced before the statute of limitation period expires, and there is typically no prior notice required before service of the writ.

10. Is there a privilege for quoting or reporting on:

a . Papers filed in court?

Yes. A good faith accounting of the content of papers filed in court is covered by the immunity provided for in Section 41 of the Law of 29 July 1881.

b. Government-issued documents?

Section 41 of the Law of 29 July 1881 provides for immunity from criminal or civil prosecution for defamation in relation to speeches made in parliament or written reports emanating from either chamber of parliament as well as all good faith journalistic accounts of such speeches or reports. The same immunity exists in relation to documents issued by either chamber of parliament.

It would not, however, immunize documents issued by a government administration or agency to the extent such documents would be defamatory. The good faith defense would, however, be available.

c. Quasi-governmental proceedings?

The immunity from prosecution provided in Section 41 of the Law of 29 July 1881 would not apply, but the good faith defense might exonerate the defendant, provided the reporter used due care in reporting. In turn, this would entail examining the reliability, reputation, and methods used by the source paper upon which the defendant is relying.

11. Is there a privilege for republishing statements made earlier by other, bona fide, reliable publications or wire services?

Not *per se,* but this would typically be a situation where a good faith defense could be articulated.

12. Are there any restrictions regarding reporting on:

a. Ongoing criminal investigations?

As a matter of principle, criminal investigations are conducted under a rule of secrecy (Section 11 of the French Code of Criminal Procedure). All those persons who participate in the conduct of an investigation (police, investigating magistrate, the clerk) are bound by the rule of secrecy. Violation of the rule by those bound to it is an offense. But this rule is not enforceable as against persons who do not participate in the investigation (such as journalists).

However, journalists may be held liable as accomplices if they participated or in some way aided or instigated persons bound by the secrecy rule to violate that rule (e.g., an investigating magistrate who gives an "interview" to a journalist). The magistrate would be guilty of violating the rule and the journalist could be held liable as an accomplice for providing the means by which the magistrate was able to violate the rule. Journalists may also be held liable for aiding and abetting the disclosure of secret documents (i.e., documents produced or obtained in the course of an investigation and which are also covered by the rule of secrecy) if they publish those documents. The Supreme Court has recently upheld this position (Supreme Court of France, Criminal Chamber, 12 June 2007, *Légipresse* 2008, III., p. 1) notwithstanding the very clear position of the European Court of Human Rights (*Dupuis et al. vs. France*, 7 June 2007, application no. 1914/02) according to which prosecution for aiding and abetting in such circumstances exceeds the authorized limits of freedom of expression as posed in Article 10 of the European Convention).

A caveat to the above is a consequence of Section 109 of the French Code of Criminal Procedure. Journalist are *not* obligated to reveal their sources. So if a journalist obtains information about an ongoing investigation from sources that are not and cannot be identified other than through the testimony of the journalist (which journalists are at liberty not to give), then prosecution for complicity in the violation of the secrecy rule (assuming the source is bound by the rule) will not be practicable.

b. Ongoing criminal prosecutions?

Criminal prosecutions are reported under the same guidelines as investigations.

Section 9-1 of the French Civil Code provides, moreover, that all persons are presumed innocent and institutes a specific action in tort and specific interlocutory relief (i.e., *inter alia,* the publication of a communiqué) in favor of any persons who, under criminal prosecution or investigation, are publicly presented as being guilty of the facts for which they have been charged, until a final judgment has been made against them. The cause of action for violation of the "presumed innocent" rule is subject to a three-month statute of limitations.

c. Ongoing regulatory investigations?

There is no general rule, but the statutes that engender regulatory agencies (e.g., AMF, Conseil de la Concurrence) contain provisions similar to the secrecy rule applied to criminal investigations according to which those persons participating in a regulatory investigation are bound to a secrecy rule. Question 12a above would therefore apply to most regulatory investigations.

d. Ongoing civil litigation, or other judicial proceedings?

With the notable exception of procedures for defamation (where the *exceptio veritatis* would not be admitted), divorce, paternity, alimony, or abortion, for which Article 38 of the Law of 29 July 1881 prohibits that accounts of these procedures be made public, there is no specific restriction in respect of civil proceedings.

13. Are prior restraints or other prepublication injunctions available on the basis of libel or privacy, and if so, what are the standards for obtaining such relief?

Yes. Section 809 of the French Code of Civil Procedure allows the President of the Court of first instance to order "any provisional and conservatory measure" to prevent an imminent injury or loss from occurring or to put an end to a clearly illicit behavior. All forms of *in limine* relief are available, including prepublication injunctions and press releases. The plaintiff has only to provide a *prima facie* case that the publication under criticism is defamatory, injurious, or generally violates an existing rule. Urgency is not a condition.

As a matter of practice, however, obtaining immediate injunctive relief on the basis of libel is complicated by the fact that, pursuant to Section 55 of the Law of 29 July 1881, the defendant must, in all cases of defamation, be granted a period of ten days from the date of service of the complaint in order to administer evidence of the truth of the defamatory statement (an additional five days being granted to the plaintiff to administer counterevidence). This provision of the Law of 29 July 1881 is a matter of public policy and applies even to applications for injunctive relief. So, as a practical matter, no hearing can take place before at least ten days from the complaint, which thus ensures that a publication will remain on the stand for at least that period of time. Likewise, a prepublication injunction, in relation to a television program, for example, will only be efficient if the plaintiff has had at least ten days' prior notice of the fact that the program will be aired. This rule, however, only applies in matters of defamation and does not apply in matters where the plaintiff invokes another rule, say, a violation of the statutes that protect privacy.

14. Is a right of privacy recognized (either civilly or criminally)?

Yes. It is recognized both civilly (Section 9 of the Civil Code) and criminally (Section 226-1 *et seq.* of the French Criminal Code).

a. What is the definition of "private fact"?

There is no academic definition of a "private fact" but it is generally considered that all aspects of a person's intimacy are protected. This includes not only events that concern someone's family life but also more generally all those aspects of a person's life that can legitimately expected to not be made public. In this respect, reproducing a photograph or voice recording of someone without authorization is a violation of privacy. It is for this reason that the French press often blurs or otherwise masks the faces of bystanders in photographs. The protection is far-reaching. For example, if a person agrees to give an interview to a magazine and reveals certain aspects of intimacy (love life, children, etc.), another magazine would not be entitled to report the same without the person's authorization.

b. Is there a public interest or newsworthiness exception?

The scope of someone's intimacy will shrink if that person is a public figure. Yet, the aspect of family life will remain private. Prince Albert of Monaco succeeded in this regard, where the Supreme Court upheld a decision that had ordered a magazine to pay damages to Prince Albert of Monaco for having divulged the fact that Prince Albert was the father of a child although the information was neither public, newsworthy, nor of public concern (Supreme Court of France, 1st Chamber, 27 February 2007, *Légipresse* 2007, III., p. 107).

c. Is the right of privacy based in common law, statute, or constitution?

The right of privacy is codified both civilly and criminally.

15. May reporters tape-record their own telephone conversations for note-taking purposes (not rebroadcast) without the consent of the other party?

Yes. As a matter of ethics, journalists should refrain from recording interviews without the consent of the interviewee.

16. If permissible to record such tapes, may they be broadcast without permission?

No. Broadcasting a tape recording of an interview without the interviewee's consent is a violation of Section 9 of the Civil Code and Section 226-1 *et seq.* of the French Criminal Code (see Question 14 above).

17. Is there a recognized evidentiary privilege preventing the disclosure of confidential sources relied upon by reporters?

Section 109 of the French Code of Criminal Procedure provides that journalists may refuse to testify and disclose their sources.[7] But the rule only applies to the journalist's testimony. It will not apply to work in progress or other documents or papers the journalist may have gathered and which are susceptible of being seized in the course of a criminal investigation. It is worth noting that the search and seizure of documents on the premises of media undertakings is, however, subject to specific rules (i.e., Article 56-2 of the Code of Criminal Procedure) intended to protect the freedom of journalists to exercise their profession. These do not apply when the search and seizure is conducted on other premises including the journalist's home, although a draft bill was recently announced by President Sarkozy to the effect of extending this specific procedure to the home of the journalist.

18. In the event that legal papers are served upon the newsroom (such as a civil complaint), are there any particular warnings about accepting service of which we should be aware?

Yes, especially with respect to a criminal complaint for defamation. A journalist (e.g., the author of an article considered as libelous) can be prosecuted as an accomplice (the "director of publications" being considered as the statutory principal offender). But service of the writ to appear before the criminal court is not valid unless delivered to the journalist himself or herself, or in his or her absence, at the place of residence. Service at the professional office is not valid. Because the statute of limitations is extremely short (three months), the invalidity of the service will often bar prosecution if it is not reinstated within the limitation period. So, as a practical matter, journalists and generally all persons other than the "director of publications" (who can validly be served at the registered office of the news medium) should never accept service at their place of work and service should never be accepted on their behalf at their place of work. Civil complaints likewise should not be accepted by the defendants or on behalf of the defendants at their place of business.

19. Has your jurisdiction applied established media law to Internet publishers?

Yes. The Law of 21 June 2004, which amended the Law of 29 July 1982, has subsequently regulated Internet publications.

20. If established media law has been applied to Internet publishers, are there any ways in which Internet publishers (including chat room operators) have to meet different standards?

Although Internet publishing is by and large subject to the same rules as those which apply to television and radio broadcasting (notably, as regards the Law of 29 July 1881 and the obligation, pursuant to the Law of 29 July 1982, as amended by the Law of 21 June 2004), Internet publishers, like television and radio broadcasters, must appoint a "director of publications" (see Note 6 below). In addition, a specific regime applies, according to the Law of 21 June 2004, to the Internet host, which is defined as the company that organizes "the storage of either signals, writings, frames, sounds or every kind of messages provided by the recipients of those services."

Hosts have immunity under the Law of 29 July 1881 if they can prove that (1) they had no knowledge of the exact content of the website *and* (2) they acted on short notice to withdraw the illegal information or restrain the access to it as soon as they were informed of its content. A host will be deemed to be aware of the circulation of unlawful information on the site, and those liable under the Law of 29 July 1881, as soon as accurate complaints are received describing the offense. The Constitutional Council has however held, in a decision dated 10 June 2004, that this presumption of liability is deemed to comply with the Constitution provided only that (1) the information described in the complaint is clearly illegal or (2) a prior judgment has ordered its withdrawal.

21. Are there any cases where the courts enforced a judgment in libel from another jurisdiction against a publisher in your jurisdiction?

To our knowledge, there are no such decisions. As a matter of principle, nothing should prevent a foreign decision from being registered in France, provided it complies with the conditions set forth, either in the relevant bilateral treaties on the enforcement of foreign decisions or, in their absence, the general rules of registration of foreign judgments.[8] A criminal judgment rendered abroad will not be enforceable in France, although if the foreign decision contains an order for the payment of damages to the victim of the offense, that portion of the decision will be susceptible to being registered in France like any other civil foreign decision.

A judgment made by a foreign civil jurisdiction will be enforceable in France provided it is registered in France.[9] The application for registration of a foreign judgment will be dismissed if the foreign decision does not comply with due process or if the rule that has been applied by the foreign jurisdiction is considered as contrary to French international public policy. In this respect, it is likely that an application for registration of a foreign judgment will be dismissed if those laws do not afford the defendant the same degree of protection as is available under French law. For example, a foreign judgment under laws that did not provide a defense based on truth would probably be considered as contrary to French international public policy.

Chapter Notes

1. Section 29 of the Law of 29 July 1881.

2. Nonpublic defamation (i.e., the making of a defamatory statement by the defendant in a private setting) is a misdemeanor.

3. The complained-of words must be susceptible to being proven as true. If they cannot be, then the offense is that of injurious language. The distinction is important from a procedural point of view because the plaintiff must choose the grounds upon which he or she acts and both actions cannot be presented in the alternative.

4. Supreme Court of France, 2nd Ch., April 8, 2004, *Légipresse,* 2004, I, p. 76.

5. There is no right of response in relation to the publication by the written medium of a photograph. The right of response for communications on television and radio is governed by Section 6 of the Law of 29 July 1982 (as amended by the Law of 21 June 2004) and the Decree of April 6, 1987. The conditions are slightly different than those that exist in relation to the written medium in the sense that the right of response for television and radio communications may only be exercised if the initial communication on the air is susceptible of being considered as defamatory. This is not the case for both the written medium and Internet, where it suffices that a person be named or cited in the article to claim a right of response. The right of response for communications over the Internet is governed by Article 6, § IV, of the Law of 21 June 2004 and the Decree of October 24, 2007.

6. The Law of 29 July 1881 has instituted a list of statutory defendants in all cases that are governed by this law. The "director of publications" is the statutory principal offender. All news media must appoint a "director of publications," who will be held personally liable for the offense (the news medium being vicariously liable for civil damages but not criminally); the "director of publications" is the chief executive officer of the company that exploits the medium. Likewise, the Law of 29 July 1982 (as amended by the Law of 21 June 2004) has instituted a similar list of statutory defendants with respect to television (including cable television), radio, and Internet communications, where each one of these mediums must appoint a "director of publications" who will be held personally liable for the offense.

7. The European Court of Human Rights has also held that an injunction ordering journalists to disclose a source is contrary to Article 10 of the European Convention on Human Rights, which protects the freedom of expression (*Goodwin v. United Kingdom,* application no. 17488/90 dated February 22, 1996).

8. There are no treaties between France and the United States on this point. As a member of the EU, France will most likely enforce judgments rendered in other EU nations.

9. Registration is obtained through an application in the French Courts either *ex parte* in the context of a treaty or *inter partes* in the absence of a treaty.

CHAPTER 17

Germany

JAN HEGEMANN AND SLADE R. METCALF
Hogan & Hartson LLP

Jan Hegemann
Hogan & Hartson LLP
Potsdamer Platz 1
10785 Berlin, Germany
Phone: +49 (30) 72 61 15-303
Fax: +49 (30) 72 61 15-106
www.hhlaw.com
jhegemann@hhlaw.com

Slade R. Metcalf
Hogan & Hartson LLP
875 Third Avenue
New York, NY 10022 U.S.A.
Phone: 212-918-3000
Fax: 212-918-3100
www.hhlaw.com
srmetcalf@hhlaw.com

Introduction to the German Legal System

Germany has adopted a traditional civil law system. The German Constitution of 1949, called Basic Statute (*Grundgesetz*), is the central document in the German judicial system. Acts of Parliament are the sole method for statutory reform and codification. Civil, private, and criminal laws are codified in separate government groups; however, all actions regarding the constitution are heard in the German Federal Constitutional Court (*Bundesverfassungsgericht*).

The German legal system does not have separate federal and state branches. There is a series of state courts, organized by subject matter jurisdiction, where actions can be brought. Appeals are heard in federal courts, and the constitutional court is accessible to any citizens claiming that their constitutional rights have been impinged.

1. What is the locally accepted definition of libel?

Under German law, libel is a broad term that describes statements in verbal, written, or other form that injure a person's reputation. A false *allegation of fact,* be it defamatory or not, enjoys no protection under German law and will, as a rule, be prohibited by the courts upon application of the person concerned. "False information," as the Federal Constitutional Court has put it, "is not covered by the right to free speech and freedom of expression." A false and, as the case may be, defamatory allegation of fact may be justified only if the person having made the allegation has acted "in the pursuit of legitimate interests."[1]

With regard to press statements, such public interest will be presumed if the journalist has observed the rules of conduct established in the case law for members of the press. However, these rules are strict and compliance with them is often difficult to prove. By contrast, *expressions of opinion* are generally free from liability (see Question 8 below). Despite the protection given to opinion under German law, courts will allow libel claims to stand where the statement is only meant to revile and vilify another person.

The following statements have been found to be defamatory by German courts: The Federal Constitutional Court (*Bundesverfassungsgericht*) held that the description of a politician by a songwriter as "such a heap of federal shit that you would not want to step into it" was defamatory. The Court further held, however, that the newspaper which had published the statement was not liable for its publication since it had sufficiently distanced itself from it.[2] Crude swear words such as "pig," "swine," or "bastard"[3] as well as unfoundedly discrediting expressions like "total loser"[4] are usually deemed defamatory. According to the Köln Court of Appeal (*Oberlandesgericht Köln*), the expression "courtesy journalism" can be defamatory if it creates the impression that the publishers of a magazine have sold their journalistic independence to their major advertising customer.[5] An unproved statement that a person has worked for the ministry of state security (*Ministerium für Staatssicherheit*) of the former German Democratic Republic is commonly found to be defamatory by the courts.[6]

The following statements have been found to be not defamatory by German courts: The statement that a politician running for the mayor's office in a small town was "a scrupulous liar who stuck to nothing and spurned the legal order" was held to be protected under the right to free speech.[7] Likewise, the expression "Stop the child-murder in mother's womb on the premises of the N. clinic. Then: Holocaust. Today: Babycaust" made by anti-abortionists with regard to the body responsible for an abortion clinic was not regarded as defamatory.[8] Yet, the action for defamation by the clinic's head physician with regard to the same expression was successful before the Federal Constitutional Court.[9] The Karlsruhe Court of Appeal (*Oberlandesgericht Karlsruhe*) held that it was permissible under freedom of speech to call a doctor who had widely criticized the methods of traditional medicine a "pseudo-religious vitamin guru," a "butcher," and a "charlatan."[10] The statement "soldiers are murderers" was held to be protected under the right to free speech by the Federal Constitutional Court.[11]

2. Is libel-by-implication recognized, or, in the alternative, must the complained-of words alone defame the plaintiff?

German law recognizes libel-by-implication. Thus, a statement does not necessarily need to defame a plaintiff expressly to be considered libelous. For a statement to be deemed libelous, it does not necessarily matter what the journalist expressly asserts. It primarily matters what the reader perceives.[12]

However, the German Federal Court of Justice (BGH) demands a high standard for claims of libel-by-implication. For such a claim it does not suffice that a reasonable reader might have concluded that the author intended to imply a libelous allegation. Rather, this conclusion must be compelling in order to be considered libel-by-implication.[13]

3. May corporations sue for libel?

German press law is not restricted to the protection of individuals: corporations may sue for libel. It also protects a corporation's reputation against defamatory criticism that evidently aims at insulting or disparaging the corporation,[14] and grants protection against inaccurate allegations of fact, especially if the statement of such facts has a negative effect on the corporation's credit rating.[15] However, a corporation's reputation enjoys less legal protection against libel than that of an individual, and German courts recognize that reports on corporations and their products are often a matter of great and legitimate public interest.[16] Thus, a corporation must accept critical reports of its performance and business standing, and courts will narrowly read a complaint for defamatory allegations to succeed. Coverage of such issues will not be considered libelous as long as it keeps to the facts and does not aim at disparaging the corporation.[17]

Besides that, it is recognized that in case of disparaging statements about an institution or a collectivity of people in general, individual members of the collectivity may successfully sue for libel if the circumstances indicate that the statements aimed not at defaming the collectivity as such (e.g., "the police"), but rather its individual members (cf. Question 5 below).[18]

4. Is product disparagement recognized, and if so, how does that differ from libel?

German law recognizes product disparagement. The standards for product disparagement do not differ from libel. Product disparagement may particularly be claimed in two cases: Either (1) a specific product is negatively reviewed in a (comparative or noncomparative) product test; or (2) a report may criticize a whole line of business and name a certain product as an example. In both cases, the report has to comply with the standards of libel law. Thus, critical commentary of a product is allowed as long as the allegations are true and do not primarily aim at disparaging the product, its manufacturer, or distributor.

A journalist who alleges, for example, that an entire line of products contains toxic substances must make sure that these allegations are true with regard to each particular product that is being singled out for the purpose of illustrating the allegations. Product tests must at least comply with a minimum of neutrality, expertise, and impartiality.[19] Higher standards regarding the objectiveness of a report apply to comparative product tests.[20]

5. Must an individual be clearly identified (by name or photograph) to sue for libel? Can a group of persons sue for libel, even though not named?

Under German law, an individual does not need to be clearly identified by name or photograph to sue for libel. The individual must only be identifiable. Similarly, a group of persons may sue for libel, even though not named, provided that the members of the group are identifiable. In many cases, a statement refers to an individual without clearly identifying him or her by name or photograph. This does not mean, however, that the individual may not sue for libel.

German courts consider it to be sufficient if the statement refers to a certain person covertly. Identification can be constituted by reference to the name, by pictures, initials, nicknames, or by a description of the plaintiff's life story, profession, or any other identifying circumstance.[21] The courts do not make high demands on showing that the plaintiff is identifiable. The test is whether a person acquainted with the plaintiff would be able to identify the plaintiff as the person referred to on the basis of the information provided by the article in question.[22]

Similarly, members of a group (but not the group itself, unless it is a legal entity) can sue for libel, even though not named, provided that they are able to show that the statements aimed not at defaming the group as such, but rather its individual members. In such a case the identification often depends on the size of the group of persons referred to. The smaller the group, the more likely it is that a court will find that each member of the group was meant to be disparaged.[23]

6. What is the fault standard(s) applied to libel?

a. Does the fault standard depend on the fame or notoriety of the plaintiff?

The fault standard does not depend on the fame or notoriety of the plaintiff. However, press coverage of famous or well-known figures will often be of public interest. Matters of public interest are subject to the heightened fault standard applied under the "public interest" defense. In that defense, even if a statement is false and defamatory, liability will not attach provided the journalist can show that: (1) the subject is indeed in the public interest; and (2) the story was crafted with a requisite degree of journalistic care.

b. Is there a heightened fault standard or privilege for reporting on matters of public concern or public interest?

The fault standard applied to libel also depends on the relief sought by the plaintiff. In cases where a plaintiff seeks injunctions or the right to retraction, libel is essentially a strict liability tort. By contrast, claims for damages require proof of at least negligence, which may be defeated by the defense of proper journalistic caution. This defense usually requires proof of careful, methodical research of the issue.[24]

7. Is financial news about publicly traded companies, or companies involved with a government contract, considered a matter of public interest or otherwise privileged?

Financial news about publicly traded companies or companies involved with government contracts is not automatically privileged. With regard to companies in general, however, German courts recognize that coverage of corporations is often a matter of great public interest, given the fact that they may be heavily unionized, publicly held, or enjoy contracts with the government.[25]

8. Is there a recognized protection for opinion or "fair comment" on matters of public concern?

German press law recognizes the defense of fair comment on a matter of public interest. Recognizing that there is no such thing as a false or untrue opinion, persons must tolerate sharp, unfair, or even insulting criticism as long as it is somehow issue-related. An expression of opinion will only be deemed libelous if it deliberately and primarily aims to injure a person's reputation.

The intentional attack on a person's reputation must clearly be in the foreground of the comment. According to the case law, this can be assumed if the statement in question, even from the critic's point of view, has no factual basis and is only meant to revile and vilify another person. Unlike U.S. law, where the more heated and hyperbolic the words, the more protection the statement may enjoy, German law does not abide by gratuitous or overly vitriolic language, and such writing may be *prima facie* evidence of an intentional attack.

Gratuitous attacks excepted, under German law, the right to freedom of expression and opinion is widely protected. There is a legal presumption that the expression of one's opinion is permissible.[26] Since this presumption does not apply to statements of fact, the distinction between allegation of fact and expression of opinion becomes crucial in determining the outcome of many lawsuits.[27]

The expression of opinion that is defamatory, however, is actionable. The degree of public interest, again, determines the standard for defamation. Thus, statements that concern a matter of public interest are more likely to be considered permissible by German courts. They even may be exaggerated and polemic as long as they still refer to the matter of public interest.[28]

9. Are there any requirements upon a plaintiff, such as demand for retraction or right of reply, and if so, what impact do they have?

In general, an action for damages or injunctive relief does not require that the plaintiff has demanded a retraction or asserted a right of reply. However, the plaintiff's damage claim may be reduced if the defendant has published a retraction without delay. In this respect, it is irrelevant if the plaintiff has demanded a retraction or if the defendant has independently retracted the statement.

10. Is there a privilege for quoting or reporting on:

a. Papers filed in court?

Coverage of public proceedings of a court is conditionally privileged. In general, the media is entitled to report on all judicial proceedings. Therefore, German press law excludes any claims arising from the coverage of judicial proceedings, as long as the coverage truthfully reports on the trial.

However, there are some restrictions of importance. First, the privilege normally extends only to the publicly available documents of the court. Accordingly, Section 353d No. 3 of the German Criminal Code prohibits literal quotations from indictments or other parts of an investigation *before* the case is brought before a public hearing. The provision does not, however, prohibit publishing of a rough summary of an indictment. In the event that a pretrial summary or contemporaneous report is published, the media must not infringe on the privacy of the persons involved in criminal cases. Thus, the accused or the witnesses may not be mentioned by name or identified by other details unless the case concerns serious crimes or other offenses that are of public interest.[29]

b. Government-issued documents?

Coverage of legislative or parliamentary debates is similarly privileged.[30] By contrast, republication of government-issued documents or proceedings and statements from government bodies are not privileged.

c. Quasi-governmental proceedings?

Basic reports on quasi-governmental proceedings are not privileged, but may satisfy the "public interest" privilege, but failure to verify facts contained therein that may be "obviously" incorrect, inaccurate description of legal terms, failure to provide for comment, and failure of other journalistic fundamentals may result in liability.

11. Is there a privilege for republishing statements made earlier by other, bona fide, reliable publications or wire services?

Yes. German law recognizes a privilege for republishing statements made earlier by other, bona fide, reliable publications or wire services, unless there is reasonable doubt about the reliability of the statement. In general, courts consider the press not to be obliged to conduct further research on a statement if the report comes from one of the established wire services.[31] However, further research is required if there is reasonable doubt that the statement is reliable. Other bona fide, reliable publications include information from public authorities like the public prosecutor or the police.[32] Such information can be relied upon unless there is reasonable doubt about the reliability.

12. Are there any restrictions regarding reporting on:

a. Ongoing criminal investigations?

Coverage of investigations and prosecutions may be permissible provided that there is a public interest in either the victim, the suspect, or the nature of the crime. Yet, the press must in any event observe the presumption of innocence, which is enshrined in the German constitution.[33] On the same principle, Section 353d No. 3 of the Criminal Code prohibits literal quotations from indictments for other parts of an investigation before the case is brought before a public hearing.

Names of the victims, witnesses, or other involved persons may only be mentioned in the case of serious crimes or in other cases that are of particular public interest.[34]

b. Ongoing criminal prosecutions?

The legal principles for reporting on ongoing criminal prosecutions are basically the same as for criminal investigations (see Question 12a above).

Again, the presumption of innocence is the central legal principle to be observed by the media. Reports that violate this principle can give rise to significant damage awards in favor of the accused person even if the accused is later convicted.

c. Ongoing regulatory investigations?

See the following section.

d. Ongoing civil litigation, or other judicial proceedings?

Reports on ongoing regulatory investigations, civil litigation, and other judicial proceedings are not subject to any particular restrictions but must still comply with the standards of general libel law.

13. Are prior restraints or other prepublication injunctions available on the basis of libel or privacy, and if so, what are the standards for obtaining such relief?

Prior restraints and other prepublication restraints on the basis of libel or privacy are available under German law. However, the standards for obtaining this sort of relief are high.

German law requires a plaintiff seeking a prepublication injunction to present substantial evidence that the defendant is likely to commit the alleged libel ("likelihood of commission").[35] Thus, the plaintiff must precisely describe the alleged libel to the court, demonstrating both its falsity and defamatory quality. In most cases, plaintiffs will not be able to adduce proof of the likelihood of commission, unless they somehow came into possession of the rough draft of the statement. The mere fact that a journalist has been doing research on an issue does not suffice to adduce such evidence.[36] If a journalist, however, expressly announces that he or she is going to publish the alleged libel, the required proof may be accepted by the court, and an injunction issued, provided the complaint meets the test laid out above.

14. Is a right of privacy recognized (either civilly or criminally)?

a. What is the definition of "private fact"?

German civil and criminal law recognize a right of privacy. It is part of the so-called general right of personality (*allgemeines Persoenlichkeitsrecht*). This all-embracing right of individuals to protection of their personality was first recognized by the Federal Supreme Court in 1954[37] and has since been further elaborated by the courts.[38] It is based in Articles 1 and 2 of the Basic Statute, which warrant the inviolability of human dignity and the right of individuals to free development of their personality. Article 13 of the Basic Statute guarantees the inviolability of the home as one specific aspect of the right of privacy. In addition, the right of privacy is protected by a wide range of statutory provisions, in civil as well as in criminal law, such as Sec. 22 of the *Kunsturheberrechtsgesetz* (KUG), which protects against the unauthorized publication of a person's image, or Sec. 201a of the StGB (German Criminal Code), which prohibits the infringements of a person's right to privacy by taking pictures of that person at home or any other secluded space.

The Federal Supreme Court held that the publication of photographs showing Princess Caroline of Monaco at a candlelight dinner in a secluded part of a restaurant infringed on her right of privacy. Even though a person did, in general, not have a reasonable expectation of privacy in a public place, the remoteness and familiarity of the place in question made it obvious to everyone that the princess wished to be left alone. The Court placed special emphasis on the fact that the pictures had been taken surreptitiously and by telephoto lens.[39] In contrast, the Courts deemed lawful the publication of pictures showing the princess in a Monaco beach club,[40] in a marketplace, or while riding a horse or a bike.[41] This finding, however, was recently challenged by the European Court of Human Rights.[42]

b. Is there a public interest or newsworthiness exception?

In general, German privacy law acknowledges three "spheres of privacy," each of which is protected to a different extent.

The *core private sphere* (*Intimsphaere*) enjoys the broadest legal protection. It must absolutely not be intruded into.[43] In particular, the core private sphere includes any information relating to the sexuality of a person.[44] Coverage of those issues is not permitted without the consent of the person concerned.[45] There is no public interest exception.

Issues that concern the *private sphere* (*Privatsphaere*) particularly include the domestic area[46] and family affairs[47] as well as a person's physical condition[48] or religious views.[49] Coverage intruding into a person's private sphere is generally prohibited,[50] but there is a public interest exception for reports on matters which are of general interest to the public and serve to shape the public opinion.[51]

The *public sphere* comprises those areas of life that by definition are open to everybody. A person enjoys least protection when acting in the public sphere.[52] Thus, a politician involved in a parliamentary debate or a lawyer who appears in a public trial cannot refer to privacy law in order to prevent coverage of his public behavior.

Newsworthiness, defined here as news that serves the public interest, may justify disclosure. Press reports about a person's marital life, including marital conflicts, adulterousness, and divorce, are usually deemed unlawful if not directly related to preeminent public interests that would justify a publication.[53] With regard to a case where Prince Ernst August of Hanover had sued a German tabloid for reports about his (then) adulterous relationship with Princess Caroline of Monaco, the Federal Supreme Court held that because the prince was an eminent representative of high nobility, because the reported facts were true, and because the foreign press had already reported about the incident, the publication was permissible.[54]

Finally, information about the relationship between parents and their underage children enjoys particular protection under German law and must, therefore, not be published except in cases where outstanding public interests exceptionally outweigh the children's interest in an undisturbed development of the child's personality.[55]

c. Is the right of privacy based in common law, statute, or constitution?

The German right of privacy is both statutory and constitutional. Its interpretation and application are left by the legislature to the courts, which has led to an ever-growing body of case law till this day.

15. May reporters tape-record their own telephone conversations for note-taking purposes (not rebroadcast) without the consent of the other party?

No. Under German law, tape-recording of a telephone conversation without the consent of the other party is generally prohibited. German privacy law grants all persons the right to decide on their own whether their words may be tape-recorded and by whom the tape may be played. Moreover, according to Sec. 201, subsec. 1 No. 1 of the German Criminal Code, tape-recording a telephone conversation without the consent of the other party is considered a criminal offense. The section applies regardless of the purpose of the tape-recording. Thus, it does not matter if it is for note-taking or other purposes.

16. If permissible to record such tapes, may they be broadcast without permission?

Section 201 of the German Criminal Code not only prohibits the tape-recording of a conversation but also the broadcasting or other uses of a tape that has been recorded without the consent of the other party.

17. Is there a recognized evidentiary privilege preventing the disclosure of confidential sources relied upon by reporters?

Under German law, plaintiffs cannot force the disclosure of any sources relied upon by reporters, nor can journalists be ordered by the court to disclose a confidential source. However, defendants, by refusing the disclosure of a source, may run the risk of losing their civil case if that confidential source is the basis by which a defamatory statement would otherwise be relied upon.

18. In the event that legal papers are served upon the newsroom (such as a civil complaint), are there any particular warnings about accepting service of which we should be aware?
There are no particular warnings about accepting service of legal papers. In general, a defendant is obliged to accept the service of a civil complaint. However, you should be aware that the acceptance of service of a legal paper often triggers a statutory time period within which a reply must be filed.

19. Has your jurisdiction applied established media law to Internet publishers?
The principles of German media law described above apply equally to Internet publications. Section 186 of the German Criminal Code declares punishable, in general terms, the publication of untrue facts, which are defamatory, about others. Likewise, the publication of private facts, if not justified by overweighing public interests, is deemed unlawful by Sec. 823 (1) of the German Civil Code in conjunction with Articles 1 and 2 of the Basic Statute. Publication means *any form* of passing on the information in question[56] by any means, including the Internet.[57] Thus, Internet publishers are, in general, equally as liable as press publishers or broadcasters for the publication of untrue, defamatory, or private facts.

20. If established media law has been applied to Internet publishers, are there any ways in which Internet publishers (including chat room operators) have to meet different standards?
According to German statutory law, different standards of liability apply for Internet service providers (ISPs) that offer their own content or adopt third parties' content as their own ("content providers") on the one hand, and ISPs that merely host or give access to third parties' content ("host providers" or "access providers") on the other hand.[58] Whereas content providers are fully responsible for the information published according to the general rules set out above, host and access providers are, in principle, only obliged to remove or disable access to the unlawful information in question.

The responsibility of ISPs in German law is governed by the Telemedia Act (*Telemediengesetz*—TMG). The TMG applies to all electronic information and communication services with the exception of telecommunication services within the meaning of the German Telecommunication Act (*Telekommunikationsgesetz*—TKG). This includes basically all kinds of online services apart from the mere carriage of electronic signals via telecommunication networks (like, for example, VoIP-services). The TMG provisions thus apply to all ISPs irrespective of whether they provide their own content or host or provide access to third-party content.

Content providers are fully responsible for the published information according to the general rules of civil and criminal law (Sec. 7 (1) TMG).

In contrast, host and/or access providers are liable only if they have initiated the transfer of the information in question or have positive knowledge of such information or the circumstances establishing its unlawfulness (Sec. 8 sqq. TMG). Providers that have been made aware of unlawful information are obligated to remove or disable access to this information without delay in order to enjoy further exemption from liability.

Finally, while there is no general obligation for host and/or access providers like, e.g., chat room operators, to monitor content under German law, it is well established in the case law that monitoring obligations arise once the provider has gained knowledge of an infringement. Such obligations include, for example, the use of appropriate filter mechanisms and other technical means in order to avoid a new infringement.[59]

21. Are there any cases where the courts enforced a judgment in libel from another jurisdiction against a publisher in your jurisdiction?

Although there are no reported cases, under German law, foreign judgments are generally enforceable if the decision has become final and binding and is recognizable according to the rules of German civil procedure.[60] Provided that these requirements are met, foreign judgments in libel cases can, in principle, be enforced on German territory.

Chapter Notes

1. Sec. 193 German Criminal Code.
2. *Bundesverfassungsgericht,* (2004) Archiv für Presserecht (AfP) 49.
3. Cf. *Oberlandesgericht Hamburg,* (1990) AfP 135.
4. Cf. *Landgericht Oldenburg,* (1995) AfP 679.
5. *Oberlandesgericht Köln,* (2001) AfP 332.
6. Cf. *Oberlandesgericht Hamburg,* Judgment of May 28, 2004 (unpublished).
7. *Bundesverfassungsgericht,* (2003) Neue Juristische Wochenschrift (NJW) 3760.

8. *Bundesgerichtshof,* (2000) NJW 3421.

9. *Bundesverfassungsgericht,* (2006) NJW 3769 sqq.

10. *Oberlandesgericht Karlsruhe,* (2002) Neue Juristische Wochenschrift—Recht-sprechungs-Report (NJW-RR) 695.

11. *Bundesverfassungsgericht,* (1994) NJW 2943; (1995) NJW 3303.

12. *Bundesgerichtshof,* (1980) NJW 2801, 2803; *Oberlandesgericht Köln,* (2000) NJW-RR 470.

13. *Bundesgerichtshof,* (1980) NJW 2801, 2803; (1994) AfP 295.

14. *Bundesgerichtshof,* (1975) NJW 1882, 1883; *Oberlandesgericht Stuttgart,* (1976) NJW 628.

15. Sec. 824 BGB (German Civil Code).

16. *Bundesgerichtshof,* (1966) NJW 1617.

17. *Bundesgerichtshof,* (1976) NJW 620.

18. *Bundesverfassungsgericht,* (2006) NJW 3769 sqq.

19. *Bundesgerichtshof,* (1987) NJW 2222; (1976) NJW 620.

20. *Bundesgerichtshof,* (1965) NJW 484.

21. *Bundesverfassungsgericht,* (2000) NJW 1859; (1971) NJW 1645; *Landgericht Berlin,* (1992) NJW-RR 1379.

22. *Landgericht Frankfurt,* (2007) NJW-RR 115, 116.

23. *Bundesverfassungsgericht,* (2006) NJW 3769 sqq.

24. *Bundesgerichtshof,* (1987) NJW 2225.

25. *Bundesgerichtshof,* (1966) NJW 1617.

26. *Bundesverfassungsgericht,* (1958) NJW 257.

27. *Bundesverfassungsgericht,* (2003) NJW 277, 278; (1983) AfP 215.

28. *Bundesgerichtshof,* (2002) NJW 1192.

29. *Oberlandesgericht Nürnberg,* (1996) NJW 530; *Oberlandesgericht Frankfurt,* (1980) 597.

30. See Sec. 5 (5) of the Berlin Press Act.

31. *Kammergericht, (2008)* NJW-RR 356; *Landgericht Hamburg,* (1990) AfP 332.

32. *Bundesgerichtshof,* (1971) NJW 698, 700; *Oberlandesgericht Hamburg,* (1977) AfP 35; *OLG Karlsruhe,* (1993) AfP 586.

33. *Bundesgerichtshof,* (2000) NJW 1036, 1037.

34. *Oberlandesgericht Frankfurt,* (1980) NJW 597; *Oberlandesgericht München,* (2003) NJW-RR 111.

35. *Oberlandesgericht Nürnberg,* (2002) NJW-RR 1471.

36. *Oberlandesgericht Hamburg,* (1992) AfP 279; (2000) AfP 188; *Landgericht Frankfurt* (1991) AfP 545.

37. *Bundesgerichtshof,* (1954) NJW 1404.

38. See *Bundesverfassungsgericht,* (1973) NJW 1221, 1223; (1984) NJW 419, 421.

39. *Bundesgerichtshof,* (1996) NJW 1128, 1130; confirmed by *Bundesverfassungsgericht,* (2000) NJW 1021 sqq.

40. *Oberlandesgericht Hamburg,* (1999) AfP 175, 176; confirmed by *Bundesverfassungsgericht,* (2000) NJW 2192.

41. *Bundesgerichtshof,* (1996) NJW 1128, 1130; confirmed by *Bundesverfassungsgericht,* (2000) NJW 1021 sqq.

42. *European Court of Human Rights,* (2004) NJW 2647; see also *Bundesgerichtshof,* (2007) NJW 1981 sq., repealed by *Bundesverfassungsgericht,* Judgment of February 26, 2008 – 1 BvR 1602/07 et al.

43. *Bundesgerichtshof,* (1981) NJW 1366; *Oberlandesgericht Hamburg* (1967) NJW 2314, 2316.

44. *Bundesgerichtshof,* BGHSt vol. 11, p. 67, 71.

45. Cf. *Oberlandesgericht Hamburg,* (1991) AfP 533.

46. *Bundesgerichtshof,* (2004) AfP 116.

47. *Oberlandesgericht Köln,* (1973) 479; *Landgericht Bielefeld,* (1975) NJW 54.

48. *Bundesgerichtshof,* (1996) NJW 984, 985.

49. *Oberlandesgericht München,* (1986) NJW 1260.

50. Cf. *Bundesverfassungsgericht,* (1997) NJW 2669, 2670; *Oberlandesgericht München,* (1993) AfP 762; *Oberlandesgericht Celle,* (1999) NJW-RR 1477.

51. *Bundesverfassungsgericht,* Judgment of February 26, 2008 – 1 BvR 1602/07 et al.

52. *Bundesgerichtshof,* (1995) AfP 404, 407.

53. Cf. *Bundesgerichtshof,* (1974) Gewerblicher Rechtsschutz und Urheberrecht (GRUR) 794; *Oberlandesgericht Hamburg,* (2000) Zeitschrift für Urheber- und Medienrecht—Rechtsprechungsdienst (ZUM-RD) 142.

54. *Bundesgerichtshof,* (1999) NJW 2893, 2894 sq.; confirmed by *Bundesverfassungsgericht,* (2000) NJW 2189.

55. Cf. *Bundesverfassungsgericht,* (2000) NJW 1021 sqq.

56. Cf. *Bundesgerichtshof,* (1996) NJW 1131, 1132.

57. Cf. *Landgericht Hamburg,* (1998) ZUM-RD 389, 390; but see *Landgericht Berlin,* (1998) NJW-RR 1634.

58. Cf. *Oberlandesgericht Köln,* (2002) NJW-RR 1700, 1701; *Oberlandesgericht München,* (2002) AfP 522, 523.

59. *Bundesgerichtshof,* (2008) NJW 758 sqq.—"eBay."

60. See Sec. 328, 722 sq. of the Code of Civil Procedure (ZPO). In 1992, the Federal Supreme Court held that U.S. judgments awarding a significant sum in punitive damages can, in general, not be recognized and enforced under German law (*Bundesgerichtshof,* (1992) NJW 3096).

CHAPTER **18**

Italy

IACOPO DESTRY
MARCO CONSONNI
Dewey LeBoeuf LLP

Dewey LeBoeuf LLP
Via Fratelli Gabba 4
Milan, 20121
Italy
Phone: +39 02 3030 9330
Fax: +39 02 3030 9340 FAX
mconsonni@dl.com

Introduction to Italian Media Law

Media-related statutes must be understood as reflecting a balance of constitutionally derived rights. In the Italian legal system, people have a constitutional right to reputation and privacy, which is balanced against the right to free expression. The rights of story subjects (called "publicity" rights) are intertwined and treated interchangeably. Although Section 21 of the Italian Constitution recognizes liberty of the press, peoples' rights of reputation, image, and honor have been deemed to have superior constitutional value.

The Structure of the Civil Court System

The main body of Italian laws governing the functioning of Italian Civil Courts is contained in the Code of Civil Procedure, which came into force in 1942.

There are two levels of courts with ordinary jurisdiction: the court of first instance and the court of appeal. Both can examine questions of fact and law. The Supreme Court (*Corte di Cassazione*) serves as a court of final appeal, which only examines questions of law. The judicial territory is divided into twenty-six districts having several courts of first instance and one Court of Appeal each. The Supreme Court is in Rome.

The civil courts with ordinary jurisdiction are:

Justice Court. This court can hear disputes where the claimed damages do not exceed 2,500 euros for personal property or 15,000 euros for personal injury claims arising out of motor or ship accidents.

Civil Tribunal. This court has general jurisdiction of first instance over civil claims other than those allocated to the Justice Court. It also hears appeals from the Justice Court. In larger cities, civil tribunals have specialized divisions (e.g., bankruptcy and intellectual property divisions). Cases are usually heard and decided by a single judge or by a panel of three judges in exceptional cases.

Court of Appeal. This court has appellate jurisdiction over decisions of civil tribunals but in some cases acts as a court of first instance (e.g., proceedings for the recognition of foreign judgments, enforcement of Italian Antitrust Law). A panel of three judges renders judgments.

Supreme Court. The Supreme Court is the court of final appeal. A panel of five judges renders its decisions. This court does not adjudicate the facts but only determines issues of law.

Constitutional Court. The Constitutional Court determines the constitutional legitimacy of laws and executive enactments, having the force of law adopted by Parliament and regions. Furthermore, the Court adjudicates conflicts of power within the State, between State and regions, and between regions.

Italian civil law provides a wide range of remedies; for example, interim relief such as injunctions and seizure orders (whenever it is necessary to take urgent measures to avoid the claimant's rights from being prejudiced). In libel cases, claimants may apply for such precautionary measures considering the harmful consequences that libelous conduct may have.

1. What is the locally accepted definition of libel?

Libel, under Italian law, is defined simply as an offense to an individual's reputation, which is in turn the opinion or esteem gained by individuals in the community where they live. The offense is based on statements about their character, talent, professional ability, physical characteristics, and/or other personal qualities. Publication to a third party is an element of any libel claim.

The Supreme Court of Cassation has found the following statements to be defamatory: to refer to a business person as "insolvent" or "unreliable"; publishing a magazine article about the president of the Italian Chamber of Deputies, with the headline "Young Ignorant"; announcing the imminent cessation of a business due to economic problems of the subject company; describing someone as having "the glance of an hired killer, and [. . .] with some flashes of sadism that promise disaster"; suggesting that a female television journalist on the Italian public television channel "advanced her career because of political connections and a close friendship with the President of the Republic."

Reporters should be aware that Italian law also provides a private right of action under criminal law: Article 596 of the Italian Criminal Code provides for imprisonment up to one year and fines up to 1,032.00 euros (such penalties may be doubled if the offense is based on allegations of defamatory fact). When the offending statement is distributed through mass media or any other means of publication, penalties may be more severe (imprisonment from six months up to one year and fines not less than 516.00 euros). Although the criminal proscriptions sound daunting, as a matter of fact, criminal proceedings are rare and claimants more often than not file civil actions pursuant to Articles 2043 (non-contractual damages) and 2059 (moral and reputation damages) of the Italian Civil Code (hereinafter Civil Code).

2. Is libel-by-implication recognized, or, in the alternative, must the complained-of words alone defame the claimant?

Yes, Italian law recognizes "allusive" libel. To determine whether a publication is libelous or not, the court will focus on the specific context in which the objectionable information is placed. When equivocal, insinuating, "allusive," or ambiguous statements and the improper combination of facts impair someone's reputation, the journalistic piece may be equally considered as falling within the scope of libel.[1]

Italian law will not harbor well a journalist's "lack of clarity," and in several decisions[2] has mentioned a number of "deceptive techniques" as examples of this defect:

a) The *clever implication*, consisting in the use of expressions with the awareness that the reading public will understand them either in a different way or even contrary to their literal meaning;
b) *Suggestive combinations* of facts that refer to persons to be cast in a bad light with other facts (that somehow negatively affect their reputation) regarding other, unrelated individuals;
c) A *disproportionately scandalized and indignant tone*;
d) *Out and out insinuations*, which are made when, even without openly stating facts or judgments, matters are related in such a way that the reader interprets them to the detriment of a specific individual's reputation.

Sloppy or careless editing of stories is a particular danger. Even though there may have been no intentional defamatory meaning on the reporter's part, if the statement at issue is capable of defamatory construction, claims may proceed. Because defenses to libel claims are often adjudicated on an objective basis (a measure of reasonable care) rather than a subjective basis (the reporter's state of mind), an innocent and unintended meaning does not raise a significant defense.

3. May a corporation sue for libel?

Yes. Corporations are legal entities[3] (*persone giuridiche*) and like many other entities, such as associations, foundations, charitable institutions, parties, and religious communities, are capable of holding a possessory interest in reputation and may seek redress.[4]

4. Is product disparagement recognized, and if so, how does that differ from libel?

Product disparagement is treated in Section 2598 c.c., n. 2, in the context of unfair competitive practices, where "news and appraisals of the products and activities of a competitor, capable to cause its or their disrepute" are disseminated, or the case where the competitor "appropriates the merits of a competitor's products or enterprise." Claims sounding in unfair competition are limited to competitors.

Italian law respects the right to publish consumer protection news and product reviews, but it is subject to a high duty of care. Italian courts have held that while publication of consumer-related testing reviews (*Warentest*) represents a manifestation of the right of criticism envisaged and protected by Section 21 of the Italian Constitution (in regard to the right of criticism, see point 6 hereunder); on the other hand, there is a limit beyond which the right of criticism interferes with the right to exercise economic activities, a right protected by Section 41 of the Italian Constitution. The publication of inaccurate product reviews falls outside the Section 21 protection because the inaccurate article is not helpful to consumers.[5] Reporting of or publishing comparison test results is considered legitimate only if and when it satisfies the demands for objectivity and accuracy. The Court of Rome has outlined clear limits to the reporting of consumer reporting:

> ". . . for publication of defamatory results of the Warentest in the press and on television to be considered a legitimate manifestation of the freedom of opinion and not involve civil liability, the following conditions must be satisfied: 1) the news must be socially useful; 2) the presentation must be formally correct; 3) the presented facts must be true (this requirement is considered satisfied when the journalist, after carefully verifying the competence of the experts and scientific seriousness of the analysis, presents the investigative methods and results in the body of the article)."[6]

5. Must an individual be clearly identified (by name or photograph) to sue for libel? Can a group of persons sue for libel, even though not named?

According to legal scholars and case law, it is necessary that the defamed person is identified or at least reasonably identifiable. Therefore, even if not specifically named, the defamatory statement must include direct or indirect elements as to unequivocally and immediately associate in the mind of the recipient a specific individual or group of persons. Note that Italian law allows *indirect* causes of action in libel.[7] For example, even though a statement might be directed at the directors and management of a specific corporation, the organization for which they work might be implicated. In one case, the inaccurately reproduced quotations of a famous political leader gave his party standing to bring an action in libel, complaining of a damaging distortion of its ideological position.[8]

Group libel is now almost unanimously recognized in Italy. Therefore associations, religious groups, parties, and in general any group of persons representing a collection of shared interests can bring suit against those uttering libelous statements and otherwise defaming such group. There are detailed limitations on damages in such instances, depending upon the nature of the claimant.[9] This will not obviously affect the individual's right to separately file an action in cases of autonomous claims arising from the conduct of the offender.

6. Please describe the fault standard(s) applied to libel, particularly:

As defamation represents an offense, a *prima facie* case is made simply on the presentation of evidence that the allegedly libelous statement was published with the intent to damage someone's reputation. However, under some circumstances, and in particular, when the expression is itself patently offensive, fault may be presumed.

(a) Does the fault standard depend on the fame or notoriety of the plaintiff?

No; however, the fame or notoriety of the plaintiff may inform the court's decision on the defense of public interest described below.

(b) Is there a heightened fault standard or privilege for reporting on matters of public concern or public interest?

The fault standard does not depend on whether the matter is of public concern or public interest.

There is, however a recognized privilege for public interest reporting of erroneous statements of fact, provided three strict criteria are met. In a leading case,[10] the Court of Cassation identified these criteria in order for a publication to be considered lawful, despite carrying a defamatory sting:

a) the social utility of the information;
b) its objective (or at least presumed) truth; and
c) a sober form in reporting the story.

If all three of these requirements are satisfied, a consolidated line of decisions[11] grant a privilege for publication and will not allow liability to attach, despite the fact that the article in question may be false and injurious to another person's reputation.

While it is certainly difficult to define, the general rule of social utility forces the judge to determine in any given case whether there is a genuine social interest in the people to be informed about the news item(s) under review. The plaintiff's status, role in society, and position of authority will inform the court as to the social utility. This should not be read as a "public figure" defense: courts recognize that even the famous and infamous have a personality right that should be protected. Courts instead ask whether journalists are fulfilling their mission to inform the public about news it needs to protect itself, rather than mere gossip or prurient interest. For example, in a case adjudicating an article about a famous television broadcaster and her allegedly improper relationship with a politician, the Court held that "no social utility could be realized from informing the readers [. . .] and the public in general" of this "alleged intimate personal relationship."[12]

(c) What are the traditional defenses to a libel claim?

Provided that specific conditions are met, reporting news and expressing opinions about specific facts may be exempted from liability as it constitutes the exercise of the right to expression as set forth under Article 21 of the Italian Constitution. That right can be exercised without incurring liabilities in cases where *all* of the following three requisite elements are met:

1) The news reported is true (or at least not provably false) and the source of such news is reliable; in any event, it is important that the news was published subject further to an accurate and appropriate check. For example, just relying on information released by press agencies could not suffice to this end. It should be noted that there is no "substantial truth" defense in Italy; the article must be correct in all statements of fact. The line of decisions equates false news to "half truths" or incomplete truths. The publication of a story that is objectively true in itself but accompanied by silence regarding other facts that are so closely related to the reported news as to distort its content "is [ruled] more dangerous than the exposition of individual falsehoods [. . .] on account of the greater ease with which

reporting or hearing a report of a patently false fact, rather than a true but incomplete fact, may be defended."[13]

2) The facts alleged must be weighed for their social importance and relevancy to serving the public interest. Some events are of public interest when they have such impact or have a certain interest for the community that they can influence public opinion. There is no blanket public interest in facts regarding private life. However, where personal information may be relevant to public issues or opinion, the journalist is allowed to report these otherwise private facts.
3) The news should be presented in an impartial and unbiased manner, and should not be aimed at denigrating or impugning someone's reputation based on the language used or the opinion expressed. This last requirement, which is also referred to as the criteria of moderation, is specified in a series of hypothetical cases considered by the court decisions in question. In particular, the press is expected to use moderated and cautious language not considered rude or discourteous or disrespectful. Articles may be considered libelous when the vitriolic language:
   i) "exceeds the proposed aim of providing information,"
   ii) "is not calm and objective,"
   iii) "tramples that minimum amount of dignity to which all individuals have a right," or
   iv) "is not characterized by sincere clarity." An important decision by the Italian Supreme Court contains the "journalists handbook" (Cass. Civ., October 18, 1984 n. 5259), which bans some forms of expressions such as a) clever implications, b) suggestive combinations, c) disproportionately scandalized and offended tones, d) outright insinuations, or e) omissions.[14]

Italian law also recognizes a *de facto* "good faith" defense, provided that an article (even if inaccurate) serves the social utility and is soberly expressed. The essential rules of conduct in the reporting of news are the subjective standards of prudence and skill. A journalist publishing an error will be released from liability *only* if he proves that he acted with a high degree of diligence, described by one court as the "fruit of serious and documented research."[15]

7. Is financial news about publicly traded companies, or companies involved with government contracts considered a matter of public interest or otherwise privileged?

Financial news regarding publicly traded companies or companies involved with government contracts would most likely be considered as information of public interest.

However, further to the implementation by Legislative Decree 62/2005 of the Directive 2003/6/EC on insider dealing and market manipulation (the "market abuse directive"), the Italian Journalists Association adopted the Charter on Economical Information Duties (*Carta dei Doveri dell'Informazione Economica*). The Charter was approved by the CONSOB (the public authority responsible for regulating the Italian securities market), and it sets forth rules with which Italian journalists are expected to comply. [16]

8. Is there a recognized protection for opinion of "fair comment" on matters of public concern?

Expression of "fair comment" is allowed under Article 21 of the Italian Constitution; provided that specific requirements set forth in Question 6 are met. Whenever it is possible to provide evidence that certain news was characterized as of public interest and correctly presented, the journalist could most likely invoke a defense grounded on the Constitution. It is worth stressing that in specific subject matters such as politics, more aggressive language would be acceptable, and consequently judges may be reluctant to find liability under this circumstance.

9. Are there any requirements upon a plaintiff such as a demand for retraction or right of reply, and if so, what impact do they have?

Yes. Italian law recognizes a right-of-reply. The Italian legal system holds that individuals whose image has been published or who have been subjected to statements they consider harmful to their dignity or contrary to the truth have the right to ask the directors of newspapers, periodicals, or press agencies to publish their replies free of charge. It has been held that the function of the correction is not to reestablish the objective truth of the published news report but rather ensure publication of the subject's point of view and publicize a possible different interpretation of the facts in the interest of pluralism in the news media.[17] Italian law allows parties who have made a written demand for a right of reply to seek judicial intervention and an order requiring the publication to publish the reply.[18]

The provisions regarding the right to publish a reply by the offended party are quite detailed as to the terms for publication (within two days from receipt) and the modalities of its presentation (number of words, position on the page, etc.).

The publication of the claimant's reply will not prevent a claim for compensation of damages and the publication of the final ruling on the libelous conduct of the journalist and the relevant media. Law No. 177 of July 31, 2005 sets forth similar provisions involving news or information published through radio and television.

10. Is there a privilege for quoting or reporting on:

(a) Papers filed in court?

Italian law does not recognize "privileged" documents. The Supreme Court of Cassation was forced to wrestle with this issue, and said that no documents, by themselves could "release the journalist from his duty of: a) examining, controlling, and verifying the facts he relates [. . .]; b) proving the care that he exercised in verifying the facts to remove all doubts [. . .] as to the truth.[19] However, accurate and fair reports of judicial proceedings may satisfy the "prudence and skill" elements required in a "good faith" defense.

When basing articles on court documents, journalists will be expected to present the information in such a way as to not side with any of the parties and not to change, modify, or incorrectly report the contents of such papers. Furthermore the information must be complete and neutral and objectively report the positions of the involved parties.

Italian law gives special treatment to the naming and depiction of minors involved in the justice process. The Constitutional Court first recognized the notion of "the minor's interest not to be publicized" as a strong value in contrast with legitimate publication: "the reporter's activity must respect personality and, therefore, there can be no dispute that the protection of minors assumes a special set of norms regarding formation of the personality."[20]

(b) Government-issued documents?

No specific privilege is provided under Italian law; such documents are usually and clearly characterized by a certain level of trustworthiness but this will not exempt the journalist from carrying out the necessary checks as to the sources of the news and the content of the information and making best efforts to present a sober and balanced story.

(c) Quasi-governmental proceedings, such as those by professional associations (for example disciplinary proceedings)?

Quasi-governmental proceedings, such as those regarding professionals, are usually characterized as having public impact. The same caveats regarding the reporter's due diligence apply.

11. Is there a privilege for republishing statements made earlier by other, bona fide reliable publications or wire services?

No. Relying solely on previously published statements and information will not exempt the journalist from liability if the reporter fails to attempt a thorough examination of the accuracy of the reported facts.

12. Are there any restrictions regarding:

(a) Reporting on ongoing criminal investigations?

Articles 114 and 329 of the Italian Code of Criminal Procedure provide that some documents cannot be published (*atti coperti da segreto*) if they relate to the investigative phase or in the alternative are specifically identified as secret or confidential by the magistrate (investigating judge). Breach of such provision might amount to criminal sanctions for the journalist under Article 684 of the Italian Criminal Code (with possible imprisonment up to thirty days and fines ranging between 51.00 and 258.00 euros).

Article 114 also forbids the publication without consent of the image of a defendant deprived of personal freedom (for example, if handcuffed or subject to other means of restraint).

(b) Reporting on ongoing criminal prosecutions?

Journalists are allowed to report on a criminal case and to quote those documents not covered by secrecy. It is worth stressing that as of this writing, the Italian legal system is undergoing changes as to the use of tape-recording of telephone conversations and of documents and information related to criminal prosecutions.

(c) Reporting on ongoing regulatory investigations?

Considering that no specific rule is provided regarding regulatory investigations, it is possible to consider that such information would be available for publication where public interest is identified.

(d) Reporting on ongoing civil litigation or other judicial proceedings?

Actually with respect to civil proceedings, because they are usually characterized as a private matter, it is not possible to quote or report on the content of the relevant papers or circumstances unless there is a public interest that would justify their publication or unless the parties authorized publication.

13. Are prior restraints or other prepublication injunctions available on the basis of libel or privacy, and if so, what are the standards for obtaining such relief ?

Yes. Under Italian law, prepublication remedies are available. Aside from prior restraints, Article 321 of the Italian Criminal Code also allows for the seizure of allegedly defamatory or invasive publications. Nevertheless, it is very difficult get a seizure order unless the intended publication to be used is considered indecent and offensive to public morality. As a consequence, such remedy is rarely sought or granted.

14. Is a right to privacy recognized (either civilly or criminally), and if so:

(a) What is the definition of "private fact"?

Private facts are not expressly defined under Italian law; but it can be considered as the result of several provisions. Legal scholarship and case law have therefore elaborated on examples of private facts, which on the whole can be defined as the right to keep private all aspects of a person's intimacy, including personal and family information.

(b) Is there a public interest or newsworthiness exception?

There is a codified newsworthiness exception: pursuant to Sections 136 and 137 of the Privacy Code, it is not necessary to obtain the express consent of the interested party for the treatment of personal data "when it is performed in the course of exercising the journalistic profession and exclusively for the purpose of pursuing relative aims."

In addition, although the information may fall within Data Protection principles, under Articles 136 and 137 of the Privacy Code journalists are not required to provide the data subjects (those subjects referred to in the piece) with an information statement and to obtain their consent for the processing of their personal data.

Information on "private facts" regarding celebrities, politicians, and opinion-makers is more easily considered as being of public interest. Nevertheless, this is an evaluation to be carried out on a case-by-case basis.

(c) Is the right of privacy based on common law, statute, or constitution? Is there a public interest or newsworthiness exception?

The right to privacy is codified in Section 2 of the Italian Constitution, which acknowledges to all citizens equal social dignity and a right to protect privacy and a right to honor, reputation, personality, and personal image.

15. May reporters tape-record their own telephone conversations for note-taking purposes (not rebroadcast) without the consent of the other party?

At the present time, Italy allows telephone recording with the consent of only one party. Such recording is deemed to have a documental nature and the fact that it occurs without one of the parties being informed of it does not represent an offense to the other party's freedom of self-determination.[21]

16. If permissible to record such tapes, may they be broadcast without permission?

At the time of this writing, the law is in a state of change. In June of 2008, the Italian government approved a bill providing for severe criminal sanctions (including imprisonment and fines up to 400,000 euros against the publisher) in case of unauthorized publication of phone interceptions and information related to the proceedings. The Italian Parliament must now approve such proposals, and they are very controversial.

17. Is there a recognized evidentiary privilege preventing the disclosure of confidential sources relied upon by reporters?

Yes, there is a qualified privilege. According to Article 2 of Law No. 69 of 1963 regarding professional journalists, reporters are not obligated to disclose the source of their information when the source provided the information on a confidential basis. Nevertheless, Article 200 of the Italian Code of Criminal Procedure states that if the source of information is necessary in order to reach a decision as to the commission of a crime, the investigating magistrate may order the journalist to disclose the source.

18. In the event that legal papers are served upon the newsroom (such as a civil complaint), are there any particular warnings about accepting service of which publishers should be aware?

According to Article 139 of the Italian Code of Civil Procedure, legal papers can also be served at the defendant's workplace. In the absence of the named defendant, it is not mandatory for the employer to accept them; nevertheless the choice to accept service depends on the specific circumstances. When legal papers are served upon the editorial office or the individual journalist, it is advisable to immediately contact a lawyer, as usually the time for appearance in response to the service of summons is quite short.

19. Has your jurisdiction applied the above law to Internet publishers?

In relation to libel published through the Internet, the Corte di Cassazione[22] stated that despite the lack of specific legislation, online libel may be punished according to the Italian criminal system. The communication between the actor and third parties fulfills the conduct requested for the perpetration of the crimes envisaged by Section 595. The crime is completed when the readers perceive the libelous expressions. Therefore, such action may as well offend someone's reputation when libelous news is published online. Publication or accessibility in Italy most likely satisfies jurisdictional requirements.

Furthermore, the Supreme Court added that online cases may be considered as potentially more damaging or offensive than paper media, because of the wider potential distribution *erga omnes* (meaning to the address of everybody—even if, in this case, only among people with the technical means to receive it).

20. If so, are there any ways in which Internet publishers (including chat room operators) have to meet different standards?
Italian law does not envisage a higher fault standard for Internet publishers regarding the event of online libel, and Italian Press Law does not address Internet publication.

21. Are there any cases where the courts enforced a judgment in libel from another jurisdiction against a publisher in your jurisdiction?
To be enforced in the Italian legal system, a foreign judgment needs to be previously recognized through a short proceeding to verify that it has all of the requirements that an Italian decision must have, which briefly are

- the punishment must not violate constitutional principles of the Italian legal system;
- the parties' right to defense has been respected; all of them had the chance to join the proceeding and to defend their arguments;
- the sentence is finally binding; and
- there is no conflict with any Italian sentence nor with pending proceedings before Italian courts.

Therefore, it is possible to enforce in Italy a foreign conviction decision for libel, both in consideration of its criminal and civil effects. However, we are not aware of any case of foreign conviction of publishers being enforced in Italy.

Chapter Notes

1. Cassation, Criminal Section, June 8, 1992, in Cassazione Pen., 1994, p. 592, 1, and in Giur. it., 1993, II, p. 518; on the same point, see also Tribunale Roma, November 24, 1992, in Dir. inf., 1993, p. 403.

2. The leading case is Cassation, October 18, 1984, n. 5259, in NGCC, pp. 84 and 214, with notes by G. Alpa and E. Roppo.

3. Tribunale Roma, June 7, 1991, in Dir. inf., 1992, 72, with note by Zeno-Zencovich.

4. Cassation, March 3, 2000, n. 2367, in Danno e resp., 2000, p. 490, with a note by Carbone, Il pregiudizio all'immagine e alla credibilità di una S.P.A. costituisce danno non patrimoniale e non danno morale.

5. Tribunale Milano, September 28, 1972, in Giur. it., 1973, I, 2, 1; Tribunale Roma, July 23, 1984, in Foro it., 1984, I, 1963; Cassation, United Sections, May 22, 1991, n. 5787, in Foro it., 1992, I, 2204, with a note by Di Via.

6. Tribunale Roma, June 18, 1997, in Dir. inf., 1998, 282, with note by G. Resta.

7. Pretura Roma [Rome Magistrate's Court], May 7, 1974, in Giur. it., 1974, I, 3227; Cassation, Criminal Section, April 27, 1998, in NGCC, 1999, I, 793, with note by Ar. Fusaro, Diffamazione dell'ente mediante offesa rivolta ad un suo componente. La lesione dell'onore della Corte dei Conti.

8. Pretura Roma, May 11, 1981, in Giust. civ., 1982, I, 817.

9. Cassation, Criminal Section, January 16, 1986, in Dir. inf., 1986, 458, with note by S. Lariccia and V. Zeno-Zencovich, Il diritto all'onore delle confessioni religiose e dei loro fedeli.

10. Cassation, October 18, 1984, No. 5259, ibid.

11. Among the most significant ones, Cassation, Criminal Section, October 15, 1987, in Riv. pen., 1989, 428; Cassation, Criminal Section, April 27, 1992, in Giur. it., 1993, II, 688; Cassation, July 25, 2000, n. 9746, in Danno e resp., 2001, 146, with note by Maccaboni.

12. Tribunale Roma, November 24, 1992, in Dir. inf., 1993, 403.

13. Cassation, October 18, 1984, n. 5259, ibid.

14. Ibid.

15. Cassation, February 14, 1984, n. 1138, in Mass., 1984.

16. In particular, the Charter provides for specific duties when reporting news regarding financial markets. To illustrate, journalists are required to correctly report, that is without alterations or omissions, all relevant information and/or to avoid any personal bias in the presentation of specific financial news.

17. Pretura Roma, April 29, 1991, in Dir. inf., 1991, 889.

18. Section 700, Code of Civil Procedure. See also, Section 8 of the Press Act, as amended by Section 42 of Law No. 416 of 1981. Failure to comply with a properly executed demand for right of right may amount to the imposition of administrative sanctions ranging between 1,549 and 2,582.00 euros.

19. Cassation, Criminal United Sections, June 30, 1984, in Foro it., 1984, II, 531. Following such decisions are the subsequent Cassation, Criminal Section, April 17, 1985, in Cassation pen., 1985, 1078; Cassation, Criminal Section, February 13, 1992, in Cassation pen., 1993, 2266.

20. Constitutional Court, February 10, 1981, n. 16, in Foro it., 1981, I, 601.

21. Cassation, April 8, 1994, in Riv. pen., 1994, 856.

22. Cassation, Criminal Section, November 17, 2000, in Dir. inf., 2001, 21.

CHAPTER 19

Netherlands

JENS P. VAN DEN BRINK
Kennedy Van der Laan

Kennedy Van der Laan
Haarlemmerweg 333
1051 LH Amsterdam, Netherlands
Phone: 00-31-20-550 68 43
Fax: 00-31-20-550 69 43
www.kvdl.nl
jens.van.den.brink@kvdl.nl

Introduction to the Dutch Legal System

The Dutch legal system has evolved from being almost identical to the French civil law system to one that incorporates several aspects of a number of different legal systems in Europe. Guided by traditional civil law principles, the Dutch system is divided into three main branches: the civil branch, the administrative branch, and the criminal branch. The court of first instance in all three branches is called the *rechtbank* (the district court). The administrative system has a number of sector-specific supreme courts, organized by subject, that hear appeals and select cases.

The civil system has a sub-district court, the so-called *sector kanton,* which has recently been made a separate department of the *rechtbank.* The *sector kanton* hears cases of lesser importance as well as real estate and labor cases. The civil and criminal branches have a court of appeals and the *Hoge Raad* (or Supreme Council), which is the Supreme Court. Appeals from both the sub-district courts and the district court are heard in the appeals court. The Supreme Court, comprised of a president, seven vice presidents, and thirty-one justices, ensures that law is being properly applied. Dutch courts do not have the authority to test an Act of Parliament or an international treaty against the Dutch Constitution. Dutch courts do test Acts of Parliament against international treaties.

Introduction to Netherlands Media Law

The Netherlands is a member of the European Convention on Human Rights (the Convention); thus, this section contains regular citations of case law of the European Court of Human Rights (ECHR). Article 94 of the Dutch Constitution contains the general principle that clauses with direct effect in international treaties override national law. Whereas the freedom of speech as laid down in Section 10 of the Convention has direct effect on press rights, Dutch courts directly apply the relevant ECHR case law in their judgments.

Conflicts relating to press publications may also be brought before the Council for Journalism, which is a self-regulatory entity. Its decisions are not binding and it cannot apply any sanctions. The Council will give its opinion on whether a journalist has operated carefully and whether a publication has exceeded the boundaries of what is acceptable in society, taking into account journalistic responsibility.

1. What is the locally accepted definition of libel?

As a criminal matter, article 261 of the Dutch penal code defines common libel as the "intentional damaging of a person's honor or good name by accusing that person of something, while aiming to make this fact public."

Slander is defined as a libel committed with the knowledge that the accusations are untrue (Article 262 of the Criminal Code). Offending a person by exposing him to rash accusations and thereby harming that person's reputation may also constitute a tort under Article 6:162 of the Dutch Civil Code.

Any limitation of freedom of speech should meet the test of Article 10 of the Convention. In short, the limitation should be (a) prescribed by law, (b) serve one or more defined legitimate aims,[1] and (c) be necessary in a democratic society. The role of the press as public watchdog will be taken into account; the press fulfills an essential function in a democratic society. The freedom of speech also entails the right to use speech that offends, shocks, or disturbs,[2] and journalistic freedom also covers possible recourse to a degree of exaggeration, or even provocation.[3] ECHR case law provides that the press even has a *duty* to impart information and ideas on all matters of public interest.[4]

If statements are unlawful or punishable by criminal law (and therefore prescribed by law), it should still be determined under Article 10 of the Convention whether the limitation of the freedom of speech serves one of the defined aims and is necessary in a democratic society. The latter will be determined by weighing the freedom of speech against the personal (or dignitary) rights of the person implicated (often the right of privacy). This is a case-by-case analysis; there is no order of priority between these rights.

The following statements have been found to be defamatory under Dutch criminal law: The accusation "that G.R. mistreats and/or threatens women on the streets" was found to be libelous (Supreme Court, November 6, 2001). By contrast, the implicit allegation that "H. may be seduced by a bag of candy" was not found to be libelous (Supreme Court, October 24, 1989).

The following statements have been found to convey defamatory meaning under Dutch civil law: a medical watchdog group calling a physician a "quack doctor";[5] accusing the president of a Dutch football club of being a "dictator who lies and cheats";[6] and accusing a Dutch TV presenter of being a "program thief."[7] The following statements have been held lawful under Dutch civil law: "mala fide trade-practices mislead agrarian entrepreneurs,"[8] "reprobate swindler," "professional liar,"[9] "trophy wife," and "gold digger."[10]

2. Is libel-by-implication recognized, or, in the alternative, must the complained-of words alone defame the plaintiff?

Yes, libel may occur by implication only.

3. May corporations sue for libel?

Yes, a legal entity can sue for libel. This has recently been confirmed by the ECHR.[11] Libel toward a company may also create criminal liability.[12]

4. Is product disparagement recognized, and if so, how does that differ from libel?

Yes, product disparagement may constitute a tort, e.g., if the reputation of the producer of that product is harmed. For example, a product may be libeled in a publication through the use of demeaning language that implies wrongdoing on the part of the producer. The abovementioned guidelines on libel apply.

If it concerns advertising that directly or indirectly mentions the product or name of a competitor, the rules on comparative advertising apply (Section 6:194a of the Dutch Civil Code). Comparative advertising is allowed if the statutory conditions are met (article 194a Civil Code, which is an implementation of European Directive 97/55/EC). This also comprises the rule that the reputation of the competitor may not be harmed and no denigrating language may be used.

5. Must an individual be clearly identified (by name or photograph) to sue for libel? Can a group of persons sue for libel, even though not named?

Even if a publication does not clearly identify an individual by name or photograph, that individual may sue for libel if that person can be identified by other means.[13] A group of persons that is not named may also sue for libel. For example, the Anne Frank Foundation has successfully acted against Holocaust revisionist publications.[14]

6. What is the fault standard(s) applied to libel?

a. Does the fault standard depend on the fame or notoriety of the plaintiff?

Yes, Dutch law holds that public figures should in general tolerate more harsh speech than nonpublic figures, especially public figures who actively seek out publicity for their own private life. Further, if a (public or nonpublic) person is accused of wrongdoings and actively seeks publicity, thereby wrongfully creating the impression that he or she has been cleared from all accusations, that may justify renewed attention for the original allegations.[15]

The limits of acceptable criticism are especially broader when it concerns politicians and when the debate is in the general interest.[16] With respect to public figures who do not exercise public functions, the "public figure" defense has recently been curtailed by the ECHR.[17]

b. Is there a heightened fault standard or privilege for reporting on matters of public concern or public interest?

Yes, the more an issue reflects on the public interest, the more freedom the press has to examine and disclose such problems.

Dutch law uses a balancing test to determine liability for potentially defamatory speech. Under tort law, it should always be assessed which interest prevails: the interest of an individual not to be confronted with rash accusations in the press weighed against the public interest involved in the exposure of wrongs in society to the general public. This balancing of interests has been given shape in Supreme Court case law,[18] which determines that journalists should take the following elements into account:

1. The nature of the accusations and the seriousness of the expected consequences for the person to whom the accusations relate;
2. The seriousness—as seen from the general interest—of the abuse that the publication tries to expose;
3. The extent to which the accusations were supported by factual material available at the time of the publication;
4. The way the accusations have been formulated;
5. The probability that the general interest that the publication strived for could have been achieved in a different, less damaging, manner;

6. The probability that the statements or accusations have been published anyway.

Similar considerations regarding the general interest will play a role under criminal law. Article 261(3) of the Criminal Code provides a ground of justification for libelous statements if the perpetrator assumed in good faith that the charged fact was true, provided that the accusation was in the general interest.

7. Is financial news about publicly traded companies, or companies involved with a government contract, considered a matter of public interest or otherwise privileged?

Yes, financial news about publicly traded companies, or companies involved with government contracts, may be considered a matter of public interest. Nevertheless, the press must not overstep certain bounds, in particular with respect to the reputation and rights of others and the need to prevent the disclosure of confidential information.[19] In each case, the balancing of interests should take place. The making public of confidential corporate documents that have been obtained through a criminal act is criminally punishable (Article 273 of the Criminal Code).

8. Is there a recognized protection for opinion or "fair comment" on matters of public concern?

According to established case law, a distinction should be made between opinions or value judgments on the one hand and statements of fact on the other. The former provide much more leniency to journalists than the latter. Whereas the existence of facts can be demonstrated, the truth of value judgments is not susceptible to proof.

Further, it is generally accepted in Dutch and ECHR case law that opinion columns have a more lenient fault standard than normal publications. A column—which inherently contains opinions—justifies stronger wordings, the blowing up of a topic, and a simplifying approach. The Dutch Supreme Court recently confirmed that this heightened protection applies to opinion-forming publications in general, and not just to columns.[20]

In the recent case of *Vereinigung Bildender Kunstler v. Austria,*[21] the ECHR set a new standard for caricatures and satire. During a 1998 art exhibition in Vienna, Austria, the painting "Apocalypse" by Otto Mühl was shown. The painting shows a collage of various public figures, such as Mother Theresa, the Austrian Cardinal Hermann Groer, the former head of the Austrian Freedom Party (FPÖ), Mr. Jörg Haider, and Mr. Meischberger, a former general secretary of the FPÖ, depicted performing various sexual acts. The ECHR ruled that Austria had breached the freedom of expression by granting Mr. Meischberger an injunction. The court stressed: "It was common ground . . . that the painting obviously did not aim to reflect or even to suggest reality. The court finds that such portrayal amounted to a caricature of the persons concerned using satirical elements. It notes that satire is a form of artistic expression and social commentary and, by its inherent features of exaggeration and distortion of reality, naturally aims to provoke and agitate. Accordingly, any interference with an artist's right to such expression must be examined with particular care." The court considered that the painting could hardly be understood to address details of Mr. Meischberger's private life, but rather related to Mr. Meischberger's public standing as a politician, while in this capacity Mr. Meischberger had to display a wider tolerance in respect of criticism. The court did not find unreasonable the view that the scene in which Mr. Meischberger was portrayed could be understood to constitute some sort of counter-attack against the FPÖ, whose members had strongly criticized the painter's work.

9. Are there any requirements upon a plaintiff, such as demand for retraction or right of reply, and if so, what impact do they have?

There is no general requirement for the plaintiff to demand some form of retraction or a right of reply before starting defamation proceedings. However, in some cases damages may be neutralized or limited by a fair and timely correction or retraction. If the plaintiff refuses a right of reply that is offered, this might be used against him or her by the court.

Dutch law does not contain a general obligation to provide the person involved with a right of reply or a right of inspection, either prior to or post publication.[22] However, serious allegations may not be expressed rashly and must be founded on the then-available facts. The more serious the allegation, the more stringently the publication should be researched. In some cases, especially when serious accusations are made, therefore, journalists may indeed be obliged to provide the person involved with a right to reply prior to publication.[23] If it can be shown that obtaining a reply or comment has been attempted but failed, this may suffice.[24] However, if it concerns serious allegations, the reporter may need to prove that he or she not only attempted to contact the person involved, but that he or she also left a message indicating the seriousness and (general) content of the allegations.[25] If the plaintiff was contacted, but refused to provide commentary, this may lead the court to conclude that the press has fulfilled its duty to investigate. Please note that if a reply is published, this does not necessarily make the publication lawful.

10. Is there a privilege for quoting or reporting on:

a. Papers filed in court?

There is no statutory privilege for papers filed in court; however, there is a common law privilege as courts have held that if it encompasses statements regarding matters of public concern from a bona fide third party source (and that would include government sources), no further research is required.[26]

Statements that are included in procedural documents of a criminal case may relieve journalists of their duty to investigate the factual basis of those statements, even if the person who made the statements withdrew them at a later stage.[27]

In the case of *Scientology v. XS4all,* a reporter published the so-called Fishman affidavit on her personal website. This affidavit was filed in a court case in the United States involving the Church of Scientology and contains parts of the written teachings of the church that Scientology claims are protected by copyright. The court of appeal of The Hague confirmed that in this case, the information freedom laid down in Article 10 of the Convention overruled the copyright of the Church of Scientology in the Scientology texts cited in the affidavit.[28] This confirms that in exceptional cases, the freedom of information may overrule copyright.

b. Government-issued documents?

There is no specific privilege for government-issued documents. As a general rule, under Dutch law, information concerning administrative matters originating from the government should in principle be available to the public. Any citizen (including journalists) may request copies of such documents on the basis of the Code Publicity Public Administration (*Wet Openbaarheid Bestuur* or WOB).

c. Quasi-governmental proceedings?

There is no specific privilege.

11. Is there a privilege for republishing statements made earlier by other, bona fide, reliable publications or wire services?

Although there is no codified republication privilege, under Dutch law statements pertaining to matters of public concern derived from bona fide third parties do not require further investigation on the reporter's part.[29]

If accusations are based on previous publications, while plaintiffs chose not to act against those previously published allegations (even if worded differently), the court may find that the accusations as published in the later publication are sufficiently substantiated by the earlier publications and thus lawful. Defendants may also use earlier publications in their own media as part of the evidence used to substantiate those same allegations repeated in a later publication and challenged by a plaintiff.[30] Passive plaintiffs who did not take action against similar accusations published in the past may therefore have less chance to get their claims awarded.

However, in some cases, especially if the third-party source makes particularly harsh or accusatory statements, the republishing of these statements may require establishing distance with the third-party source, e.g., by explicitly stating that it concerns statements from a third-party source.

12. Are there any restrictions regarding reporting on:

a. Ongoing criminal investigations?

Generally, no. However, publishing (or even obtaining) government documents that should be kept classified in the interest of the State constitutes a criminal offense (Dutch Penal Code Articles 98–98c). Please note that in exceptional circumstances, those asserting the freedom of speech might prevail.

b. Ongoing criminal prosecutions?

No.

c. Ongoing regulatory investigations?

Articles 10 and 11 of the WOB define circumstances that provide for an exception to the duty of the public administration to supply information as laid down in the WOB. These exceptions include information the disclosure of which would endanger the safety of the State or criminal investigation and/or prosecution and/or the privacy of persons.

In the "King Kong" case,[31] a journalist requested a copy of government information, which the Dutch State regarded as classified. The court decided that, although the files concerned the Dutch secret service, and thus the safety of the State, this information did not contain information that would *per se* endanger the State when made public. Therefore, the documents had to be provided to the requesting journalist.

There are no special restrictions regarding reporting on ongoing regulatory investigations.

d. Ongoing civil litigation, or other judicial proceedings?

There are no special restrictions regarding reporting on ongoing civil litigation or other judicial proceedings and/or criminal prosecutions.

However, such reporting often implicates the privacy of persons involved in a criminal case. For that reason, in most cases, the names of the defendant and the convicted in a criminal case are only mentioned by using initials (this is customary, and not laid down in a statute). Please note that the full name may be provided under certain circumstances, e.g., to warn the public, if the person involved cooperated with the publication, or if the full name is already published by other media.[32]

13. Are prior restraints or other prepublication injunctions available on the basis of libel or privacy, and if so, what are the standards for obtaining such relief?
Article 7(2) of the Constitution provides that prior restraint is not allowed. However, in the case of repeated broadcasts or publication, or if the content is known to a sufficient extent prior to the broadcast or publication, it may be forbidden on the basis of libel or tort law.[33]

14. Is a right of privacy recognized (either civilly or criminally)?
Yes, the right of privacy has been recognized both in civil (Article 8 of the Convention, Article 10 of the Constitution, and the Act on the Protection of Personal Data) and in criminal law (Articles 138–139g of the Criminal Code). Further, the right of privacy has been indirectly laid down in the so-called portrait right clauses of the Dutch Copyright Act (Articles 19–21). If a portrait has not been made at the request of the person portrayed, that person may prevent the publication of the portrait if he has a reasonable interest that opposes such publication. This reasonable interest is usually privacy related.

a. What is the definition of "private fact"?
"Private fact" as such is not defined under defamation law nor in the fundamental right of privacy as laid down in the Dutch Constitution and the Convention. However, the Convention defines the right of privacy as follows: "Everyone has the right to respect for his private and family life, his home and his correspondence." Further, the Dutch Act on the Protection of Personal Data provides that personal data are any data concerning an identified or identifiable natural person.

b. Is there a public interest or newsworthiness exception?
There is no absolute, general public interest exception. When a publication is accused of infringing on the right of privacy, a balancing of interests will have to take place. If the infringement of privacy is necessary in the public interest, it might be a lawful infringement. Circumstances mentioned in case law that specifically relate to the balancing of interests in case of a privacy infringement comprise the following:

- the seriousness of the privacy infringement;

- the nature and extent of intimacy;
- the length of the period within which the infringement took place;
- the nature and importance of the published facts;
- the extent to which the published facts shed new light on what is already known;
- the persons involved;
- whether the person involved actively pursued public interest for his or her private life; and
- the position of the person involved; and
- the aim and the nature of the publicizing medium.

The following cases have been found to be unjustified intrusions upon privacy: the use by a welfare institution of a report on a woman who was on social security, which was the result of information provided by her neighbor (also director of a social security institution) who regularly "spied" on her;[34] publication of stories and photos by a gossip magazine about the children of a Dutch princess who the magazine had also followed around;[35] publication of a photograph of a woman engaged in a sexual act in public;[36] and the publication of pictures of the wife of the Dutch crown prince and their children, while sunbathing in bathing suits on a public beach.[37]

The following have been found to be justified publications of private facts: the publication of a photographic portrait of the killer of Gerrit-Jan Heijn (brother of the founder of the famous Dutch supermarkets Albert Heijn), due to the high newsworthiness of the portrait and the special quality of the picture (which won a prestigious photographic prize);[38] publication of a summary of gossip concerning the editor of a famous gossip magazine (allowed in part because of the manner in which the person exposed worked as a journalist himself);[39] and the publication of tax forms of the director of Peugeot (allowed because of the public interest and because the facts substantiated the accusations made against the executive).[40]

c. Is the right of privacy based in common law, statute, or constitution?

The right of privacy has been statutorily recognized both in civil law (Article 8 of the Convention, Article 10 of the Constitution, and the Act on the Protection of Personal Data) and in criminal law (Articles 138–139g of the Criminal Code).

15. May reporters tape-record their own telephone conversations for note-taking purposes (not rebroadcast) without the consent of the other party?

Yes, provided the reporter is a party to the conversation. This has been confirmed in civil law case law[41] and is laid down in articles 139a and b of the Dutch Criminal Code. However, reporters relying on such documents to defend their case may have to surrender such a recording during court proceedings. Even though Dutch law does not have a "discovery" principle as known under Anglo Saxon law, a party in a legal dispute may ask for submission of exhibits by the other party under article 843a of the Dutch Code of Legal Procedure. The foregoing means that in case an interview has been recorded, the one being interviewed may request a copy of the recording in order to assess whether the interview has been correctly reproduced. Depending on the circumstances, such an application may be granted.[42]

16. If permissible to record such tapes, may they be broadcast without permission?

This will depend on a balancing of the interest of: (a) the individual involved not to be confronted with rash accusations in the press; and (b) the public interest in exposing wrongs in society to the general public. Broadcasting such a conversation may, depending on the circumstances and content of the tape, be a wrongful act due to an infringement of the right of privacy.

In one case,[43] a journalist published the contents of an illegally recorded telephone conversation (to which he was not a party). The court found that the freedom of speech overruled the criminal provisions on illegal taping. Therefore, even the broadcasting of illegally recorded phone conversations might be allowed.

17. Is there a recognized evidentiary privilege preventing the disclosure of confidential sources relied upon by reporters?

Yes. Although Dutch law does not provide for a statutory right of nondisclosure for journalists, case law does. According to the Supreme Court, the protection of journalistic sources is one of the basic conditions for press freedom, to prevent sources from being deterred from assisting the press in informing the public on matters of public interest. Journalists may only be forced to reveal a confidential source if this would be justified by an overriding requirement in the public interest.[44] The reporter's privilege is not limited to preventing merely the disclosure of the name of the source, but pertains to all information that may lead to the source, directly or indirectly.[45]

Following the recent ECHR ruling in *Voskuil v. The Netherlands,*[46] in which The Netherlands was criticized for taking the reporter's privilege too lightly, a statutory basis for the reporter's privilege is being prepared, although it is still the subject of parliamentary discussion.

18. In the event that legal papers are served upon the newsroom (such as a civil complaint), are there any particular warnings about accepting service of which we should be aware?
No.

19. Has your jurisdiction applied established media law to Internet publishers?
The European E-Commerce Directive (2000/31/EC) contains limitations of liability for intermediaries providing mere conduit, caching, or hosting services. For example, an Internet service provider that merely hosts information is not liable for the information transmitted. However, liability does arise if the ISP, as soon as knowledge of apparent illegal activity or information is obtained, fails to act expeditiously to remove or disable access to that information.

This exception has been implemented in Article 6:196 (c) of the Dutch Civil Code and Article 54a of the Dutch Criminal Code. This rule is based in part on a landmark Dutch case (*Scientology v. XS4all,* http://www.spaink.net/cos/verd2eng.html), in which the same rule was found to apply in general to service providers that merely pass on information, without making a selection or adapting the information.[47] Please note that a publisher who acts in the more traditional sense and selects or adapts the content of its publications will normally be liable for the content it distributes.

Extensive case law with respect to Internet publications exists. In general, the same rules that apply offline also apply to online publications.

There have been several cases relating to various forms of hyperlinking. Generally, it could be said that a regular hyperlink is allowed and does not infringe the copyright of the owner of the content to which the link leads. Deeplinking is normally also allowed. As a general rule, inline and framed linking (whereby content actually remains on the server of the owner but is visually copied to the website containing the link) is not allowed.

In the *Deutsche Bahn* cases, a website of a left-wing group contained a manual for sabotaging the German railways. The Amsterdam court of appeal found that this publication constituted a tort and ordered the Dutch ISP of the website to shut it down.[48] However, mirror sites with the same content had already appeared. On its website, Indymedia provided a hyperlink to one of those mirror sites, which contained the same manual. Indymedia was summoned by the German Railways to remove the hyperlink. The court found that, by knowingly linking to material that a court had already deemed tortious, Indymedia committed a tort itself.[49] In arriving at this conclusion, the court also noted that the text that accompanied the hyperlink encouraged the visitors to use the link and visit the connected website (with wrongful content).

Recently, the Dutch Supreme Court published an important Internet defamation verdict, in the case of *Van Gasteren v. Hemelrijk,* which actually relates back to events taking place during the Second World War. On May 24, 1943, during the Nazi occupation of the Netherlands, Oettinger, a Jewish man in hiding in Amsterdam in the house of Mr. Van Gasteren, now a noted Dutch filmmaker, was murdered by his host. Van Gasteren later claimed to have been part of the Dutch resistance. He said the killing was necessary to prevent him and other members of the Dutch Resistance from being exposed by Oettinger. In 1990, the Dutch newspaper *Het Parool* published a story on the subject, casting doubt on Van Gasteren's explanation of the killing. Van Gasteren sued for libel. The Supreme Court found in favor of Van Gasteren finding that the news articles contained an implicit accusation that Van Gasteren had committed "a (common) robbery and murder."[50]

On November 2, 1999 Dutch reporter Pamela Hemelrijk published an "Open Letter to the Supreme Court" on her private website, which begins as follows:

> Dear Supreme Court,
>
> I am writing to you on a subject matter which, if I may believe the lawyers, I can never mention again. Well, I may do so but, according to these lawyers, I will immediately be sued for enormous damages, which case I am definitely going to lose. Why am I bound to lose this case? Because I am not allowed to drag up the past of movie maker Louis van Gasteren anymore. . . . Strangely enough, Louis himself can drag up his past as much as he likes . . .

In the letter Hemelrijk expressed her doubts about Van Gasteren's statement that he was a member of the Resistance and that killing Oettinger was a result thereof.

> I know better than to speculate about Van Gasteren's real motives to kill this person in hiding. It is an established fact, though, that this person in hiding owned a small fortune of money, which he carried with him day and night. . . . . Just like me, the Supreme Court is also aware that shortly after the murder witnesses have seen Louis with a large amount of money, which looked like it had been in the water. If I remember well, he was busy hanging the bank notes out to dry. But I am not going to speculate about Louis van Gasteren's real motives. I know better than that. Let the readers draw their own conclusions . . .

In 2001, Van Gasteren sued Hemelrijk, claiming that she acted unlawfully by repeating allegations which the Supreme Court had found libelous in the *Het Parool* judgment.

Under the circumstances (including the fact that Van Gasteren sought publicity for the subject himself), the Supreme Court found that the freedom of speech prevailed over Van Gasteren's right of privacy. An important question facing the Court was whether this "open letter" published online actually deserved the same protection awarded to "regular" offline press publications. After all, that would mean extending the special position of the press, which deserves extra protection because of its function as public watchdog, which deserves more leniency. The Supreme Court argued that partly because of the rise of the Internet, no exact definition of press can be given. Through the advent of the Internet, private persons can also easily address the public. With the open letter, Hemelrijk addressed a wide audience and expressed her doubts about the act of resistance claimed by Van Gasteren. Hemelrijk acted in the public interest, and the Supreme Court found that the Court of Appeal had rightfully put the private online letter on a par with a press publication.

20. If established media law has been applied to Internet publishers, are there any ways in which Internet publishers (including chat room operators) have to meet different standards?

As soon as an Internet publisher obtains knowledge of an apparent illegal activity or information, it must act expeditiously to remove or disable access to that information.

There is no general monitoring duty for Internet publishers that publish third-party content, either through chat rooms, blogs, or otherwise. The more monitoring activity the publisher undertakes, the bigger the chance that it will be held liable for third-party content whose distribution it facilitates.[51] On the other hand, a certain duty of care is expected. And even though there is no formal requirement to adopt a notice and takedown procedure, this will certainly aid in fighting liability for third party content.[52]

21. Are there any cases where the courts enforced a judgment in libel from another jurisdiction against a publisher in your jurisdiction?

Such case law has not yet been decided. Foreign judgments in libel cases have the same status as "normal" judgments. This means that a judgment given in a foreign jurisdiction is not enforceable in the Netherlands, unless such foreign country has entered into an agreement thereto with the Netherlands. Within Europe, the EEX Regulation[53] provides that judgments given in E.U. member states may relatively easily be executed in the Netherlands. Please note that no bilateral agreement exists between the United States and the Netherlands concerning the execution of U.S. judgments in the Netherlands.

In case of libel through a publication in several E.U. member states, the offended person may take the publisher to court in the jurisdiction where the publisher is incorporated, or in the jurisdictions where the publication was disseminated and where damage was done to that person's reputation.[54]

Chapter Notes

1. Article 10 (2) of the Convention defines the following interests: territorial integrity or public safety, for the prevention of disorder or crime, for the protection of health or morals, for the protection of the reputation or rights of others, for preventing the disclosure of information received in confidence, or for maintaining the authority and impartiality of the judiciary.

2. ECHR, April 26, 1979, NJ 1980/146 (*Sunday Times*).

3. ECHR, April 26, 1995, Series A no. 313 (*Oberschlick v. Austria*).

4. ECHR, September 23, 1994, Series A no. 298, p. 23 (*Jersild v. Denmark*).

5. Court of Appeal Amsterdam, October 19, 2000, Elro no. AA 7654.

6. President Court of Utrecht, September 20, 2001, Elro no. AD 3844.

7. President Court of Amsterdam, April 5, 2005, LJN no. AT 3177.

8. President Court of Breda, July 15, 1991, KG 1991/260.

9. President Court of Assen, 1994, Mediaforum 1994, p. B68.

10. Court of Amsterdam (summary proceedings), October 26, 2006, KG 06-1809 OdC, (*Girlfriend Endstra v. Balans*).

11. ECHR, February 15, 2005 (*Steel and Morris v. the UK*).

12. Supreme Court, April 22, 1986, NJ 1986/827.

13. Cf. Court of Arnhem, April 1, 1999, Mediaforum 1999–5, nr. 27.

14. Court of Appeal Amsterdam, April 27, 2000, Mediaforum 2000–7/8, nr. 45.

15. Supreme Court, January 18, 2008, no. C06/161HR, (*Van Gasteren v. Hemelrijk*).

16. ECHR, July 8, 1986, NJ 1987, 901.

17. ECHR, June 24, 2004, Mediaforum 7/8, nr. 27 (*Caroline of Monaco*).

18. Supreme Court June 24, 1983, NJ 1984, 801 (*Council Member X*).

19. ECHR, May 20, 1999, no. 21980/03 (*Bladet Tromso*).

20. Supreme Court, *Van Gasteren v. Hemelrijk*, see note 15 above.

21. ECHR, January 25, 2007, no. 68354/01 (*Vereinigung Bildender Kunstler v. Austria*).

22. Cf. Court of Appeal The Hague, May 25, 1993, Mediaforum 1993, p. B62 and Court of Appeal Den Bosch, February 18, 1999, Mediaforum 1999–3, nr. 17.

23. Supreme Court, January 6, 1995, NJ 1995/422 (*Parool v. Van Gasteren*).

24. ECHR, May 2, 2000, NJ 2001/65 (*Bergens Tidende*).

25. Court of Amsterdam (summary proceedings), July 28, 2005, Mediaforum 2005/9, 312 (*Camp Kleyn v. Het Parool*).

26. ECHR, *Bladet Tromso,* see note 19 above, and Supreme Court, June 15, 1990, NJ 1990/432 (*McDonalds*).

27. President Court of Maastricht, January 28, 1998, KG 1998, 81.

28. Court of Appeal The Hague, September 4, 2003, NJ 2003/664 (*Scientology v. XS 4ALL et al*).

29. ECHR, *Bladet Tromso*, see note 19 above, and Supreme Court *McDonalds*, see note 26 above.

30. Court of Appeal Amsterdam, July 26, 2007, case no. 05/1788 (*Knoop v. Het Parool*).

31. Council of State (judiciary department), January 2, 1986, AB 1986, 216.

32. Cf. ECHR, January 11, 2000, NJ 2001/74 (*News Verlag*); Court of Appeal Amsterdam, February 25, 1960, NJ 1960/502; Court of Amsterdam, August 14, 1996, Mediaforum 1997–5, B78–82; President Court of Amsterdam, December 1, 1988, KG 1989, 15.

33. Supreme Court, May 2, 2003, Mediaforum 2003/6, nr. 30 (*Storms v. Niessen*).

34. Supreme Court, January 9, 1987, Computerrecht 187–2, 110–15.

35. Supreme Court, March 4, 1988, NJ 1989/367 (*Children De Bourbon Parma*).

36. Court of Amsterdam, July 10, 1996, Mediaforum 1996–10, pp. B136–B138 (*Wasteland*).

37. Court of Amsterdam, February 6, 2008, case no. 07-1942 (*Royal Family v. Audax*).

38. Supreme Court, January 21,1994, NJ 1994/473 (*Ferdi E.*).

39. Court of Haarlem, August 19, 1997, Mediaforum 1997–9, pp. B130–B132 (*Van der Meyden*).

40. ECHR, January 21, 1999, NJ 1999, 713 (*Fressoz and Roire*).

41. Court of Amsterdam, October 28, 1998, NJ 1990/440 (*Huibregtsen v. De Volkskrant*).

42. Court of Appeal, Amsterdam, June 22, 1989, KG 1989/344 (*Nieuwe Revu v. Stuart*).

43. Court of Amsterdam, January 2, 1996, Mediaforum 1996–2, pp. B30–B35.

44. ECHR, March 27, 1996, NJ 1996/577 (*Goodwin*) and Supreme Court, May 10, 1996, NJ 1996/578 (*V.d. Biggelaar v. Dohmen en Langenberg*).

45. Court of Appeal Den Bosch, July 11, 2006, Mediaforum 2007–1, 27 (*Van Helvoirt/Toering v. Top Oss*); Court of Appeal The Hague, July 27, 2006, Mediaforum 2006–9, 270 (*NRC reporters v. Voûte*).

46. ECHR, November 22, 2007, no. 64752/01.

47. Court of The Hague, June 9, 1999, Computerrecht 1999, pp. 200–205. Confirmed on appeal, Court of Appeal, The Hague, September 4, 2003, Mediaforum 2003–10, nr. 45.

48. Court of Appeal, Amsterdam, November 7, 2002 (*Deutsche Bahn v. XS4ALL*).

49. Court of First Instance, Amsterdam, June 20, 2002 (*Deutsche Bahn v. Indymedia*).

50. Supreme Court, *Parool v. Van Gasteren*, see note 23 above.

51. Court of Zwolle, May 3, 2006, case no. 05–211 (*Stokke v. Marktplaats*).

52. *Idem.*

53. Council Regulation (EC) No 44/2001 of December 22, 2000, on jurisdiction and the recognition and enforcement of judgments in civil and commercial matters.

54. European Court of Justice, March 7, 1995, NJ 1996/269 (*Shevill v. Presse Alliance*).

CHAPTER 20

Poland

CHARLES J. GLASSER JR.*
Bloomberg News

Introduction to Polish Media Law

The court system in Poland is composed of trial (or common) courts and the Supreme Court. Common courts are divided into: (i) district courts established for the territory of one or more local communes and, in certain circumstances, for part of the territory of a local commune; (ii) regional courts established for the territory of at least two district courts; and (iii) appeal courts established for the territory of at least two regional courts.

The adjudication of a civil case by the relevant district or regional court depends on the subject matter and size of a claim. In principle, district courts decide on all matters unless the law provides that the regional court is the correct authority. Venue in district trial courts is strictly defined in the civil procedure code and includes cases involving proprietary rights if the value of the dispute exceeds PLN 75,000 (approximately USD 26,500), non-proprietary rights (including libel, privacy, and press law actions), and intellectual property cases. Although subject matter jurisdiction is reached by the amount of damages in question and is

* The author gratefully acknowledges the assistance and research help of Mr. Paweł Bajno of the Warsaw offices of Dewey LeBouef LLP, and Bloomberg intern Lucas Kelly-Clyne, Johns Hopkins University (class of 2010).

normally pleaded by the plaintiff, the court has the discretion to evaluate the amount in controversy.

Poland maintains a civil law system (*prawo cywilne)* guided by constitutional principles (*prawo konstytucyjne).* In addition to the Civil Codes, Poland's Press Law of 1984 applies to all publications in Poland and requires that publications distributed in Poland register at a local court.[1] New statutes are published in the Official Gazette of the Republic of Poland. As a member of the European Union, Poland is a signatory to the European Convention on Human Rights, and rulings by its Supreme Court may, in free expression cases, be subject to review under Article 19 of the European Convention for Human Rights.[2]

1. What is the most widely accepted definition of libel?

Poland's Civil Code (specifically Article 23)[3] reflects the broad notion that persons have a dignitary and proprietary interest in their reputation, privacy, and likeness. These provisions seek the protection of those interests. A libel is simply a statement upon which the good name of a subject is threatened. Polish law readily provides complainants the ability to seek injunctive relief to protect those dignitary rights.[4]

Although Article 14 of the Constitution of 1997 guarantees freedom of the press, the Civil Codes allow fines or imprisonment of up to two years for one who "publicly insults or humiliates a constitutional institution of the Republic of Poland."

The most famous case tried under this law found President Aleksander Kwasniewski suing the newspaper *Zycie* for insinuating the president had contacts with "Russian spies." Additionally, individual citizens and businesses as well as government officials can use provisions of the Criminal Code to punish defamatory speech.[5]

Defamatory meaning under Polish media law ranges from the traditional to the expansive. The following publications have been found capable of defamatory meaning: allegations of involvement in corruption;[6] having been an informant under the old Soviet-controlled regime;[7] insinuating a relationship between the President and a former Russian KGB agent;[8] being compared to a potato;[9] and publishing a photo of a female bystander sitting next to a person accused of being a client of a prostitution ring.[10]

2. Is libel-by-implication recognized, or, alternatively, must the complained-of words alone defame the plaintiff?

Yes. The protected dignitary rights can be infringed by a sense of the entire publication, not only by particular phrases. The structure of the publication does not free the journalist from the obligation to act with the utmost diligence and fairness in collecting and using information.

3. May a corporation sue for libel?
Yes, a corporation can sue for libel. The good name of any legal entity as well as its dignity and reputation is recognized as one of the personal possessions of that entity.

4. Is product disparagement recognized, and if so, how does that differ from libel?
Yes. Recent judgments of the Supreme Court indicate that a breach of moral rights (statements impacting the good name of a legal entity) under Article 24 of the Civil Code may have the form of "dissemination of untrue and inadequately verified information regarding the product."

It should be added that the Act on Combating Unfair Competition may in some instances apply to publishers of newspapers and magazines. Disseminating untrue or misleading information concerning another business (e.g., disseminating untrue information regarding manufactured products) may constitute an act of unfair competition.

5. Must an individual be clearly identified (by name or photograph) to sue for libel? Can a group of persons sue for libel, even though not named?
No Civil Code or Supreme Court precedent addresses this question. As a practical matter, it would be difficult for an unnamed group of persons to have standing to file a lawsuit; therefore it would appear that groups or unnamed individuals could not sue for libel.

6. Please describe the fault standard(s) applied to libel, particularly:
The existence of fault is not necessary for libel to occur. There are defenses to libel (detailed below) but Polish jurisprudence does not take fault into consideration.

(a) Does the fault standard depend on the fame or notoriety of the plaintiff?
No.

(b) Is there a heightened fault standard or privilege for reporting on matters of public concern or public interest?
Yes. Article 5 of the Civil Code recognizes that the dignitary interests affected by a defamatory statement may be justified by the public interest, if it serves the implementation of citizens' rights to be accurately informed about such issues. The Supreme Court has required that in mounting such a defense the journalist serves a "justifiable public interest, and exercises the utmost diligence and fairness in collecting and using the materials."

7. Is financial news about publicly traded companies or companies involved with government contracts considered a matter of public interest or otherwise privileged?

Such information is not privileged in any particular manner; however, the public interest defense may apply if the statements at issue were made in order to protect public interests and examine consumer rights protection practices.

8. Is there recognized protection for an opinion of "fair comment" on matters of public concern?

Yes, with restrictions. Criticism that contains defamatory statements is protected only when it is substantive and fair, and intended to protect the public interest.

9. Are there any requirements on a plaintiff, such as a demand for retraction or right of reply, and if so, what impact do they have?

Yes, Poland recognizes a Right of Reply. Pursuant to the Press Law, the subject of a story has a right to demand the publication of a correction or in the alternative, a statement of reply. This also applies if the plaintiff believes a previously published correction or statement in reply was insufficient. Claims for rectification cannot be filed beyond one year from the date the offending material was published.

The Right of Reply is not a condition precedent to filing a civil claim against the media; however, journalists should be aware that Art. 24 § 1 of the Civil Code does provide aggrieved parties with the ability to seek injunctive relief against publication.

10. Is there a privilege for quoting or reporting on:

(a) Papers filed in court?

Yes. Pursuant to the Act on Access to Public Information, all information on public matters shall be made available to the public, and the Press Law protects the publication of truthful and accurate accounts of public sittings of Parliament and local councils and their executive arms, as well as other governmental bodies.

(b) Government-issued documents?

Yes (see below).

(c) Quasi-governmental proceedings, such as those by professional associations (for example disciplinary proceedings)

The entities obliged to provide public information include public authorities and other entities performing public duties, in particular public authorities, economic and professional self-government authorities, entities representing the State Treasury pursuant to separate regulations, as well as entities representing other state organizational units or local government units, entities representing other persons or organizational units performing public tasks or which are responsible for public property, and legal persons in which the State Treasury, local government or business or professional self-government units hold a dominant position within the meaning of the regulations governing the protection of competition and consumers. In addition, labor unions, employers' organizations, and political parties are obliged to provide information to the public.

As long as the statement is a quotation of publicly available information released to the press on the grounds of the obligation as described above, it should not be held actionable.

The right to public information is subject to certain restrictions:

(i) with regard to classified information and other information protected on the basis of statutes;

(ii) for reasons of privacy of a natural person or business secrets of an entrepreneur. (This limitation does not apply to information about persons holding public office, connected with the holding of such office, including the circumstances in which they were entrusted with, and hold, such office, and in instances when a natural person or entrepreneur gives up the right vested in them.)

11. Is there a privilege for republishing statements made earlier by other, bona fide reliable publications or wire services?

Yes, but it is limited. Pursuant to the Press Law, an editor is not responsible for the content of news supplied by the Polish Press Agency (PAP) or for the content of official communiqués from the supreme or central state authorities, including supreme and central state administration bodies, or for the contents of rulings or court judgments that are no longer subject to appeal, or the contents of wanted persons' notices. Publishers and editors are also not legally responsible for the content of advertisements published on a commercial basis.

12. Are there any restrictions regarding:

(a) Reporting on ongoing criminal investigations?

Pursuant to Article 241 § 1 of the Criminal Code, it is punishable to publicly disseminate (e.g., through the mass media) any information exclusively learned through those proceedings prior to such information being disclosed in the court proceedings.

In order for the above provision to apply, the disseminated information must be sourced from preparatory proceedings, i.e., the files of, or persons conducting or supporting, such proceedings ex officio (e.g., a policeman, an employee of a prosecutor's office) and refer to more than the mere fact that such proceedings are pending. It does not amount to an offense under Article 241 of the Criminal Code to collect information on an event subject to preparatory proceedings, in any other manner, e.g., by a private investigation undertaken by a journalist. Unlike Contempt of Court laws in the United Kingdom, a journalist has a right to undertake a private investigation of a current trial and to disclose its results. Therefore it is not forbidden to report on ongoing preparatory proceedings, provided that the disclosed information is not uniquely sourced from such proceedings.

(b) Reporting on ongoing criminal prosecutions?

Pursuant to the Press Law, it is prohibited to articulate in the press any opinions regarding the outcome of legal proceedings before a ruling in the first instance is issued. It is also prohibited to publish in the press the personal data and images of persons against whom an investigation or court proceedings are in progress or the personal data and images of witnesses, or injured parties, unless such persons give their consent thereto. However, the relevant prosecutor or court may authorize, on the grounds of valid public interest, the disclosure of personal data and images of persons against whom an investigation or court proceedings are under way.

(c) Reporting on ongoing regulatory investigations?

See above.

(d) Reporting on ongoing civil litigation or other judicial proceedings?

None.

13. Are prior restraints or other prepublication injunctions available on the basis of libel or privacy, and if so, what are the standards for obtaining such relief?

Yes. Prior restraints are granted in Poland with some regularity. The plaintiff may file a motion for an injunctive order to be issued by the court demonstrating the likelihood of success of a libel suit and thereupon be granted a prior restraint. In 1998, Amway, the U.S.-based household goods manufacturer, obtained an injunction against the distribution of *Welcome to Life*, a documentary alleging high-pressure sales techniques.[11]

14. Is a right to privacy recognized (either civilly or criminally)?

Polish law conflates reputation with privacy under the more expansive notion of possessory dignitary rights. The Polish Constitution recognizes the rights of privacy and data protection. Article 47 states, "Everyone shall have the right to legal protection of his/her private and family life, of his/her honor and good reputation, and to make decisions about his/her personal life." Article 49 states, "Freedom and privacy of communication shall be ensured. Any limitations thereon may be imposed only in cases and in a manner specified by statute." The right to privacy is also protected on the basis of Arts. 23 and 24 of the Civil Code, as a personal possession.

Additionally, various sectional laws deal with the issue of the right to privacy. There are also laws in place to deal with the processing of medical data. The Act on the Profession of Doctor imposes on medical professionals a duty of confidentiality, subject to certain exceptions, in relation to patient information. With respect to financial data, the Banking Act imposes a requirement of secrecy on banks in relation to an individual's banking activities and identity, and limits the exchange and disclosure of personal data among banks and third parties, except for the purpose of assessing credit risk or investigating fraud. The Penal Code stipulates that unauthorized access to computer systems, computer eavesdropping, interference with data, and computer sabotage are crimes punishable by up to eight years' imprisonment. This code also prohibits telecommunications fraud, the handling of stolen software, computer espionage, and causing harm from interference with automatic data processing.

(a) What is the definition of a "private fact"?

Private facts constitute circumstances of private life as well as family life that are disclosed to close relatives and friends and which are essentially destined for this group of people. Within private facts, facts from intimate life are distinguished, i.e., facts relating to the individual's experiences that are not disclosed even to close relatives and friends. These facts are strongly protected.

(b) Is there a public interest or newsworthiness exception?

Yes, provided that the intrusion into the private sphere was performed in defense of a demonstrable public interest. The Press Law stipulates that it is forbidden to publish, without the consent of the person concerned, any information or data concerning such person's private life, and any such publication must be directly connected to the person's public activities.

15. May reporters tape record their own telephone conversations for note-taking purposes (not rebroadcast) without the consent of the other party?

Although there is no prohibition on making such a recording, the dissemination of that recording may have various legal effects. Article 14.1 of the Press Law prohibits the publication or other dissemination of information recorded by visual or sound recording means without the consent of the person providing the information. The prohibition applies regardless of whether the recording was made with or without the consent of the recorded person. Violation of this prohibition may constitute a criminal offense under Article 49 of the Press Law, and carry the risk of a criminal fine or "restriction of liberty" (lesser criminal sanctions). In practice, we have not heard of any recent examples of actions being brought by a public prosecutor under Article 49 in connection with violation of Art. 14.1.

16. If permissible to record such tapes, may they be broadcast without permission?

No. Pursuant to Article 14.1 of the Press Law, publishing or/and otherwise disseminating information recorded in any form whatsoever (including videotaping and sound recording) requires the consent of the person concerned. Article 14.5 of the Press Law also stipulates that a journalist may not publish the information if the source stipulated prior to publication that it is not to be published for reasons of official or professional secrets.

17. Is there a recognized evidentiary privilege preventing the disclosure of confidential sources relied upon by reporters?

Yes, although the law is qualified and not absolute. Pursuant to the Press Law, a journalist is obliged to keep confidential:

- (i) any data making it possible to identify the author of material appearing in the press, a letter to the editor or other material of a similar nature, published or released for publication, if such persons demanded that such data remained confidential; and
- (ii) any information the disclosure of which could prejudice the interests of third parties protected by law.

Pursuant to the Criminal Procedure Code, persons obliged to keep business secrets or secrets connected with practicing a profession or with the post held may refuse to testify in respect of the circumstances covered by this obligation, unless the court or prosecutor relieves such persons from the requirement to keep such secrets. The court will more than likely hear the testimony of such persons in camera.

Additionally, persons obliged to maintain journalistic secrecy may be questioned regarding the facts covered by such secrecy if a judge is convinced that it is indispensable for the due process of law and if the facts needed cannot be determined from other sources.

18. In the event that legal papers are served on a newsroom (such as a civil complaint), are there any particular warnings about accepting service of which we should be aware?

Submissions or rulings addressed to a legal person or an unincorporated entity are delivered to a body authorized to represent them before a court or to an employee authorized to receive correspondence. Submissions addressed to entrepreneurs and shareholders in commercial companies, entered in the court register under separate regulations, are delivered to the address indicated in the court register entry, unless the party supplies a different service of process address.

19. Has your jurisdiction applied established media law to Internet publishers?

Yes. A number of libel cases involve Internet versions of traditional publications, and there have also been cases where the speech at issue was solely digital in nature. In September 2007, a twenty-three-year-old computer programmer was charged with criminal defamation after he created a computer program (called a "Google bomb") that caused any Polish search for the word *penis* to direct the searcher to the president's website.[12]

20. If established media law has been applied to Internet publishers, are there any ways in which Internet publishers (including chat room operators) have to meet different standards?

Given the stringent standards of media law in Poland, we do not see any significant difference in due care that is distinguishable from that required of traditional media.

21. Are there any cases where the courts enforced a judgment in libel from another jurisdiction against a publisher in your jurisdiction?

None reported, although it is feasible that a valid judgment in any E.U. nation could be enforced against assets in Poland.

Chapter Notes

1. http://www.obp.pl/03-raport/2001/LegalFrame.htm.

2. http://conventions.coe.int/treaty/en/Treaties/Html/005.htm; http://www.hri.org/docs/ECHR50.html#C.Art14.

3. Article 23 of the Civil Code stipulates that the personal rights of a human being, in particular health, freedom, dignity, freedom of conscience, surname or pseudonym, image, secrecy of correspondence, inviolability of home, and scientific,

artistic, inventor's and rationalizing achievements, shall be protected by civil law independent of protection envisaged in other provisions.

4. Article 24 § 1 of the Civil Code stipulates that a person whose personal rights are threatened by another person's activity may demand the cessation of that activity unless it is not illegal.

5. http://www.pressreference.com/No-Sa/Poland.html.

6. http://www.freemedia.at/cms/ipi/freedom_detail.html?country=/KW0001/KW0003/KW0075/.

7. http://www.freemedia.at/cms/ipi/freedom_detail.html?country=/KW0001/KW0003/KW0075/.

8. http://www.policy.hu/kaminski/LawPoland.html.

9. http://www.mywire.com/pubs/AFP/2007/12/07/5129152?extID=10037&oliID=229.

10. http://www.policy.hu/kaminski/LawPoland.html.

11. "Ban on Film Has Poland Debating Censorship," *New York Times,* June 14, 1998, http://query.nytimes.com/gst/fullpage.html?res=9A07E7D7163DF937A25755C0A96E958260/.

12. "Linking President to Penis May Put Pole in Prison," Reuters, September 14, 2007, http://africa.reuters.com/odd/news/usnL14702855.html/.

CHAPTER **21**

Russian Federation

NELLIE ALEXANDROVA, ANNA OTKINA,
EKATERINA PETROVA AND ANTON PUSHIN
Denton Wilde Sapte

Denton Wilde Sapte—Moscow Office
Bolshaya Dmitrovka 7/5
Building 2
Moscow
Russia
125009
Phone: +7 095 255 7900
Fax: +7 095 255 7901
moscow@dentonwildesapte.com
anna.otkina@dentonwildesapte.com
ekaterina.petrova@dentonwildesapte.com
anton.pushin@dentonwildesapte.com

Denton Wilde Sapte—London Office
One Fleet Place
London EC4M 7WS
United Kingdom
Phone: +44 (0) 20 7242 1212
Fax: +44 (0) 20 7246 7777
nellie.alexandrova@dentonwildesapte.com
www.dentonwildesapte.com

Introduction to the Russian Legal System

The Constitution of the Russian Federation of 1993 spurred a significant reform of the Russian legal system. The Russian system, based on the tenets of civil law, has a three-branch court system. The three branches include a four-level "regular" court system with a court of last resort—the Supreme Court of the Russian Federation (the *Supreme Court*) for civil and criminal actions, a three-level arbitration court system for business-related actions, and a constitutional court system composed of one Supreme Court for constitutional actions.

The "regular" court system is similar to the traditional hierarchical structure in many other countries, and it includes the courts of general jurisdiction that adjudicate civil and criminal matters as well as administrative disputes. There are four levels of courts: the Supreme Court as the highest court of the courts of general jurisdiction, supreme courts of the republics, *krai* and *oblast* courts, and courts of cities of federal level. The lower courts of general jurisdiction hear disputes involving individuals regarding civil, family, labor, and other relationships. They also may recognize and enforce the decisions of the foreign courts and foreign arbitral awards.

Almost every civil or criminal action is initially heard in the People's Court. Each city, or area, has a People's Court that, unlike many other civil law systems, does not organize courts by the subject matter of the case being tried. The appeals process is in a hierarchical structure, from an intermediate court to the Supreme Court.

There are several methods of determining a verdict in a case. The most common structure of adjudicating bodies consists of either a panel of three judges or a single judge. The reform of the mid-1990s led to experimentation with twelve-member juries, which came into existence as such but are currently reserved for serious crimes that are designated to *oblast* courts.

1. What is the locally accepted definition of libel?

Libel is a criminal offense, and defamation is a civil offense as explained below:

Criminal Law

The Criminal Code of the Russian Federation No. 63-FZ dated June 13, 1996 (the *Criminal Code*) defines libel in Section 17 as "Crimes against the freedom, honor and dignity of a person" by "spreading (circulation) of deliberately false information denigrating the honor and dignity of a person or undermining his reputation."[1] "Spreading or circulation" is understood by the Criminal Code as communication of information to one or more persons other than the claimant in written, oral, or video form.[2]

The Criminal Code has been read to mean that "disseminating deliberately false information" means that the speaker knows the information is false or that it could be false.[3]

Under the Criminal Code, the statement itself must be capable of defamatory meaning, and has been read to require a statement of a fact evidencing that the subject of the publication is in breach of the law or of any moral values. This requires that the sued-upon statement must be specific and contain factual statements capable of being verified. By contrast, a statement that someone is "bad" is a matter of personal opinion and is not sufficiently specific to constitute criminal libel.

Like other criminal laws, libel is also capable of being an aggravated offense, and two specific instances are most likely to occur: (1) "libel contained in a public speech or in a work performed in the public or in mass media" and (2) "a defamatory statement alleging that a person has committed a grave crime." An aggravated libel is punishable by either four or six months' detention or by up to three years' imprisonment. (An ordinary libel is punishable by a fine,[4] in the amount of the defendant's monthly income, or up to one year of penitentiary work.)

Accusing a person or entity of committing a serious crime is the basis of most criminal libel claims. *A and B v. D* (1999) is such a case, wherein the Lomonosov Regional court of the city of Arhangelsk found that in an interview to a newspaper and his letter to the president of the Russian Federation, Mr. D "circulated deliberately false and denigrating information regarding Mr. A. and Mr. B., stating that they had committed a serious crime."[5] According to Mr. D., in 1989 Mr. A. and Mr. B., being employed by the state legal entity "Arkhangelskribprom," sold to another legal entity in Germany a batch of crayfish for the value of US$740,000. Mr. D. alleged that this money was subsequently stolen by Mr. A. and Mr. B. and used to establish their own business. Mr. D. was convicted of aggravated libel. On appeal, the guilty verdict was reversed. Mr. D. was found innocent and the decisions of the lower courts were reversed. In its decision the Supreme Court looked at the factual as well as formal requirements of part 3 Article 129 of the Criminal Code. Criminal libel requires that the circulated information must be distributed with knowing falsity: a difficult standard to meet. According to the facts of the case, Mr. D. had been in charge of an investigation related to embezzlement at Arkhangelskribprom and had documents indicating that Mr. A. and Mr. B. were directly involved in receipt of the money in the transaction in question. However, the criminal investigation of the matter by the local prosecution office was not completed. Recognizing the difference between an error and an intentional falsity, the Supreme Court concluded that under the circumstances Mr. D. could have been genuinely confused as to the real circumstances of the case and therefore found him not guilty of libel.

By contrast, in *Antoshin v. Rzhevsky* (2003), the trial court of the city of Kalitva found Mr. Rzhevsky guilty of aggravated libel. The court found that in July 2002, during a meeting of the city council in the presence of 147 people, Mr. Rzhevsky publicly claimed that Mr. Antoshin, the deputy mayor of the city, was guilty of embezzlement of RUR 10 million (approximately USD 365,000) granted as part of federal support of the coal mining industry of the city of Kalitva. The court found that the allegation of embezzlement had been the subject of a previous investigation by the local prosecutor's office and was found to be untrue. Before making his defamatory statement, Mr. Rzhevsky had already obtained written conclusions from the office of the prosecutor to this effect. Therefore, at the time of making the statement, Mr. Rzhevsky knew that he was circulating deliberately false and denigrating information and was therefore guilty of criminal libel.[6]

In practice, few courts in the Russian Federation actually apply the criminal sanctions to libel because of the difficulty of proving the knowing falsity that the law requires. It should be noted, though, as a civil law jurisdiction, Russian courts do not recognize court precedent as a formal source of the law, and, although the lower courts generally take account of and follow the recommendations and legal practice of the Supreme Court, each case is reviewed independently on its merits and with reference to the provisions of the relevant law.[7]

Civil Law

Unlike in the criminal context, the defamatory meaning required in civil law to trigger liability is considerably broader: a statement simply "discrediting the honor, dignity or business reputation" made in the mass media.

The civil law and, more specifically, the Civil Code of the Russian Federation No. 51-FZ dated November 30, 1994 (the *Civil Code*) is designed to protect persons against defamation under the heading of "protection of freedom, dignity and business reputation" (Article 152 of the Civil Code). The Article provides as follows: "any person has the right to demand in court the refutation of communications defaming his honor, dignity, or business reputation, unless the person who disseminated such communications shows that they correspond to reality."

By contrast to the criminal courts, the commercial courts of the Russian Federation[8] hear annually a substantial number of cases on protection of freedom, dignity, and business reputation. The courts are mindful of the right of the mass media to fair comment, as provided by the Law "On Mass Media" No 2124-I of December 27,1991 (the *Mass Media Law*), and, thus, many claims are unsuccessful, on the basis that the statements in question are either true or within the protection for fair comment.[9]

In *Alliance Group v. Publishing House of Rossiskaya Gazeta* (2004), the publicly traded Alliance Group filed a claim against Publishing House of Rossiskaya Gazeta. The claimant asked the court to rule the publication of an article to be false and discrediting its honor, dignity, and business reputation. The article in the newspaper *Rossiskaya Gazeta* said that Alliance Group, using "dodgy methods of business," corrupted officials and participated with criminals to the detriment of the Russian economy. The Commercial Court of the city of Moscow found the newspaper liable for defamation and ordered it to publish a retraction of the allegations made in the article. The appellate court reserved its decision and reviewed the case de novo. In its decision, the appellate Federal Commercial Court of the Moscow Region stated that the lower court failed to give sufficient weight to the following points: (1) whether the claimant had proved that the allegations made in the article were false; and (2) whether the statements made in the article in fact could be considered "an opinion" of the journalist and thus would fall within the definition of fair comment.[10]

2. Is libel-by-implication recognized, or, in the alternative, must the complained-of words alone defame the plaintiff?

The Criminal Code and the Civil Code each take the position that, in order to constitute a libel, the defamatory statement has to be clear and precise and must make factual allegations, the truth of which is capable of verification.

3. May corporations sue for libel?

Yes. Any legal entity can sue for libel. Criminal proceedings for libel are brought by a public prosecutor following a complaint of a person or a legal entity. A civil lawsuit is initiated by a claimant for protection of honor, dignity, or reputation.

In its Resolution No. 3 dated February 24, 2005, "On Judicial Practice on Protection of Honor, Dignity and Business Reputations of Individuals and Legal Entities," the Supreme Court directs that, if the dissemination of false and dishonoring information meets the criteria of the crime of libel set out in Article 129 of the Criminal Code, victims may initiate criminal proceedings and simultaneously bring civil proceedings seeking protection of their honor, dignity, or business reputation.

Should the court dismiss criminal charges, this will have no negative effect on the civil claim for protection of honor, dignity, and business reputation arising out of the same circumstances.

4. Is product disparagement recognized and, if so, how does it differ from libel?

Product disparagement is implicitly prohibited by Article 5 of the Federal Law No. 38-FZ dated March 13, 2006 (as amended), "On Advertising" (the *Advertising Law*), which deals with unfair advertising practices and explicitly requires any advertising to be "in good faith and accurate. Advertising not made in good faith or inaccurate is not allowed."[11]

Advertising is *not considered to be in good faith* if *inter alia* it contains inappropriate comparisons of the advertised product with other product(s) produced by other manufacturers or sold by other sellers (Article 5, part 2, para 1) or discredits the honor, dignity, or business reputation of another person including competitors (Article 5, part 2, para 2).

Examples of *inaccurate advertising* are information given on advantages of the advertised product in comparison with products manufactured by other producers or sold by other sellers as well as on characteristics of the advertised product, if such information differs from the actual situation (Article 5, part 3, paras 1 and 2).

There are two ways of bringing actions against unfair advertising: either to file a complaint with the Federal Antimonopoly Service (an administrative process) or to initiate litigation in a court of general jurisdiction or a commercial court (a civil law process). The possible remedies in each case include a refutation,[12] fine(s), and/or damages.[13]

5. Must an individual be clearly identified (by name or photograph) to sue for libel? Can a group of persons sue for libel, even though not named?

The claimant must be ascertainable by name or by photograph to be able to sue for libel. The right to bring an action is of a personal nature and is vested only with a natural person (who can appear in a court in person or via a representative) or a legal entity (which can be represented in a court).

A group of individuals, which might be identified by certain criteria (e.g., religion, profession, employment by the same company, etc.) cannot bring an action for libel. Such action must be brought by each individual, who will have to prove that the defamatory statement concerns him or her personally (and not him or her as a member of the group). However, where all suits are brought against the same defendant, they can all be brought at the same time, and a judge can decide to adjoin the cases.

However, in *Ramenskiy OJC v. Regnum LLC* (2007), Ramenskiy sued for protection of its business reputation and asked to recognize as false and dishonoring the information distributed by Regnum via the Internet that the juice Lyubimiy Sad contained mercury. The claim of Ramenskiy had previously been dismissed by an appellate court because the claimant was not the sole producer of the juice under the trademark "Lyubimiy Sad" and the distributed information had never referred to the business name of the claimant, Ramenskiy Milk Enterprise. The Commercial Court of the Moscow Region set aside the decision of the appellate court on the grounds that giving business reputation a legal protection should not depend on whether or not the false information explicitly identifies the name of the firm or a person concerned. It is for the court to decide whether or not the disseminated information directs to the particular person on the basis of all the circumstances of the case and the evidence given in the court provided that in accordance with general civil procedure rules a burden of proof lies on the claimant.

At the same time, according to *the Resolution of the Supreme Court of the Russian Federation*, No. 3, February 24, 2005, "On Judicial Practice in Cases of Protection of the Honor, Dignity and Business Reputation of Individuals and Legal Entities," judicial protection of the honor, dignity, and business reputation of a person in respect of whom abusive and discrediting information has been disseminated is possible even if the person who spread the information is unidentifiable (e.g., anonymous letters or dissemination of information via the Internet). In such situations the court may recognize the information as false and defamatory in a special proceeding (*osoboye proizvodstvo*).

6. What is the fault standard(s) applied to libel?

In order to be liable for libel, the person has to have acted in bad faith, although there is not much direction as to what constitutes "bad faith." It has been suggested that, in the civil context, reporters will be held liable for careless, sloppy, or reckless reporting techniques that result in a false and defamatory publication. In criminal libel, the laws require that the publisher acts with knowing falsity.

a. Does the fault standard depend on the fame or notoriety of the plaintiff?

No, the fault standard has no relevance whatsoever to the social standing of the claimant. However, the Supreme Court's overview of the court practice regarding the protection of honor, dignity, and business reputation and the right to privacy of public persons in the spheres of politics, art, and sport (published in *The Bulletin of the Supreme Court of the Russian Federation*, No. 12, 2007) gives some guidance to the courts.

The Supreme Court established, in particular, that the private life of public persons is often subject to offense, and it is sometimes a source of profits for the mass media. The suit for protection of honor, dignity, and business reputation, as well as other intangible wealth, is as a rule filed together with a damage claim—so called "compensation of moral damage." In determining the value of such moral compensation, the personality, social position, and work status should be taken into account together with other circumstances of the case.

In the case *B. v. Arbat and Co.,* B. claimed that the magazine published by Arbat and Co. LLC contained abusive information that discredited the claimant's honor, dignity, and business reputation and caused him moral suffering. The author of the article alleged that what was described in the released information had in fact taken place. In the decision dated October 31, 2005, the district court of Moscow city took a view that B. was a public person and for that reason, any information concerning him was broadly discussed in the mass media and by the public. B.'s professional and charitable activity was common knowledge, and so dissemination of false information was likely to affect his business reputation. The court required that "Arbat and Co." refute the information and pay damages for "moral suffering."

The Supreme Court also established that the courts, when deciding cases on the protection of honor, dignity, and business reputations of state officials or other persons who hold positions in governmental or local bodies, take into consideration the provisions of the Declaration of Freedom of Political Discussion in Mass Media dated February 12, 2004, adopted by the Committee of Ministers of the European Union. Following this Declaration, courts conclude that state officials implicitly and voluntarily subject themselves to public scrutiny and possible criticism to the extent that this relates to their public duties, because this is the way to ensure public responsibility.

In *M v. The Tula News and H,* M. sued for protection of honor, dignity, and business reputation and for compensation for moral damage. The court established that the claimant was the head of the local authority and that the published article had an evaluating, ironic character and expressed the personal opinion of the author with regard to the prospects of his reelection should the claimant wish to be re-elected. The speculations included in the article could not be checked for their validity and, therefore, could not be the object of denial. The court decided that the author discussed problems of public interest and merely wanted to draw public attention to the ongoing administrative reform, and on this basis the publication did not contravene the Declaration of Freedom of Political Discussion in Mass Media.

b. Is there a heightened fault standard or privilege for reporting on matters of public concern or public interest?

There is no diversity of fault standard depending on whether the matter is of public concern or public interest.

7. Is financial news about publicly traded companies, or companies involved with a government contract, considered a matter of public interest or otherwise privileged?

Not generally. Furthermore, all Russian open joint stock companies are subject to various reporting and disclosure requirements, particularly in relation to their major financial results and corporate governance events.[14] The standards for such disclosure are much higher in situations of public offering and placement of stocks and bonds,[15] or when securities are listed and traded at stock exchanges,[16] or reporting of banking institutions.[17] Information on corporate mergers and acquisitions in excess of 20 percent of stock is also subject to reporting and disclosure requirements.[18]

Finance and banking businesses and those focused on investment activities are restricted in the types of information they can include in their advertisements by the Advertising Law. For example, it will be contrary to the Advertising Law if such a company makes representations or promises on its profitability in the future, or guarantees dividends on its ordinary stocks, or makes any statements as to the future growth of the market value of its securities.[19] Consistently, a similar requirement is contained in the Federal Law No. 39-FZ dated April 22, 1996, "On Securities Market," specifically in relation to the public offering of stocks, bonds, and derivatives.

8. Is there a recognized protection for opinion or "fair comment" on matters of public concern?

Yes. The right of fair comment as well as the prohibition of any kind of censorship is provided for in the Mass Media Law.[20] However, this right is balanced against the limitations set out by the Criminal and Civil Codes on libel discussed above. The rights guaranteed to publishers are not absolute and must also be balanced against the prohibitions of disclosure of state secrets and any other statutorily protected information.

In *AN Rosbuilding LLC v. closed joint stock company Publishing House Ekonomicheskaya Gazeta* (2004), the defendants published an article stating that "sooner or later it is possible to become a victim of skillful speculators like Rosbuilding." The claimant sued, alleging that the statement discredited its honor, dignity, and business reputation. The claim was dismissed with reference to Article 47 of the Mass Media Law and the right of the journalist to fair comment. The court did not find that the statement was defamatory, because the statement did not allege provably false facts, and was found to be the personal view of the author of the article. The court offered its linguistic analysis of the statement and found that the words "skillful speculators" can be viewed only as the author's personal opinion and are allowed under the Mass Media Law as a matter of personal comment, whether positive or negative.[21] The appellate court upheld the decision.

In *Sablin v. Yurbusinessinizaitiva and Babak* (2005), the Commercial Court of the Moscow Region emphasized that the source of information cannot be regarded as the criterion for evaluating its content. The court should base its decision on whether a particular text provides facts (events, actions) or represents only the opinion (proposition, assumption) of the author on the analysis of the meaning of the text alone.

The source of information may, however, be grounds for exemption from liability. For example, Article 57 of the Mass Media Law establishes that an editorial board, chief editor, and journalists are exempt from liability for dissemination of false information that discredits the honor and dignity of individuals and legal entities, or violates their rights and legal interests, or for abuse of right to comment, if such information is:

- included in obligatory messages;
- received from information agencies; or

- contained in the answer to a request for information or in materials of press services of state bodies, organizations, offices, enterprises, public associations, and so forth.

In *Russkiy Textil OJC v. Kommersant Publishing House CJC* (2007), the Commercial Court of the Moscow Region decided that refutation under Article 152 of the Civil Code of the Russian Federation concerns only information that appears to be a statement of fact, i.e., information about real, true events that can be characterized by such factors as certainty of action, a particular date, or composition of subjects.

9. Are there any requirements upon a plaintiff, such as demand for retraction or right of reply, and if so, what impact do they have?
Article 43 of the Mass Media Law provides that claimants have a right to demand retraction of any audio, video, or printed publication. The retraction should be made in the same form as the defamatory statement. For example, if the statement was made in a printed form, the retraction should be published on the same page as the original statement, and, if broadcast, it should be broadcast at the same time and by the same method.

The right of retraction does not exclude the rights of the claimant to bring an action to court. Retraction is regarded as a remedy of supplementary nature and does not prevent the claimant from claiming full damages or loss, including moral damage, that has resulted from the defamatory publication.

10. Is there a privilege for quoting or reporting on:

a. Papers filed in court?
Provided that the republication is accurate, Russian law provides immunity for statements made in these contexts. According to Article 57 of the Mass Media Law, liability for dissemination of false or dishonoring information shall not arise if the mass media organization proves that it has merely reproduced a press release issued by a state body, an organization, an institution, or a social association, or, alternatively, that the information has been reproduced from an official response to a request sent by such mass media organization.

b. Government-issued documents?
Yes, the same as above.

c. Quasi-governmental proceedings?
There are no particular privileges on such materials. As a matter of practice, the mass media often follow the exact wording of press releases

in relation to quasi-governmental proceedings, because this most likely relieves them of any liability under Article 57 of the Mass Media Law.

11. Is there a privilege for republishing statements made earlier by other, bona fide, reliable publications or wire services?

Yes. Under the Mass Media Law, the mass media organization is exempted from liability for republication where: (1) the statement republished is a word-for-word copy of the information or the statement previously made by another public source; and (2) this source can be located and, if false and defamatory, held liable under Russian law.[22]

In *Pentakom LLC v. NPF Softvideo LLC* (2002), Pentakom filed the claim against NPF Softvideo in the Commercial Court of the Moscow Region, claiming that the defendant broadcast false and denigrating information on the claimant's business activities. In the television program in question, a reference was made to different newspaper articles as the source of information. The claim was dismissed. In its decision the court referred to the Mass Media Law and stated that the publishing house or the news agency is not liable for any defamatory information where the latter was reproduced from another media publication, and the latter could be located as the source of information.[23]

In *OJC Vladivistok Avia v. noncommercial organization Parlamentskaya Gazeta* (2006), the Commercial Court of the Moscow Region confirmed that, due to the operation of Article 57 of the Mass Media Law, the mass media organization takes no liability for dissemination of false or dishonoring information to the extent that it was a word-for-word representation of information already disseminated by someone else.

12. Are there any restrictions regarding reporting on:

a. Ongoing criminal investigations?

Yes. Reporting on ongoing criminal investigations is not allowed unless consented to by a public prosecutor or by an investigator in charge. Dissemination of such information may lead to criminal liability under Article 310 of the Criminal Code. Presidential Decree No. 188 dated March 6, 1997 (the *1997 Presidential Decree*) introduced a "List of Types of Information Regarded as Confidential," which covers information obtained during a criminal investigation.

In the event that an investigatory search of a home brings to light certain circumstances of a person's intimate life, the investigator is obliged by law to take steps necessary to prevent further disclosure of such private circumstances to the public.[24] If a criminal investigation requires any intrusion into a person's private life (for example, by conducting a personal search or a search of a person's home, removing personal belongings, seizing correspondence, recording conversations, etc.), such actions need prior approval of a public prosecutor, or, alternatively, a court decision. The option for a public prosecutor's *post factum* approval, previously existing in law, no longer applies.[25]

No information obtained during a criminal investigation may be disclosed unless such disclosure has been specifically approved by an investigator in charge and only to the extent it is justified by good reason. No disclosure of information relating to the private life of parties to a criminal investigation or criminal prosecution can be made without their consent.[26]

b. Ongoing criminal prosecutions?

If a criminal case is heard in open court, there are no specific restrictions on covering it in the press. A journalist attending the hearing may take notes (including shorthand notes), or make sketches, or even make audio recordings, unless this interferes with the proceedings.

However, specific permission of a judge is required for filming, taking photographs in a courtroom, or broadcasting proceedings on radio and television.[27] Similar rules apply in relation to commercial litigation in a commercial court[28] and to proceedings on civil law matters in a court of general jurisdiction.[29] A judge can make a decision to permit or not to permit these actions, either on his own initiative or in response to a request of any party to the proceedings.

When a criminal case is heard in a court, judges traditionally deal with protection of privacy, for example by ruling on holding closed hearings, particularly where facts of intimate personal life will be discussed.[30] Similarly, the identity of crime victims may not be disclosed without consent prior to publication.[31]

In 2007, Perviy Kanal OJC contested the decision of the Federal Service of Supervision of Mass Communications and Protection of Cultural Heritage *(Rosohrankultura)*. Perviy Kanal broadcast the television program "Man and Law" about a juvenile girl, A.R. The program discussed a range of issues raised in the context of the private life of the girl: her physical injuries, psychological trauma, and abuse caused by her stepmother, her illness and surgery, and finally her adoption and biological parents. All these facts taken together allowed for the clear identification of that girl. Rosohrankultura considered such distribution of information a violation of Article 4 of the Mass Media Law, which prohibits the use of mass media for dissemination of information containing state and other legally protected secrets such as that "directly or indirectly allows the identification of a juvenile victim without the consent of this person or his/her legal representatives" (Article 41 of the Mass Media Law). The court that heard the case had taken a view that information broadcast in the program "Man and Law" was confidential by nature and should not be distributed in the mass media, particularly in the absence of any relevant consent for release of such information to the public.

c. Ongoing regulatory investigations?

There is no specific regulation of this issue, but it is customary to hold regulatory investigations in closed proceedings.

d. Ongoing civil litigation, or other judicial proceedings?

Most proceedings in a civil law court are of open character; however, the law requires that civil or administrative hearings be held closed if the discussions may lead to the exposure of facts of the person's private life or any other secrets protected by law.[32] Examples are a case involving a state secret or a secret of adoption where a judge is expected to rule on keeping the proceedings closed (which means that no information leaves the courtroom). Judges have discretion to keep the proceedings closed in other circumstances too, for example responding to a request filed by one of the parties, if it is motivated by prevention of disclosure of a commercial secret, protection of private life, or any other right or interest the court deems legitimate.[33] Similar rules are provided by the Commercial Procedure Code in relation to litigation in a state commercial court.[34]

Covering cases involving juveniles requires special care. The Mass Media Law provides for additional protection for young persons (those under eighteen years old) who are involved in criminal or administrative proceedings. Their identities are treated as confidential information in itself. Editors may not bring to the public any information that leads explicitly or implicitly to the identification of a young person who has committed a crime, or is suspected in the commission of a crime, or has committed an administrative offense or any other action of antisocial character, without the consent of the person in question or a legitimate representative.

13. Are prior restraints or other prepublication injunctions available on the basis of libel or privacy and, if so, what are the standards for obtaining such relief?

Generally, interference or restraint prior to the publishing of any materials or information is not allowed.[35] However, secrecy is required by legislation in certain situations. For example, the Mass Media Law provides that mass media sources may be restrained in relation to "disclosure of any information constituting a state secret or other secret information specifically protected by law."[36] If a mass media source discloses information regarded as a state secret, this will qualify as "a misuse of freedom of information" under Article 59 of the Mass Media Law and could lead to a range of criminal and administrative penalties and liabilities.

The same approach is taken by Federal Law No. 5485-1 dated July 21, 1993, "On State Secrets," which limits access to and reporting on any information related to state secrets to persons with due authorization.

In case of pending litigation, injunctive relief (such as restraining a defamatory publication) may be sought under Article 91 of the Commercial Procedure Code, or Article 140 of the Civil Procedure Code, which contain identical rules on this issue. Both laws allow the judge to "prohibit a defendant from taking certain actions before hearing the case if this is necessary in order to prevent further violation of somebody's rights."

14. Is a right of privacy recognized (either civilly or criminally)?

Yes. The Constitution of the Russian Federation (the *Constitution*) recognizes a right of privacy as a fundamental right of an individual: "Everyone shall have the right to the inviolability of private life, personal and family secrets, the protection of honor and good name."[37] The Constitution further provides that "The collection, keeping, use, and dissemination of information about the private life of a person shall not be allowed without his or her consent."[38]

Violation of privacy may be actionable on different grounds and incur civil, administrative, and criminal liability. For example, it is a criminal offense to illegally collect or disseminate information on the private life of a person which is his or her personal or family secret.[39] Alternatively, a civil action may be brought in order to protect the inviolability of private life and personal and family secrets, and such claims are often coupled with claims for moral damage. In case of a positive outcome, compensation at the discretion of the court and retraction may be awarded (although sometimes courts also award apologies, which are, strictly speaking, not on the legislative list of potential remedies).

If privacy has been violated by a state body, an official, or a nongovernmental organization, the action may be brought on the basis of Article 2 of the Law "On Challenging to Courts any Actions and Decisions that Violate Rights and Freedoms of Citizens," No. 4866–1 dated April 27, 1993.

Truth is not a defense to privacy claims, and the law seeks to redress the intrusive nature of the crime or tort. One recent example was a claim based on the filming of a couple during their wedding. The seven-second fragment of the film was featured in a television program devoted to marriages, and also appeared in promotional spots for the program, which turned on the theory that "all marriages via advertisements are 'calculated marriages.'" Broadcasting of the film in such a program suggested that these newlyweds met each other through a marriage advertisement, which was actually true, but nevertheless was considered an unwanted intrusion into their private life, heightened by the negative comment on such marriages made in the program. The court ruled in favor of the couple, taking into account that they were recognizable in the video recording included in the program, although no names or other personal data were broadcast in the program.

This area of Russian law has recently been further developed by introduction of the Federal Law No. 152-FZ dated July 27, 2006 "On Personal Data" (the *Data Protection Law*). The law introduces and regulates the concept of *personal data*. It provides a detailed definition of personal data, sets out rules prohibiting personal data processing (including disclosure to third parties) without the consent of the individual concerned, sets out reporting requirements for state authorities, and provides for a range of non-compliance measures. It also reinforces the general civil law entitlement of an individual to claim compensation for any substantial damage caused to him or her by improper use of personal data. This is in addition to other options existing in criminal and administrative laws. Thus the Code on Administrative Offenses of the Russian Federation No. 195-FZ dated December 30, 2001 provides that, if the procedures for gathering, storing, utilizing, and distributing personal data prescribed by law are breached, this may lead to fines in the amount of several minimum monthly wages (the amount depends on the status of the offender). The Criminal Code imposes criminal liability for any illegal gathering or dissemination of personal data with a range of penalties, from fines to compulsory work and detention.

a. What is the definition of "private fact"?

There is no commonly recognized legislative definition of a "private fact" per se.

The 1997 Presidential Decree does not contain the term "private fact," but effectively outlines this concept by qualifying as confidential "any information on facts, events or circumstances of the private life of an individual that allows his/her personality (personal data) to be identified, except for any information that is subject to dissemination in mass media in the circumstances set up by Federal laws." A non-exhaustive list includes: information with limited accessibility derived from professional activity (such as a medical secret[40] or an attorney-at-law's secret); correspondence; telephone, postal, or telegraph communications; a secret of adoption;[41] a secret of confession;[42] a secret of will and other actions of a notary;[43] a secret of monetary deposits;[44] and a secret of personal data. This also extends to impermissibility to have a person shadowed and to have private conversations overheard.[45]

The Data Protection Law has introduced a detailed definition of personal data. In accordance with the general provisions of Russian law, in the event of conflicting regulation between the 1997 Presidential Decree and the Data Protection Law, the latter will have priority in application as a specific and more recent piece of legislation.

Under the Data Protection Law, personal data is defined as follows: "any information relating to an identified, or identifiable on the basis of the given information, individual (personal data subject), including his/her surname, name, patronymic, date and place of birth, address, marital and/or social status, material circumstances, education, profession, income and any other information."[46] The list of information qualifying as personal data is not exhaustive. Since the Data Protection Law is relatively new (having come into effect as of January 2007), it has not yet received any significant interpretation in legal practice, nor are there any subordinate regulations or clarifications. Therefore, it is currently unclear what "other information" could also be considered as "personal data" and who would make such a judgment.

Furthermore, the Data Protection Law distinguishes between various degrees of sensitivity of information about an individual by creating separate types of personal data that are subject to separate or additional regulation that is more restrictive. The "personal data falling within specific categories"[47] includes information as to the racial or ethnic origin of the individuals concerned, their political opinions, their religious or philosophical beliefs, their physical or mental health, and their sexual life. The "biometric personal data"[48] consists of information on the physiological characteristics of a person on the basis of which he/she can be identified.

One of the main and most significant principles introduced by the Data Protection Law is the requirement to obtain the consent of a personal data subject prior to the processing of personal data (where processing includes "collection, systematization, accumulation, storage, updating, utilization, dissemination (in particular, transfer), depersonalization, blocking and erasure"[49]) by a personal data operator.

The law "On Information, Information Technologies and Protection of Information" No. 149-FZ dated July 27, 2006 (the *Law on Information*) takes a similar approach as to the consent for processing information related to privacy. It states that "it is prohibited to demand that a citizen (an individual) give any information on his private life, including any information that contains a personal or family secret, and to obtain such information against the will of a citizen (an individual), unless otherwise established by Federal laws."[50] Under the Law on Information, it is mandatory to observe the confidentiality of any data to which access has been restricted by law or in respect of which the owner of such data has introduced a commercial secret regime.

b. Is there a public interest or newsworthiness exception?

In general, the Data Protection Law provides for the principle of confidentiality with regard to personal data.

However, there is an exception for any personal data that is available in the public domain, i.e., accessible by an unlimited number of people. Such information is not covered by the confidentiality requirements, and its processing does not require the consent of the personal data subject. This exception applies, among other things, when the personal data processing: (1) is performed for the purpose of fulfilment of an agreement, provided the personal data subject is a party thereto; (2) is necessary for protection of life, health, or other vital interests of the personal data subject, provided the consent of such individual cannot be obtained; (3) is performed for the purpose of the professional activity of a journalist, or for scientific, literary, or other creative activity, provided the rights and freedoms of the personal data subject are not breached.

Moreover, there is a common understanding of the situations that would justify intrusion into someone's private life for the sake of the public interest. Examples are as follows: (1) investigation of a crime or other serious offense; (2) protection of health or public security; (3) protection of the public from a fraud attempted by a person or by an organization through any word of mouth or any actions; (4) bringing to the public's attention the significant incompetence of an official. In each case, proportionality between any action and the public interest served is required.

c. Is the right of privacy based in common law, statute, or constitution?

The right of privacy is based primarily on the Constitution as discussed above. It is further supported and developed by the Data Protection Law and the Law on Information.

15. May reporters tape-record their own telephone conversations for note-taking purposes (not rebroadcast) without the consent of the other party?

No. Article 49 of the Mass Media Law requires that journalists must let sources know that they are being recorded.

16. If permissible to record such tapes, may they be broadcast without permission?

The broadcasting of tape recordings made without the consent of the source of information (as set out in Question 15 above) is admissible in the following situations:

1. if such broadcasting does not violate the constitutional rights of an individual, for example by identifying him or her;
2. if it is necessary for protection of a public interest and all measures have been taken not to identify a third party without a good reason; or
3. if such broadcasting is based on a court decision.[51]

17. Is there a recognized evidentiary privilege preventing the disclosure of confidential sources relied upon by reporters?
There is a limited shield law, but prosecutors would most likely succeed in overcoming it.

18. In the event that legal papers are served upon the newsroom (such as a civil complaint), are there any particular warnings about accepting service of which we should be aware?
No, except those that relate to general civil procedure. Under the Civil Procedure Code of the Russian Federation No. 138-FZ dated November 14, 2002 (the *Civil Procedure Code*), the service of summons is effected either via registered mail or by personal delivery. The time of delivery is reflected in the receipt, which is returned to the court. The summonses are served either on a particular journalist or, if the claim is against a company, on its authorized representative (e.g., an editor in chief). One can refuse to accept the summons, in which case the person effecting delivery makes a note on the receipt, and for the purpose of litigation this is regarded as effective service.

19. Has your jurisdiction applied established media law to Internet publishers?
There is no specific legislation regulating the rights and obligations of Internet publishers, which prompted Russian courts to apply to Internet publishers the general rules of the Mass Media Law. However, in the absence of a system of precedents, current court practices vary with and do not show consistency in their approach.

There could be three different parties involved in administering an Internet site: (1) the domain owner—the person in whose name the domain is officially registered; (2) the person providing the technical support or content of the Internet site; and (3) the person on whose behalf the Internet site provides the information. It is not uncommon that all three parties are separate legal entities or individuals, in which case allocation of responsibilities among them (particularly in case of a defamatory statement) is not an easy matter. The courts by and large take a view that those who benefit from the site (i.e., administered for their benefit) should be held responsible in such circumstances. Although a domain name may be actually registered with someone else, such "beneficiaries" are seen as the owners of the sites.[52]

Another hot issue is which law applies to Internet publishers. Technically an Internet publisher does not fall within the Russian law definition of a mass media source as it is limited to "printed publications, radio, television, video and documentary film programs" (Article 2 of the Mass Media Law). As a result, publishers sometimes try to avoid the liability associated with registered mass media by using statements/disclaimers to the effect that: (1) they are not required under law to register; and (2) the Internet Web pages are merely their "hobby."[53] The courts, however, increasingly take an approach that (1) the legislation on libel as well as on protection of freedom, dignity, and business reputation should be applicable to Internet publishers independently of their legal "status"; and (2) Internet publishers should be regarded as an electronic mass media source.

The Supreme Court in its Resolution No. 3 dated February 24, 2005, "On Judicial Practice in Cases of Protection of Honor, Dignity and Business Reputations of Individuals and Legal Entities" directs that, if the defamatory information was placed on the Internet on an information resource registered under Russian law as electronic mass media, it will be subject to general mass media requirements and regulations.

In at least one case, it appears that Internet site operators who host chat rooms may not avoid liability even where they are allegedly unaware of the content of postings in those rooms. In *Troyka Steel v. Megasoft LLC* (2004), Troyka Steel filed a claim against Megasoft, claiming that the information posted in a chat room hosted on its Internet site, www.metaltorg.ru, denigrated its honor and dignity and undermined its reputation. The substance of the postings aside, Megasoft argued that: (1) it cannot be considered an entity circulating the information on the Internet site www.metaltorg.ru because neither the site nor the respondent can be considered a mass media source; and (2) the fact that the site belongs to the respondent does not mean that it should be responsible for the denigrating information published in the chat room of the site. The Federal Commercial Court of the Moscow Region ruled in favor of the claimant, applying the provisions of the Civil Code and stating that: (1) the liability for publishing information denigrating the honor and dignity of a person or undermining his or her reputation is not directly linked with the status of the legal entity as a mass media source; and (2) the fact of creating and supporting the site by the defendant made it possible for such denigrating publications to take place.[54]

In *Ramenskiy OJC v. Regnum LLC* (2007) the Commercial Court of the Moscow Region stated that the claim to delete the discrediting information from the Internet site does not represent a new or independent means of protection of rights, but adapts part of the initial claim for refutation of dishonoring information to the technological peculiarities of the Internet where the dishonoring information was placed. The court also emphasized that the data placed on Internet sites is present on the respective sources constantly and continuously, and for this reason dissemination of such information can be stopped only if the respective pages of such sites are removed.

In *OOO Group of companies Metalloinvest-Market v. Mr. A. I. Gusev,* heard by the Moscow Commercial Court on December 8, 2006, the company filed a law suit against Mr. Gusev, an administrator of domain http://www.ruscable.ru seeking to protect its business reputation and claiming 10 million roubles in moral damages. The cause of the action appeared to be an article published on the Internet site that contained unfavorable comments and allegations with regard to the top executives of the claimant company, the company's business practices, and its relationships with commercial partners. The claimant claimed that the published information was false. The court, however, dismissed the claim on several grounds, one of the main ones being that it was not obvious that the information on the site with all certainty pointed to the claimant and was irrelevant to other companies in similar circumstances in the region. In addition, according to the court, a successful claim for protection of business reputation must prove all of the following: (1) the fact of dissemination of information; (2) the defamatory character of the information; and (3) the information is not supported by the facts. The court did not agree that the information was totally of a defamatory nature (as opposed to merely not favorable or critical). Damage to the business reputation was not proved either, due to a lack of causation. The case appears to be a good indication that Russian courts do not regard a disputable situation differently simply on the basis that the information has been released via the Internet.

20. If established media law has been applied to Internet publishers, are there any ways in which Internet publishers (including chat room operators) have to meet different standards?

No. The analysis in Question 19 above applies.

21. Are there any cases where the courts enforced a judgment in libel from another jurisdiction against a publisher in your jurisdiction?

We are not aware of any such cases. Any foreign judgment in the Russian Federation is enforced on the basis of a convention for the mutual recognition of judgments. Currently Russia has entered few such conventions, except with the countries of the former USSR.

Chapter Notes

1. Article 129, the Criminal Code.

2. Article 129, the Criminal Code.

3. Article 129, the Criminal Code.

4. A statutory minimum wage currently amounts to 100 rubles (approximately US$3.40).

5. The Decision of the Supreme Court of the Russian Federation dated June 29, 1999 (abstract from the ruling).

6. "Rzhevsky guilty of libel," *Perekrestok,* November 20, 2003.

7. The review of the cases by the Supreme Court or any other high court of the Russian Federation is intended only for the purpose of observing diligent and accurate interpretation of the law by the relevant courts. Constitution of the Russian Federation 1993, Chapter 7.

8. The word "commercial" in this context is used only for the purpose of defining the type of courts, called, confusingly, "Arbitrazh courts," which hear disputes relating to the business activity of companies and private entrepreneurs including defamation issues.

9. For more detailed analysis of the matters related to fair comment, see the discussion in Question 8 of this chapter.

10. The decision of the Federal Commercial Court of the Moscow Region dated October 14, 2004 No. кГ-А40/8331-04.

11. Article 5, the Advertising Law.

12. Article 36, the Advertising Law.

13. Article 38, the Advertising Law.

14. Article 92 of the Federal Law No. 208-FZ December 26, 1995 "On Joint Stock Companies" specifies the major types of information subject to disclosure and reporting requirements; the detailed procedure is governed by "Procedure for Publication of Annual Book Accounts by Open Joint Stock Companies" approved by Ministry of Finance on November 28, 1996 No. 101.

15. "Provision of Disclosure of Information by Issuers of Capital Issues," approved by the Order of the Federal Service for Finance Market (FSFM) No. 06–117/pz-n dated October 10, 2006.

16. "Provision of Activity of Organization of Trade in Stock Market," approved by the Order of the FSFM No. 07—102/pz-n dated October 9, 2007.

17. "Provision of Order for Keeping Records and Submission of Information on Affiliated Persons of Credit Organizations," approved by the Central Bank of the Russian Federation on July 20, 2007, No. 307-P.

18. See Note 15.

19. Articles 28, 29, the Advertising Law.

20. Article 3, the Mass Media Law.

21. Decision of the Federal Commercial Court of the Moscow Region October 5, 2004, No. кГ-A40/8753-04.

22. Article 57, the Mass Media Law.

23. Decision of the Federal Commercial Court of the Moscow Region dated February 21, 2002, No. кГ-A41/609-02.

24. Article 182, the Criminal Procedure Code.

25. Articles 29 and 182–186, the Criminal Procedure Code.

26. Article 161, the Criminal Procedure Code.

27. Article 241, the Criminal Procedure Code.

28. Article 11, the Commercial Procedure Code.

29. Article 10, the Civil Procedure Code.

30. Article 241, the Criminal Procedure Code.

31. Article 41, the Mass Media Law.

32. Article 10, the Civil Procedure Code; Article 24.3, the Code of Administrative Offenses; Article 241, the Criminal Procedure Code.

33. Article 10, the Civil Procedure Code.

34. Article 11, the Commercial Procedure Code.

35. Articles 3 and 57, the Mass Media Law.

36. Article 4, the Mass Media Law.

37. Article 23, the Constitution of the Russian Federation.

38. Article 24, the Constitution of the Russian Federation.

39. Article 137, the Criminal Code.

40. Protection of medical secrets has been consistently dealt with in a few other sources, such as Articles 30 and 61 of the Basics of Health Protection of Citizens; Article 9 of the Law "On Mental Help and Guarantees to Individuals Taking

It"; Article 52 of the Federal Law "On Sanitary-Epidemiological Well Being of Population"; and Article 12 of the Law "On Avoidance of Spreading out of Tuberculosis in Russian Federation."

41. Article 139, the Family Code; Article 155, the Criminal Code.

42. "On Freedom of Conscience and Religious Associations," Article 3 of the Federal Law.

43. Article 1123, the Civil Code.

44. Article 857, the Civil Code; Article 26 of the Federal Law "On Banks and Banking Activities."

45. Article 9, the Law on Information.

46. Article 3, the Data Protection Law.

47. Article 10, the Data Protection Law.

48. Article 11, the Data Protection Law.

49. Article 3, the Data Protection Law.

50. Article 9, the Law on Information.

51. Article 50, the Mass Media Law.

52. "Retraction of the information on the Internet: legal peculiarities," V.V. Bulichev, *Zakonodatelstvo,* N9, October 2004.

53. "Internet will be viewed as Mass Media," dated July 8, 2004, http://www.media-online.ru.

54. Decision of Federal Commercial Court of Moscow Region dated March 9, 2004 No. кГ-А41/390-04.

CHAPTER 22

Spain

ALMUDENA ARPÓN DE MENDÍVIL
Gómez-Acebo & Pombo

Gómez-Acebo & Pombo
Paseo de la Castellana, 216
28046 Madrid, Spain
Phone: (34) 91 582 91 00
Fax: (34) 91 582 91 20
www.gomezacebo-pombo.com
aam@gomezacebo-pombo.com

Introduction to the Spanish Legal System

The Spanish Constitution of 1978 provides the framework for the Spanish legal system, and the Organic Law of the Judicial Power contains that country's fundamental laws. As described in the Constitution, the General Council of the Judiciary (*Consejo General del Poder Judicial*) is the sole group controlling the Judicial System. The Council is composed of twelve judges and eight lawyers and other established legal professionals. Council members serve a five-year term and may not serve beyond one term.

Spain is divided into several levels of geographical judicial areas. These areas, from smallest to largest, are municipalities, judicial districts, provinces, and autonomous communities. Municipalities only have courts of the peace, judicial districts have courts of first instance, provinces have provincial courts, and autonomous communities have a high court of justice. The Supreme Court and the National Court are the only courts with complete jurisdiction.

Spanish courts are also organized by subject matter. Civil and commercial issues are addressed in civil courts, criminal offenses are heard in criminal courts, social security and employment issues are heard in social courts, and the administrative court is used for public administrative issues. The courts are in a hierarchical structure where lower court decisions can be appealed to higher courts, and higher court opinions override those of the lower courts.

1. What is the locally accepted definition of libel?

The Dictionary of the Royal Academy of the Spanish Language defines libel as "the act of discrediting someone by publishing something against his/her good opinion or fame."

Under Spanish law, defamatory meaning is broad, and libel is most often defined as "an illegitimate intrusion in someone's right of honor" under the Organic Law 1/1982, of May 5, on Right of Honor and Privacy (hereinafter, Law 1/1982). If serious enough, and if the communication in question is made in a public forum, it may also constitute a criminal offense sanctioned by the Spanish Criminal Code, which defines libel as "the action or statement that injures someone's dignity, discrediting his/her fame or as an attack on his/her own esteem."

The Constitutional Court, in Judgment 223/1992, defines libel as "harming the reputation of someone within the public consideration, as a consequence of statements expressed with discredit or disrespect or that were considered as an offense within the public context."

Slander is a higher or aggravated degree of libel, essentially the publication of a statement that similarly injures reputation, but is also made with the knowledge that the statement is false. Slander is also an offense under the Criminal Code.

Spanish law is also unforgiving with regard to hyperbolic language that might be seen as "insulting." For example, in Judgment 1882/2002, the Supreme Court found the following statement defamatory, in this case, made by Ramón Mendoza, a former president of Real Madrid Football Club: "There are people who manipulate the public opinion, and the biggest bastard of them is José María García, who, by means of lies and defamations, creates suspicion and doubts among Real Madrid supporters. . . . Maybe when Mr. García speaks about some people's private life and their economic reputation he is trying to protect his friends, who are seated on the bench."

By contrast, in Judgment 3927/2000, the Supreme Court did not find defamatory an economic magazine calling a group of financial companies a "gang of swine" under the title "How to Hide Money." The Court held that these words could be defamatory, but not within a context referring to a well-reported financial scandal, which was of public significance and related to persons who held professions with a public scope. The Court also stated that the journalists carried out the required diligence in order to verify what they published. (See the discussion in Question 6 below.)

2. Is libel-by-implication recognized, or, in the alternative, must the complained-of words alone defame the plaintiff?

Libel-by-implication is recognized under Spanish law even though no reference is made in this regard in Law 1/1982. In order for the plaintiff to sue for libel, the individual needs to prove that the statements expressed in relation to himself or herself are defamatory within the context in which they were stated.

For example, the Supreme Court found a newspaper liable for publishing a letter that criticized, without evidence, how the principal of a school was appointed, and accused the principal of getting his job through means that did not comply with all legal requirements. Although the words used were not libelous by themselves, these words, when taken as a whole, were found defamatory, and the newspaper that published the letter was held liable for defaming the teacher (Judgment 679/2004).

3. May corporations sue for libel?

The Constitutional Court has established in various judgments that corporations may sue for libel.[1]

4. Is product disparagement recognized, and if so, how does that differ from libel?

Disparagement of products is generally limited to statements made by or between competitors in the marketplace, under Article 9 of the Law on Unfair Competition. Unfair competition may be found simply when the statement is capable of damaging the product's reputation within the relevant market. Likewise, publicity disparaging a competitor's product may also be considered as "unfair publicity" under Article 6 of the Law on General Publicity.

Product disparagement itself cannot be considered an illegitimate intrusion in the right of honor since only persons (either natural or corporate), and not products, are holders of dignitary rights. However, in very extraordinary cases, denigration of a product could be considered a libel upon the manufacturer's reputation.

5. Must an individual be clearly identified (by name or photograph) to sue for libel? Can a group of persons sue for libel, even though not named?

An individual does not need to be clearly identified to sue for libel as long as that person's honor, privacy, or image is damaged. A group of persons can also sue for libel, even though not named.[2] Group libel was recognized in 1991 when Spanish Jews brought a successful libel claim upon a statement made by a German World War II veteran: "If there are so many

Jewish people, it is difficult to believe that they left crematoriums so alive; the problem with Jewish people is that they always want to be the victims, if they do not have enemies, they invent them . . . We need a leader . . . but nowadays there is not a person like the Fürher." (Constitutional Court Judgment 214/1991).

6. What is the fault standard(s) applied to libel?

It is worth noting that Spanish law conflates to a degree the right of privacy and the right to be free of defamatory falsehoods. In order for liability to attach, the defendant must have published either:

1. The disclosure of facts relating to private life, which affect a person's reputation and good name; or
2. The attribution of facts or the expression of statements that injures someone's dignity, discrediting his or her fame; and
3. Either of the above publications must be unprivileged, that is, "an illegitimate intrusion" into the dignitary rights of the subject.

In civil libel, the fault standard is objective, not subjective; thus the author's state of mind is not relevant to a defense. The Constitutional Court defines "illegitimate intrusion" in the following manner:

- The facts or expressions do not serve the public interest.
- The information lacks the requirement of veracity (i.e., genuine efforts to verify the truth of the report, and generally accepted reportorial technique).
- Clearly humiliating, insulting, or opprobrious language with no relationship to the factual matter of general interest is used.

As regards the press and the freedom of speech, Spanish case law is still debating whether or not to apply a subjective standard in favor of the press, i.e., to exonerate the publication of untrue news when the media has used reasonably required efforts in order to find out the truth.

a. Does the fault standard depend on the fame or notoriety of the plaintiff?

In principle, no. However, the fault standard depends on the notoriety of the plaintiff in the sense that the greater the popularity of the affected person, the less right the person has to privacy.

b. Is there a heightened fault standard or privilege for reporting on matters of public concern or public interest?

Yes. Spanish law recognizes a public interest exception to defamation. This is narrowed by an examination into the truth-finding efforts of the reporter. News stories, even if defamatory, may not be the subject of liability when a historic, scientific, cultural, or public interest exists.[3] Public figures have also been deemed to have a limited right of privacy compared with ordinary individuals.[4]

In the civil context, truth is not an absolute defense to libel. If the public interest is not served by the publication, then liability may still attach. Truth is a defense to criminal libel in the narrow instance that the subject of the story is about government employees and relates to facts regarding the exercise of their public function or the commission of either criminal or administrative offenses.

7. Is financial news about publicly traded companies, or companies involved with a government contract, considered a matter of public interest or otherwise privileged?

Financial information regarding important known corporations and publicly traded companies is generally considered to be of public interest. The criteria applied to news about corporate activity do not differ from the general criteria applied to individuals. If the information published is in the public interest and the veracity of what is published was duly checked, the right of the press would prevail over the right of honor.

8. Is there a recognized protection for opinion or "fair comment" on matters of public concern?

Freedom of speech and the right to express opinions are fundamental rights recognized by the Spanish Constitution. Truthfulness of the opinion or the implications that an opinion might engender are not subject to the ordinary degree of diligence, as might be the case with a traditional news story.

However, the freedom of speech and opinion is not absolute. Therefore, if the opinion expressed by a reporter includes humiliating expressions directed at a person (natural or corporate), then an illegitimate intrusion in the right of honor may have occurred.

Protection of the freedom of speech and right to opinion is greater when opinions refer to matters of public concern or toward persons who hold a public service or profession. For example, the Supreme Court did not find defamatory the following statements included in a Spanish Socialist Party's press release: "The company La Palma TV is acting in a sectarian and partial way . . . The news broadcasted does not comply with the necessary pluralism and impartiality . . . they do what Coalición Canaria (the party in the government) orders them to do." The Court explained that damage to La Palma TV's honor did not occur since what the Socialist Party disseminated was criticism protected by the freedom of speech and right to opinion (Judgment 4937/2004. See also Judgments 336/1993 and 79/1995).

9. Are there any requirements upon a plaintiff, such as demand for retraction or right of reply, and if so, what impact do they have?
Yes. Aggrieved parties may make application to the Court for a right of reply. There is no requirement upon plaintiffs to demand a retraction before they file a complaint for libel. Section 2 of Article 9 of Law 1/1982 enumerates the remedies available to prevailing plaintiffs to put an end to the illegitimate intrusion against the right of honor and to be compensated for damages. The subject of a news story can choose one or more of the remedies granted by Law 1/1982:

- ***Right of reply:*** The right of reply is established by a judgment on the facts. The purpose of this remedy is to rectify and clarify the untrue facts and statements disseminated by the defendant. The right of reply is usually carried out in the terms specified by the Court in its judgment against the publisher.
- ***Money damages in tort:*** Both Law 1/1982 and the Constitutional Court recognize the right of the plaintiff to receive pecuniary compensation for the moral and material damages suffered. Presumed (or "Moral") damages are allowed (*iuris tantum presumption*); however, claims for actual damages (called "material damages") must be supported by proof.
- ***Retraction right:*** Law 2/1984 on Right of Retraction establishes that anyone has a right to demand a retraction of the information published in relation to facts about the subject that the individual considers false and the disclosure of which can injure that person's right of honor.
- ***The dissemination of the judgment:*** This remedy is aimed at compensating the plaintiff for the moral damages suffered. The judge shall decide whether the defendant has to publish the whole judgment or only some part of it and the specific media where the judgment has to be published.

Notwithstanding the above remedies, other measures can be requested by the plaintiff and granted by the judge.

10. Is there a privilege for quoting or reporting on:
In general terms, in reporting on matters of a governmental nature, as long as public persons are involved, and provided the journalist is diligent with regard to the veracity of the information reported, the right of information shall prevail over the right of honor. Thus, statements that within a different context might be considered libelous will not be seen as an illegitimate intrusion.

a. Papers filed in court?

Under Spanish law, governmental and judicial documents are not the proper object of copyright. Therefore, unless a secrecy obligation exists with regard to judicial proceedings or judgments (see the answer to Question 12 below), there are no particular restrictions on the reporters to be able to quote or report on documents issued by the courts. By the same token, the general contours of media law still apply to reports from judicial proceedings; thus, insulting or offensive language may not be tolerated.

Documents filed by lawyers are the subject of copyright and, consequently, they cannot be freely disclosed or broadcasted absent the lawyer's consent.

b. Government-issued documents?

Article 71 of the Spanish Constitution establishes that members of Parliament and senators shall enjoy immunity for the statements declared during the course of their public functions. Similarly, under Article 8 of Law 1/1982, statements made by competent government authorities according to law shall not be considered an illegitimate intrusion in someone's right of honor. Thus, official statements from government agencies acting within their lawful capacity may not be the basis of a defamation claim.

Except in the case of insulting or opprobrious language, the public interest privilege would almost always be satisfied by basing reporting on documents issued by the government. As stated above, legal documents generated by the Court or government agencies are not the object of copyright.

c. Quasi-governmental proceedings?

No statutes or cases have treated statements made by these kinds of bodies as on equal footing with government statements; therefore, reporters are urged to act with due diligence in reporting any such statements.

11. Is there a privilege for republishing statements made earlier by other, bona fide, reliable publications or wire services?

Yes. This principle is known in Spain as the "neutral report doctrine." This doctrine allows reporters to accurately quote other, earlier publications, as long as the report is a matter of public concern or public interest (see, e.g., Judgments 232/93, 136/99, and 134/99).

12. Are there any restrictions regarding reporting on:

a. Ongoing criminal investigations?

Yes. In accordance with Article 301 of Law on Criminal Procedure, criminal investigations conducted by the investigating judge (called a "magistrate") shall be carried out in secret until the opening of the oral proceedings.

b. Ongoing criminal prosecutions?

There are no restrictions for reporting on the existence, development, and outcomes of ongoing criminal prosecutions.

Article 680 of Law on Criminal Procedure states that criminal litigation shall be public during the oral proceedings. However, the president of the Court can require secrecy when so required due to reasons of morality or public order, or out of respect for the victim or the victim's family.

c. Ongoing regulatory investigations?

There are no restrictions regarding regulatory investigations.

d. Ongoing civil litigation, or other judicial proceedings?

Except for reporting on matters referring to minors, marital status, or other very personal rights, such as adoptive parents' names, there are no restrictions regarding civil proceedings.

13. Are prior restraints or other prepublication injunctions available on the basis of libel or privacy, and if so, what are the standards for obtaining such relief?

Precautionary measures are expressly allowed in Article 9 of Law 1/1982. These interim measures are aimed at preventing an alleged illegitimate intrusion into someone's right of honor. However, granting interim relief only occurs in very extraordinary cases.

In order for a precautionary measure to be granted by the courts, applicants must provide preliminary proof of the violation of their right of honor and must also post a bond to make good the damages that the precautionary measure might cause to the defendant if the libel claim is unsuccessful.

14. Is a right of privacy recognized (either civilly or criminally)?

Yes. This right is recognized and protected both by Law 1/1982 and by the Spanish Criminal Code. The Constitutional Court considers that the information disclosed represents an illegitimate intrusion into someone's right of privacy when the disclosure is not consented to, and lacks public interest, regardless of the veracity of the information.

The Constitutional Court has held that the following facts represented an illegitimate intrusion into the right of privacy: broadcast of a videotape from an ambulance depicting the agonizing death of a famous bullfighter who was mortally injured in the ring (Constitutional Court Judgment 231/1988); disclosure of the identity and activities of the natural mother of a child adopted by a well-known artist (Constitutional Court Judgment 134/1999); disclosure of the fact that an architect suffered from AIDS (Constitutional Court Judgment 20/1992); and publishing unauthorized photographs of the interior of a famous person's home and detailing that person's personal likes and dislikes in his or her home life (Constitutional Court Judgment 115/2000).

a. What is the definition of "private fact"?

It is a constitutional doctrine under Article 20 of the Spanish Constitution that a "private fact" is that kind of fact found within someone's personal and reserved sphere, kept private by the right's holder, and "necessary to keep a minimum quality of human life." Usual examples are intimate family or medical information, details about children, and financial information.

b. Is there a public interest or newsworthiness exception?

Yes. The public interest is the dispositive criterion to assess whether certain information deserves protection under the right of privacy or, on the contrary, constitutes a legitimate exercise of the right of freedom of information.

Thus, when certain information refers to a public matter, that is, to facts or an event that affects the whole of the citizens, then the information does not represent an illegitimate intrusion in someone's right of privacy.

c. Is the right of privacy based in common law, statute, or constitution?

The right of privacy (as well as the right of honor) is based on the Spanish Constitution, which considers this right fundamental and, therefore, subject to the highest legal and judicial protection.

15. May reporters tape-record their own telephone conversations for note-taking purposes (not rebroadcast) without the consent of the other party?

Yes. Although Article 7 of Law 1/1982 prohibits secret placement of tape-recording devices with the aim of recording someone's private life, the Constitutional Court has also held that persons may tape-record their own conversations without the consent of the other party.

By contrast, a third party may not record without consent a conversation to which he or she is not a party.

16. If permissible to record such tapes, may they be broadcast without permission?
In principle this would represent an illegitimate intrusion in the right of privacy. However, in the right context, the public interest exception may apply. If the person involved in the conversation was a public figure and the recording related to a matter of public interest, it may be justified.

17. Is there a recognized evidentiary privilege preventing the disclosure of confidential sources relied upon by reporters?
Yes. Pursuant to the Reporters' Statute, reporters are obliged to keep secret the identity of their confidential sources. Reporters may not be compelled to disclose their sources to their employers, the public authorities, or judicial authorities except in extraordinary cases, when, as a consequence of the disclosure, the commission of an offense against someone's life, integrity, health, freedom, or sexual freedom can be prevented.

In most circumstances, a reporter summoned to reveal a source's identity in a judicial proceeding must invoke the right to confidentiality. Breach of the promise to a confidential source can be considered an offense under the Criminal Code.

18. In the event that legal papers are served upon the newsroom (such as a civil complaint), are there any particular warnings about accepting service of which we should be aware?
No. Article 155 of the Law on Civil Procedure establishes that the defendant's residence for the purposes of the first summons can be that person's place of work. Thus, it is common in Spain that legal papers are served upon the newsroom and no consequences will arise by accepting service.

19. Has your jurisdiction applied established media law to Internet publishers?
Law 1/1982 protects the right of honor and privacy and constitutes a limit to the right of information regardless of the nature of the media (radio, television, press, Internet, etc.). For example, the Court of First Instance number 43 of Barcelona found "Leading Activities at Canadian Abroad Network Online Associates, S.A." liable for publishing false information on its website regarding the alleged sexual affairs of some members of a football team in a Madrid hotel. The company was ordered to pay damages to the football players and to publish the judgment on its website (Judgment 23/2003).

20. If established media law has been applied to Internet publishers, are there any ways in which Internet publishers (including chat room operators) have to meet different standards?

The standards that Internet publishers have to meet are the same as those explained above. No distinctions are made regarding the media used to diffuse the information.

21. Are there any cases where the courts enforced a judgment in libel from another jurisdiction against a publisher in your jurisdiction?

As far as we know, there are no cases where Spanish Courts enforced a judgment in libel against a publisher from another jurisdiction. However, this does not mean that it is not possible.

Chapter Notes

1. See, e.g., the Constitutional Court Judgment 139/1995 or the Supreme Court Judgment 751/2004, which found the Socialist Party liable for some statements in which it accused the plaintiff, Radio Television La Palma, S.L. (limited corporation), of being partial on political matters. More recently, Supreme Court Judgment 20238/2006 dated November 17, 2006.

2. The Jewish associations B'nai B'rith de España and Amical de Mauthassen had standing to bring an action against the author of a comic book considered xenophobic (Constitutional Court Judgment 1761/1995).

3. As the Constitutional Court Judgment, 22/1995, of January 30, 1995, states: "it is reiterated constitutional doctrine that only the information referred to facts of public concern and obtained and contrasted with a minimum of diligence, that is, truthful information, can be protected by Article 20.1.(d) of the Spanish Constitution (which guarantees the freedom of information right) and prevail over the right of honor guaranteed by Article 18.1. of the Spanish Constitution."

4. Thus, the Constitutional Court has held that the right of honor is weakened when the holder of the right is a public person, a person who holds public functions, or a person who takes part in matters of public concern, because that person is obliged to bear the risk of his or her right of honor being discredited as a consequence of expressions or statements of public interest (Constitutional Court Judgments 165/87, 107/88, 20/92, and 320/94).

CHAPTER **23**

Switzerland

ROLF AUF DER MAUR
VISCHER

VISCHER
Schützengasse 1
P.O. Box 1230
CH-8021 Zurich
Switzerland
Phone: +41 (44) 254 34 00
Fax: +41 (44) 254 34 10
www.vischer.com
ram@vischer.com

Introduction to the Swiss Legal System

Switzerland is divided into twenty-six states, called cantons. Each canton has significant law-making powers, which are evident in the mixture of cantonal law and federal law in each individual canton. Courts are divided into civil, criminal, and administrative courts. As a general rule, cantonal courts serve as courts of first instance and appeal courts, whereas the Federal Supreme Court constitutes the court of last resort. The Federal Criminal Court and the Federal Administrative Court have jurisdiction over particular cases in the fields of criminal law and administrative law, respectively. Procedural law is generally canton-specific, while more substantive laws tend to be federal laws. In recent years, federal codes of procedure have been developed for criminal and civil proceedings, to replace the existing twenty-six cantonal procedures currently in force. The Federal Code of Criminal Procedure and the Federal Code of Civil Procedure are scheduled to enter into force in 2010.

1. What is the locally accepted definition of libel?

Various federal statutes provide civil and criminal sanctions against libel, slander, defamation and, in more general terms, disparaging statements.

Whereas the freedom of speech (*Meinungs- und Informationsfreiheit*) and the freedom of the media (*Medienfreiheit*) are guaranteed by Articles 16 and 17 of the Federal Constitution (herein referred to as "FC"), these civil and criminal sanctions constitute limits to the media that are clearly distinctive from those applicable in other European countries or in the United States.

Three statutes are of particular relevance: (1) the Civil Code of December 10, 1907 (herein referred to as "CC"), for the protection of personality rights; (2) the Penal Code of December 21, 1937 (herein referred to as "PC"), for the protection of the right of honor; and (3) the Unfair Competition Act of December 19, 1986 (herein referred to as "UCA"), for the protection of fair competition. Additionally, the Data Protection Act of June 19, 1992 (herein referred to as "DPA") may also have to be considered.

As a consequence, there is no single definition of "libel," "slander," or "defamation," but rather a framework of legal provisions, which must be examined on a case-by-case basis. Ultimately, these provisions incorporate (and are construed by the courts in accordance with) the constitutional rights to human dignity (Article 7 FC, *Menschenwürde)*, privacy (Article 13 FC, *Schutz der Privatsphäre*), and the right to enjoy free access to and free exercise of private economic activities (Article 27 FC, *Wirtschaftsfreiheit*).

Infringement of the Personality Right (Civil Law)

Article 28 CC protects the rights connected with the personality of an individual or legal entity, i.e., all aspects making a person or entity unique. The personality right includes the right to live, the right to physical integrity, the right to personal freedom, the right to bear a name, the right to one's own image and voice, the right to privacy, and the right to be recognized as a person of dignity. More specific rules relating to the protection of personal data are set out in the DPA. It is noteworthy that the DPA does not only relate to personal data of individuals but also to those of legal entities.

Anyone whose personality is injured by a wrongful act can seek judicial measures against any person who takes an active part in the injury. An injury is illegal when it is not justified (1) by the injured person's consent, (2) by a prevailing private or public interest, or (3) by the law.

Article 28a CC provides for (1) injunctive relief, (2) removal of an existing infringement, (3) a declaratory judgment (if the effect of the infringement is continuing), and (4) a claim for rectification or publication of the judgment. Furthermore, the injured party may ask for compensatory damages and/or for an account of profits and for moral compensation. Damages are only due if the offender was acting with fault, i.e., with intent or with negligence.

In a widely noted recent case before the Federal Supreme Court, the father of the well-known Swiss tennis player Patty Schnyder sought judicial remedies against a Sunday paper for infringement of his personality rights. The paper had, in particular, described the plaintiff as a "Taliban" to characterize his attitude towards his daughter and had accused him of criminal behavior. In addition to the publication of the judgment, the Federal Supreme Court awarded an approximated account of profits to the plaintiff. The Court accepted that the causal relation between the violation of personality rights and the profit gained from the media campaign was virtually impossible to prove. Since many factors determine circulation figures, the exact amount of profits resulting from a specific article in a newspaper cannot be determined. However, the Court ruled that such profit can be approximated, e.g., by taking into account readers and sales figures, the number of violations, and by the positioning as well as the format of the news coverage. In particular, the Court found that the tabloid reporting style cultivated by the newspaper in question raised the readers' expectation of regular sensational articles about celebrities. Since the perpetuation of this expectation and its regular fulfilment increase the newspaper's circulation, the causal link between the violation of personality rights and the profits gained thereby was deemed to be established. The Court further ruled that compensatory damages and account of profits can be awarded cumulatively in certain cases and that even the cost of proceedings before the self-regulatory body of Swiss media (*Presserat*, see below) can be eligible for compensation.[1] The determination of the amount to be paid to the plaintiff in the Schnyder case was left to the cantonal appeal court. Eventually, the parties settled out of court.

Infringement of the Right to Dignity (Criminal Law)

The object of legal protection in criminal law is the right to dignity (i.e., the moral reputation of a person as opposed to the social or professional reputation). Social and professional reputations are protected only by Article 28 CC (and to some degree through the UCA, as outlined below).

The two most important criminal law provisions regarding defamation are slander, Article 173 PC (*Üble Nachrede*), and libel, Article 174 PC (*Verleumdung*). Both provisions apply to the dissemination of false and dishonorable information vis-à-vis a third party or the public. Article 174 PC applies only if the false statement is made knowingly (i.e., the infringer knows that the statement is not true), whereas Article 173 PC includes cases where the defendant is unaware of the statement's inaccuracy.

The dissemination of a defamatory value judgment (e.g., the allegation that someone acts like a "clown") as opposed to a statement of fact, or the dissemination of a factual statement only to the subject of the statement (i.e., not to third parties or to the public) will be qualified as an insult, in accordance with Article 177 PC (*Beschimpfung*).

For lawyers and other professionals bound by statutory duties, it can be argued that their duty obliges them to make certain statements, e.g., about the opposing party, even if such statements might be considered defamatory (Article 14 PC in conjunction with Article 12 lit. a Lawyers' Act, *Anwaltsgesetz*). Yet, there is no absolute exception for such professional statements. Rather, professional statements are required to be appropriate, not unnecessarily offending or against better knowledge. Presumptions have to be declared as such.[2]

Article 173 PC contains a so-called proof of exoneration, which consists of a "proof of truth" and a "proof of good faith": to avoid criminal sanctions, offenders must show either that the defamatory statement was true (proof of truth) or that they had good reasons to believe, in good faith, in the truth of the defamatory statement (proof of good faith). The proof of exoneration can also be applied to Article 177 PC, if a statement of facts is concerned.

With regard to statements published by the media, Article 28 PC determines the allocation of criminal responsibility (*Strafbarkeit der Medien).* Generally, solely the author of the incriminating statement is liable to prosecution. If the author cannot be identified or prosecuted by the Swiss authorities, the responsible editor or the person responsible for the publication according to Article 322bis PC regarding the non-prevention of a criminal publication (*Nichtverhinderung einer strafbaren Veröffentlichung*) is liable to prosecution.

The period of limitation for the prosecution of the above-described offenses according to Articles 173, 174, and 177 PC is four years starting with the day the offense is committed or the day the violation ends, whichever is later (Article 178 Para. 1 in conjunction with Article 98 PC). If a court of first instance rules before the end of such period, the offense cannot be time-barred anymore (Article 97 Para. 3 PC). The Federal Supreme Court held that, in case of publication of a slanderous book, the offense was committed by such publication and the limitation period starts on the respective date.[3]

The following represent some examples of media defamation cases.

A weekly business magazine accused a manager of dubious business practices. The manager resigned from his professional position before the defamatory article was published. As a result of the defamatory article, he was not able to find new employment. The Federal Supreme Court held that the article in question infringed the manager's personality rights and granted compensation for damages of CHF 1.7 million (approximately USD 1.4 million).[4]

A daily newspaper published an article about criminal proceedings that dated back twenty years ago and published the name of the then-juvenile delinquent who had been successfully reintegrated into society by the time of the publication. The Federal Supreme Court held that the media company infringed the personality rights of the former delinquent and argued that there exists a "right to forget." The Court awarded the plaintiff moral compensation of CHF 40,000 for suffering severe depression after the publication of the defamatory article.[5]

The different scope of protection in civil and criminal law can result in situations where a civil personality right (Article 28 CC) is violated, but the elements of the respective criminal offenses are not fulfilled. In the case of a foreign investment in a Swiss holding, a Swiss newspaper described the investor as someone who tried to smuggle money away from the shareholder and into his own pocket. The Federal Supreme Court ruled that such statement was no criminal offense, but that it violated the investor's civil personality rights.[6]

In addition to civil and criminal proceedings, questions of media ethics can be submitted to the self-regulatory body of Swiss media (*Presserat*) in the form of a complaint against unethical media reporting. The *Presserat* is not competent to impose sanctions or award damages, but issues statements which are published on its website and can have effects on the reputation of the respective company (http://www.presserat.ch).

2. Is libel-by-implication recognized, or, in the alternative, must the complained-of words alone defame the plaintiff?

Defamation-by-implication is recognized, i.e., even if a statement is not by itself defamatory, it can become actionable if it is put in a libellous context.

3. May corporations sue for libel?

Corporations may sue for defamation under both civil and criminal law. There is a dispute, however, as to the extent a corporation's "honor" can be infringed under Articles 173, 174, and 177 PC.

4. Is product disparagement recognized, and if so, how does that differ from libel?

Under Article 3a UCA, it is considered unfair (and therefore illegal) to disparage another person or entity, its products, works, services, prices, or other business affairs by making false, misleading, or unnecessarily infringing statements. The disparaging statement must be of some gravity and it must have influence on the competition between the person or entity and other market participants.

Contrary to laws against unfair competition in most other countries, the UCA also applies to parties who are *not competitors* (e.g., to media reporting on businesses, thereby impairing the latter's competitive status). An aggrieved party may initiate civil (Article 9 UCA) and criminal (Article 22 UCA) actions against the infringing party.

Thus, the dissemination of false, misleading, or unnecessarily infringing statements about products, which affect the competitive status of the products, may be subject to civil and criminal sanctions. In a newspaper interview, the manager of a sewing machine company was quoted as saying that a competitor's technical standards were outdated and that his own products were "always technically ahead." The Federal Supreme Court held that the journalist infringed Article 3a UCA by publishing the interview.[7] However, the European Court of Human Rights (herein referred to as "ECHR") has in the past reversed similar judgments under Swiss law. A scientist wrote in an academic journal that food prepared in microwaves is a health hazard. The Federal Supreme Court held that the statement infringed Article 3a UCA.[8] The ECHR reversed the judgment of the Federal Supreme Court, arguing that the statement of the scientist was protected by Article 10 of the European Convention for the Protection of Human Rights and Fundamental Freedoms of November 4, 1950 (herein referred to as "Convention").[9]

5. Must an individual be clearly identified (by name or photograph) to sue for libel? Can a group of persons sue for libel, even though not named?

It is sufficient if the aggrieved party is *identifiable* by the public concerned in the context of a defamatory statement. An explicit identification (i.e., by name, photograph, voice, etc.) is not required.

A group of persons can sue in civil and criminal actions if organized as a legal person (e.g., as a corporation). Unincorporated groups without legal capacity do not have standing to bring actions in Swiss law for defamation (e.g., boards of directors, governmental administrations, or ethical or social groups), and each person must file a lawsuit individually.

6. What is the fault standard(s) applied to libel?

The verification of the source of potentially defamatory information is a significant part of the journalist's professional duties of care. If severe allegations are to be published, the journalist is required to submit the allegation for comments to the person concerned prior to publication and to publish such comments along with the allegation, unless there is not sufficient time for obtaining the comment of the person concerned (principle of *audiatur et altera pars,* stipulated as principle no. 3.8 of the guidelines relating to the Swiss charter of journalists, published by the *Presserat.* See above, Question 1).

Swiss law recognizes a "good faith" defense. The headline in a tabloid, "Rightist Extremist Works for the Protection of the State," was not found to be infringing the right of honor because the defendant could show that he believed with good faith in the truth of the statement.[10]

Each case requires an assessment of the public interest versus the interest of the person concerned. Overall, the reporting style of Swiss media is rather reserved and unaggressive. Exceptions to this common practice, such as the publication of photographs of a government minister in his swimming trunks in 2006, caused a stir in the Swiss media environment. (It did not, however, lead to judicial proceedings.) Yet, a certain tendency towards more aggressive reporting can be identified. The *Schnyder* case (see Question 1, above) illustrates that the courts might not be willing to tolerate this development.

a. Does the fault standard depend on the fame or notoriety of the plaintiff?

The fault standard does not depend on the fame or notoriety of the plaintiff.

b. Is there a heightened fault standard or privilege for reporting on matters of public concern or public interest?

Yes. Reporting on matters of public concern or public interest is privileged under both civil and criminal law, and such publications may be defended from monetary damages by "good faith," namely, by showing that the article was published without malicious intent or negligence, and that it was subjected to a sufficient degree of fact-finding and scrutiny or truth-seeking by the reporter. When the issues at stake concern matters of public interest or public concern, the courts will more readily admit good faith and acquit the defendant on that basis, provided that the journalist has acted in accordance with the "professional duties of care."

Under civil law, the Swiss jurisprudence follows the so-called theory of spheres that distinguishes between the person's (1) intimate sphere, (2) private sphere, and (3) public sphere. A further distinction is made between persons of public interest, where the doctrine further distinguishes between "absolute and relative persons of contemporary history" (*absolute und relative Personen der Zeitgeschichte*) and private persons in whom the public has no interest.

"Absolute persons of contemporary history" (such as the president of a state, a minister of national importance, a CEO of a [multi]national corporation, or a leading celebrity or artist) can only in exceptional cases prevent the media from reporting on them.

"Relative persons of contemporary history" (i.e., persons who are temporarily in the public eye or only in relation to a limited subject matter, such as a scientist) can prevent the publication of any facts that are not related to their public function.

Private persons can challenge the publication of any facts about them unless such facts are part of public life (e.g., a picture taken of a person who is part of a crowd in a sports stadium).

In criminal actions against the infringement of the right to dignity and against insult, the public interest is taken into account as part of the "proof of exoneration" (see above, Question 1).

In either a civil or criminal action, based on Article 3c UCA (see above, Question 4), public interest is taken into account when assessing whether a statement is "unnecessarily infringing."

7. Is financial news about publicly traded companies, or companies involved with a government contract, considered a matter of public interest or otherwise privileged?

There is no particular privilege, as such, protecting the publication of financial news, neither with respect to publicly traded companies nor with respect to companies involved with a government contract. A public interest, however, in information related to publicly traded companies and companies involved with government contracts is likely to be inferred.

8. Is there a recognized protection for opinion or "fair comment" on matters of public concern?

An opinion is not as such actionable as defamation under criminal law (Articles 173, 174 PC), but it can be actionable under civil law (Article 28 CC and Article 3a UCA). In cases where an opinion amounts to a defamatory value judgment, criminal prosecution under Article 177 PC is possible. The line between an opinion expressed by a journalist and a defamatory statement can be a fine one. Good faith is a defence upon which the defendant could rely under criminal law ("proof of exoneration" under Articles 173 and 177 PC; see above, Question 1).

9. Are there any requirements upon a plaintiff such as demand for retraction or right of reply, and if so, what impact do they have?

In civil law, persons who are affected (but not necessarily infringed) in their personality rights by the publication of facts (as opposed to value judgments) in periodically published media, in particular, the press, radio, or television, are entitled to publish a counter-statement (*Gegendarstellung,* right of reply, Article 28g CC). The text of the counter-statement must be brief and restricted to the subject matter of the publication to which the right to reply applies. The person concerned must send the text of the counter-statement to the media company within twenty days from having taken notice of the published facts, but in no case later than three months after the publication. The media company must immediately inform the person concerned, stating when the counter-statement will be published or stating the reasons why it is rejected. When the purpose of the right to reply can only be achieved through the publication of a picture instead of a text, the applicant can request that the media company publish the picture.[11]

The counter-statement shall be published as soon as possible and in such a manner that it reaches the same audience as the facts to which it relates. The counter-statement must be marked explicitly so that it can be recognized as such. The media company is entitled to add a declaration, clarifying whether it maintains the previously published position, and it may also add the sources of its findings. The counter-statement must be published free of charge. If a media company refuses to publish a counter-statement or if it is published incorrectly, the person concerned may file a request with the court.

The law does recognize a mandatory right of reply; however, neither civil law nor criminal law requires a plaintiff to demand retraction of an infringing statement or to exercise a right of reply prior to taking legal action.

A request for criminal prosecution for defamation needs to be filed within three months from the day when the injured party becomes aware of the identity of the infringer (Article 31 PC).

Demanding publication of a counter-statement can be in abuse of law (*rechtsmissbräuchlich*) if the person affected was offered the opportunity to provide comments on the facts before the respective publication.[12]

10. Is there a privilege for quoting or reporting on:

a. Papers filed in court?

There is no privilege for quoting or reporting on papers filed in court. Such reports are still subject to due diligence of responsible reporting.

b. Government-issued documents?

There is no privilege for quoting or reporting on government-issued documents.

In 2006, the new Publicity Law (*Öffentlichkeitsgesetz*; herein referred to as "PL") introduced the principle of publicity for the federal administration. The PL was adopted to improve access to official documents. According to the PL, anybody—including the media—is in principle entitled to access to official documents. Yet, numerous exceptions apply, in particular where business secrets, other legally protected secrets, personal data, overriding public interests, overriding personal interests, or ongoing proceedings (civil, criminal, or administrative) are concerned. In short, although the PL does in principle facilitate access to official documents, it has in fact a rather narrow field of application.

Truthful media reporting about public official negotiations and public communication of official authorities cannot trigger prosecution. However, journalists quoting from official governmental documents legally declared secret by the appropriate authorities may be subject to criminal prosecution for indiscretion (Article 293 Para. 1 PC, *Veröffentlichung amtlicher geheimer Verhandlungen*). This provision of the Swiss PC has been criticized because it criminalizes the media for disseminating information even if the public is interested in this information. In the case *Stoll v. Switzerland,*[13] the ECHR annulled a fine of CHF 800 imposed on a journalist for the publication of a classified document by the then Swiss ambassador in the United States, in connection with unclaimed Jewish accounts. The court found the fine to be in breach of the right to freedom of speech.

Publication of information obtained from a public official bound by official secrecy obligation can result in conviction for incitement to breach such obligation. In *Dammann v. Switzerland,*[14] a journalist was fined CHF 500 for sending a list of names to the prosecutor's office shortly after a high-profile robbery and asking a clerk to provide information regarding the criminal record of the persons on the list. As in the *Stoll* case, Switzerland was found to be in breach of the right to freedom of speech. In both cases, the ECHR found the public's interest in publication of the respective information to prevail.

c. Quasi-governmental proceedings?

There is no privilege for quoting or reporting on quasi-governmental proceedings, such as those issued by professional associations.

11. Is there a privilege for republishing statements made earlier by other, bona fide, reliable publications or wire services?

There is no privilege for republishing statements made earlier by other, bona fide, reliable publications or wire services. The "proof of exoneration" according to Articles 173 and 177 PC, however, may be successful in certain contexts (see above, Question 1).

12. Are there any restrictions regarding reporting on:

a. Ongoing criminal investigations?

Criminal investigations and prosecutions are currently governed by cantonal laws (but a federal law is scheduled to take effect in 2010). All cantons stipulate that criminal investigations shall be conducted secretly. A public official who infringes the secrecy obligation is committing a criminal offense, namely, violation of the official secret (Article 320 PC, *Verletzung des Amtsgeheimnisses*). A journalist who publishes secret information obtained from an official who broke the secrecy obligation can be prosecuted for indiscretion or for incitement to infringe a secrecy obligation (Article 293 Para. 1 PC; see above, Question 10b). A conviction for the latter was, however, found to be in breach of the right to freedom of speech in *Dammann v. Switzerland*. (See above, Question 10b.)

b. Ongoing criminal prosecutions?

Pretrial prosecution is conducted secretly and is subject to the same secrecy obligations as criminal investigations. (See above, Question 12a.) Criminal court proceedings are open to the public: "the court hearing shall be public, and the judgment shall be publicly proclaimed" (Article 30 Para. 3 FC; Article 6 Para. 1 Convention). The public has the right to attend criminal trials. This right includes neither the media's right to make sound or picture recordings nor their right to broadcast the trial to the public. Proceedings under the Juvenile Penal Code (herein after referred to as "JPC") are not generally open to the public, but can be opened to the public if demanded by the juvenile or by public interests (Article 39 Para. 2 JPC).

The public and the media may be excluded from all or part of any criminal trial in the interest of morals, public order, or national security; where the protection of the parties' private lives prevails; or under special circumstances when publicity would prejudice the interests of justice (Article 6 Para. 1 Convention). All cantonal statutes enumerate exceptions to the rule of publicity, within the scope given by the Convention.

c. Ongoing regulatory investigations?

Regulatory investigations are conducted secretly, but the authorities may make public any investigation of public concern. Some laws, including Article 25 of the Federal Antitrust Act (*Kartellgesetz*), provide explicitly that the authorities must respect the secrecy of investigations under Article 320 PC. (See above, Questions 10b and 12a.) A journalist who publishes information obtained from an official who breaks the secrecy rule may be sentenced for indiscretion or for incitement to infringe a secrecy obligation (Article 293 Para. 1 PC; see above, Questions 10b and 12a). A conviction for the latter was, however, found to be in breach of the right to freedom of speech in *Dammann v. Switzerland.* (See above, Question 10b.)

d. Ongoing civil litigation, or other judicial proceedings?

As a general rule, civil litigation or other judicial proceedings are open to both the public and the media (Article 30 Para. 3 FC; Article 6 Para. 1 Convention). Sound and picture recordings or broadcasts to the public are not allowed. Most procedural rules provide that secret proceedings are to be conducted if legitimate reasons are at stake, such as morality or family interests. The latter applies in particular to divorce cases.

13. Are prior restraints or other prepublication injunctions available on the basis of libel or privacy, and if so, what are the standards for obtaining such relief?

Prior restraints and other prepublication injunctions are available on the basis of defamation and privacy. Article 28c CC states that persons may apply for precautionary measures if they can substantiate that their personality rights have been infringed by an illegal act; that such infringement is imminent; and that from such infringement a disadvantage that cannot be easily compensated later will arise.

Where an infringement is caused (or imminent) by periodically published media (i.e., by press, radio, or TV), the court can only take steps to restrain or to remove the infringement if: (1) the personality rights infringement involves a particularly serious disadvantage to the aggrieved party; (2) there exists obviously no justification for the infringement; and (3) the prepublication injunction does not appear to be disproportionate (Article 28c Para. 3 CC).

Yeslam Binladin (the half-brother of Osama Bin-Ladin) and his company, Saudi Investment Company, SICO Corporation, applied successfully for precautionary measures (ban of publication) at a cantonal court before the distribution of a book in Switzerland, published by French authors and entitled *The Forbidden Truth: The Involvement of the USA with Osama Bin-Ladin.* The Federal Supreme Court repealed the decision after examining the defamatory meaning complained of, holding that neither Yeslam Binladin nor his company were put in the perspective of terrorism; the publication was therefore neither capable of harming their reputation nor violating their personality rights.[15]

14. Is a right of privacy recognized (either civilly or criminally)?

Yes. Swiss law recognizes a right of privacy, which is stipulated in Article 13 FC. (See above, Question 1.) As mentioned above (Question 6b), under civil law, Swiss jurisprudence follows the so-called theory of spheres that distinguishes between the person's (1) intimate sphere, (2) private sphere, and (3) public sphere. A further distinction is made between persons of public interest, where the doctrine further distinguishes between "absolute and relative persons of contemporary history" (*absolute und relative Personen der Zeitgeschichte*) and private persons in whom the public has no interest. The object of legal protection in criminal law is the right to dignity (i.e., the moral reputation of a person as opposed to the social or professional reputation; see above, Question 1).

a. What is the definition of "private fact"?

No definition of "private fact" is found in any legal statute. All aspects of a person's intimate and private life are protected as "private fact." This concerns all those aspects of life which a person can legitimately expect not to be made public. Private facts include photographs and/or recordings of private or intimate situations, information on health, on social security measures, or on sexual preferences. Information has, perhaps, held the public's interest at the time it initially occurred, but this interest may dissipate over time.

b. Is there a public interest or newsworthiness exception?

The protected scope of a person's privacy is reduced if that person is active in matters of public concern. (See above, Question 6.) Private aspects may only be published if a public interest is given (e.g., it is of public interest when a person with a pedophiliac past is applying for a position for the protection of children's rights within the local government; on the other hand, purported romantic involvements of celebrities are generally not a matter of public interest).

c. Is the right of privacy based in common law, statute, or constitution?

The right of privacy is based in the Constitution (Article 13 FC) as well as in statutes (Article 28 CC; Article 173 ss. PC; Article 1 DPA).

In one case, a journalist took a photo of a man involved in a criminal proceeding and who had just been released from a pretrial confinement. The subject was standing in the doorway of his house and explicitly told the journalist that he did not want to be photographed. The Federal Supreme Court held that taking a picture of someone against his will, in the doorway of his house, is a violation of this person's privacy right. Note: the plaintiff sued the journalist for infringing his intimate and private sphere through use of a tape recorder.[16]

15. May reporters tape-record their own telephone conversations for note-taking purposes (not rebroadcast) without the consent of the other party?

According to Article 179ter PC (*unbefugtes Aufnehmen von Gesprächen*), without the consent of the other party, reporters may not tape-record telephone conversations for note-taking purposes. This law even applies if the conversation or extracts of the conversation is not intended for rebroadcasting.

16. If permissible to record such tapes, may they be broadcast without permission?
No. (See above, Question 15.)

17. Is there a recognized evidentiary privilege preventing the disclosure of confidential sources relied upon by reporters?
Article 28a PC recognizes the evidentiary privilege of confidential journalistic sources (*Quellenschutz*). The privilege includes the right to refuse to testify in court, to disclose research material, and to reveal journalistic sources. The privilege may be suspended, however, if specific, legally protected interests of importance are at stake.

The privilege can be suspended in connection with certain offenses, if necessary for the prosecution of the crime. The law contains a comprehensive list of such offenses including, in particular, murder (Article 111–113 PC); armed robbery (Article 140 no. 4 PC); sex crimes (Article 187, 189–191 PC); hardcore pornography (Article 197 no. 3 PC); membership in a criminal organization or financing of terrorist organizations (Article 260ter and 260^{quinquies} PC); money laundering and related crimes such as lack of care within financial transactions (Article 305bis and 305ter PC); corruption (Article 322ter–322^{septies} PC); serious drug trafficking (Article 19 no. 2 of the Narcotics Act, *Betäubungsmittelgesetz*); and any other offense carrying a minimum sentence of three years imprisonment. The same applies as last resort in cases of immediate danger to a person's life or health (Article 28a Para. 2 PC).

The legal doctrine also requests that a test of proportionality be conducted in each case before a journalist is requested to disclose research material and sources. In case 132 I 181, the Federal Supreme Court denied the suspension of the privilege, since the public interest in disclosure was not found to outweigh the journalist's interest in legal certainty. The case concerned a criminal investigation in connection with the death of a patient following the transplantation of a heart with an incompatible blood type. After the patient's death, a newspaper published articles containing details about the operation that only insiders could have known. The Federal Supreme Court ruled that, since all insiders had already been interrogated, even the suspension of the evidentiary privilege would not likely result in the resolution of the case. Therefore, the cantonal court's decision ordering the suspension of the evidentiary privilege was repealed.

18. In the event that legal papers are served upon the newsroom (such as a civil complaint), are there any particular warnings about accepting service of which we should be aware?

In Switzerland, the delivery of legal documents is carried out by the courts and not by the parties themselves. In general, the courts deliver legal papers to the defendant at the address provided by the plaintiff.

Should delivery fail because the defendant rejects receipt of the legal documents, effective delivery may be presumed under the applicable cantonal or federal procedural law. If delivery fails because the defendant has no domicile or habitual residence at the address the plaintiff provided, the court may ask the plaintiff to provide an accurate address.

If legal documents in criminal or civil matters against a media company are delivered to the premises of the media company, receipt should not be rejected (because it may otherwise be deemed to have taken place). The documents should be forwarded directly to the person who can make the appropriate decisions on the proper course of action, such as local counsel.

If legal papers in criminal or civil matters against a journalist, whether employee or regular contributor, are delivered to the media company's premises, these documents should be received and forwarded to the proper person. If the journalist is not a regular contributor, receipt should be rejected by explicitly stating that the defendant is not related to the media company. It should be taken into account, however, that legal documents may be published (and thereafter deemed delivered) if these documents cannot be delivered to the defendant.

Receipt of legal papers at the media company premises does not prevent the journalist from appealing the validity of the service at a later stage. Further procedural rules should be considered in accordance with the cantonal laws applicable at the media company's domicile.

19. Has your jurisdiction applied established media law to Internet publishers?

The above law applies to Internet publishers, but there has been no specific precedent of the Federal Supreme Court to this effect.

20. If established media law has been applied to Internet publishers, are there any ways in which Internet publishers (including chat room operators) have to meet different standards?

Internet publishers do not, as such, have to meet different standards, but they may be held liable for content contributed by users and published in discussion forums or chat rooms. Therefore, Internet publishers need to establish clear rules as to the nature of the content that may be published by users. They should also establish appropriate monitoring procedures to ensure that no illegal content can be published by users and that noncompliant content is removed immediately upon the publisher being made aware of it.

Legislation that stipulates a primary responsibility of the publisher and grants relief from criminal prosecution to access providers and (to a lesser extent) to hosting providers has been extensively discussed by the legislator in the past years, but will not be implemented in the near future as, according to the Federal Council of Switzerland (federal executive), the existing laws are sufficient. This finding contrasts with the lack of legal certainty experienced by access and hosting providers. In the absence of clear law, providers are well advised to cooperate closely with the Cybercrime Coordination Unit Switzerland (*Koordinationsstelle zur Bekämpfung der Internetkriminalität; KOBIK*) to avoid criminal prosecution for illegal online content.

21. Are there any cases where the courts enforced a judgment in libel from another jurisdiction against a publisher in your jurisdiction?

There are no publicly reported cases in Switzerland where the courts enforced a judgment in libel from another jurisdiction against a Swiss publisher.

Chapter Notes

1. Federal Supreme Court, BGE 133 III 153; David Rüetschi, *Anmerkungen zu* BGE 133 III 153, sic! 6/2007, p. 440–442; Peter Studer, *Bundesgericht: Erstmals Herausgabe eines (geschätzten) Gewinns an ein Medienopfer, in: Jusletter* of October 1, 2007.

2. Federal Supreme Court, BGE 131 IV 154 and case 6P.174/2004 / 6S.453/2004, May 2, 2005, all referring to Article 32 old PC.

3. Federal Supreme Court, case 6B.67/2007, June 2, 2007, see also BGE 119 IV 199, 97 IV 153, and 93 IV 93.

4. Article 28 CC, Article 41 Code of Obligations, Federal Supreme Court, BGE 123 III 385 and case 5C.57/2004, September 2, 2004.

5. Article 28 CC, Article 49 of the Swiss Code of Obligations, Federal Supreme Court, case 5C.156/2003, October 23, 2003.

6. Federal Supreme Court, case 6S.83/2007, May 17, 2007, and case 5A.78/2007, August 24, 2007.

7. Federal Supreme Court, BGE 117 IV 193.

8. Federal Supreme Court, BGE 120 II 76.

9. *Hertel v. Switzerland*, 59/1997/843/1049.

10. Articles 173 and 174 PC, successful "proof of good faith," Supreme Court of the Canton of Zurich, case DF30002/U, March 1, 2004.

11. Federal Supreme Court, BGE 130 III 1.

12. Federal Supreme Court, BGE 120 II 273.

13. *Stoll v. Switzerland*, no. 69698/01, decision of the ECHR of April 25, 2006.

14. *Dammann v. Switzerland*, no. 77551/01, decision of the ECHR of April 25, 2006.

15. Federal Supreme Court, case 5P.362/2002, December 17, 2002.

16. Article 179 PC, *Verletzung des Geheim- oder Privatbereichs durch Aufnahmegeräte*, Federal Supreme Court, BGE 118 IV 41.

APPENDIXES

I. Special Issues for Book Publishers

II. Shooting Stars: Privacy Claims in the UK

III. Cross-Reference Chart

IV. Recommended Reading

Appendix I

Special Issues for Book Publishers

SLADE R. METCALF
Hogan & Hartson LLP

Hogan & Hartson LLP
875 Third Avenue
New York, NY 10022 U.S.A.
Phone: 212-918-3000
Fax: 212-918-3100
www.hhlaw.com
srmetcalf@hhlaw.com

Libel rules affecting book publishers under U.S. law are significantly different from the rules applicable to newspaper publishers, primarily due to the fact that almost all authors of books are independent contractors and accordingly there are separate bases of liability for authors and book publishers. Unlike the employer/employee relationship with most newspaper publishers and the rather simple written agreements between magazine publishers and writers, book publishers generally enter into detailed written agreements with their authors, who are considered independent contractors. These detailed contractual relationships determine the rights and liabilities of book publishers and authors. This is not always the case in non-U.S. jurisdictions, especially those where a strict liability standard may apply. Book publishers should carefully consider the libel laws of the various nations presented elsewhere in this book, and consult with counsel prior to publication. As a starting point, publishers should ask themselves where the book will be published, and whether or not the potential plaintiff has a significant relationship to that country.

Book publishers face more than libel claims in terms of the legal issues they confront. Although most book publishers use, at least as a starting point, a standard-form written agreement, most authors—particularly the more celebrated ones—can negotiate certain clauses and adjust certain provisions to suit their needs. The following discussion will treat various aspects of the book publishing agreements as well as other issues arising outside of the publishing agreement.

Author Agreements and Electronic Publishing

A book publisher is usually aware of the separate rights that it can acquire from an author in a written agreement. Generally, a trade book publisher will acquire at least exclusive first rights to publish the author's manuscript (the "Work") in the hardcover edition for a specific geographic area, whether the United States, North America, or worldwide. Some of those rights that a book publisher can acquire are as follows:

- Softcover or paperback rights
- Syndication rights for newspapers or magazines
- Anthology rights
- Abridgement or condensation rights
- Foreign language rights
- Rights to subcontract publication in other countries
- Motion picture rights
- Derivative rights
- Theatrical rights
- Book club rights
- Rights for publication in Braille or large-size type
- Audio rights
- Electronic rights

It is important for book publishers to consider the scope of the electronic rights that they may be acquiring. If there is a negotiation as to particular electronic rights, some of the rights to be considered should include:

- Electronic retrieval rights such as Nexis or other subscription data services
- Rights for the publishers' websites
- Electronic commerce (or e-book rights)

With the commercial viability of e-books seemingly on the rise, all book publishers, to the extent that they obtain electronic rights, should clarify that they are receiving rights to publish the Work in e-book format.

Noncompetition Clauses

Book publishers may from time to time preclude certain authors from having manuscripts published that are competitive with a book already under contract to the publisher. These prohibitions on competitive works are subject, of course, to reasonable time restrictions. Such a competitive restriction would not be upheld, for example, for the life of the copyright of the published Work. These competitive restrictions are more likely to be upheld as reasonable if they preclude books by other publishers on the same or similar topics as the initial book published. With respect to "similar" topics, it is helpful to describe and delineate the scope of the subject matter that is restricted. Frequently, a book publisher will obtain from the author an option to publish the next book or books by the author, or secure the right of first refusal or a right to match a competing offer made to the author.

Publishers' Obligations and Warranties

The publisher generally accepts the responsibility in good faith to edit, print, bind, and distribute the Work as submitted by the author. However, courts routinely determine that standard publishing agreements grant publishers "wide discretion in the performance of [these] obligations." Indeed, in one case, a court found that a book publisher's decision to terminate its publishing agreement with the actor Tony Curtis was reasonable despite Curtis's allegation that the publisher did not provide him with adequate editorial services. The court found that, while the publisher had a duty to exercise good faith "in its dealings" with Curtis, this general duty did not "include a duty to perform skillfully." Specifically, the court held, in the absence of an explicit contractual provision, it would not impose a duty on the publisher "to perform adequate editorial services." The court reasoned that "[t]o imply such a duty . . . would . . . represent an unwarranted intrusion into the editorial process." As one later case noted, however, while courts will not impose a duty on a publisher to provide reasonable editorial services, this obligation can be modified by express contractual language.

The publisher rarely, if ever, takes on the obligation to ensure that the facts contained in the manuscript are accurate. Occasionally, the publisher will take on the obligation to "use its best efforts" to market the Work. However, the publisher, except in those cases when a contract is with a very well-known author, will assume the exclusive rights to determine such aspects as the distribution of the book, layout of the book, quality of the paper, price of the book, nature of the binding, advertising efforts, markets for distribution, and publicity relating to the ultimate publication. However, one court noted that, notwithstanding an express contractual provision leaving the number of copies of a work to be published and the advertising budget to the publisher's discretion, a publishing agreement implies an obligation upon the publisher to promote a book it publishes and to provide an "advertising budget adequate to give the book a reasonable chance of achieving market success in light of the subject matter and likely audience." But, the court noted, once the obligation to perform initial promotional activities has been fulfilled, a publisher's business decision to limit further printings or the advertising budget should not be overturned.

Authors' Obligations and Warranties

First and foremost, the author agrees to provide a publishable manuscript within a certain deadline and of a certain length, both of which are set by the publisher. The author generally agrees to obtain appropriate releases and permission forms for photographs and illustrations or reprinted material, which will be included in the published book. The author also warrants and represents that the manuscript as submitted is original to her or him and will be free from any claims of libel, invasion of privacy, and copyright infringement, and that it will not be harmful to the reader. Frequently, a book publisher will require an author to certify that the manuscript is accurate to the best of the author's knowledge. The author also generally agrees to indemnify the book publisher for any costs, including reasonable attorney's fees, which arise as a result of any claims made against the published work. Some book publishing agreements limit the indemnification only to those occasions where a claimant *successfully* pursues a claim against the publisher or the costs arise from a breach or alleged breach of the author's warranties.

The issue of warranties and indemnification should be addressed at the commencement of any libel, invasion of privacy, or copyright suit. To the extent that the publisher agrees that it is appropriate to have the same outside counsel represent both the book publisher and the author, it is important to discuss and specify with the author the nature of the relationship with the joint outside counsel and how the indemnification might work. Sometimes a book publisher will "freeze" the royalty account of the author so that there will be a fund to pay the legal expenses at the end of the case. Both the book publisher and the author should resolve the questions of what might happen if their interests diverge as the suit proceeds. For example, it may turn out that the author was aware of certain information but did not share it with the publisher. That might well impose increased liability on the author, and the publisher might prefer to make a significant issue of the failure of the author to disclose that relevant information.

Insurance Coverage for Authors and Publishers

Book publishers commonly have insurance policies for the books that they publish. Those policies may also provide coverage for the authors who are independent contractors. The policy may spell out the deductible (or retention) under the policy, which is the maximum amount of money for defense costs and settlement that will be owed by the publisher. The book publisher, in turn, may have an arrangement with the author in the written agreement, whereby the publisher and the author pay the retention amount on a certain percentage basis. For example, if there is a $200,000 deductible and the publishing agreement provides that the author and the publisher would share the retention on a 50/50 basis, then the author would be obliged to reimburse the publisher in an amount of up to $100,000. That amount might well be deducted from the author's royalty account, if there are any monies owed or to be owed to the author. The insurance policy may provide that the publisher (or insured) can select counsel to represent it with respect to claims filed against it, but that right is often subject to the approval of the insurance company. The policy may or may not specify whether the insurance company will pay for separate representation of the author in the event that the interests of the publisher and the author diverge during the course of the lawsuit. The author will always have the option of retaining his or her own counsel, but such representation would be at the expense of the author. In order for the insurance company to cover the cost of separate representation, the conflict between publisher and author generally needs to be material.

Differences in Liability between Author and Publisher

Unlike the newspaper business, because the author is not generally an employee of the book publisher, there is no *respondeat superior* manner of responsibility or liability. As an independent contractor (which the publishing agreement usually specifies), the author has her or his own basis for liability. The separate basis often translates into a heightened level of protection for the book publisher. Libel in the United States differentiates between public persons and private figures. Individuals (and corporations) who are deemed to be public figures or public officials must satisfy the onerous burden to show by clear and convincing evidence that the publisher and/or author either knew that the offending language was false or had serious doubts about the truth of that language. This so-called "constitutional malice" standard for public persons frequently means that the book publisher will avoid liability because the publisher generally relies on the *bona fides* of the author and the representations and warranties in the publishing agreement that the author has taken appropriate steps to ensure the accuracy of the manuscript. The publisher may incur liability if it is put on notice prior to publication that certain facts in the manuscript are false and defamatory, and the publisher takes no steps whatsoever to obtain assurances that the material is in fact accurate. For example, if a book publisher were provided with a tape recording of a meeting that directly contradicts the author's portrayal of that meeting in the manuscript, and the publisher takes no steps to obtain independent corroboration or modify the wording of the manuscript, then the book publisher may be held liable under the constitutional malice standard. On the other hand, the author may be subject to liability even in a libel suit brought by a public person if that author was a part of a particular event and it was shown that the author's rendition of that particular event was false. The plaintiff will argue that the author knew that the portrayal in the manuscript was false because the author participated in the event and therefore must have known that the wording was contrary to the actual facts.

When a libel suit is brought by a private person, the standard to be imposed in a particular case is dependent on the law of the appropriate state that governs the proceedings. That standard of liability may range from a simple negligence standard (as in most states) to a gross negligence standard (as in New York State) to a constitutional malice standard (as in Colorado, Indiana, and New Jersey). Where a negligence standard applies, it is extremely difficult for a libel case to be dismissed prior to trial. Courts will generally allow a jury to make a determination whether the publisher and/or the author used reasonable care in researching, writing, and publishing the offending language. Such evidence would thus be evaluated under the negligence standard. Frequently, book publishers will submit testimony from professional editors or other journalists to show that what the book publisher and author did with respect to the book at issue in the lawsuit was reasonable under the circumstances and that the efforts of the defendants evidenced reasonable and due care.

Product Liability

From time to time, purchasers and readers of books claim that they have been physically injured or have suffered some kind of economic damage from material contained in a book. Although infrequent, those claims can have a severe adverse impact on a book publisher and its authors. For example a cookbook might contain a recipe that inadvertently contained the wrong ingredient or incorrect amount of the ingredient. If the misnamed ingredient was in fact dangerous, it could certainly cause health hazards to the reader.

Indeed, in one unfortunate case, a book contained the wrong name of a mushroom to be picked and eaten, and a reader died from ingesting poisonous mushrooms. In another case, a medical textbook contained the wrong name of a chemical substance to be injected for an enema. A nurse relied on the book and used that incorrect chemical when she self-administered an enema. The incorrect chemical burned her insides. United States courts have generally found in those circumstances that the book publisher does not have a duty to the reader to ensure the accuracy of the information contained in the books. In other nations, particularly those without a constitutional right to press freedom, publishers of instructional, how-to, and other informational books may be held liable for incorrect information that results in monetary loss or physical harm. Again, it is strongly suggested that publishers consult with local attorneys prior to distributing books in multiple jurisdictions.

It is also worth noting that even in the United States, courts have not been so clear that the individual author does not owe a corresponding duty of care to the readers. In the case involving the self-administered enema, the court dismissed the book publisher from the case but did not dismiss the author from the case.

Courts have also rejected claims when certain financial information turns out to be untrue. For example, incorrect listings of prices of securities have not provided a basis for a claim based on negligent publication. As an example, a book publisher came out with a book about battered women. The book contained a listing of attorneys who were familiar with the area of the law. One of the attorneys listed turned out to have been sanctioned by a state disciplinary organization. A reader who relied on the book in selecting the attorney learned, unfortunately, that the attorney had ignored her case and that the statute of limitations had expired on her claim. The court found that the book publisher again did not have a duty of care to the reader and, although the information about the attorney was not current, the plaintiff could not pursue any claim. For whatever reason, the plaintiff in that case chose not to sue the two authors of the book and therefore the court did not have occasion to decide whether the authors had a duty to take reasonable steps to make sure the information in the book was accurate.

A separate category of cases in this area arises when a publisher endorses or guarantees the quality of a product or a service. For example, a court declined to dismiss a case against *Good Housekeeping* magazine when it placed its "Good Housekeeping Consumers Guaranty Seal" on a product that allegedly was defective. Courts on rare occasions have found that certain advertising that contains harmful information can be grounds for a lawsuit. However, those cases are generally restricted to the commercial speech or advertising context. A rare exception concerned the manual called *Hit Man: A Technical Manual for Independent Contractors.* There, the author gave precise instructions on what to do in the event you wanted to kill someone. A man looking to obtain his son's $2 million trust fund, derived from the settlement of a personal injury suit, hired an assassin to murder his ex-wife, his son, and the son's nurse. The assassin succeeded. Certain relatives of the decedent wife and son sued the book publisher on the theory that the publisher aided and abetted the assassin. A federal appellate court found that the publisher could be held responsible for information that was so clearly offensive and dangerous on its face.

Print-on-Demand Publishing Agreements

A new but increasingly common type of book publishing agreement is the "print-on-demand" self-publishing agreement. "Print-on-demand" agreements differ significantly from typical publishing agreements and, while current case law interpreting "print-on-demand" agreements is sparse, these differences are likely to effect the duties and obligations courts will impose on "print-on-demand" printing companies. For instance, in a typical publishing agreement, the book publisher will select and pay certain authors to write a book for the publisher, and, as noted above, the publisher will have the duty to publish, edit, distribute, and promote the book. However in a "print-on-demand" agreement, the author, typically an unknown author without a significant budget, pays the printing company to print a limited number of copies of the author's manuscript, which the author will then purchase from the printing company and distribute and promote independently. The printing company does not review, edit, or fact-check the author's manuscript before printing it, and, unlike typical book publishers, the "print-on-demand" printing company is not selective; it typically prints any manuscript submitted to it. Moreover, in a "print-on-demand" agreement, the relationship between the author and the printing company differs considerably from the relationship in a typical book publishing agreement. In a typical book publishing agreement, the publisher will work closely with the author to develop, publish, and promote the book. In a "print-on-demand" agreement, on the other hand, the author has minimal contact with the printing company. Indeed, typically the author simply submits a PDF-formatted manuscript to the printing company over the Internet, which the printing company will then print for the author.

In one recent case, a court held that due to the unique and distant relationship between the author and the printing company in a "print-on-demand" publishing agreement, it would not impose the same duties on a "print-on-demand" printing company as it would on a typical book publisher. In that case, the court determined that the "print-on-demand" printing company could not be liable for defamation based on the statements contained in a book that it printed because the company was not an active participate in the preparation of the defamatory statements and it did not know or have reason to know that any of the statements in the book were defamatory. The court reasoned that the printing company did not have any actual knowledge that any of the statements in the complained-of book were defamatory because, although the company published the manuscript and made it available on its website, as was typical for "print-on-demand" companies, it never read, reviewed, or edited the manuscript. Further, the court held that the printing company did not have any duty to inspect the work for defamation. The court reasoned that because these types of printing companies print any manuscript submitted to them, imposing a duty on "print-on-demand" printing companies to review each and every manuscript submitted to them would be too great of a burden and would impair a company's ability to print the works of lesser known authors at affordable prices. However, the author would still have the same responsibilities and be subject to the same legal exposure as if she or he had entered into a traditional agreement with a book publisher.

Appendix II

Shooting Stars: Privacy Claims in the UK

AMBER MELVILLE-BROWN

David Price Solicitors & Advocates

David Price Solicitors & Advocates
21 Fleet Street
London EC4Y 1AA
United Kingdom
Phone: +44 (0) 7793 001 023
Fax: +44 (0)20 7353 9990
www.am-b.co.uk
am-b@btconnect.com

Introduction

"A picture paints a thousand words" according to American actor Telly Savalas, or more important perhaps, according to the UK's House of Lords in the notable privacy case of British supermodel and secret drug addict, Naomi Campbell.[1] Since that seminal case, privacy claims have continued to gain viability in the UK, most notably against tabloid or celebrity-centered publications. But what will generate a complaint is not always obvious. Complaints have been made over unauthorized, long lens photographs of soccer star David Beckham in his underwear on a private Portuguese balcony,[2] and of British radio presenter Sara Cox, honeymooning in a private villa in the Seychelles and snapped naked in her Jacuzzi by a photographer from a boat offshore.[3] But complaints have also been made over depictions of everyday matters such as skiing and horseback riding—*Caroline von Hannover v. Germany* (*von Hannover*)[4]—and by a mother pushing her toddler in a pushchair down an Edinburgh street; this was no ordinary mother—it was the multimillionairess author J.K. Rowling who famously guards the privacy of her and her family with ferocity.[5]

These types of cases are gaining ground, despite the fact that there is no English constitutional right to privacy. Historically, there has been no free-standing tort of privacy and little parliamentary appetite for legislation. But the implementation of the Human Rights Act 1998 (the HRA)[6] incorporating into UK law the European Convention of Human Rights (the Convention) guaranteed not only the Article 10 right to free speech,[7] but also the Article 8 right protecting privacy.[8] In *Douglas v. Hello* concerning the unauthorized publication of wedding photographs of Hollywood royalty Catherine Zeta-Jones and Michael Douglas, the UK Court of Appeal recognized "for the first time" that post the ECHR case "the courts have a duty to recognise and protect privacy rights."[9]

Anyone who flips through the pages of the British tabloid press or any number of the magazines that jostle for position in the thriving celebrity magazine market may think that the courts are not taking that duty sufficiently seriously. A closer look, however, will show that this is far from the case and that the courts are coming down hard—or as hard as legislation currently allows—where it finds that privacy rights have been unnecessarily infringed. One might deduce, therefore, that the bare buttocks and unsightly cellulite that do grace these pages are either authorized, or are at least tolerated by their owners in compliance with the Faustian pact that they have signed with the media. But if this is the case, how can the reporter and editor up against deadline, or the photographer on the street, and the picture editor back in the office know what will generate a successful complaint and what won't get off the ground? While every case is always decided on its facts, months of legal wrangling after the event in those cases that do get before the courts can help others, prepublication, get a better view of whether their exposé will expose them to legal action.

The law is evolving fast in the UK in spite of, or perhaps precisely because of, the fact that the shelves of every newsagent and supermarket are groaning under the weight of celebrity-obsessed publications. Focusing on photographs, this chapter aims to give an insight to those operating at the coal face of the industry, making daily decisions as to the content of their publications, into how to protect their freedom of expression while not unnecessarily infringing the rights of others.

The Human Rights Act: Synching Up with Europe

The implementation of the HRA significantly impacted UK privacy laws, which until then had been a mish-mash of causes of action including trespass, copyright, and breach of confidence. Incorporating into UK law the European Convention's twin rights of freedom of expression and the right to respect for private and family life, *aka* "privacy," it required the courts, as set out by Nicholls LJ in *Campbell,* "to recognise that the values enshrined in Articles 8 and 10 are now part of the cause of action for breach of confidence." Indeed, born out of the long-standing cause of action of breach of confidence, privacy got its full name at a christening by Lord Nicholls in Campbell, when he said: "Information about an individual's private life would not, in ordinary usage, be called 'confidential.' The more natural description today is that such information is private . . . The essence of the tort is better encapsulated now as misuse of private information." Like two naughty siblings, Articles 8 and 10 have been fighting for supremacy ever since. But neither has automatic precedence and the UK courts must balance the two rights in circumstances where they are both at play.

Any discussion about privacy without reference to Naomi Campbell's case is like a treatise on the history of English literature ignoring Shakespeare. While the internationally famous and frequently photographed supermodel could not complain about being outed as a drug addict by the *Mirror* newspaper—she had lied about her addiction publicly so had to accept that there was a legitimate public interest in exposing her as a hypocrite—in this case, the devil was in the detail. She complained that the combination of photographs of her taken on the steps of the Narcotics Anonymous (NA) and the inclusion of details about her treatment infringed her privacy rights. She had to fight all the way to the UK House of Lords, but was eventually successful albeit on a three to two majority. The judicial disagreement turned on the application of the law to the specific facts and the "margin of appreciation" to be allowed to the editor in adding color to the story that it legitimately proposed to publish. The senior judges Lords Nicholls and Hoffman were in favor of dismissing the claim, while the other three, Lords Hope and Carswell and Baroness Hale, upheld it. Despite an inability to reach agreement on the facts of the case, useful and significant general principles were stated:

- the right to freedom of expression and the right to respect for a person's privacy, enshrined respectively in Articles 10 and 8 of the European Convention on Human Rights, lie at the heart of liberty in a modern state;
- neither Article 8 nor Article 10 has precedence over the other;
- the "touchstone" of private life is whether the subject had a reasonable expectation of privacy with regard to the disclosed fact;
- in deciding whether there is an invasion of privacy, it is important to distinguish between the question as to whether Article 8 is engaged, and subsequently, the question as to whether the subject's rights are nevertheless not infringed as a result of the combined effect of Article 8(2) and Article 10.

Von Hannover and the ECHR Ruling

Meanwhile in Europe, privacy law was being put through its paces in *von Hannover v. Germany*. Princess Caroline von Hannover, the eldest daughter of Prince Rainier III of Monaco, had, during the 1990s and beyond, brought a number of actions over the publication in Germany of photographs that she said invaded her privacy and, contrary to the German Basic Law, infringed her right to the protection of her personality rights. These pictures featured her going about her normal daily business—with her children, at the end of a secluded courtyard—and they were found in one landmark decision in the German Constitutional Court in 1999 to have breached her rights under German law. But whereas other pictures taken in France of her horseback riding, skiing, shopping, and so on would have breached stricter French privacy laws, published in *Bunte, Freiseit,* and *Neue Post* in Germany they did not. The German courts found that as a public figure "par excellence" she had to tolerate photographs of her in public places, be they at any public functions or otherwise. If she could not show that she was in a secluded place out of the public eye, she would have to put up with what she maintained was constant harassment from photographers cataloguing virtually her every movement.

But the ECHR—in whom the matter was entrusted after numerous hearings throughout the various German courts—did not find this acceptable, referring in its judgment with obvious distaste to the way in which the photographs were taken and "the harassment endured by many public figures in their daily lives." On June 24, 2004, the ECHR found that Princess Caroline's rights guaranteed by Article 8 of the Convention had been infringed and that the laws of Germany had not sufficiently protected her.

A deciding factor in balancing the protection of private life against the right to freedom of expression was the contribution that the publication of the photographs made to "a debate of general interest," the court said. The photographs here—taken in public but without her consent—did not refer to any public function but merely to Princess Caroline's private life. There were no special circumstances to justify their publication and even as a public figure Caroline had a legitimate expectation that her private life would be protected. The ECHR seemed to draw an important distinction between Caroline the Princess and Caroline the woman:

> A fundamental distinction needs to be made between reporting facts—even controversial ones—capable of contributing to a debate in a democratic society relating to politicians in the exercise of their functions, for example, and reporting details of the private life of an individual who, moreover, as in this case, does not exercise official functions. While in the former case

> the press exercises its vital role of "watchdog" in a democracy by contributing to impart[ing] information and ideas on matters of public interest . . . it does not do so in the latter case.

Albeit that Princess Caroline was not a private individual and that the public might be interested in seeing the photographs, the court found that the photographs of complaint did not concern her taking part in any official functions and were purely to "satisfy the curiosity of a particular readership regarding details of the applicant's private life." Accordingly, even though they were relatively anodyne in subject matter and even though they were taken in a public place, they did not contribute to a debate of general interest and, accordingly, they were private.

What has clearly come out of *von Hannover* is that the courts have an obligation to protect individuals from invasion of privacy by others, and that although the press will be praised for its role as Watchdog of Society, it will be reprimanded where it extends that role and acts to the detriment of others as lap-dog to the public's prurient interest for pure entertainment and titillation.

So, if a publisher can be prevented from publishing photographs of an internationally famous woman out and about in public doing nothing in particular, one might imagine that *von Hannover* rang a death knell for the tabloid newspaper and celebrity magazine market. That was certainly not the immediate result, although a certain amount of self-censorship does appear to have subsequently occurred, which may have been the result either of confusion over which way the legal wind was blowing or simply to avoid costly and time-consuming litigation with celebrities' lawyers.

Is there a better response? In order to avoid confusion or unnecessary self-censorship, the best that anyone publishing in the United Kingdom can do is to try to anticipate how the courts will assess their publication if they end up defending it in the witness box. And to do that it is helpful to know just what the courts are likely to take into consideration. In other words, as part of their risk assessment—"Is George Bush really likely to sue over the publication of that photograph?"—publishers must ask themselves what the court would make of it if they were unlucky enough to find themselves on trial defending their publication after the event, or trying to fend off an injunction.

Assessing a Claim in Privacy

First, the court will assess whether the claimant gets over the threshold of establishing a *prima facie* claim to privacy. If the claimant does, the court will balance that claim against any other rights that might be affected, which in the case of the media is often going to be the Article 10 right to freedom of expression.

Getting over the threshold requires the claimant to show that their Article 8 rights to privacy are engaged; in other words, that they have a "reasonable expectation of privacy" in respect of the material that they are seeking to protect. The publisher can't avoid liability by simply pointing to the fact that the photograph was taken in public and arguing that, accordingly, no reasonable expectation exists—the cases of *Campbell* and *von Hannover* are evidence of that. How then, can this be assessed? There are probably as many ways of doing it as there are legal minds out there grappling with the concepts. But the important thing for any publisher is to take into account in respect of each of the elements which the media wishes to publish *all* the surrounding circumstances—none of which on its own is necessarily going to be decisive—including the nature of the information that the claimant is seeking to protect, who the material concerns, and where and how it was obtained.

Where the proposed publication includes photographs, the publisher should assess, specifically and separately, whether the subject has a reasonable expectation of privacy in relation to that material. Sure, the publisher has a margin of appreciation in the manner in which he illustrates his articles. But that does not give him *carte blanche* to ride roughshod over his subject's private life. An unnecessarily invasive photograph may invade the subject's privacy where a straightforward relating of the facts may not. The House of Lords in *Campbell* gave the hypothetical example of a story that disclosed a sexual relationship between a politician and someone who they had appointed to public office. While it might be in the public interest to disclose the relationship, it might be a step too far to illustrate the story with a photograph: "The addition of salacious details or intimate photographs [might be] disproportionate and unacceptable," the court said.

A real life example is the case brought by British children's television presenter Jamie Theakston.[10] He had complained over a prominent exposé in *The People* newspaper, a British Sunday tabloid, of a trip after a drunken Christmas party to what he said he was told by his taxi driver was a late night drinking venue, and which turned out to be a brothel. So the story went—although he could not remember much about it—he was taken to a private room where "a sex act" was performed on him before someone burst into the room and took a photograph. Mr. Theakston was unsuccessful in his application for an injunction to prevent the publication of the story in the public interest, but he was successful in preventing the publication of the photographs, which the judge said would "constitute an intrusion into his private and personal life and would do so in a particularly humiliating and damaging way."

What, Who, How, and Where?

All manner of material might be captured on film which would titillate and entertain the public—even inform and educate them—but at the same time would horrify the subjects and cause them to reach for their lawyers. There is no exhaustive list, but a look at recent cases will give an indication of the sort of information that should ring alarm bells.

What?

Material of a medical or quasi-medical nature, as noted in the case of *Campbell*, is almost certainly going to be high on the list for public policy reasons. Who would visit the doctor, seek counseling, or engage in therapy with organizations such as Alcoholics or Narcotics Anonymous if they believed that details of their treatment and therapy, or photographs of them undergoing the same, were fair game for the media? A distinction can be drawn, however, between treatment and drug abuse itself, which could be exposed, equally in the public interest; "the possession and use of illegal drugs is a criminal offense and a matter of serious public concern," said Baroness Hale in the Campbell case. "The press must be free to expose the truth and to put the record straight."

Photographs of the naked body and of people engaged in sexual activity will not be far down on the list of protected material. Model daughter of Rolling Stones Mick, Elizabeth Jagger sought the protection of the court when a nightclub owner sought to publish photographs of her and footballing legend George Best's son, Callum, engaged in sexual activity taken from CCTV footage inside his club.[11] The court accepted her evidence that they had been in a discreet corner of a dark and secluded room of the club and that she had a reasonable expectation of privacy as regards her sexual conduct there. As with Jamie Theakston, the court took into account the humiliation that such a publication would cause. In 2008, the actress Sienna Miller obtained £37,500—reportedly the highest sum so far for a photographic privacy action—for the unauthorized publication in the *News of the World* and *The Sun* of photographs of her in costume on a closed set of her new film, *Hippie Hippie Shake*. The problem here was that the costume was her "birthday suit."[12]

Who's who?

The publisher must also consider the identity of the subject. Just because John Doe has never engaged with the media before, it doesn't mean that as a private person he will automatically be protected where there is a public interest, for example, in the material to be exposed. Equally, celluloid celebrities are not always going to be fair game; their attitude and history with the media, their own self-exposure or privacy protection will be relevant. In *Campbell*, Lord Hoffman referred to the symbiotic relationship that Ms. Campbell had with the media: "She and they have for many years fed upon each other. She has given them stories to sell their papers and they have given her publicity to promote her career." By contrast, Princess Caroline of Monaco rarely carried out any official functions and attempted to live as normal a life as possible; her status as a princess did not deprive her of the right to protect her private life as a woman.

Real care has to be taken over photographing children. This is not necessarily because there is anything intrinsically private about the face of a child, but for the practical reason that parents get emotional about their kids, which increases the possibility of a complaint; and given that the courts are keen to protect the vulnerable in society, this in turn can increase the prospects of those complaints being upheld. Of course, not all children are the same. Those of some celebrity parents—Madonna, Angelina Jolie, and Brad Pitt—are instantly recognizable and are not hidden from public view. Other parents—Michael Jackson and British actor Ewan McGregor for example—are fiercely protective of their children's privacy.

The most significant case to come out of the British courts concerning children was that brought by Harry Potter author J.K. Rowling on behalf of her toddler, David. She sued over unauthorized photographs of him in a pushchair with her and her husband on a street in Edinburgh. The judge at first instance said that she was attempting to carve out "a press-free zone for children [of celebrities] in respect of absolutely everything they chose to do." But, while sympathetic, he was not able to find that a walk down the road was capable of attracting a reasonable expectation of privacy for the boy; "there remains an area of innocuous conduct in a public place which does not raise a reasonable expectation of privacy." The Edinburgh stroll he felt, fell into this category; "If a simple walk down the street qualifies for protection then it is difficult to see what would not," he said. He struck out the claim. Needless to say, Rowling appealed and in May 2008 the Court of Appeal overturned Patten J's decision, reinstating the action so that the issues could be dealt with at a full trial. While it will therefore be for any ultimate trial judge—unless the matter settles—to decide the case having assessed the facts, the Court of Appeal judgment is an important statement of the law of privacy when it comes to children. It reiterated that in determining whether an Article 8 right has been infringed, *all* the circumstances of the case have to be taken into account, and if the subject of the alleged invasion is a child, that circumstance must necessarily be thrown into the mix for deliberation.

"The question whether there is a reasonable expectation of privacy is a broad one," said the Master of the Rolls, giving the Court of Appeal's judgment, "which takes account of all the circumstances of the case. They include the attributes of the claimant, the nature of the activity in which the claimant was engaged, the place at which it was happening, the nature and purpose of the intrusion, the absence of consent and whether it was known or could be inferred, the effect on the claimant and the circumstances in which and the purposes for which the information came into the hands of the publisher." Importantly he went on to add that "in the case of a child the position is somewhat different from that of an adult."

A word of warning may be inferred from the manner in which the court referred to the way the relevant test might apply to the pictures in question, suggesting that the court should consider whether "David had a reasonable expectation that commercial picture agencies like BPL would not set out to photograph him with a view to selling those photographs for money without his consent, which would of course have to be given through his parents." The Court of Appeal also noted the UK's Press Complaints Commission Code of Conduct, which states, "Editors must not use the fame, notoriety or position of the parent or guardian as sole justification for publishing details of a child's private life." Out of this the court drew the general principle: "If a child of parents who are not in the public eye could reasonably expect not to have photographs of him published in the media, so too should the child of a famous parent."

This judgment is helpful in that it clarifies the way in which children should be dealt with. But it is not helpful if it is to be read to imply that children should not be touched with a barge-pole. How this will play out in practice will necessarily be seen over the coming months and years in the pages of the glossy magazines.

How did you do it?

There is no doubt that there is a judicial distaste for information obtained by deception, harassment, or subterfuge and particularly surreptitious, long-lens photographs. It's unlikely that the UK courts will take too kindly to an argument from a photographer that the use of a long lens was merely an attempt to be discreet and not cause the subject distress by getting too close. In *von Hannover*, the ECHR clearly objected to the harassment to which it accepted Caroline had been subjected and it disapproved highly of photos taken in "a climate of continual harassment which induces in the person concerned a very strong sense of intrusion into their private life or even of persecution." A practical problem for photographers in the modern competitive news industry is that while one photographer working independently may be acting entirely properly and may cause the subject no concern, the moment that same photographer becomes part of a media scrum, things change. En masse, the scrum appears to the subject—and certainly may well appear to the court assessing the matter post publication—

to be a dangerous, snarling beast. A seething mass of people and cameras was seen to have contributed to the death of Diana, Princess of Wales.

And where?

Photographs of individuals in a state of grief or shock will also gain judicial sympathy, wherever that might occur. The case in 2003 against the United Kingdom was a firm slap on the wrist by the European Court for the country's then lack of privacy protection.[13] Here Mr. Peck, suffering from depression, was spotted walking down Brentwood High Street with a knife in his hand, on the Council's new closed circuit television (CCTV). When he attempted suicide, the police were called, he was detained under the Mental Health Act, and he was treated by a doctor before being released without charge. Some stills from the CCTV were then included in a press release issued by the local council, boasting of the effectiveness of CCTV in preventing "a potentially dangerous situation."[14] It was followed up by local newspaper and television reports, none of which pixilated Mr. Peck's face. The ECHR found that the footage had been seen to an extent that far exceeded any exposure to a passer-by that he could have expected and, accordingly, despite the fact that he had been in public, his Article 8 rights had been interfered with.

Balancing the Rights

Just because the privacy claimant gets over the threshold of establishing a reasonable expectation of privacy, doesn't mean that the game is over for the media. The court then assesses whether this Article 8 right should be protected if it means curtailing the Article 10 right also at play. And accordingly, when assessing whether he is likely to get his fingers legally burned, the publisher needs carefully to assess his own arguments in favor of publication.

Public Domain

Publishers may try to argue that the material is already in the public domain (although in cases involving exposés and exclusives this is unlikely). In *Spycatcher* Lord Goff said that in order for the material no longer to be confidential, it must be "so generally accessible that, in all the circumstances, it cannot be regarded as confidential." And this is something that Formula One boss Max Mosley found out to his cost.[15] The president of the governing body of motor sport worldwide, the Federation Internationale de l'Automobile, sought an injunction to prevent the publication on the News International website of secretly obtained film of him engaged in sexual activity with five prostitutes at a private residence. The story had already run in the British tabloid the *News of the World* and by the time he applied for his injunction, there had been 435,000 hits on the online version of the article of complaint, with the video footage viewed approximately 1,424,959 times.

Mr. Mosley did not challenge that the events took place—although he did vehemently challenge the characterization of the events as Nazi role-play—but he also argued that their publication infringed on his right to privacy. If he could show that he had a greater than 50 percent chance of obtaining an injunction in privacy/breach of confidence at trial, then he would be entitled to an injunction preventing publication in the interim. However, while Mr. Justice Eady easily found that the claimant's Article 8 rights were engaged and came into conflict with the defendant's Article 10 rights, the judge had to ask himself "whether in respect of the information contained in the edited footage, Mr. Mosley any longer has a reasonable expectation of privacy, having regard to everything which has happened since the original publication." There was no public interest in revealing the material powerful enough to overcome Mr. Mosley's Article 8 right, he found; the only reason the photos and footage were of interest was because they were "mildly salacious" and provided an opportunity "to have a snigger" at the participants' expense. There was "no legitimate element of public interest which would be served by the *additional* disclosure of the edited footage."

However, Mr. Mosley was not able to breathe any sigh of relief. Notwithstanding this, the judge had to go on to consider whether the information "has lost its privacy to the extent that there is nothing left for the law to protect." And unfortunately for Mr. Mosley, he found that it had. The footage had already been seen by thousands of people around the world and should anyone wish to see it they need only search the Internet where it could still be accessed, notwithstanding any order of the court against NGN. "The court should guard against slipping into playing the role of King Canute," said Eady. And, accordingly, he had no option but to find that "the material is so widely accessible that an order in the terms sought would make very little practical difference." Mr. Mosley no longer had the required reasonable expectation of privacy as regards the material he sought to protect. Although it was intrusive and demeaning, "the granting of an order against this Respondent at the present juncture would merely be a futile gesture."

Trivia

Another argument that the media may run, to outweigh the claimant's Article 8 rights, is that the material is just too trivial or anodyne to warrant protection. The judge striking out *Murray* had said that his starting point was "a strong predisposition that routine acts such as the visit to the shop or the ride on the bus should not attract any reasonable expectation of privacy." But the Court of Appeal did not accept that this was the correct approach. While the triviality of some activities is a factor to be taken into consideration, *all* circumstances must be considered and triviality cannot be applied to classes of information in order to act as a trump card.

Public Interest

And then of course, all publishers worth their salt are going to try to argue that what they want to publish is in the public interest. Not everything that is of interest to the public is a matter of public interest—there is a difference between what might satisfy the public's prurient interest for salacious gossip and that which contributes to public debate—but the argument is one that can be raised. For example, it can be in the public interest to correct a false image; lying about her drug addiction meant there was a public interest in exposing the truth about Naomi Campbell. However, this may not extend to "exposing" a celebrity where they have simply fallen short of their own personally imposed standards. In a case brought by a Canadian folksinger[16] over what was effectively an unauthorized biography by a former friend, the trial judge Mr. Justice Eady said, "for a claimant's conduct to trigger the 'public interest defense' a very high degree of misbehavior must be demonstrated . . . all of us try to behave well, no doubt for most of the time, but hardly anyone succeeds in achieving that ideal. The mere fact that a 'celebrity' falls short from time to time, like everyone else, could not possibly justify exposure, in the supposed public interest, of every peccadillo or foible cropping up in day to day life."

Getting Results

Damages in defamation cases, while not as high as they were in the heyday of the 1980s, can still top £200,000, while damages in privacy claims usually struggle to get into double figures. But it is not damages that the publisher should concern himself with when assessing whether he wants to take a chance and publish, but the prospect of an injunction. An injunction is not available in defamation cases where the defendant intends to plead an arguable defense, due to the long-standing principle of "publish and be damned." But not so in privacy cases. Injunctions will be granted to preserve the status quo where the claimant can establish a threat of unauthorized publication and that he is "more likely than not" to succeed at trial. This can lead to significant expenditure on the part of the publisher, both in time to find other suitable stories at the last minute and in costs to recall articles that have already been printed and distributed.

Conclusion

Privacy in the UK has come a long way since its tentative beginnings more than one hundred and fifty years ago. The courts have finally accepted that they have an obligation to protect an individual's right to privacy from interference by others, and they are laying down, case by case, a series of guidelines as to what may be considered private material as well as how and in what circumstances privacy may be invaded.

Is it likely that the battle between the rights of the individual and the rights of the media will ever result in a truce? It is arguable that to some extent that is already happening. On the one hand, even before *Murray,* publishers were exercising self-restraint and self-censorship when it comes to the photographs of children, not necessarily out of any altruistic desire not to harm the little darlings, but to ensure that they do not offend their celebrity parents whose faces still sell magazines worldwide. On the other hand, some in the public eye themselves have conceded some ground, allowing photographs that they might otherwise prefer not to be seen, as they clamber up the slippery pole to stardom, as "any publicity is good publicity." Once there, however, having used the media attention to grab their space in the spotlight, they appear all of a sudden slightly more protective of their privacy.

And perhaps that is only to be expected. Mr. Justice Eady was impressed by the evidence of Loreena McKennitt when she told him how she felt as the media encroached upon her; "she valued what privacy was left to her more and more as the demands of fame and publicity encroached upon her; [drawing] the analogy of an animal living within an ever diminishing area surrounded by deforestation."

Every case is different. The subject of the story, the nature of the material, where and how it was obtained, and whether there is any overriding reason why it should be published are all matters that the courts will take into account after the event or on an application for an injunction. They are matters that any sensible publisher publishing in the United Kingdom should also take into account. But needless to say, while the sands shift and the tides turn, it's dangerous out there. While this chapter should raise awareness of the issues to be considered, the law moves too quickly for any overview to remain seaworthy for long. A combination of common sense, an eye to detail, and access to the lifeline of a lawyer are the requirements for any publisher intending to set sail on these choppy seas.

Chapter Notes

1. *Campbell v. MGN Limited* [2004] UKHL 22 on appeal from [2002] ECWA Civ 1373.

2. In June 2004, complaint was made by the Football Association (FA) over unauthorized photographs, published on the print pages of two UK tabloids, *The Sun* and *The Star*, of the then-captain of England's football team, David Beckham, in his underwear on the balcony of his hotel room, taken during the European cup in Portugal. They had been taken with a long lens despite an exclusion zone around the hotel complex precisely to protect the privacy of the players.

3. *Sara Cox v. MGN Limited [2005].* The claimant complained to the PCC over a breach of the PCC code, the relevant provisions of which provide that "(i) Everyone is entitled to respect for his or her private and family life, home, health and correspondence. A publication will be expected to justify intrusions into any individual's private life without consent. (ii) The use of long lens photography to take pictures of people in private places without their consent is unacceptable. Note—private places are public or private property where there is a reasonable expectation of privacy." She followed this by proceedings for breach of confidence, which were settled with a reported payment of £50,000 damages.

4. *Von Hannover v. Germany* (application number 59320/00) June 24, 2004.

5. *Murray v. Big Pictures (UK) Ltd.* (CA) [2008] Civ 446.

6. http://www.hmso.gov.uk/acts/acts1998/19980042.htm.

7. Article 10 ECHR. Article 10—Freedom of expression. 1. Everyone has the right to freedom of expression. This right shall include freedom to hold opinions and to receive and impart information and ideas without interference by public authority and regardless of frontiers. This article shall not prevent States from requiring the licensing of broadcasting, television or cinema enterprises. 2. The exercise of these freedoms, since it carries with it duties and responsibilities, may be subject to such formalities, conditions, restrictions or penalties as are prescribed by law and are necessary in a democratic society, in the interests of national security, territorial integrity or public safety, for the prevention of disorder or crime, for the protection of health or morals, for the protection of the reputation or rights of others, for preventing the disclosure of information received in confidence, or for maintaining the authority and impartiality of the judiciary.

8. Article 8 ECHR. Article 8—Right to respect for private and family life. 1. Everyone has the right to respect for his private and family life, his home and his correspondence. 2. There shall be no interference by a public authority with the exercise of this right except such as is in accordance with the law and is necessary in a democratic society in the interests of national security, public safety or the economic well-being of the country, for the prevention of disorder or crime, for the protection of health or morals, or for the protection of the rights and freedoms of others.

9. *Douglas v. Hello Ltd. (no 8) (HL)* The Hollywood actors Michael Douglas and Catherine Zeta-Jones sued for breach of confidence and breach of the Data Protection Act 1998 over the publication of unauthorized photographs of their private wedding at the Four Seasons Hotel in New York, taken surreptitiously by an infiltrator to the wedding, notwithstanding the security measures taken. The couple had entered into an exclusive deal with *OK!* magazine to license exclusively for nine months photographs taken by the couple's chosen photographer that they authorized for release. *OK!'s* rival *Hello!* proposed to publish the surreptitious shots taken by the infiltrator, and the couple initially obtained an injunction to prevent *Hello!* from publishing. However, this was lifted on appeal and the photographs

were published in *Hello!*. *OK!* then attempted to mitigate the damage by the loss of the scoop by changing their plans, which were to run the photographs over two weeks and they rushed to get their issue out on the same day as *Hello!* On the substantive claim for breach of confidence and under the DPA, Mr. Justice Lindsay awarded the couple damages for distress and for wasted costs in relation to the work that had to be undertaken to get authorized photographs approved for the earlier deadline; the sum, £14,600 each. He awarded *OK!* damages for the loss of the scoop; the sum just over £1 million. On appeal to the Court of Appeal, the court upheld the damages award to the Douglases to compensate them for the invasion of privacy, but overturned the award to *OK!* on the grounds that it had no claim to compensation in respect of photographs to which it was not entitled under its agreement with them. On appeal to the House of Lords, the damages award was reinstated. The House heard *OK!* argue that it too was owed a duty of confidence in respect of any photographic image of the event, and that publication of the unauthorized photographs constituted an unlawful interference with its business. *Hello!* argued that any confidence in the photographic representation of the event was destroyed when *OK!* published its own authorized photographs. The majority found for *OK!* in the confidence claim. While *OK!* had no claim to privacy, either its own or "parasitic upon" that of the Douglases, the obligation of confidence imposed on the photographic images of the wedding was for the benefit not only of the Douglases, but also of *OK!*, which had paid handsomely for the ability exclusively to photograph the event. According to Lord Hoffmann: "The point of which one should never lose sight is that *OK!* had paid £1 million for the benefit of the obligation of confidence imposed upon all those present at the wedding in respect of any photographs of the wedding. . . . Provided that one keeps one's eye firmly on the money and why it was paid, the case is, as Lindsay J. held, quite straightforward."

10. *Theakston v. MGN Limited,* [2002] EMLR 398.

11. *Jagger v. Darling*, Unreported, UKHC, Bell J, March 9, 2005.

12. *Sienna Miller v. Warren Richardson* (Unreported) Settlement.

13. *Peck v. United Kingdom* (2003) 36 EHRR 41; [2003] EMLR 297.

14. Id.

15. *Mosley v. News Group Newspapers* [2008] EWCH 687 QB.

16. *McKennitt v. Ash* [2006] EWCA Civ 1714; [2007] EMLR 113; *The Times*, December 20, 2006.

CROSS-REFERENCE CHART

ISSUE	AUSTRALIA	BELGIUM	BRAZIL	CANADA	CHINA	ENGLAND & WALES	FRANCE	GERMANY
Truth as Absolute Defense?	Y	Y	Y	Y	N	Y	Y	N
Libel by Implication?	Y	Y	Y	Y	U	Y	Y	Y
May Corporations Sue for Libel?	Y	Y	U	Y	Y	Y	Y	Y
Product Disparagement?	Y	Y	Y	Y	Y	Y	N	Y
Group Libel?	N	Y	Y	N	U	N	Y	N
Higher Public Figure Fault Standard	N	Y	N	N	N	N	N	N
Public Interest Defense?	Y	Y	Q	Q	N	Y	Y	Y
Company Reporting as Public Concern?	Y	U	Y	N	Y	Y	N	U
Fair Comment or Opinion?	Y	Y	Y	Y	N	Y	Y	Y
Right of Reply?	N	Y	Y	U (varies by province)	N	N	Y	N
Privilege for Government Documents?	Y	N	Y	Y	Y	Y	Y	Y
Wire Service Defense?	N	Y	Y	N	N	N	N	Y
Contempt of Court?	Y	N	N	Y	N	Y	Y	Y
Prior Restaints?	Y	Y	N	Y	Y	Y	Y	Y
Privacy Recognized?	N	Y	Y	Y	Y	Y	Y	Y
Shield Law?	N	Y	Y	N	N	Y	Y	Y
Law Applied to Internet?	Y	Y	U	Y	Y	Y	Y	Y

Key: Y = Yes, N = No, U = Unclear, Q = Qualified or Limited

	HONG KONG	INDIA	ITALY	JAPAN	KOREA	MALAYSIA	NETHERLANDS	POLAND	RUSSIA	SINGAPORE	SPAIN	SWITZERLAND	THAILAND	USA
	Y	Y	N	Y	Y	N	Y	N	Y	Y	N	Y	N	Y
	Y	Y	Y	N	Y	Y	Y	Y	N	Y	Y	Y	Y	Y
	Y	Y	Y	Y	Y	Y	Y	Y	Y	Y	Y	Y	Y	Y
	Y	Y	Y	N	Y	Y	Y	Y	Y	Y	Y	Y	N	Y
	Y	N	Y	N	Y	U	Y	N	N	N	Y	N	N	N
	N	Y	N	N	N	N	Y	N	N	N	N	N	N	Y
	Y	Y	Y	Y	Y	Y	Y	Y	N	Y	Y	Y	Y	Y
	Y	U	Y	N	N	Y	Y	Y	N	Y	Y	N	Y	Y
	Y	Y	Y	Y	Y	Y	Y	Y	Y	Y	Y	Y	Y	Y
	N	N	Y	N	Y	N	N	Y	Y	N	Y	Y	N	N
	Y	Y	N	N	N	Y	N	Y	Y	Y	Y	N	Y	Y
	N	N	N	N	N	N	N	Y	Y	N	Y	N	N	Y
	Y	Y	Y	N	Y	Y	N	Y	N	N	Y	Y	N	N
	Y	Y	Y	Y	Y	Y	N	Y	N	Y	Y	Y	N	N
	U	Y	Y	Y	Y	N	Y	Y	Y	N	Y	Y	Y	Y
	Y	Y	Y	N	Y	N	Y	Y	Y	N	Y	Y	N	Y
	Y	Y	Y	Y	Y	Y	Y	Y	Y	Y	Y	Y	Y	Y

RECOMMENDED READING

Abrams, Floyd, *Speaking Freely: Trials of the First Amendment.* New York: Penguin, 2006.

Fiss, Owen, *The Irony of Free Speech.* Cambridge: Harvard University Press, 1998.

Friendly, Fred W., *Minnesota Rag: Corruption, Yellow Journalism, and the Case That Saved Freedom of the Press.* Minneapolis, MN: University of Minnesota Press, 2003.

Gatley, John Clement Carpenter, *Gatley on Libel and Slander.* London: Sweet & Maxwell, 2001.

Goldstein, Norm, *The Associated Press Stylebook and Briefing on Media Law: Revised Edition.* New York: Basic Books, 2007.

Hart, Jonathan D., *Internet Law: A Field Guide—Fourth Edition.* Washington, DC: BNA Books, 2007.

Hooper, David, *Reputations Under Fire: Winners and Losers in the Libel Business.* London: Little, Brown Book Group, 2001.

Jarrow, Gail, *The Printer's Trial: The Case of John Peter Zenger and the Fight for a Free Press.* Honesdale, PA: Calkins Creek Books, 2006.

Kovach, Bill, and Tom Rosenstiel, *The Elements of Journalism: What Newspeople Should Know and the Public Should Expect—Revised Edition.* New York: Three Rivers Press, 2007.

Lewis, Anthony, *Make No Law: The Sullivan Case and the First Amendment.* New York: Vintage, 1992.

Media Law Resource Center Staff, *MLRC 50 State Survey—Media Libel Law.* New York: Media Law Resource Center, 2008.

Media Law Resource Center Staff, *MLRC 50 State Survey—Media Privacy and Related Law.* New York: Media Law Resource Center, 2008.

Metcalf, Slade R., *Rights and Liabilities of Publishers, Broadcasters, and Reporters.* New York: McGraw-Hill, 1982.

Pearlstine, Norman, *Off the Record: The Press, the Government, and the War over Anonymous Sources.* New York: Farrar, Straus and Giroux, 2008.

Robertson, Geoffrey, and Andrew Q.C. Nicol, *Robertson and Nicol on Media Law: Fifth Edition.* London: Sweet & Maxwell, 2007.

Sack, Robert D., *Sack on Defamation: Libel, Slander and Related Problems—Third Edition.* New York: Practising Law Institute (PLI), 1999.

INDEX